CHAINED EAGLE

SERIES EDITORS
Walter J. Boyne and Peter B. Mersky

Aviation Classics are inspired nonfictional and fictional accounts that reveal the human drama of flight. The series covers every era of military and civilian aviation, is international in scope, and encompasses flying in all of its diversity. Some of the books are well-known bestsellers, and others are superb but unheralded titles that deserve a wider audience.

Other Titles in the Aviation Classics Series

Ploesti: The Great Ground-Air Battle of 1 August 1943
by James Dugan and Carroll Stewart

Thirty Seconds Over Tokyo
by Capt. Ted W. Lawson

Operation Overflight: A Memoir of the U-2 Incident
by Francis Gary Powers with Curt Gentry

CHAINED EAGLE

The Heroic Story of the First American
Shot Down over North Vietnam

EVERETT ALVAREZ, JR.,
and
ANTHONY S. PITCH

Potomac Books, Inc.
Washington, D.C.

Originally published in 1989 by Donald I. Fine, Inc. Copyright © 1989 by Everett Alvarez, Jr., and Anthony S. Pitch.

Library of Congress Cataloging-in-Publication Data

Alvarez, Everett, 1937–
    Chained eagle : the heroic story of the first American shot down over North Vietnam / Everett Alvarez, Jr. and Anthony S. Pitch.—1st ed.
        p.   cm.—(Aviation classics)
    Originally published: New York : D.I. Fine, c1989.
    ISBN 978-1-57488-558-3 (alk. paper)
    1. Alvarez, Everett, 1937– 2. Vietnamese Conflict, 1961–1975—Prisoners and prisons, North Vietnamese.   3. Vietnamese Conflict, 1961–1975—Personal narratives, American.   4. Prisoners of war—United States—Biography.   5. Prisoners of war—Vietnam—Biography.   I. Pitch, Anthony.   II. Title.   III. Aviation classic series (Washington D.C.)
    DS559.4.A48   2005
    959.704'37'092273—dc22
    [B]   2005043032

Potomac Books, Inc.
22841 Quicksilver Drive
Dulles, Virginia 20166

First Edition

10 9 8 7 6 5 4 3 2

TO THE MEN WHO SUFFERED CAPTIVITY AS
PRISONERS OF WAR IN NORTH VIETNAM, WHO
SHARED THE PAINFUL EXPERIENCE, WHO CAME
HOME WITH THEIR DIGNITY AND PERSONAL
INTEGRITY INTACT. . . . AND TO THOSE WHO DID
NOT RETURN.
TO THEIR LOVED ONES WHO WAITED. . . . AND
ENDURED.
AND TO THOSE WHO STILL WAIT.

ACKNOWLEDGMENTS

FOR THE HELP I RECEIVED IN PREPARING THIS BOOK, I want to thank my former cell mates from the POW camps in North Vietnam who graciously gave their time to relive painful memories in order to substantiate events and circumstances, namely Lt. Col. Thomas Barrett, USAF (Ret); Lt. Col. Kyle Berg, USAF (Ret); Capt. David Carey, USN (Ret); Capt. Gerald Coffee, USN (Ret); and Capt. William Metzger, Jr. USN. I want to thank my friend, Capt. John Nicholson, USN (Ret), who was flying with me the day I was shot down, and who never gave up on me.

I am eternally grateful to my Mom and Dad, and to my sisters, Delia and Madeleine, for reliving painfully emotional experiences a decade and a half after my return from Vietnam. I never knew their story, and they never knew mine, until now. I am grateful to my aunt Cecilia and cousins Linda and Albert for the time they took to assist with the manuscript and recreate events, and to the extended Sanchez family for their supportive efforts over the years, especially the long, long hours spent collecting signatures in the petition drives.

I want to thank Tony Pitch for his strong commitment and dedication to this effort over the past three years.

Finally, I want to give special thanks to my wife, Tammy, and my sons, Marc and Bryan, for their patience and understanding. Most of what appears in this book was new to them. Things they learned of their husband and dad were from a different time, a different place. I owe all to Tammy, to whom I am lucky to be married, for if it had not been for her urging and steadfast support this story would not have been told.

Everett Alvarez, Jr.

For their guidance towards overall improvement of the early draft manuscripts, and for their encouragement during the long haul that lay ahead, I wish to thank my friends whose judgment I value so highly: Milton Kapelus, Allan Mendelowitz, Rona Mendelsohn and Rudi Munitz.

To Everett Alvarez, Sr., Soledad Alvarez, Delia Alvarez, Madeleine Schramm, Cecilia Sanchez, Albert Sanchez, and Linda Espinosa my gratitude for their warm Californian hospitality and their readiness to sit for long interviews, even while tears flowed and hearts ached in the remembrances.

My apologies and appreciation to my wife, Marion, and my children, Michael and Nomi, who suffered much neglect during the years it took to structure and write this book. Without their tolerance it would not have been possible to indulge the selfish creative process.

Anthony S. Pitch

CONTENTS

PROLOGUE

WHEN MY CO-AUTHOR ASKED ME IN THE SUMMER OF 1986 whether I wanted to collaborate on this book I accepted immediately. The time was right. Thirteen years had passed since my liberation and return to the USA. Saigon had fallen to the enemy eleven years back. The post-war years had allowed me to get on with my life, remarry, raise a family, and distance myself from the carnage and horrors of captivity. Older and wiser, I could look back on those years with a deeper understanding and dispassionate reflection. I also had the advantage of reviewing thousands of declassified documents relating to the war. There was much to tell and messages to impart. The book would record the past and perhaps enlighten posterity. It would be my personal testament to successive generations and to many high school and college students around the country, for whom the Vietnam War is little more than aging history.

In the intervening years our country had also begun to heal. Americans in opposite camps of the divisive war were more receptive to seeing the total picture. There was a readiness to separate individuals from the politics of the conflict. The most vivid expression of this new mood came with the construction of the Vietnam Veterans Memorial in our nation's capital. Veterans Day 1982 was cold and blustery when I had the honor to address the multitudes gathered for the dedication, but there was a special warmth in our hearts. I knew that I spoke for millions when I said, "With this long overdue week of activities, with this parade today and especially with this dedication, America is saying, 'Welcome home!'"

More than two million Americans served in Vietnam, most of them accepting their duty unselfishly and heroically. Even though the public at large still had a difficult time dealing with the effects of the war, no one should have been debating the sacrifice of those who fell while serving. "No one can doubt," I continued, "that the Vietnam Veterans Memorial will be an eternal touchstone for the conscience of this nation. It will tell us, as no words can, of the awesome responsibility we have as members of a free and democratic society."

Not a single man I met during all my years in captivity agreed with the conduct of the war. As military men we were told we could not strike certain harbors, airfields, missile sites and other targets. That was no way to win a

1

war. The lesson we should learn from Vietnam is that if we are going to get involved in a foreign war again, let's make up our minds as a country that the cause is worth fighting for, then let's go in and do it right and win. Otherwise, we shouldn't get involved in the first place.

If wars bring the ultimate destruction, they also present the noblest challenges. Prolonged captivity under brutal conditions in a hostile land pits a man against overwhelming odds. My survival depended on much more than trying to satisfy a craving for food, and overcoming the emptiness of isolation and the pain of torture. My strength came from holding fast to my faith in God and belief in the values enshrined in our Constitution: duty, loyalty, unity, integrity, honor, allegiance, courage and hope. Without my absolute belief in these core virtues of our heritage I don't believe I would have pulled through alive and sane.

In this book I have tried to convey the human interest side of the story, relating what everyday life was like for myself and those around me and how beliefs and faith were constantly put to the test. Though sharing a common fate of bondage within dank cells and patrolled perimeters, we remained individual characters with our own quirks and foibles. There were jokers and loners, dreamers and realists, some who were reckless and others who were cautious, men with guts and high principles forced to live cheek by jowl with a few shameful POWs who collaborated with the enemy.

I have also tried to portray the war's effects on my own immediate family. My parents and two sisters were drawn into the whirlpool of war from day one of the conflict, when my fighter-bomber was shot down over the Gulf of Tonkin. Their lives lurched sharply off course from then on. They labored obsessively to remind the public of the fate of the POWs and worked relentlessly to hasten our release. During the eight and a half turbulent years I was held captive, they were consumed by anguish and suffering. For reasons I explain in later chapters, we never talked it over until this book compelled us to draw on memories and read the harrowing letters we wrote each other. Distant though the conflict may now seem, it was not easy opening up to each other and stirring the embers of years marked by so much rage and killing. I am left with a new awareness of the infinite love they felt for me as they tried, in their different ways, to secure my safe return.

I was not alone in returning to a broken home, forsaken by a loved spouse. Many more were robbed of the joys of watching their children grow into adolescence and adulthood. It was not uncommon for men to return and learn of the demise of their parents. The years had brushed us aside and passed on forever. Yet we were not wholly without reward. For those of us who survived with honor, there was a feeling of uncommon pride. Shakespeare well understood this emotion when he wrote King Henry V's lines to his lieutenants on the eve of the battle of Agincourt:

If we are marked to die, we are enough
To do our country loss: and if to live,
The fewer men, the greater share of honor.

—*Everett Alvarez, Jr.*
June, 1989

1
CONFLICT

THE JUNIOR OFFICERS' WARDROOM BEGAN FILLING UP shortly before the screening of the evening movie aboard our aircraft carrier, U.S.S. *Constellation.* Pilots from our attack squadron 144, nicknamed the Roadrunners, ambled down to the forward section where our "turf" was staked out with bright orange-colored baseball caps plopped on the chairs. Already some of our guys were exchanging friendly insults with the blue-capped aviators in our sister squadron, clustered around a table in their own adjacent territory.

It was Tuesday, August 4, 1964.

I reached for the telephone, ringing above the din of hooting and catcalls. It was our squadron duty officer.

"Nick, it's for you!"

Lt. Cmdr. Nick Nicholson, our squadron operations officer, took the call without comment. But as he hung up he muttered, "Oh crap! What now?" and abruptly left the room.

When the phone rang again the room was already darkened and I was munching popcorn as the credits rolled for the start of the movie.

"Alvie, get dressed on the double!" Nick ordered. "AI (Air Intelligence) wants three attack pilots in full gear. We've got three planes (Skyhawk A4s) standing by. I'm taking one and I want two guys with me. You and Ronnie Boch."

As Ronnie and I made for the exit I glanced back, tripping over an extended leg as I did so, but still managing to read the title of the grade B movie, *The Night Has A Thousand Eyes.*

In the AI room they briefed us on a furious sea battle going on about 450 miles to the west. North Vietnamese torpedo boats had two of our destroyers, the U.S.S. *Maddox* and U.S.S. *Turner Joy,* under attack in the thick of a stormy night. The naval conflict was raging more than 60 miles away from the North Vietnamese coast, in the Gulf of Tonkin.

We had cut short our shore leave in Hong Kong and were already racing towards the battle zone because two days earlier North Vietnamese boats had tried to sink the *Maddox* as it sailed alone in the Gulf waters. The enemy had launched torpedoes and opened fire with a machine gun in broad daylight. It seemed like a reckless act or brazen contempt for a superpower, especially as Washington explained that the *Maddox* had been on a routine patrol in international waters when it underwent an unprovoked attack. The stern but measured response from Washington warned of grave consequences that would follow another unprovoked attack.

Nobody told us that the Joint Chiefs of Staff had ordered the *Maddox* to conduct electronic surveillance of special types of enemy radar in case we had to operate against North Vietnam. Nor was there a word about the *Maddox* steaming up and down the same route along which unmarked patrol boats from South Vietnam had sailed several nights earlier, arousing North Vietnamese radar and other defenses as the southern intruders blasted the enemy's military targets. The operation marked a heightened level of warfare between the two Vietnams. It was the first time South Vietnam had opened fire on its enemy from the sea. Approval had come from the highest political level in Washington. President Lyndon Johnson had given the go-ahead for an escalating series of highly classified covert sea and air operations. The object was to strike back against North Vietnam and make it pay a price for infiltrating men and materiel into South Vietnam.

Our briefers passed on the stark facts as they knew them: North Vietnamese gunboats were trying to torpedo U.S. destroyers in international waters. They told us that other planes were standing by on the U.S.S. *Ticonderoga* in the South China Sea. In case they needed us, we should also stand by, prepared to launch and head to the Gulf of Tonkin. Once there, we had to check in on the ships' frequency for further guidance.

"Ronnie and I have rockets. You take the flares, Alvie," said Nick, knowing that I was one of the few in our squadron who had dropped the magnesium flares at night in previous exercises.

"Here we go again," I thought as I slipped into my flight gear and remembered all the times we Navy pilots had stood by and never launched. Once we had stood by for three days, ready to bomb a target in the Plain of Jars in Laos. Then the Air Force had gone in and struck the wrong target, hitting instead a meeting of the International Control Commission, supervising government by three warring factions in Laos. So here we were, first night out of Hong Kong, all dressed up and ready to go, and we might end up sitting for hours in the cockpit before they'd call it off and we'd have to climb out.

Ready Room 3 was in Condition Red, with every bright light switched off and replaced with subdued red bulbs to accustom us to night vision. It took about half an hour for our eyes to adapt and we had to guard against carelessness. Turning on just one bright light would be like looking point blank at a camera's exploding flashbulb.

Suddenly a message came in that airplanes had launched from the *Ticonderoga*. Then, unexpectedly, a voice crackled over the intercom: "Ready 3. Have your pilots man the planes!"

We scrambled.

There wasn't a star to be seen and it was pouring out on the flight deck, with thunderbumpers (thunderstorms) all around. "What a lousy night to pull this kind of a drill!" Nick shouted to his plane captain, the enlisted man who would help him into the cockpit and make sure everything was set. If we did launch, we would have to keep our wits about us because the turbulence was likely to toss the planes all over the place.

Vision was limited on the flight deck though I easily made out the familiar silhouettes of immobile aircraft and the ghoulish-looking deck crew in red-lensed goggles. The shadowy outlines of men scurrying about their tasks, beaming red-lensed flashlights or conical-shaped signaling wands, resembled participants in some secret nocturnal rite, more so as the sound of their speech and movements were drowned out by the driving rain and the hiss of the heaving sea.

My A4-Skyhawk jet was already positioned over number 3 catapult's shuttle in a state of alert. If need be we could launch in less than a minute. I walked around the plane on a preflight external check, shining my flashlight to see that nothing had been left in the intake, glancing at the tires and making sure everything was secure. Once up the ladder and strapped into the cockpit I did the preliminary pre-start checks and settled in for what I expected would be hours of tedious inactivity.

To my surprise, I got the wave to start the engines. Maybe this was going to be more than a drill! We had never actually started our engines in past drills. I flicked on the red cockpit lights, strapped on my hard hat, closed the canopy and did a rapid post-start check, scanning the oil pressure, temperatures, gauges, radios and electrical equipment. The oxygen flow was normal.

Nick had already launched and Ronnie was starting up, his Skyhawk defined by the steady wing lights—red on port, green on starboard. A red anti-collision beacon rotated above his fuselage behind the cockpit, well ahead of the tail light.

Swiftly, the deck crew attached thick steel cables to my aircraft and the hold-back bar, then signaled the catapult handlers on the catwalk. At the instant one of them pushed a button, the cables tightened, the shuttle locked and the plane jerked. It was like being held in the taut gut of an archer's expanded bow.

The catapult officer circled his red-tipped wand. I applied full power, with the plane still held back by the cables. I ran the throttle all the way forward to max thrust, gripping a bar at the same time so my arm didn't accidentally fly back and reduce power. Simultaneously, I "wiped the cockpit" with the control stick, making sure it moved unimpeded in all directions. I checked the elevators at the back, kicked the rudder, and glanced over the engine instruments. The headings on my radio magnetic indicator corresponded with those on the standby compass.

My heart thumped. My left hand clutched the bar near the throttle in a death grip as I flipped a switch turning on a light under the fuselage. It was the final night signal to the flight deck officer letting him know I had gone through the check list and was ready to go. He drew an arc in the air with his wand, a catapult crewman pressed the button and I was off! Whoosh!

It was like being shot from a sling. The initial surge pinned my head and body back against the seat. My eyeballs rattled and my vision blurred. In those split milliseconds I was powerless to stop the aircraft. As it careened down the 120 foot run, I heard myself shouting "Agghhhhhh!!!" This was more exhilarating than the heady plunge of a rocketing roller coaster. But it was explosively dangerous at such screaming velocity, especially at night without benefit of the familiar references of sea and sky, or even the ship's flight deck. In the dark there was but a single guardian—my illuminated instrument panel.

The lights down the catapult track seemed to blur and hurtle towards me. I couldn't see the edge of the angled deck. But the sensation of rapid acceleration to about 170 knots per hour eased off at the end of the track. Using all the instincts honed from countless takeoffs, I felt a comforting sensation when the shuttle pulled up abruptly at the end of the deck and the thick cables slipped loose from their hooks under the fuselage, dropping ponderously onto the deck with a thud drowned out by my jet turbine. Instantaneously, the plane seemed suspended. At that precise moment my vision returned clearly. I got control of the stick and brought it to a neutral position. If I had pulled it too close to me, the plane would have risen sharply and stalled. If the stick had gone too far forward, the nose would have dropped and I would have lost altitude. My eyes were glued to the rate of climb indicator and the altimeter. They looked good. I was climbing about 500 feet per second. Quickly, I released my grip on the bar and hit the handle to pull up the wheels.

Nick was orbiting at about 10,000 feet as he waited for Ronnie and me to join him. Then we all climbed to about 30,000 feet before leveling off.

Now my adrenaline really began to flow, pumping and surging through my body. Here I was, a 26-year-old lieutenant j.g., speeding into combat for the first time! I had been flying for four years and felt supremely confident. I knew I had a natural flair for flying. After one debriefing in flight training an instructor had told me, in our slang, that I was "really smooth." He congratulated me for doing well, then confided, "Some other guys get a death grip on the stick. You've got to be smooth with the controls of a plane."

It took us just over an hour to cover approximately 450 miles from the *Constellation* to the two beleaguered destroyers because we had to fly a dog's-leg route around Hainan Island—a piece of Chinese territory on the eastern flank of the Gulf of Tonkin.

When we switched over to the destroyers' frequencies I was startled to hear so much bedlam and confusion. There were bursts of frantic commands and shouted reports from both ships as they desperately gave ranges, courses and torpedo bearings. Pilots from the *Ticonderoga* were trying to pin down the destroyers' positions in the rain and thick overcast. "What's your position?" the pilots asked. We had to strain to catch the reply because three or four people on the ships were shouting simultaneously: "Torpedo bearing . . .", "Turning hard to port," "Sonar bearing . . .," "Radar contact! Radar contact!"

The weather was foul and the night opaque. Usually the Skipper of the *Turner Joy,* Cmdr. Robert Barnhardt, could pick out the silhouette of another ship at close quarters during nocturnal maneuvers, but on this night it was so dark he couldn't see the *Maddox.* And the air was so charged with static electricity that Lt. Cmdr. Everett Southwick, one of the *Ticonderoga* pilots already on scene, saw the freak atmospheric conditions give rise to a rare instance of *St. Elmo's Fire,* in which a bluish-orange glow appeared to dance on the rim of his canopy. Periodically blinded by flashes of lightning, he and his wingman avoided each other by keeping an eye on the red and white wingtip lights on Southwick's plane and the rotating red beacon on the fuselage of the other aircraft.

The chaotic radio transmissions from the ships might have continued much longer were it not for the intervention of one of the pilots who spoke in a commanding tone. Years later, while still a POW, I learned this was Cmdr. James Stockdale, whom I had met when his squadron came aboard our carrier in the South China Sea a month before the *Maddox* incident. It was clear, then, how much his men respected him for being in control of everything.

"I'm trying to help you! Can you turn your lights on?" Stockdale interjected with firm authority. "Can you shoot up a flare to show us where you are?"

We waited briefly, then saw the flare illuminate the swirling overcast. But it didn't clear up the hysteria down below. Freak atmospheric conditions for the past two days had played *ducting* tricks with the radarscopes. Radar beams were either curving over the horizon, enabling radarmen to pick up objects and shapes at very great distances, or the beams were bending straight up so that not even the closest objects registered on the scope. Such fickle performances resulted in a disorderly succession of excellent, poor, or totally blank readings on the screens.

Stockdale asked the ships if their lights were on. When they replied in the negative he said he'd seen a light and was rolling in on it. He had no sooner announced this than a voice from one of the destroyers yelled: "Our lights *are* on! Our lights *are* on!"

Other *Ticonderoga* pilots circling overhead were equally bewildered by the frenzied voices crackling over the frequency shared with the ships. Cmdr. Wesley McDonald, in a delta-winged Skyhawk, spotted the faint red aircraft warning lights, lit for several minutes atop the *Maddox* to guide the airmen. McDonald also briefly saw the *Maddox's* wake churned into white froth by her high speed propeller screws and the vessel's spasmodic turns.

When the controller aboard the *Maddox* directed him to suspected enemy craft, McDonald radioed: "I don't have anything to shoot at." Soon after, he saw a wake, climbed to about six thousand feet and was about to roll in for a strike when he changed his mind, unsure whether he had sighted friendly or hostile craft.

Suddenly the *Turner Joy* directed him and his wingman to a target the ship marked with five-inch shells streaking out like red globs. McDonald saw neither boats nor wakes yet slammed his pod of nineteen visually-guided rockets into the blackness below. The water swallowed them up without even a hint that they had struck anything. He returned to the *Ticonderoga* upset and frustrated that he had not found any enemy craft.

Two other pilots from the *Ticonderoga,* Cmdr. George Edmondson and his wingman, were diving to 700 feet and then climbing to 1500 feet in their propeller-driven Skyraiders when they saw gun flashes on the surface of the water. They reported bursts of light anti-aircraft fire at their approximate altitude. Unknown to them, they were being targeted by some gunnerymen on the *Maddox* who, apparently assuming their ship was under attack, fired as soon as the plane's blips appeared on the radar screens.

Nick radioed our arrival. "This is *War Paint* 401. We're a flight of three Skyhawks. We have flares. Can we help out?"

"Roger, 401. Send 'em on down," Stockdale ordered.

"Okay Alvie," said Nick, "go on down. We'll be up here."

I was already descending when Stockdale asked my position.

I called out my altitude.

"Roger, I see your lights," he said.

"I *don't have* any lights on!" I corrected, amid the crackling commotion from the ships.

I was down to about 5,000 feet when a voice from the ship announced, "we're going to fire a broadside."

Could that be in my direction? I hoped they didn't fire too high. At 2,500 feet I called Stockdale.

"I'm still in the soup but I'm going to drop a flare."

"Okay."

I pushed the button and the flare drifted down on its parachute, burning incandescently yellowish-white. It lit up enough to show I was still enveloped in thick clouds.

"I've gotcha," said Stockdale. "You're too far north. Come on back down here."

I dropped down to 1,500 feet, at about the base of the overcast, and "pickled" another flare.

"Right on! Beautiful!" exclaimed Stockdale.

I dropped four more flares in a semi-circle and looked back. I could see that I was northwest of the two bobbing, twisting destroyers. In the rainswept, tempestuous water, beyond the ships and my plane, I saw a bunch of what might have been U-shaped tracks. But I couldn't make out whether they were formed by the wild turnings of the destroyers, the rough sea, or whatever.

Nick and Ronnie meanwhile had descended to the base of the overcast and had also seen what appeared to be two white marks resembling the churned water of wakes. Neither of them knew if they belonged to the destroyers.

"I have two fast movers on the surface at eleven o'clock!" Ronnie announced.

"Roger, I have them in sight," said Nick, who immediately asked the destroyer below to verify its heading.

The strained, nervous voice of the young man on the ship gave the surface Navy lingo for a northerly course: "We're heading zero, zero, zero."

"Confirm your heading," Nick asked.

"Zero, zero, zero."

"Roger," said Nick, looking at the wakes going in a southerly direction, "we have two fast movers heading one eight zero. These contacts are moving one, eight, zero, at high speed!"

"Take them under attack!" the ship's air controller ordered.

"Arm your weapons!" Nick directed Ronnie as he himself prepared to fire, in a single salvo, the pod of eighteen 2.75 inch diameter rockets clipped under his fuselage. A second later Nick added, "Okay. One in position to roll in."

At that critical moment, when he was on the verge of diving down, the frantic air controller screamed, "Hold fire! Hold fire! Hold fire! Our heading is one, eight, zero! One, eight, zero!"

Miraculously, Nick and Ronnie peeled off in time. But now they were gun shy. If the air controller down below could make a mistake of that magnitude they would have to be extra careful in taking his orders. Nick had no doubt from the controller's behavior that he genuinely thought the destroyers were in jeopardy. But the sudden 180-degree switch spoke volumes for the man's nervousness and inexperience.

I looked down at my instrument panel. The fuel gauge was down to bingo, leaving me just enough to make it back to the *Constellation*. I called the flight from our sister squadron.

"Do you have any flares?"

"Rog, but I'm at 30,000 feet."

"Well come on down because you can use them here," I said.

I called Nick. "I'm bingoing."

"Okay, see you back on the ship."

Nick and Ronnie were so low on fuel that they had to jettison anything acting as a drag on the Skyhawks. When he was certain they were well clear of the destroyers, Nick radioed Ronnie, "Go ahead and fire in this area. If there's anything down there at least let's let them know we have the capability."

The rockets slammed harmlessly into the swirling ocean.

"Clean your wings. Jettison everything and let's get up to a high altitude," Nick ordered.

That meant dumping the empty fuel pods. The internal 20 mm. ammunition remained because it was not a wind drag.

I was climbing to about 25,000 feet when an authoritative voice from the ship cut into the din of sonar soundings, torpedo bearings and radar contacts. The anonymous voice was calm, steady and strong: "Tell all the aircraft to go on back home. We don't need them."

"What the heck is this? What's he talking about?" I thought to myself, surprised by the sudden turn of events and even confused, wondering where the order had come from.

Other pilots were similarly amazed by the order. "Say again," radioed one pilot in a questioning tone of voice.

"Tell all the planes to go on back. We don't need them," the voice repeated decisively. To this day, I'm not sure who it was—possibly one of the senior officers in one of the command centers aboard one of the ships or one of the ships' captains.

It was a strange conclusion to a night of havoc but I had to concentrate immediately on flying through the fiercest thunderstorm I'd ever encountered. My A4 was buffeted and the airspeed showed zero because I had neglected to turn on my pitot switch to de-ice the little probe sticking out of the wing which measured my air pressure. As a result, it had frozen over. By the time I came out of it I was far south, way off course, and low on fuel. I climbed again to 37,000 feet and made it back to the carrier with what I estimated was just enough fuel left for one pass. A little luck would also help since a lot could always go wrong landing on a carrier. I would have to be damn careful. An F4 had once landed on our flight deck and almost ground to a halt when the thick, steel restraining cable snapped. The plane slid helplessly overboard and the crew was lost. Simultaneously, the cable slashed backwards with deadly velocity, scything limbs off a number of the flight deck crew. No matter how many night landings I'd made I always had to have my wits about me because of such unforeseen hazards. This time, as the carrier control approach (CCA) directed me down by radio and I approached the ship, I knew they really weren't ready to take me on. I saw a plane taking off and knew they wouldn't have time to clear the deck. When they turned me back out I was concerned because once before, when I had been in a similar pattern, they lost me through clutter on the scope. I didn't want them to keep me going around this time on account of my low fuel.

"Hey, you guys are running me out of fuel!" I exclaimed.

"Where are you?" CCA asked.

In that instant I recognized the voice of Lt. Cmdr. Roger Sheets, the very able CCA officer in charge. I knew if he was in control nothing untoward would happen. Sure enough, within seconds Sheets' voice came over the headset, "We have you."

Fortunately, everything went well and I landed without incident. It was about 1 A.M. and I clambered out of the plane wearily. Some three hours had passed since launch.

Back in the air intelligence room we briefed Adm. William Guest, the Task Force commander, who had been listening in on all the monitored radio transmissions.

"Well, did anybody see anything?" he asked in his usual gruff manner.

"No, sir."

"Alvie dropped flares," Nick said.

"See anything?" the admiral asked again.

"I saw the two destroyers and something that might have been tracks. But I didn't see any torpedo boats, sir."

He was obviously irritated. "Well, do you think they're *lying* on the destroyers? They were shooting broadside at their radar targets."

No one could offer an explanation, except to say we couldn't see much because of the storm, the fog, and the absence of moonlight or stars.

"Sir," said one of the pilots, "they told us to go on back to the ships. They said they didn't need us."

There was a strained silence but the admiral nodded his head, giving the impression he already knew about the order to return to the *Constellation*.

"Okay, well thanks a lot, boys," said the admiral. "That'll be all."

Air intelligence told us to write out detailed debriefs. They had to be accurate, someone noted, because they were to be used as supporting evidence at the United Nations.

We sat around in our ready room, still stupefied at how hysterical they'd been on the *Maddox* and *Turner Joy*. We had been there to help yet they had shown little ability to coordinate in their wild disorder. None of us had seen any PT boats and it seemed the destroyers were battling phantom targets.

"Nick," I said, "did you hear that guy tell us to go home?"

"Yeah, that was strange."

Still bewildered but very tired, we got to bed about 3:30 A.M. By then, both Capt. John Herrick, commander of the Seventh Fleet's destroyer division 192, and the *Maddox's* skipper, Cmdr. Herbert Ogier, had become suspicious at the number of sonar contacts. The destroyers had reported twenty-two torpedoes though each North Vietnamese PT boat could carry only two torpedoes and the *Turner Joy* had recorded a running battle with only four to six high speed patrol craft. Herrick, who was also aboard the *Maddox*, put the destroyer into full turns and discovered that the sonarman reported hearing torpedoes. It turned out that it was the echo of the ship's outgoing sonar beam hitting the rudders, which were then full over, and being reflected back into the receiver. It would be some time, however, before Herrick relayed his findings and doubts to higher military authorities.

2
REPRISAL

AT 8:14 A.M. ON TUESDAY, AUGUST 4, A TELEPHONE RANG AT
the Defense Intelligence Agency in the Pentagon. The caller spoke from the
top secret National Security Agency which intercepted, translated and distributed communications intelligence from around the world. He warned
that North Vietnam, ahead by twelve hours in the time differential, planned
imminent naval action, possibly against the *Maddox* and *Turner Joy*.

During the call, the text of the secret intercept came over the DIA's cable
channel for high priority, sensitive traffic. A courier dashed to deliver copies
to Defense Secretary Robert McNamara and the Chairman of the Joint
Chiefs of Staff, Gen. Earle Wheeler. By the time McNamara telephoned the
president to relay the communications intelligence, an hour had passed since
the NSA alert. Lyndon Johnson was caught in a routine breakfast meeting
with congressional leaders, but he acted swiftly and resolutely.

In a mood now markedly serious, he turned the discussion to Vietnam and
consideration of a congressional resolution which would empower him to use
armed forces in Southeast Asia.

When the meeting was over, Majority Leader Carl Albert (D-Okla.) remained behind and overheard the president giving telephone instructions to
someone whom he believed to be Gen. Wheeler. The president said, "I not
only want retaliation. I want you to go all the way in to the shore establish-
ments, the supporting elements of these boats, and bomb them out of existence. Go get 'em and not only get 'em but get the things that feed and
supply 'em!"

At about 11 A.M. Defense Secretary McNamara telephoned the president
for the fourth time that morning. He had sketchy but momentous news: The
Maddox and *Turner Joy* were under torpedo attack.

Johnson was furious that the North Vietnamese had the audacity to attack
American ships. At a lunch meeting with top advisors he authorized aerial
bombing of oil tanks at Vinh and patrol craft bases bordering the Gulf of

Tonkin. McNamara estimated the warplanes would head for North Vietnam about 7 P.M. Washington time.

Then, astonishingly, a message from Captain Herrick aboard the *Maddox* cast doubt on the earlier attacks, stating:

> *Review of action makes many recorded contacts and torpedoes fired appear doubtful. Freak weather effects and over-eager sonarman may have accounted for many reports. No actual visual sightings by Maddox. Suggest complete evaluation before any further action.*

Later that afternoon, however, Herrick relayed another message; even though the evidence was confusing, he was now "certain that original ambush was bonafide."

At a hastily convened meeting of the National Security Council, the president pointedly asked CIA chief, John McCone, "do they want war by attacking our ships in the middle of the Gulf of Tonkin?"

"No," replied the gray-haired McCone. "The North Vietnamese are reacting defensively to our attacks on their offshore islands. They are responding out of pride and on the basis of defense considerations. The attack is a signal to us that the North Vietnamese have the will and determination to continue the war. They are raising the ante."

The scant evidence of torpedo attacks troubled Carl Rowan, Director of the U.S. Information Agency. "Do we know for a fact that the North Vietnamese provocation took place?" he asked. "Can we nail down exactly what happened? We must be prepared to be accused of fabricating the incident."

Though the bombing was scheduled to take place in less than three hours, McNamara replied: "We will know definitely in the morning."

As far as McNamara was concerned, highly classified intercepts of North Vietnamese military communications were "unimpeachable" evidence of the naval attacks. But Dr. Ray Cline, the CIA's Deputy Director in charge of Intelligence, felt a "sort of gnawing uncomfortableness" as he scanned the same intercepts. He regarded it as an imperfect intelligence operation because policymakers wanted quick action rather than a close analysis. It would be several days before he openly expressed his reservations.

Meanwhile, the countdown had begun for the historic inaugural bombing of North Vietnam by the United States.

Lyndon Johnson presided in vintage form at a meeting of the congressional leadership. These were the people he understood best, and from whose ranks he had emerged with an awesome reputation for kneading the congressional psyche with artful persuasion and manipulative skill. Seated in his high-backed, black leather chair, the president simplified the options: "We can tuck our tails and run, but if we do, these countries will feel all they have to do to scare us is to shoot at the American flag. I think I know what the reaction would be if we tucked our tails."

He asked their support for a congressional resolution empowering him to use U.S. armed forces in Southeast Asia. House Speaker John McCormack assured it when he declared, "Congress has a responsibility and should show a united front."

Lyndon Johnson wanted to show he was in complete and absolute control, before the North Vietnamese could present their version of the incident. Yet television prime time slipped by as events beyond control forced postponement. There was a communications lag with the *Ticonderoga*, and the *Constellation* was not close enough to launch its strike aircraft.

Tension rose as the night wore on. The president was losing his east coast audience as viewers retired to bed. Yet the reprisal raid could not be postponed until the morning because it would then be dusk in Vietnam, making visibility difficult for American pilots. By then, too, the Vietnamese would have time to issue their own version of events.

Finally, at 11:20 P.M., Adm. U.S. Grant Sharp, Jr., commander of U.S. Pacific Forces (CINCPAC), briefed McNamara. "She *(Ticonderoga)* got her planes off." He said it would take the aircraft about one hour and fifty minutes to reach their destination over the oil tanks at Vinh.

Johnson was visibly frustrated and testy. He had been held up and he desperately wanted to get it done his way. He walked to the Fish Room, near the Oval Office and, with a somber look, he began his speech at 11:36 P.M.

> *My fellow Americans. As president and commander-in-chief, it is my duty to the American people to report that renewed hostile actions against United States ships on the high seas in the Gulf of Tonkin have today required me to order the military forces of the United States to take action in reply . . . . . . Air action is now in execution against gunboats and certain supporting facilities in North Vietnam which have been used in these hostile operations . . . . . . Our response, for the present, will be limited and fitting. . . . . We still seek no wider war . . . . . .*

In reality, the only planes airborne for the retaliatory strike when the president announced "air action is now in execution" were four lumbering Skyraiders still 350 miles short of their target. These Skyraiders, the first of

59 U.S. planes that would fly off to North Vietnamese targets that day, peeled off towards their destinations a single minute before Lyndon Johnson began his televised speech. The president had unwittingly warned the North Vietnamese of the reprisal strikes, code-named *Pierce Arrow*, 99 minutes before the first bombs fell and three-and-one-half hours before the *Constellation*'s aircraft would strike.

The short, sharp ring of the telephone roused me from a deep sleep at 10 o'clock on the morning of Wednesday, August 5. It was the squadron duty officer.

"Alvie, they want you in AI. You're going to fly a mission."

"I'll be right there!"

Impatient to find out what was up, I hurriedly dressed in the same khaki flight suit I had worn on the night mission, dropping flares over the *Maddox* and *Turner Joy*. I got to AI just before the carrier air group (CAG) commander walked in to brief about twenty pilots already assembled.

"Gentlemen," he said, sliding open the information board to reveal a large map of North Vietnam, "this is a contingency plan for strikes against North Vietnam, in retaliation for what happened last night."

It was the first really good look I'd had of a map of North Vietnam. He pointed out targets by working his way up from the southernmost one near the DMZ. I was in a group of A4s from our squadron assigned to hit the naval base at Hon Gai harbor, about twenty-five miles northeast of Haiphong and only fifty miles south of the Chinese frontier. We were all amazed. We knew next to nothing about Vietnam and the briefing was so scant it left gaping holes in vital information on target layouts and area defenses. Nothing at all was said about search and rescue.

It was hard to believe we were heading for North Vietnam! Until now it had been strictly hands off. We couldn't even go near it. We'd been extra careful to fly only over South Vietnam on our missions to Laos. But in one of our flight exercises a few weeks back we had simulated penetrating the North Vietnamese coast with low level flights to avoid detection. We practiced popping up at the last moment, just before attacking supposed North Vietnamese bridges, so that we would maintain the element of surprise and minimize our exposure to enemy fire.

"Gosh, Alvie, just think of that!" Nick had said then as he gazed at the wall maps after one briefing. "Bombing bridges on Route I, over North Vietnam! I wonder what's going on."

Now we were not only going to fly over North Vietnam. We really were going to *bomb* it—for the very first time! It was long overdue. All of us knew where the real trouble stemmed from. Finally we were going to go in and do something about it.

About an hour after the briefing began, the CAG came back in. "We just got the word from Washington! This is a GO!"

The *Constellation* was south of Hainan Island and about 350 miles away from the target, as the crow flies. It would be high altitude flying all the way, to make the best use of fuel because there would be no refueling in the air. Four slower Skyraiders were set to launch an hour and a half before us so we would arrive on target simultaneously. As soon as we got through planning our hops I went down to the wardroom for a sandwich. I sat across the table from Roger Sheets, who'd been in charge of directing me down from the Tonkin Gulf flight the night before.

"Busy night last night, Alvie," he commented.

"Yeah. Did you have me?"

"God, of course, Alvie. You panicked."

"Panicked? No way. I was just concerned about being so low on fuel."

I didn't remind him about that earlier landing when they'd lost me on the scope because of sea clutter.

Just then one of the F4 pilots, who'd slept through the entire night mission, walked in, sat next to Roger and looked puzzled.

"What's all the activity? What's going on?"

"Well, our destroyers were attacked by torpedo boats last night," the assistant operations officer said casually as he continued his meal.

"Son-of-a-bitch!" said the pilot. "Aren't we *ever* going to do anything about it?"

"Yeah," said Roger, nodding towards me, "they're going right now."

The pilot swiveled towards me. "Where are you going?"

Roger cut in. "They're going up north."

"NO SHIT!"

I was in the first of two Skyhawk launches, scheduled for 2:30 P.M.! This was going to be live ammo—not flares—against live targets, in broad daylight! It was at once both chilling and invigorating, reminding me of our brush with Soviet pilots the previous year, when we became the first U.S. ship in the Pacific to be targeted for reconnaissance overflights by the long-range heavy Russian "Bear" bombers. They wanted to prove their capabilities but we weren't taking any chances. Our planes were ordered to intercept and as ten "Bears" flew over, at altitudes ranging from 100 feet to 10,000 feet, several of our fighters were on their wings. Our instructions were clear: open fire if they open their bomb bays. This aerial rendezvous ended light-heartedly when some U.S. and Soviet pilots flying alongside each other took pictures, while others waved greetings, or gave one another the bird. The brief confrontation highlighted the grim training given us in flying nuclear bombs. The reality of perhaps having to fly with primed nuclear cargo was awesome. Everyone knew we would be flying suicide missions because even if we dodged the nuclear blast, the carrier would assuredly have been wiped out before our return.

"Wow! Imagine that! Nuclear weapons! It's crazy, isn't it," one of my colleagues exclaimed at the time.

If things ever got to that point, well, it was our job; I just hoped that sane people would be in control and that they would at least have exhausted every alternative course open to them before ordering a nuclear attack.

I was brought back sharply to the present by the high-pitched whistle of a general quarters alarm over the speakers.

"General quarters! General quarters! This is not a drill!"

Without a pause, the captain disclosed orders for the imminent raid by the carrier's planes. He announced that attack aircraft had already launched from the *Ticonderoga* for similar strikes. The captain said he had sounded general quarters to be prepared in case the enemy tried a reprisal raid against our carrier. The announcement galvanized the crew. Deck hands, flight crew, everyone seemed to be running to don combat gear, man the guns and effect emergency procedures.

I raced to put on my G-suit, lacing it up tightly so that it fit like a corset around my waist and legs over my combat flight suit. Though weighted down with about thirty pounds of gear, I was eager and restless in the ready room as I quickly reviewed the briefing by intelligence officers. Our target, Hon Gai, was a bay city from where the Vietnamese shipped out coal. But the briefing had been vague and flimsy. An intelligence officer had pointed to the unfurled map and said, "Look around here, the PT boats may be at wharves on the northeast side of the mouth of the bay. If you don't see anything, then look over at this location. . . ." He didn't know for sure where the anti-aircraft artillery might be, nor whether we might confront enemy aircraft. Our specific targets, however, were torpedo boats.

None of us knew then how concerned the top U.S. brass had been about the possibility of our clashing with Chinese warplanes. Intelligence believed the Chinese had seventy-nine jet fighters on Hainan Island and, unknown to us, there were reports that some of these had flown down as far as Danang, on the South Vietnamese coast, during the night. That was why the northernmost of our original targets, Port Wallut, lying only 25 miles south of China, was hastily scratched after our briefing. A recorded telephone conversation that morning between the Chairman of the Joint Chiefs of Staff, Gen. Wheeler, and the Commander-in-Chief, Pacific, Admiral Sharp, highlighted their concern about the Chinese as they spoke in guarded language over secure phones:

Wheeler: "You are going to have to lose out on those northern ones."

Sharp: "Just one. Just the most northern one. Now for two reasons. It's pretty close to the other country."

Wheeler: "I got you."

Sharp: "The weather's bad and they would have difficulty locating the target and might stray. We also know that we got some people coming down from that other country."

Wheeler: "I see. I understand."

Sharp: "You know?"

Wheeler: "Yes, I see."

Sharp: "And we've got some opposition to bother about."

Wheeler: "Right."

The order came through crisply at 2 P.M. "Man aircraft!"

I slipped my arms and legs through the torso harness and zipped it up over my G-suit. Part of it held my survival vest with shark repellant, magnesium flare, food rations, knife, shroud-cutter and whistle. As I put on my gloves I noticed my wedding ring. Survival school instructors had warned us not to wear them in combat because communists would inflict further mental torture on a captured married pilot by fabricating stories about the aviator's wife abandoning him for another man. Rapidly, I debated whether to leave it with a colleague standing next to me. Oh, what the hell, there wasn't time, and I'd always flown with it, just like the St. Christopher medal I conscientiously detached from my key ring and put in my sleeve pocket before every flight.

I had the same plane I'd flown the night before, and of the fifteen Skyhawks scheduled to take off at 2:30 P.M. for Hon Gai and Loc Chao, I was to be the very first launch. Our call sign was *War Paint* and I was 411.

Everyone on deck seemed to be excited and energized by the combat missions. A gung ho crewman sat on the wing of my plane and patted the skin. "Don't break it, sir! She's the best plane we've got!" he joshed in his thick Brooklyn accent.

At that moment the captain announced over the bullhorn that the twenty-two aircraft from the *Ticonderoga* which had struck other North Vietnamese targets at 1:15 P.M. were already on the way back to their ship. So far there was only one damaged plane and it was heading for Danang.

Lawson, the plane captain who acted as a kind of pilot's valet, positioned the ladder and helped me climb up into the tiny cockpit. He hooked my torso harness to the seat's twin D-rings. He'd already checked out my parachute and life raft attached to the seat.

I pulled out the two safety pins with red ribbons from the alternate ejection handle and gave them to him. He removed another from behind me for the main ejection face curtain, held it up to me, then rolled up all three and stuffed them in a side panel. I strapped on my knee-board, slipped on my helmet and fastened the face mask. A flip of the toggle switch brought on a hiss and a steady flow of oxygen. I made a radio check. Transmission was good.

"Okay?" Lawson asked.

"Fine."

"Go get 'em, sir! Good luck!"

He climbed down and took the ladder over to the catwalk. I closed the canopy. Ahead, a flight deck crewman swiveled his wrist, signaling me to start the engines. After I heard the familiar rush of air into the turbine I went through the post-engine check.

As I taxied up to the catapult, a crewman stuck the small protrusion at the end of the steel tiller bar into the center of the nose wheel, then steered the Skyhawk so that its nose wheel rolled up and just over the shuttle. Deck crew attached the weighty cables to the plane and the hold-back bar. Seconds later the cables strained and the aircraft seemed to vibrate in the steely grip of the stiffened catapult. As the engines roared to a crescendo I gave the customary "all clear" salute with my free right hand. The flight deck officer looked to see that the deck was clear, gave me a thumbs-up sign for good luck, then drew an arc in the air with one arm. Boom! Off I went, pulled by the mechanical shuttle and flung from the deck as my engines thrust and screamed. It was no wonder many aviators joked about the best thing to say at the moment of lift-off: "Thank you, God—I have it now! I'm flying!"

All ten Skyhawks assigned to attack Hon Gai rendezvoused at 20,000 feet before climbing to 30,000 feet for the seventy-minute flight northwest to the target.

"Holy smokes!" I thought to myself. "This is war! We're going into battle! My God! This could be the start of something really big!" Yet I wasn't scared, just a little jittery. It reminded me of the butterflies I'd felt running track in high school, just before the starter's gun went off.

I was flying wing on Cmdr. Bob Nottingham, our flight leader, when we broke through to clear blue skies after half an hour. North Vietnam's coastline, with the port of Haiphong over on the left, spread out before we began our descent. Nottingham broke radio silence. "When we go in, everybody drop back. Alvie and I'll go in first."

According to the vague briefing, we might find the boats on the right side of the bay.

"Okay, everybody, check your switches," said Nottingham as we powered back during descent.

I turned on the switch for the pod of nineteen rockets clipped under the fuselage on my center-line rack. Simultaneously we heard the leader of the four aging, single-engine propeller-driven Skyraiders, which had launched an hour-and-a-half before us to link up for the combined attack. "Okay boys, let's give her the gun. Let's add throttle. Check your switches."

From the lone F4 flying fighter-cover over us came a short, stirring war cry: "Go get 'em, tigers!"

I couldn't have looked too closely at the briefing map because only now did I become aware of the proliferation of tiny rocky islands off the coast. The bay had a narrow mouth. Over to the right were the docks, but there were no boats there, as our briefers had guessed. We streaked in at about 500 miles per hour in a shallow, fifteen-degree dive.

The flight leader and I must have seen them at the same time, to our left: four torpedo boats lined up next to a much larger coastal patrol ship.

"Good God! Shoot!" Nottingham yelled as he flew by, too late to open fire.

I was flying in loose formation, about seventy feet behind him. I kicked the plane over a bit, pointed the nose and squeezed the trigger. There was no time to see if my rockets hit home. As I pulled off sharply to the right, staying inside the bay, I called over the mike to the other A4s: "They're sitting inside the bay, on the west side! Four torpedo boats and a big one!"

"Rog, Alvie," Nick acknowledged.

"Look out! They're shooting at you!" warned the F4 pilot as the third A4 screamed in on the boats.

As I looked back the whole world seemed to be firing at me. The Skyhawks zeroed in, one after the other at two-second intervals. I flew through streams of black flak peppering the sky from the naval craft and AAA batteries on the hills behind. This was heavier flak than we'd anticipated and they opened up so quickly it was obvious they'd been on alert. But I felt as if I was operating like an old pro. I was neither distracted by nor scared of the flak.

As the last of the Skyhawks rolled in and pulled off Nottingham radioed, "I'm going in again." I had not yet fired my 20mm ammo, so I quickly flipped on my gun switch, set the gunsight for a shallow strafing run and re-checked that my master armament switch was on. I followed Nottingham in again because I'd had it drilled into me that a good wingman always sticks to his leader.

Down below the PT boats were burning and smoke wafted lightly out of the bigger craft. Nottingham came in on a run almost identical to his first pass, fired his rocket pod and called "Pulling off!" I couldn't see whether he hit anything.

"I'm in!" I announced, as I came in on a low, strafing run on the largest boat while silent tracer bullets swept by me. My first few rounds hit just below the water line but I held it, in spite of the heavy flak, and walked the fire up the side of the boat until it struck the bridge. I held it there as pieces of the bridge fragmented and flew off. I could have done more damage but the pressure gave on the trigger. Either I had run out of ammunition or the guns had jammed.

I was pulling up when Nottingham said, "I'm staying on the deck." He was low and turning full bore to the right. I pulled down and couldn't have been more than 100 feet above the water as I tried to stay on the inside of his turn to catch up with him. He leveled his wings as we zoomed across land to the eastern side of the bay. We skimmed over the trees and red-tiled rooftops. "How quiet and peaceful," I thought, "but that's enemy territory down there!"

We were passing over the southern edge of the town, approaching a hilly ridge overlooking the sea, when I heard a sound like *poom* followed by a big yellow flash on the port (left) side of my windscreen. The plane shook violently, rattling and clanking as if someone had thrown a bucket of nuts and bolts into the engine. All my fire and hydraulic warning lights flashed on. Smoke filled the cockpit, the hydraulic system lost power and the stick froze. Strangely, though, everything appeared to be taking place in slow motion. It must have been my imagination but I could not seem to move my hands, key the mike button, or even talk as fast as the crisis demanded.

I keyed the mike.

"409, this is 411. I've been hit!"

"What's your position?" Nottingham asked.

"Right behind you!"

I pulled my emergency flight disconnect when all the hydraulic lights came on and immediately deployed my emergency generator. My ears buzzed from electrical static in the headset. I pulled the jettison to dump everything I had on the wings, even though I didn't know if the explosion had knocked off part or all of a wing. The crippled Skyhawk banked to the left.

Again I keyed the mike.

"I'm on fire and out of control!"

Frantically I fought the stick to try and level up. It was obvious the plane was coming apart. If I had to eject I would have to level the wings. But the more I tried to bring the plane over to the right, the more it toppled left. I was losing the little altitude I had.

Nick Nicholson's voice came into the headset: "You know what to do, Alvie!"

"Right," I replied amid the confusion.

But as soon as I spoke I wondered what on earth he could have meant. There was no time for questions and answers. The best bet would be to try and hit the stick all the way to the left and roll it over completely so I'd come out level, and punch out going straight up. The plane rolled upside down and was coming up right when the nose dropped. This left me hanging in the strap, almost inverted, at an angle of about forty-five degrees to the terrain. If I hung in any longer I would crash with the plane. I could see I was only about 500 feet above land. If I ejected now I'd have a chance to live—with, at best, a couple of broken bones.

I keyed the mike, not knowing if it would transmit. "I'm getting out! I'll see you guys later!"

I grabbed the ring of the face curtain behind my head and yanked hard. The canopy shot off and the rocket blasted my seat up the rails and out of the doomed plane. The air stream ripped the face curtain out of my hand and pinned my arms and legs back as I dropped head down and spread-eagled. I felt whoozy and almost blacked out. Something tugged my body. I heard the *pop* of the pilot chute as it pulled out the main parachute with a louder clap while the metal seat automatically fell away. Within one or two seconds, I hit water, and not land, as expected.

3
CAPTIVITY

I PULLED AWAY MY FACE MASK, RIPPED OFF MY HELMET and pushed down on the two levers to release the parachute, which sank quickly. Instantly I was covered in the oozing black dye of shark repellant, whose container accidentally broke loose in my survival vest. Unknown to me, our planes picked up the signal from my beeper, which transmitted automatically for almost a full minute from the moment I ejected. But none of the aviators had seen my parachute as I dropped a few hundred yards away from the coastline.

Further out to sea, about 200 yards away from me, were a couple of sampan fishing boats with sails. I couldn't help thinking of Tangee, my bride of seven months, and Mom. What would happen to them? My poor wife. And how would Mom cope? She was scared to death of flying and always worried about me. I had to get out of here but, fearing capture, I feverishly took off my wedding ring and dropped it in the Gulf of Tonkin. "Don't worry, sweetheart," I thought, "Someday I'll get you another one."

At the same time, God knows why, I remembered a pilots' briefing a few years earlier when they told us about a wild Laotian tribe that would shoot if we were armed and ask questions later. I undid my .38 pistol holster and let it fall to the ocean bed. Then I unhooked my seat pack with life raft and survival kit and dragged it along as I tried to swim underwater, away from shore. But the current dragged me towards land. When I came up gasping for air I was startled by a gush of water just behind me. They were firing from 150-foot-high cliffs. I saw that they were trying to hit a Skyraider which made a fast right turn about 100 feet over me before heading further out to sea and out of sight. I was unaware of how much time had passed but I felt exhausted. There seemed to be no one around so I decided to inflate part of the life jacket to help keep me afloat. I pulled a toggle, forgetting this would inflate the entire greenish-yellow jacket. All of a sudden I stuck out like a sore thumb.

As I worked feverishly to unscrew the stopper to deflate my vest, I heard a zinging noise. Something cut through my flight suit and nicked my elbow. When I looked up I saw a sampan circling some thirty yards away. Four of the fisherman pointed rifles at me. A fifth leveled a pistol and the sixth clutched a hand grenade. The little boat edged closer as they fired again, this time over my head. I let go of the seat pack.

"Don't do that!" I shouted.

One of the scrawny fishermen stood up and motioned me to raise my hands. They pulled alongside, looped my hands and neck with ropes and yanked me aboard. Roughly, they stripped off my boots, socks, and G-suit, and trussed me up with the same fervor that fisherman would apply to subdue a snared shark. Everyone was shouting except for the one with the hand grenade, who stood and trembled.

When they were satisfied I had been rendered harmless, they relaxed a bit, standing back to put on their green pith helmets pinned with military insignia. Most probably they were also part of the coastal militia. The one who gave orders glared at me, then stuffed a cigarette in my mouth.

I was drenched through with sea water. My legs ached and short stabs of pain shot through my back with every slight move. While they chattered and gesticulated excitedly, I lay mute and numb, tired and reeling from the shock of events. What would they do? Hang me by my ankles? Rip off my skin? Castrate me? Lop off my head? I had no fight in me and did not fear sudden death. But I began to pray silently:

Our Father, who art in heaven. Hallowed be Thy name. Thy kingdom come. Thy will be done. . . .

As the little boat drifted slowly around the crash site, they reached overboard to retrieve some of the floating debris. They brought aboard my hard hat and the liquid oxygen tank. Then one of them shouted and his cries were picked up by the others as they called out across the water. Answering voices filtered across from a distance. Soon I heard the *put-put-put* of a diesel motor as a tug boat loomed large over us, its deck bristling with militiamen clutching obsolete bolt-action rifles. Four of them jumped down into our boat. They glowered at me and jabbed my prostrate body with bayonets.

I didn't understand any of their questions which were put to me brusquely and repeatedly. Perhaps to confuse them and to try and conceal my identity, I answered reflexively in Spanish.

"Que? No entiendo. No entiendo."

One of them coaxed, wondering if I were Vietnamese: "Vietna? Vietna?"

The others looked at the length of my body and shook their heads. I was too tall to be a native. I lay there, with a cigarette drooping from my mouth because every time it burned down my captors stuck in another. The newcomers left abruptly and their tug boat pulled off and away. I tried to sit up and look around but a fisherman pushed me down.

A while later the whirr of another motorized craft grew louder and my captors waved and shouted. A torpedo boat drew alongside and the engine idled. Some of the crew jumped aboard. The officers, identifiable by insignia on their white shirt collars, wore navy blue trousers. The other ranks were dressed in traditional black-striped bibs and white caps, like British sailors, banded in blue with tassels hanging down one side. With dispatch and discipline, they carried me to the torpedo boat deck, where they covered all but my face with a tarpaulin. Two sailors stood over me, their rifles aimed at point blank range. Another crew member had a blood-stained bandage over one ear. Perhaps, I thought, he'd been injured during our aerial raid. I saw them bring aboard my personal gear and the recovered wreckage. An officer scribbled something on a note pad and gave it to the commander of the fishermen, who nodded obediently. Maybe it was an address where he could claim his reward.

A man in civilian clothing stood over me and began quizzing in Vietnamese. Again I replied in Spanish. Nonplussed, he went off to confer with an officer.

When he returned he asked: "Parlez-vous Francais?"

"Que? Que? No entiendo."

They shook their heads, utterly perplexed about my nationality. But now they were rifling through my flight gear and found my wallet with ID. They all looked my way as the civilian approached.

"Me? Me?"

"No entiendo."

While the others looked over my billfold and Geneva Convention card the man questioning me wrote the letters MY and drew a little curlicue over the Y to pronounce it ME. Then he wrote down on the same piece of paper the letters U.S.A. and pointed to the paper and then to me.

"U.S.A.?" he asked.

"Uh huh," I nodded.

His jaw dropped and his eyes dilated.

"Me! Me!" he shouted to the others. It was Vietnamese for American.

The word rippled off the lips of the rest of the incredulous crew. At once everyone looked around, searching the skies for more Americans. Now they knew who had bombed their naval base.

They were all silent as they steered back to Hon Gai. I glanced up to see black smoke billowing skywards. The sailors looked pensive and sad and a young enlisted man near me seemed on the verge of tears. He glanced at me as if to say, "See, look what you did." When I raised my head to get a better look, other sailors hastily pushed me down and covered me with the tarpaulin. The people I had seen gathered on the coal-loading docks broke out into loud hand-clapping applause after our crew yelled out something, presumably news of my capture.

They blindfolded me so well I couldn't see a thing, then they untied my legs and led me off the boat by the rope around my neck. My hands were still bound tightly together. Denied my eyesight, my other senses sharpened and I became aware of something more malodorous than the smell of cow-sheds. This was the unmistakable whiff of human excrement, which the Vietnamese had used since generations past to fertilize arable soil. It hung offensively in the windless heat of the tropical land.

The guards sat me down then removed the blindfold. A picture of Ho Chi Minh hung like Orwell's omnipresent "Big Brother" in the austerely furnished room. There were only two tables and straight-backed wooden chairs, looking like they'd been pulled from an old schoolroom. I sat for some five hours, feeling barefoot and broke. Night had fallen and the large, naked light bulb hanging from the ceiling threw gloomy shadows around the dingy room. Ordinary townspeople, more curious than hostile, poked their heads in the doorway. Occasionally a child peeked in. I'd smile and he'd smile back before withdrawing shyly. Militiamen in identical brown uniforms and pith helmets, without distinguishing badges of rank, ambled in and out to get a glimpse of the downed American flyer.

Two older men came in, one clutching a camera. Gracelessly, they motioned me to look down submissively. Far from wanting to treat me like an object of fun and ridicule, they seemed intent on debasing and demeaning me pictorially. To press the point, the cameraman stood on the table and, as he towered above, he gleefully commanded me to hang my head. My exhaustion made me more compliant. I could barely keep my eyes open and my head up as I struggled to stay awake. Nevertheless, I was relieved to see them go.

My mind wandered back to the guys in the squadron. By now they must have reported me downed and captured. Maybe they'd already relayed the news to Mom, Dad and Tangee. I remembered how quickly they'd reported one of the *Ticonderoga*'s planes damaged on their earlier raids that afternoon. I'd actually heard it broadcast over the bullhorn speakers as I climbed into my cockpit.

My thoughts were interrupted when a thin, elderly man, with fragile features, sat down next to me. He was dressed in civilian navy blue pants, white shirt and sandals.

"And now you must answer some questions," he said, alternately expanding and contracting syllables, so that words seemed to slide from his lips with the same motions which propelled a garden worm forward.

I tried to level my glazed, weary eyes to look him in the eye. It was no use. I was so drowsy it was an effort merely to keep awake. He was very relaxed, sitting cross-legged and smoking a cigarette, with one elbow on the table.

"You are . . . an American. You must tell me your name."

"Everett Alvarez, Jr."

"How do you spell?" he asked, preparing to write it down.

I told him.

"What is your grade in U.S. Navy?"

"Lt. j.g."

"What plane did you fly?"

I didn't answer.

"You must answer my questions," he said with the same controlled geniality.

"I cannot."

"Well, now," he oozed, "are you injured?"

"Yes. I hurt all over." By now I also noticed blood on my arm from the bullet that nicked me in the sea. And the rough hemp rope tightly wound round my wrists, bit into my skin.

"Are you hungry? Thirsty? You want some tea?" he asked, his lean face lighting up.

"I'd like some tea."

"You would like some nice, warm food? Are you hungry?"

"Yes."

The only food I had eaten all day was a sandwich shortly before launch. Being fond of Chinese food, I envisioned they would bring me a full plate of succulent sweet and sour pork with a mound of steaming-hot fried rice.

Then he ordered me to take off my clothes so they could search me. I ached as I painstakingly moved my limbs out of the cloyingly wet flight suit and underwear. Ejection at high speed had pulled on my arm and leg joints and they hurt so much they felt like I had been stretched over a medieval rack. Coupled with severe back pain, also resulting from the bail-out, I moved very slowly and stiffly, as if I had been dipped in quick-drying concrete. It would be several months before my body healed and I moved like a normal person.

My condition drew no special sympathy from two elderly guards who searched my naked body so zealously that they even picked at my scalp in the manner of monkeys grooming each other. They pried under my finger and toe nails, ran their fingers inside my mouth, and made me bend over to continue their tactile check, uninhibited by the presence of the militiamen and peasants. Satisfied, they handed me a pair of blue and white striped pajamas. When I had dressed they tittered and giggled *Hee! Hee! Hee!* What was obviously a large pair of pajamas for Vietnamese, reached down just below my knees.

"You may sit," said the interrogator. "We bring you some warm food."

A barefooted peasant girl, with baggy pants corded around her waist, set down a plate of thick, dark gravy with a chunk of water buffalo meat. Though famished, I could not swallow the meat. It was bland and nauseating and smelled awful. I pushed it aside and sipped the tea, but it was so brackish and foul that I almost spat it out.

"You did not eat," the interrogator observed. "You not hungry?"

"No, I can't. Hey, I have to go to the bathroom. You know, I have to . . ."

"Ah, you make water?"

"That's it."

"One minute."

He shouted an order. A militiaman approached with what looked like a wide-spouted teapot. The interrogator gave it to me.

"What's this," I asked.

"You make water."

"Oh, yeah. But where?" I asked, looking around for privacy.

"There," he said, pointing towards the wall. "You stand there."

"What about all these people," I said, gesturing to the crowds poking their heads in and the militiamen milling around. He shooed them away.

His familiarity with English made him the only comfortable link I had with my own culture.

"What's going to happen to me now?"

"Oh, we do not know."

It began to dawn on me that perhaps arrangements were being made for U.S. officials to come and get me.

He pointed to my gear laid out on the floor.

"Now, you tell me, what is this?"

"My helmet, my boots."

"Yes, it is your equipment. What type of plane were you flying?"

"I can't tell you."

He spoke to some of the others in the clipped accent and staccato delivery of the vernacular.

"Maybe you like to clean and wash? You like nice bath?"

"Yeah."

"You sit there. We will take you. You will have nice bath."

He got up and left. I rested my head on the table and closed my eyes. Some time later I heard a vehicle pull up noisily.

"You not sleep here," said the old man. "You must come with us. We go."

"Where am I going?"

"To have nice bath. You want bath?"

"Yes," I nodded, imagining, in my drowsiness that I would soon be wallowing in the warm waters of a hotsie bath, and that my bruised and aching body would be tended by solicitous females.

They handcuffed my wrists tightly together and walked me out into the darkness.

"You sit between the guards."

One of the militiamen smiled at me as I got in the back of the jeep. The interrogator sat in the front. In silence, we crossed through darkened streets to the mouth of the bay, drove aboard the ferry and then through deserted streets in Hon Gai. Many of the small buildings appeared to be lit from the inside by coal-burning furnaces. We passed over a dirt road and drew into a compound of brick buildings whose walls had been smoothed over with mortar and painted a yellowish color. Barbed wire fencing surrounded the entire perimeter.

I followed the guards obediently, impatient to get into the bath. We walked through several gates, down a hill and into another barbed wire compound within which was a long, low building. With consternation, I realized this was a jail only when we passed alongside the rows of identical cells with barred windows. My escort stopped abruptly, removed my handcuffs, and opened a door. Two Vietnamese men, dressed only in shorts, registered surprise. They sprang up quickly and respectfully the moment they saw the guards. The cell was seven feet wide by almost ten feet long, with a large barred window rising from the bed level to the ceiling. The single bed was a flat wooden slab, partly covered with straw mats, which almost filled the entire cell. In the small space at the end of the slab was a rusty bucket filled with water. One of the guards handed me a rag.

"Take bath," said the old man who had quizzed me.

"Bath?"

"Yes! Take bath. They will help you," he said, and turned to leave.

"What's your name," I rasped, fearful of losing my sole English-language communicator.

"Not necessary," he replied, as he vanished forever from my sight.

I tried to bend over to reach the bucket but was pulled up short by the stiffness throughout my body and an excruciating back pain. I felt so groggy that I could have fallen asleep standing up. I bent down again. The water was cold. Gingerly I dabbed my face and hands before slumping against the wall. The two prisoners hurried to remove my pajamas, then washed me with infinite tenderness.

One of the prisoners spoke English. He said the guard wanted me to lie face up so they could manacle my legs. I was so limp with fatigue that they handled me like a Raggedy Ann doll. They placed open iron collars over the bottom of my legs and then ran a long metal bar through holes in the sides of the collars and under my ankles so that it effectively locked my legs in a fixed position. It was now impossible to roll over or even to turn on my side. I took one quick glance at my trapped legs before collapsing into a deep sleep.

Sometime during the night I awoke. The naked light bulb shone remorselessly, grimly illuminating my plight. I was handcuffed and tented inside a mosquito net. My cellmates lay asleep on either side of me, each covered by a mosquito net tucked under separate mats.

Fragments of a conversation I'd had in Pearl Harbor, Hawaii, some months earlier came back to me. I was visiting my former college roommate, Lt. Jack Purl and his wife, Kathy, when he had suddenly exclaimed, "I wish I could fly! I wish I hadn't dropped out of flight training. It was really neat. That's where the excitement is!"

"Oh, Jack!" Kathy had interjected, as if to bring him out of his romantic reverie.

"No, Jack," I corrected, "you're better off where you are as a submarine officer."

"Why do you say that?"

"Jack, you're just safer."

"Why, do you think there's going to be something?"

"Yeah, I think there's going to be something."

"Like what?" they asked in unison.

"I don't know. But whatever it is, you're better off in subs; better off than I am."

The sun was up when the English-speaking prisoner gently tugged me awake.

"You have to go with him," the prisoner urged, looking towards the guard.

The door was open and a guard bent over to release my legs from the shackles. Every move I made to try and get up sent acute pangs through my body. My legs remained almost rigid, my neck felt stiff and my arms and chest ached as if they'd been pummeled and punched.

The guard was oblivious to my pain. He snapped on the single-framed handcuffs which cut into my skin, fumbled for an interminable time with the key as he tried to lock them, then led me, barefoot and dressed in pajamas up the hill we'd descended during the night. Before we entered the room he tried unlocking the handcuffs, and it was then that I first felt the frustration at their ineptitude with keys. Whenever and wherever I was handcuffed in Vietnam, the turnkeys had the same problem.

Two military officers sat behind the table. One of them looked very young and handsome with even white teeth and wavy black hair. He wore a navy uniform with blue pants and white shirt. Much later, when we POWs gave nicknames to many of our captors, he became known as Little Boy Blue. The other officer, dressed in Army khakis with dark brown boots, would be called Owl because his hook-nose, surprised eyes and short-cropped, upstanding hair so closely resembled the nocturnal bird of prey. Aged about forty-five and standing perhaps 5 ft. 5 in. high, Owl had a smooth complexion, stubby fingers, and a trim and muscular athlete's build.

"Sit down," Owl commanded, pointing to the stool. "What is your name?"

"Lt. j.g. Everett Alvarez, Jr. Serial number 644124, born December 23, 1937."

"What ship were you on?"

I sat mute.

"Are you married?"

Silence.

"Do you have any children?"

I looked him in the eye, my lips sealed.

"Do you understand?"

"Yes."

"Why don't you answer?"

"I can't answer those questions."

"Why can't you?"

They offered a cigarette. I hesitated, then took it. But when they offered me beer I declined, figuring they were trying to pull something on me. Vainly, they tried again to get some answers. They looked at each other.

"Why don't you answer?" Owl asked.

"I don't have to. I have already given my name, rank, serial number and date of birth."

They huddled and spoke in low voices.

"Why did your planes come here to bomb and kill our people? Why?"

"To retaliate for your torpedo boat attacks on our ships."

Again they spoke in hushed tones to each other.

"You fool! There were no torpedo boats out there on the night of August 4," said Owl, whose persistent smirk was another of his facial characteristics.

"It is a fabrication! It is a lie! You have been used!" he sputtered angrily.

I thought to myself that they could not possibly know what had happened. If our government declared that our ships had been attacked, then there was no doubt about it. They must have been attacked. Several years later, when I briefly and casually discussed the Tonkin Gulf incident with a few other POWs, we had some doubts whether the U.S. destroyers had in fact been attacked by torpedo boats. After all, none of us flying that night had seen any North Vietnamese boats. But if pressed, not one of us would have admitted to the Vietnamese that our government could have been mistaken. We might admit to doubts as free men, but not while they held us captive. Fortunately, neither Owl nor any other official ever questioned me again about the flare-up in the Gulf of Tonkin.

Owl and the other officer conversed solemnly as they looked out the window behind me towards a hill.

"What do you think of your situation?" Owl asked.

I thought for a couple of seconds. "I am a prisoner of war," I said with some defiance.

"You are not a prisoner of war. There is no war," Owl stated with dramatic simplicity.

"My God!" I thought. "Is he right? There is no declared war!"

"Are you sick," asked Owl.

"I think so. I hurt."

"You want medicine? A doctor?"

"Yes."

"We will bring you a doctor."

Back in the cell they shackled my ankles.

"Your food is here," said the English-speaking prisoner.

"No, I don't want any food," I mumbled as I fell off to sleep.

But not long after they led me up the hill once more to Owl, who sat beside another, slightly older officer.

"This is the commanding officer of our District," said Owl. "He has come to see you."

Owl translated the newcomer's questions.

"He wants to know if you have seen the doctor. How do you feel?"

"I'm very tired."

"Do you have family? Do you have a wife?"

I didn't answer.

"Do you know the damage your planes have caused here? Many lives. Much damage."

He addressed the militiaman.

"You can go back."

They were manacling my legs in the cell once more when I asked the English-speaking prisoner if it was really necessary.

"Yes, for now," he said.

"It's very uncomfortable."

"I know, I know. I had those on for months."

"You?"

"Yes."

"Here," he said with concern, "your food is here. You must eat."

The white metal bowl was decorated with floral motifs. Using chopsticks, I took a few bites of what seemed like rice mixed with corn.

"How do you feel?"

My anguished look said it all.

"Ah, yes. We did not know you were hurt. We could have helped you. Tonight you sleep with this for a pillow," he said, indicating his little fishnet sack of belongings hanging from a nail on the wall.

"What about you?"

"I use this book. Look."

He took it out of the little sack, where he also kept his reading glasses and toothbrush.

"My wife brings me books." There was a studied pause then he looked at me quizzically. "What's your name?"

I hesitated, thinking "Who is this guy?"

Guardedly I answered, "Al."

"Ah! Mr. Al! Mr. Al!" he said exuberantly, as he paced back and forth on top of his side of the bed, his expressive hands resting on his hips, and his head cocked at a jaunty angle.

"Who are *you*?" I asked.

"My Vietnamese name means Sea. His name means Blue," he said, nodding towards the other inmate, who squatted cross-legged on the bed, absorbed in crocheting his little bag of earthly possessions. "You have a wife? Children?" he asked.

I didn't answer.

"Can't talk, eh?" He paused. "Mr. Al! Mr. Al!" he repeated with relish. "We'll take care of you," he said, slapping his thighs as if he had just discovered gold.

"How long have you been here?" I asked.

"Three-and-a-half years."

"THREE-AND-A-HALF YEARS!" I looked around the cell. "Three-and-a-half years!"

"Mr. Blue, he has been here four-and-a-half years," he said with a lunatic grin.

"FOUR-AND-A-HALF YEARS! But how . . . !"

I looked him over carefully for tell-tale signs of long incarceration. All he had on was a pair of blue shorts. He was thin but not emaciated and there was no stoop in his 5 ft. 4 in. frame. Mr. Sea was perhaps fifty years old, about ten years younger than the pensive Mr. Blue, but there was nothing in their lean faces and bodies indicating prolonged physical abuse.

"What did you do to be here so long?"

"I was in military. I was jeep driver. Jeep blew up."

He would not elaborate.

"How did you learn English?"

"Oh, English, I learned it."

I looked out the yard, suddenly aware of the group of inmates digging with picks and shovels.

"What are they doing?" I asked.

"They are digging holes for defense," said Mr. Sea.

"Foxholes?"

"For air attacks." He paused. "Yesterday we saw you."

"What did you see?"

"The airplanes, diving in." He pointed out the window. "Right over there, where the ships are."

"You saw it?"

"Oh, yes. The planes coming in and the shooting. You are a pilot?"

I didn't reply.

"Ah! Can't talk, eh? Can't talk. Wait, wait. The news is coming on!" he said as if it was a daily ritual he did not want to miss. "They are announcing now. It tells what happened."

A female's high-pitched voice crackled over the loudspeaker system.

He stood by the window and strained to catch every word.

"Ah, yes! We shot down eight airplanes!"

"How many?"

"Shhh! Listen!"

Eight airplanes!

"They captured one." He paused. "That's you! That's you!" he exclaimed with childlike glee at having his suspicions confirmed. "Ah! Yes!" he said pensively, his eyes glazing over with a faraway look. "Vietnamese people very heroic!" It sounded, even across our cultural divide, like heavy sarcasm.

Eight airplanes! I knew the *Ticonderoga's* planes were on their way back when we launched and that their lone damaged aircraft had been diverted to Danang. They didn't lose any. That meant that the eight had to come from the *Constellation!* If I was the only one captured that meant of the ten Skyhawks and four Skyraiders attacking Hon Gai, only six had made it back to the ship! Holy smokes! The squadron had been shattered, almost wiped out! What happened to Nick? Was he shot out of the sky too? His wife, Evelyn would be devastated. I had seen their devotion to each other whenever I visited their home at Lemoore Naval Air Station, our home base in California's central San Joaquin Valley, to watch weekend TV football games. One night, when I was still a bachelor, Nick had loaned me his red, canvas-topped sports car for the four-hour drive north to see Tangee. We had just finished night field carrier landing exercises and it was midnight.

"Alvie, you sure you don't want to take a flashlight or some food?" he asked.

"Nah, thanks. I'll be there real soon. Don't worry about it Nick."

I'd made the trip home from the jet air base so many times that I knew all the back roads and short cuts. But it was very dark and raining, and so late that every place I stopped at for coffee was closed. I drove on, over the mountains of Pacheco Pass and was crawling down the west side of a snaking descent, following a very slow semi-truck, when I neared the bottom. The next portion of the road was so familiar that I knew a mile-long stretch lay ahead. I pulled out to overtake and was immediately blinded by the onrushing headlights of a truck. Instinctively I swiveled the wheel in the opposite direction but the road was slick with rain and I got locked in a broadside spin. The truck hit the car's rear end and spun me around before the momentum carried the auto into a ditch. It struck the bank then popped back onto the road in a reverse spin, positioning itself like a patsy to be punched again by the truck. The lightweight British car slammed back into the ditch, buckling so grotesquely that the hood faced up while the rest of the crumpled metal pointed downwards. I felt a blow on my head as my face struck the steering wheel. At the first whiff of gas I lunged for the ignition, turned it off, then flipped the light switch to prevent an electrical spark.

Dazed and bruised, I stumbled out into the cold, black vault of night. Oh, for Nick's offer of a flashlight! Both trucks had vanished. There wasn't a sound or a light at either end of the road. I started to walk back in the direction I'd come from when I saw two moving shafts of light pierce the darkness. It was so black that the two men carrying flashlights passed right by without seeing me. They were peering into the car as I came from behind.

"Looking for something?" I asked.

"The driver."

"That's me."

They were the driver of the truck that had struck me, and his passenger.

"You okay? Are you hurt?"

"No, just a couple of bruises."

"You sure you're okay?"

"Yeah."

He shone his flashlight up and down my khaki uniform and leather flying jacket, stitched with my rank, name tag and squadron patches.

"You a pilot?"

"Yeah."

He swung the flashlight beam over the car. "It doesn't fly very well, does it," he deadpanned. "We saw you in the mirror. Your headlights were spinning around."

"Yeah, I must have hit a slick spot or something."

A few hours later I called the base. "Nick, I've got bad news."

"What happened!"

"I wrecked your car."

"You okay?"

"Yeah. But Nick, your car's demolished."

He brushed it aside. "Don't worry about the car! Are you really okay?"

That was Nick. A fine pilot, a good friend and a real gentleman.

I prayed fervently that he was among the six pilots who had made it back safely to the *Constellation.*

Drowsily I closed my eyes and saw a replay of our aerial attack on Hon Gai. I had always been especially good at gunnery, rolling in on a dive and "getting the picture" by adjusting if I was too shallow or too steep. I was convinced I had performed well. Certainly I had not panicked nor recklessly exposed myself to danger. As I drifted off to sleep, I relived my most frightening hours in the sky some years back, and remembered the wise words of warning that followed from my veteran flight instructor. It had all happened after I finished a training hop at Kingsville Naval Air Station in Texas and didn't feel too well. Anyone feeling drowsy is rushed for blood analysis to check for contamination from oxygen inhaled through face masks. I checked out okay but I still felt blurry-eyed, probably from fatigue. From that moment on, my instructor, a hardened old Marine, Capt. Gregorczyk, better known to all of us as Captain G, called me "Cousin Weakeyes".

Ol' Deadeye Ev's not Deadeye, today!" he'd gloat. "He's Cousin Weakeyes!"

After that episode, any time we'd go up and I'd drop the bombs really close on target he'd exclaim, "Ol' Cousin Weakeyes really was on today!"

One weekend I appeared at sunrise for a scheduled training flight even though I had partied all night without any sleep. A cold shower had not yet cleared my head.

"You ready to go?" Captain G asked as I stood near the F9F-8T dual-seat jet trainer.

"Right," I said, straining to clear my head and wondering how I'd feel inhaling 100 percent oxygen.

I sat in the back seat and pulled the opaque hood over the cockpit so I couldn't see a thing, apart from the instruments. This method of simulating real conditions was the best way to practice for actual instrument flying. The instructor had all the fuse panels and could fail any of my instruments. It was then up to me to compensate by quickly finding an alternative way of getting out of the scrape. I had control of the plane at all times but he could take over any time he chose. From the moment of take-off he began failing instruments. I had no sooner solved the problem when something else went wrong. He must have failed everything he could lay his hands on as he put me through the wringer. Fortunately, the oxygen intake cleared my head.

He took advantage of the light Sunday traffic at Kingsville by making me do one approach landing after the other until we were just about out of fuel. Only then did he give the go-ahead to land. We pulled up, shut down and I climbed out of the cockpit. It was sizzling hot and the sun was blinding. Now that I was off the oxygen my head seemed to spin again. As I stumbled out I felt sick and heaved, while he stood by and guffawed. Even after I'd spilled my guts he continued to rib me.

"Cousin Weakeyes, what's wrong with you, huh? You sick, Cousin Weakeyes? Don't you feel good?"

I went in and cleaned up. Then he called me over for the debrief.

"Let that be a lesson to you!" he said sternly. "We Navy and Marine pilots can go and have a good time. But when it's time to fly that plane, you've got to fly!"

I never forgot.

The fact that I lay shackled in a Vietnamese prison could not be attributed to any flight error on my part. Try as I might I could not find fault with any of my maneuvers. I had made no mistakes, taken no extraordinary risks. It was just pure bad luck that some wild flak had struck my plane. This was a natural hazard of combat missions which no amount of training could prevent.

When I woke up, it was dark.

"Doctor has come. He wants to know how you feel?" said Mr. Sea.

"Very sore."

They unshackled me as the white-coated doctor came in holding a stethoscope. After a brief examination he talked with the other inmates and gave them a black plastic vial containing a gel-like salve which smelled like mentholatum.

"We will help you. Mr. Blue and I, we will massage you and make you feel good. You will feel much better," said Mr. Sea reassuringly.

Both Mr. Blue and Mr. Sea dabbed the gel on their fingers and gently rubbed it into my arms and legs. They massaged with a quiet and considerate rhythm for half an hour, moving to my chest and neck and even rubbing the ointment along each of my fingers.

"It feels so good," I murmured.

"If you had told us before, we could have helped you last night. We want to help you," said Mr. Sea, as I drifted off to sleep.

When I awoke Mr. Sea was sleeping with his head resting on his book. I was greatly impressed with his genuine kindness in sacrificing his more comfortable pillow. Much later that night he roused me as he rolled up my mosquito net.

"You have to go with the guard," said Mr. Sea.

They took me up the hill, barefoot and handcuffed, through the darkness to Owl.

"It is not safe for you here," Owl announced with the finality of a jury foreman announcing a verdict. "We must take you to another place."

He sat in the front seat of the jeep as we crossed the bay by ferry and drove along the coast. "We're going home!" I thought. "They've arranged for my release and I'm being taken to a ship!" My spirits rose. I felt sure they had made a deal with the United States to turn me over and that we were on our way to the rendezvous point. I even allowed myself to feel a little perky as we drove up, over and around the hills. Moonlight reflected off the coastal waters and I kept a lookout for a ship that would be docking to take me home.

But we veered inland, taking winding roads until we drew up at a decrepit but spacious, single story brick farm house with many rooms. Owl led the way in with a flashlight. He shone the beam into a room furnished only with a metal-framed bed with wooden slats, a table, chair and an oil lamp.

"The Chinese man who owns this house has allowed you to stay here," he said. "He understands you have been duped and used by the imperialists and that it will be safer for you here." Owl showed me how to put the mosquito net up. "Be sure you tuck it under your mat," he advised as he turned and left.

They locked me in, clanking the keys for what seemed like minutes. A window at the back of the room was barred and shuttered. I tried to pry the shutters open but they didn't budge. I blew out the lamp and in the darkness got into bed and tucked in the net. There was a sudden commotion outside and I heard them trying irritably to open the lock to my room. Three or four men flung it open and almost stampeded to get to my bed. They shone their flashlights over me. One of them lit the lamp as Owl walked in.

"You must not put the lamp out!" he threatened. "It must stay on at all times."

They followed him out and sealed me in again. I went to sleep on Thursday, August 6, 1964, my second night in Vietnam, thinking of Mom, Dad, and Tangee. They must know I'm held captive. Surely, someone must have notified them by now? Drowsily, I recalled the few words of comfort I'd spoken to a downhearted Tangee as the time neared for me to ship out.

"Don't ever worry, sweetheart. I may not come home right away, but I'll be coming home."

The night before the *Constellation* pulled anchor at San Diego, Tangee and I had dined and danced atop the swank El Cortez Hotel overlooking the city.

"I'll always remember this night," I told her.

She tried to lighten our pain. "You'll be home by Christmas."

She was already crying when Delia, the eldest of my two sisters, joined us for the drive to the carrier. They had come aboard for a short while until all visitors were escorted off. Our final embrace was tight and tearful.

I stood on the flight deck, sad and melancholy. As the *Constellation* pulled out of the channel I saw Tangee and Del standing on Point Loma. They were waving. I knew they could not see me because the ship was colossal and hundreds of men stood on deck. But I raised my arm and waved back fondly.

4
MISSING IN ACTION

MOST EAST COAST TELEVISION VIEWERS HAD GONE TO BED by the time Lyndon Johnson announced the air raids. But he held a large captive audience in California and other states where the night was still young.

Lalo and Chole Alvarez, at home in Santa Clara, believed their son was due for shore leave in Hong Kong. There was no reason they should feel particularly concerned. The conflict in Vietnam was rarely on the front pages and few but the military and academics kept abreast of those distant events. To Lalo and Chole there wasn't even a Vietnam. They knew that vague geographical mass by its more familiar name of Indochina. Chole, however, had always feared the obvious dangers facing pilots like her son. Though lost in the technical jargon of aviators, she knew that an airborne pilot did not have to be all that close to hostilities to wind up in the center of the conflict. Her son, she realized, flew a plane that could cover 500 miles in less than an hour.

"Oh, my son!" she frequently moaned in the presence of Lalo, her husband.

Deep down, Lalo worried too. A hard-nosed sheet-metal welder and pattern-maker in a missile plant, he put on a steely mask and in his slow, gravely bass voice offered words of masculine assurance. "Nothing's going to happen. Nothing at all. And if it does, we'll know about it real fast. Anytime you see a black limo parked in front of the house, you'll know we've got real problems."

The president's televised speech did not fill them with any special anxiety. He had not mentioned that their son's carrier was steaming westwards to launch air attacks against North Vietnam. Yet hours later, when Chole was already asleep and a drowsy Lalo prepared to turn out the lights, he caught some mention on the radio of U.S. pilots being shot down. It was disturbing

42

news, but it didn't knock him off balance. There were thousands of U.S. pilots and besides, Everett should be out of range of the conflict. Nevertheless, his own son being a pilot, he instantaneously felt sympathy for the young men's parents. They were all part of a very large family, and, though unknown to each other, the mothers and fathers felt bonded by common perils.

The next morning, Chole busied herself in the kitchen preparing breakfast with her youngest daughter, Madeleine, twelve. Out of earshot in the living room, Delia, twenty-three, noticed her father do something uncharacteristic. He switched on the television. The two of them stood transfixed as the announcer reported that warplanes from the aircraft carriers *Constellation* and *Ticonderoga* had bombed North Vietnam. Two pilots were lost, one in each of the two downed aircraft, according to Defense Secretary McNamara. Without comment, Lalo turned off the set. Father and daughter avoided each other's eyes and neither uttered a word. Both were careful not to mention anything about the newscast to Chole or Madeleine.

By the time Delia, a social worker, arrived at her office, she had read an account in the newspaper about two pilots not returning from their combat missions. There were no names and neither of the aircraft was identified. With a faint attempt at laughing off her nagging sense of unease, she quipped to colleagues, "It would be just my luck, with so many pilots out there, to have my brother get shot down!"

She felt queasy thinking about his fate because they had been close since childhood. The tiny home on Pearl Street in Salinas where they grew up was no more than thirty feet long by twenty-five feet wide: they had shared a bunk bed tucked alongside one of the thin walls, with Everett sleeping up top because only he was big enough to make the climb. There were no girls in the sparsely populated neighborhood so Delia, a tomboy, had hung around with Everett. They had fought like most young siblings but he had been very protective of her, once chasing off some kids who'd struck her with a stone during a standoff. When they were indoors they listened together for hours to mystery programs and the Lone Ranger on the crackling family radio, or they played Chinese Checkers—the only board game they owned. Though the newspaper arrived every day, books were a rarity and for years the sole permanent book in the house was the thick dictionary on Delia's chair which she sat on to reach up to the kitchen table. Then, suddenly, she began to notice other books as Everett brought home westerns and adventures. His influence upon her grew, particularly as he was three grades ahead of her and didn't mind helping with her homework. But in those pre-television days they were more often outdoors in the yard, running between the weeds and rows of corn playing Cowboys and Indians. Other times they made up war games with Everett seated in the old car pretending to be a tank commander. Perhaps the most fun times of all were when they were out on their bicycles, peddling for all they were worth and then coasting down the dusty, bare mounds of earth between the scattered dwellings. They both looked forward to Fridays because it was their Dad's pay day, and that meant cash to buy meat to make the evening meal different from every other night.

The bonds intensified with the years. When Everett was desperately short of tuition funds in his last college semester, Delia loaned him all of her $350 savings, accumulated over the years working after school as a grocery clerk at one dollar an hour. Everett was equally supportive of Delia in the duel with their parents over whether she could leave home while studying at San Jose State University. The parents held steadfastly to the traditional Hispanic view that the only proper time for a female to leave the family home was after marriage. Everett challenged this as outmoded, especially since she intended moving in with three female roommates. He offered to pay her share of the rent and, true to his word, came forward punctually every month with her $35. Now, she vividly recalled his last words to her, just before boarding the *Constellation* ten weeks earlier: "By the way, Del, that money you owe me. It's okay. Forget it. You don't have to pay me back."

Sixty miles south, back in Salinas, Chole's younger sister, Everett's aunt, Cecilia Sanchez, awoke full of foreboding. She, too, had heard the President's televised speech and gasped to her husband, Albert, that she hoped it didn't have anything to do with their nephew. The news weighed heavily on her during a fretful night and in the morning she turned on the radio, only to learn the dreadful news that two U.S. planes had not returned. "Albert," she beseeched, "don't go out of the shop today. Stay close to the phone because I have a feeling my sister will be calling from Santa Clara and we might have to make a trip up there."

Then she phoned her daughter, Linda.

"I don't want you to leave home today," she urged, "because I have this strange feeling that Everett is one of those pilots. I want you to be ready if I have to call again."

Linda felt a flash of terror rush up her spine. Newly married and still childless, she also had listened to LBJ's speech. She hadn't thought much about it, but now she fretted because of her mother's call. Linda was highly sensitive to her mother's anxieties and also felt that somehow Everett must be involved. She also feared for the safety of George, her husband, a private in the army reserves. He was away at summer camp and she felt he, too, might be sent off to the war zone.

Both Albert and Linda had good reasons to be alarmed and to take Cecilia's premonition seriously. Fifteen years earlier, she had dreamed of a death in the family and within days her healthy first-born, Danny, eleven, died from an unaccountable mass of destroyed brain cells.

Now, as she busied herself painting screens for her rental properties, she feared the worst about Everett. It was impossible to concentrate. She tried unsuccessfully to convince herself that there was not a shred of evidence to justify her fears. She picked up the receiver to telephone Chole but put it back abruptly. Telling Chole how she felt would only make her sister panic.

Albert returned home at lunchtime and looked glumly at his wife's red-rimmed eyes. He tried to comfort her but she resisted. Powerless to help, he returned to work.

Tangee, meanwhile, was at her sister Emily's home, taking care of her two nieces when she looked up and saw her brother-in-law, Babe, talking to two men in military uniforms. At first she couldn't imagine why they were there. Then it hit her like a wallop to the solar plexus. The officers were gentle with the pale bride of seven months. They told her Everett was one of two pilots missing in Vietnam. One was probably dead. The other may have been captured. There was a fifty-fifty chance her husband might be alive. After she came to, the family tried to comfort her but her body shook spasmodically. They gave her sedatives and she lay down, praying hard that he had been taken prisoner.

It was mid-afternoon that Wednesday, August 5, when Babe led the two respectful naval officers to Chole's single-story house on Bohannon Drive, a quiet curving street in a leafy residential quarter of Santa Clara, near a busy commercial strip of restaurants and shops. Chole was doing laundry in a room overlooking her neat back garden, scented with avocado and orange trees and now a riot of color from the myriad California flowers. Above the noise of the radio she always carried with her from room to room, she heard the doorbell ring. Unconcerned, she walked into the living room, with its wide picture window looking out on the street. Chole pulled up with a start as she saw the military car parked outside. There was no mistaking it beyond the see-through curtains. She knew they had come about her son and her frail body stiffened. Filled with dread, she opened the door.

"It's Everett, isn't it?" she asked, barely audible.

"Yes," Babe replied.

Chole cried a little when they sat down. The naval officers, deferential and soft-spoken, tried to explain that though his plane had gone down there was not much to go on. They did not know what had become of him.

The telephone rang and Cecilia dashed to answer it.

"Tia (Aunt)?" said Delia.

"I know! You're calling me about Everett! Something happened to him, I know!"

"Yes. The officers came and told us. He's missing."

Without ado, Cecilia phoned Linda. Her instructions were brief and chilling. "We have to go to Santa Clara. Don't say anything to anyone. Just pack a little suitcase."

Madeleine had a fun time swimming with schoolfriends that sweltering hot afternoon. She had no need of the summer sun to make her enviably tanned all year round because she had the natural dark brown coloring of her grandmother, MaMona. Though the youngest of the three siblings she had always felt like an only child because of the age disparity. Everett, fourteen years her senior, was more than twice her age, and Delia was a full decade older. Madeleine looked upon them as her second set of parents. With her quiet, reserved, and slightly shy nature she did at least feel a kinship with Everett but her personality stood in sharp contrast to her sister's bubbly effervescence. Yet already Madeleine carried her slender form with a grace and poise that gave her a dignity well beyond her years.

As soon as she walked into the house that August afternoon, she sensed, with her pre-teen's sharp instincts, that something was wrong. Her mother was ironing in the heat of the afternoon, and muttering over and over, "I have to keep busy. I have to keep busy." The television was on and they seemed to be waiting impatiently for a news bulletin. Someone tried to explain that Everett had been shot down and might even be dead, but Madeleine didn't comprehend. She didn't even know he was flying a special mission. Nor could she make head or tail of who had shot him down or why they would have done this to her brother. She had no idea where Vietnam was, nor what Everett was supposed to be doing there. Nothing made sense to her and no one seemed to have the patience or tranquility to sit down and bring her fully into the picture. She didn't want to make things worse by irritating them with questions. Nor did she want to feel more left out by withdrawing to her room. Caught between the neglect of her elders and the innocence of her youth, Madeleine began to feel very scared and infinitely lonely.

By evening, more members of the family had arrived. Linda's brother, Al, an architectural student, raced down from Berkeley. Though two years younger than his cousin, he had in his own mind adopted Everett as his older brother, to try to replace Danny. But it was a big void to fill because the ingenious and intuitive Danny had spoiled his little brother, putting together model airplanes and always being around to play with. Everett, the substitute, was also considerate—but a lot different. They had such markedly different personalities. Al was restless and energetic, loud, garrulous, always coming on strong, and above all, mischievous and playful. By contrast, Everett was bookish and serious, silent, punctual, obedient and respectful. The two boys never argued or fought, though Everett might occasionally snap at his wilder cousin, bringing him into line and cutting him short with the prerogative of age.

The two families were so close that the children had even exchanged homes for a lengthy period. When Everett's family left Salinas for Santa Clara in 1958, Delia stayed behind to finish high school and moved into Cecilia's home. Simultaneously, Al went to junior college in Santa Clara and stayed for a year with the Alvarez's, sharing a room with Everett, then in his fourth year at the University of Santa Clara. But now there was a noticeable slackening in communication between the two. Everett, absorbed in his studies, kept things to himself. Besides, he had his own circle of friends from the engineering school. Al admired his cousin's trait of being single-minded in pursuit of goals. It seemed that once Everett set his heart on something he devoted himself to it with a dogged commitment. With such an attitude, thought Al, there seemed to be little Everett could not overcome and master. And he always did it in his inimitably quiet and unobtrusive manner. Sometimes, though, Al thought Everett was a mite too studious. He wished his cousin would loosen up and perhaps invite him out to share a beer and cruise downtown to look for girls. Everett, however, was far happier camping out with college friends under the giant Redwoods at Big Sur. The soaring trunks and splayed branches took on the appearance of an open-air cathedral and whenever he stood dwarfed at the base of the Redwoods, he felt especially close to God. There was a particularly peaceful hush to this forest that lured Everett back time and again.

As Al accelerated down the East Bay that August afternoon, he remembered how he and Everett had taken their first airplane flight when they were not yet teenagers in Salinas. Everett's family had moved to a house across the road from the airfield and light planes periodically sputtered overhead, almost clipping the long grass leading up to the runway. The airfield was home base for a fleet of about a dozen bi-winged Stearman cropdusters. A few of the other old Stearmans in the hangers were cannibalized for spare parts. Sometimes, Everett climbed into one of the rickety aircraft, pushed the rudder, moved the stick back and forth and pretended to be a daredevil pilot high up in the sky.

One of the airplane mechanics, Fergie, was a former World War II pilot who flew occasionally. He was a friend of the cousins' families and one day asked the boys if they wanted to go up for a spin. Would they! The boys' fathers came over to watch and cousin Al went up first. The plane had a single engine and looked as if it had been put together in someone's spare time. Young Al sat in the back and experienced all the thrills and fears of a greenhorn. When he touched down he was a little giddy but ran over to his cousin and exclaimed breathlessly, "You'd better watch it, you're going to wet your pants!"

The engine was idling as Everett climbed in. He was tingling with anticipation when Fergie helped strap him in. "Relax and just do what I say," Fergie cautioned. "Don't worry about anything, we're just going to circle the field." They taxied down and lumbered off as Everett clung white-knuckled to the rods running down the side of the plane. The little aircraft dipped and rose in the air currents. Fergie turned and saw the fright on his passenger's face. "Relax," he shouted above the noise of the chugging engine. "Sit back and take it easy. Look up at the sky. We're going to have a nice, steady ride. There'll be a few more air bumps, but nothing bad." Everett found it hard to believe that Fergie could be so calm and effortlessly steer the plane while smoking a cigarette! But in no time at all the boy noticed he himself was less taut and tense. And then, amazingly, he seemed totally at ease. It was exhilarating! The speed, the breadth of view, the altitude! They were only about 1500 feet up as they circled the airfield when Fergie said, "Let's go and take a look at the city." Salinas had a population then of about ten thousand but it seemed from Everett's altitude that they were hovering over a huge metropolis telescoped into a little neighborhood. What a revelation! What fun! He was wildly excited by his new view of the world and when they touched down the whoosh of wind was no match for the rush of his blood. He was obviously hooked.

Neither Everett nor cousin Al dared ask for a second ride because they knew the Stearmans didn't belong to Fergie and he had done them a very special favor by taking them up just that one time. The magic lingered with Everett and everytime he went to see one of the movies about flying, like *God is my Co-pilot, Flying Hellcats* or *Hell's Angels,* he knew exactly how the pilots felt!

Al also recalled the day, years later, when his cousin had walked him through the University of Santa Clara campus. Everett had been working on some kind of computer. He demonstrated his abilities to Al, causing the machine to play back, in rhythmic sounds, a reasonable likeness of the Star Spangled Banner. Al was awed and Everett looked justifiably proud. But Everett never gave the impression of being overly enthusiastic about being an engineer for the rest of his life. Al suggested he find a more exciting job, such as policeman, fireman—or even a jet pilot.

It wasn't long after that Everett indeed surprised them all by announcing he had signed up to be a Navy pilot. No one was more astonished than Everett's own father. When Everett told him he was going to join the Navy, Lalo was momentarily lost for words.

"What are you talking about? You spend all this time in college just to go in the Navy!"

"No, Dad," Everett replied. "I'm going to be a pilot—a carrier jet pilot. It's what I wanted to do ever since I was a little kid!"

Only then did Lalo flash back to the day his son had flown in the old Stearman with Fergie. Everett had never said anything about how much of a lasting impression it made. Lalo was so stunned by the turn of events that he wondered a bit how well he really knew his own son.

He would have been stunned even more had he known that another reason Everett signed up was to learn social etiquette and behavior. Everett had never forgotten the day his college roommate casually remarked that the Navy taught its officers the social graces. He realized then that the Navy would be his tutor for he had learned to his deep shame and embarrassment that he was little more than a coarse country bumpkin. On the one occasion he had invited a date to dine at a fashionable restaurant she had giggled and he had cringed when he didn't know which of several forks to use, nor that he was meant to taste the wine and respond to the waiter standing next to him.

Cousin Al was not as tongue-tied as others and enjoyed teasing Everett after he got his wings.

"What's your plane like? How big is it? Can I wear your helmet?"

Everett usually didn't respond. But one time, when Everett was visiting from nearby Lemoore Naval Air Station, Al goaded his cousin with a flurry of questions about the A4D Skyhawk. What was its wingspan? Didn't it fly at such and such a speed? Wasn't this its fuel consumption, and this the ordnance capacity, and this the maximum altitude? Everett was in no mood to be tweaked. He wanted to know where Al had gotten his information.

"What you won't tell me, what seems to be a government secret, is all in *Time* magazine," Al snickered.

"Then quit asking me and read your *Time* magazine!" Everett snapped.

Al chuckled. He meant no harm. Deep down he had a lot of respect for his cousin. It was just that sometimes he took things much too seriously.

All this changed when Everett fell in love. Sometimes he would visit with Tangee and while cousin Al and his wife, Virginia, looked on, Everett volunteered vivid and lively anecdotes about his plane, down to the smallest details he'd once been so gruffly secretive about. He was so proud of flying jets off the decks of aircraft carriers and his enthusiasm was refreshingly boyish. Al and Virginia looked on this new candor with knowing smiles. Before their very eyes the child of few words had become a compulsive, outgoing talker as he courted the woman by his side.

There wasn't a trace of boastfulness. Everett just seemed to want to share his sense of well-being with all around him. He was a good storyteller and his small audience listened captively as he spun hilarious stories about the guys in the squadron and their escapades. The lush, dark-haired beauty with fair skin and deep brown eyes had sent him into such a tailspin that merely being in her presence transformed him. She laughed a lot, girlishly and spontaneously, and Everett showed his adoration by being excessively attentive to her every need.

Their relationship had been easy from the start, even though family members had awkwardly prodded them to get together. Everett was a twenty-two-year-old college senior, three years older than Tangee, and they seemed naturally compatible. Besides, they were already distantly linked by marriage since one of Everett's cousins, Babe, was married to one of Tangee's sisters. When Everett joined the Navy he wrote to her often and saw her more regularly than he might otherwise have done because of the frequent family get-togethers. Though they later split up and dated others, they found they missed each other. It was only a question of time, once they got together again, before they announced their wedding plans.

Everett's bachelor party kicked off at Al's house where Everett and half a dozen buddies from his squadron careened over the furniture, their arms extended like the wings of planes as they simulated the hissing sounds of jet engines. Al caught snatches of muffled pilot lingo: "Wing, follow this. . . . Fly right. . . . Make this adjustment. . . ." In the thick of the sputtering and giggling, Everett seemed to be the ringleader, egging everybody else on.

Cousin Al eventually wrestled them down and stuffed them into the car for the ride to a San Francisco nightclub. By pre-arrangement, one of the slinky hostesses was supposed to lure Everett onto the dance floor, but when the moment arrived he was more than game, lunging out and whirling her around. It was vintage Everett in the months before his wedding, when he was both silly and blissfully happy.

After his December marriage he continued to shower goodwill and bonho-
mie. He delighted in playing with his baby goddaughter, Denise, the firstborn
child of Al and Virginia. Once, when they drove him back to Alameda Naval
Air Base, he was in high spirits and impishly stopped the car when a couple
of passing seamen failed to recognize an officer. He got out and stood proudly
before them, the trace of a smile on his lips, making sure the young seamen,
now ramrod straight, recognized his lieutenant junior grade bars and saluted
smartly.

Instead of waving good-bye to his cousins, Everett asked Al and Virginia
if they'd like to join him in the flight room. They were taken aback because
they didn't think they would even be allowed onto the base let alone into the
pilots' inner sanctum. But Everett pulled one surprise after another. "We'll
see if we can't get you in there," he said, nodding towards the pilots' ready
room.

Everett seemed to be overdoing the welcome but then he was back again,
looking dashing in his zipped-up orange flight suit and radiating confidence.
He invited them to look over his aircraft and they tittered like kids at
Disneyland when he had them chauffeured out in a jeep to the parked jet.
They walked around the metal bird and looked inside as Everett explained
some of its features. Then he led them to the tower and asked the officer in
charge if Al could keep radio contact with him as he took off. "Keep your
eye on that plane down there," Everett said, pointing to one among the many
gleaming warplanes. "That's the one I'll be flying."

While Everett strapped himself in and did his pre-flight check, the men
in the tower treated Al and Virginia like VIPs on a ceremonial inspection
tour. Al never forgot the special warmth he felt in his heart that day as
Everett's Skyhawk streaked off the runway and a voice crackled over the
airwaves: "Sign off to Al and Virginia Sanchez."

By the time cousin Al arrived at his aunt and uncle's home in Santa Clara
the phone was ringing incessantly. Most of the calls were from the media,
pressing for reaction from the family and background material on Everett.
Friends and strangers called to offer to run errands, do shopping chores.
Anything.

Someone shouted for quiet as a radio bulletin reported that one of the two
American pilots was understood to have survived and was being held in
captivity. The other aviator was believed to have died when his plane crashed.
The radio announcement gave no names. Worse still, nothing was official and
the family couldn't even track down the source for their flicker of hope. They
lived from one moment to the next, anxiously suspended between hope and

dread. All the while they prayed with such intensity that if miracles had depended on the strength of their pleas, Everett would have popped out of a smokescreen, safe and sound.

Chole prayed only that Everett would be captured alive. But then she had second thoughts, wondering what they would do to her son if they held him prisoner. Later she had feelings of guilt and told Delia, "I am selfish to be praying to God that the one captured alive be my son. What about the mother of the other pilot?" Delia had no such qualms. "Don't feel that way, Mom! The other mother is praying just like you are for *her* son."

Dawn found them haggard and tired after a virtually sleepless night. They were listening to both the television and the radio as they dug in for another grim day of waiting it out. There seemed to be no holding back the thickening crush of journalists and cameramen who'd been staking out the inconspicuous house since the day before. Madeleine was terrified of the unknown faces appearing at windows and the strange men with probing lenses who tried to push the curtains aside or sneak into the back yard. Thrust into the national limelight, but untutored for any such role, the family floundered in vain for privacy. They took the only protective measure they could and drew the curtains closed. It helped somewhat but the press maintained its vigil.

At mid-morning the mailman stopped by. Incredibly, he had a letter from Everett addressed to Delia. It was dated August 3, and mailed in Hong Kong. Delia winced as she read, *"Hi, Del—how is everything? Everything is O.K. here. Tomorrow we leave here and go out to sea. . . ."*

She was still reading the letter when the telephone rang. A *New York Daily News* correspondent relayed a Reuters report from a Japanese correspondent monitoring Hanoi Radio, that Everett was alive and a prisoner of the North Vietnamese! They shrieked and screamed joyously, hugging and kissing and laughing and crying as they released the tensions of the long night. Their prayers had been answered. He was alive!

But when the flush of exultation wore off they were left with the sober reality that Everett was being held captive in a hostile country in Asia. It sent a chill through all of them. Scores of reservists from Salinas had been captured by the Japanese in the Philippines during World War II. Many had died on the infamous death march from Bataan to the prison camps. Their remains lay in Asia but their fate was still fresh in the minds of the townspeople because of the fearful monument in the city park. It was enough just to see the long barrel on the rusting tank to recall the rows of names of the dead, memorialized in metal below. The Alvarez and Sanchez families knew the kin of some of those who did not return. Now they worried what Everett might be up against. They hoped that the quiet strength of his personality would stand him in good stead, and that his religious faith would sustain him for the trials ahead.

Lalo vividly remembered the last conversation he had with his son as Everett prepared to drive down to San Diego to rejoin the *Constellation* for maneuvers in the western Pacific. "Maybe you'll be going to Vietnam," said Lalo as he gave his son a farewell embrace.

Everett had laughed. "No chance, Dad. We're not going there. We've got our own missions—in Hawaii, Japan and the Philippines."

"Well, hell, they just sunk one of our ships in Vietnam," Lalo said, handing Everett the newspaper and pointing out a story about the Vietcong blowing a hole in a transport ship, the U.S.S. *Card*, in the Saigon River.

"That's not us, Dad. That's military transport. It's not our stuff."

"Well, you never know," Lalo said gravely.

Lalo secretly wondered whether his son had the staying power to overcome physical torture. He hated even to think about it, but he wondered. . . . There were those nagging memories stretching back to Everett's early childhood when he seemed to be so timid and cried so easily. Sure, Lalo knew his rough and gravelly voice must have been scary to a child, especially when he was strict with his children. But when he told his son he didn't like him running around the living room or jumping on the couch, the boy, then only about four years old, had looked at him with watery eyes. Lalo remembered bending down and tipping his son's chin up. "Look, son, men don't cry. Keep your chin up."

On Christmas, maybe in that same year, his father gave him a pair of boxing gloves and helped slide them over the boy's tiny hands. Then the father got on his knees and taunted, "C'mon! C'mon! Protect yourself, junior! Hit me!" The four-year-old thought it was fun and made a few jabs. But somehow he landed a glove right in the eye of his unsuspecting father and watched horrified as his Dad winced and the flesh quickly discolored a bluish black. Little Everett started to cry.

"Hey, junior," his father said, reaching out to hug the startled, sobbing boy, "Don't worry about it. It doesn't hurt."

In later years, when the son was still a pre-teen, the father had enjoyed arm-wrestling him on the floor of the living room. Squat and stocky, the father never relaxed his grip nor gave his son any advantage. It was his way of teaching the boy to measure up. He didn't want young Everett to grow up into a bully. He just wanted him to be able to take care of himself.

Sometimes the wayward father, who bellowed his family into line even while disregarding the turbulence he wrought with his own partying and drinking, showed a gentler, sensitive nature. The only thing he had ever stolen in his life was a gold-colored book-marker he'd found in a library when he was 13. It wasn't so much the color as the wonderful words he read upon it. They were from Rudyard Kipling's poem "If," and he thought the words added up to noble advice:

> If you can keep your head when all about you
>   Are losing theirs and blaming it on you,
> If you can trust yourself when all men doubt you,
>   But make allowance for their doubting too;
> If you can wait and not be tired by waiting,
>   Or being lied about, don't deal in lies,
>   Or being hated don't give way to hating,
>   And yet don't look too good, nor talk too wise:
>
> If you can dream—and not make dreams your master;
>   If you can think—and not make thoughts your aim,
> If you can meet with Triumph and Disaster
>   And treat those two imposters just the same;
> If you can bear to hear the truth you've spoken
>   Twisted by knaves to make a trap for fools,
> Or watch the things you gave your life to, broken,
>   And stoop and build 'em up with worn-out tools:
>
> If you can make one heap of all your winnings;
>   And risk it on one turn of pitch-and-toss,
> And lose, and start again at your beginnings
>   And never breathe a word about your loss;
> If you can force your heart and nerve and sinew
>   To serve your turn long after they are gone,
> And so hold on when there is nothing in you
>   Except the Will which says to them: "Hold on!"
>
> If you can talk with crowds and keep your virtue,
>   Or walk with Kings—nor lose the common touch,
> If neither foes nor loving friends can hurt you,
>   If all men count with you, but none too much;
> If you can fill the unforgiving minute
>   With sixty seconds' worth of distance run,
> Yours is the Earth and everything that's in it,
>   And—which is more—you'll be a Man, my son!

He vowed that if he ever had a son he would give him the bookmark. Through all his early years of nomadic struggle he kept it. When Everett was in 10th grade, he handed over the gilded bookmark with the solemn advice to keep it and learn from it. "Anytime you have any doubts or problems, read it. Try and remember the words. I think they will do you good."

Now that Everett was in real trouble, Lalo hoped his son could gain some encouragement from the poem. He guessed Everett would recite the words to himself. He would surely remember them. He had a good head. He had always been a bright kid. He had even made the National Honor Society. Lalo remembered well how they had sat down to discuss his future at the beginning of Everett's senior year in high school. Lalo asked what he planned on doing after graduation.

Everett shrugged. A close friend, a cousin and some other neighborhood boys had been talking about the Navy. Everett hinted he might go that route but his father encouraged him to consider college. A number of Everett's schoolmates had gone on to Hartnell, the local junior college, to learn a trade. That was probably what Lalo had in mind, but in his enthusiasm, Everett assumed his dad was referring to the University of California (Berkeley) or Stanford.

Everett caught the college bug; he was impatient for answers. First he went to his student counsellor, who also thought he meant Hartnell.

"No, no, no," Everett said. "I mean like Cal or Stanford! I want to be an engineer."

"Then you have to take physics, chemistry and more math."

Everett doubled up his workload. Lalo knew his son would make it because anytime he had a goal he put his heart and soul into attaining it.

During Christmas vacation that year, Lalo lent Everett the family car for the 100-mile drive up to Berkeley. He was awed by the stern old fortress of the engineering building, with its elaborately carved twenty-foot high double doors, and its cavernous entrance hall with solemn black beams high up on the ceiling. Yet Everett, seventeen, was able to summon up enough courage to arrange a short visit with the dean, who sat behind a forbiddingly large desk. The dean was forthcoming and gave Everett an idea of what it would take to enroll.

Everett had not felt so pumped-up since his first airplane flight with Fergie. He hadn't learned anything new but he had spoken with the dean and walked around the campus! That sure beat leafing through the bulky catalogue in Salinas! He returned home with a full report on course requirements and tuition costs. That was when his mother started to work long hours full-time, getting up before sunrise to pack farm produce in the cannery. Everything she earned was put aside for Everett's college tuition.

That summer following high school graduation was a memorable one; it far surpassed the day trips to Los Angeles, which were the only vacations he had ever known. Bill Kearney, the school track coach he admired so much and who was like a second father to him, had invited Everett to help out at a summer camp for underprivileged kids in the mountains. It was a healthy and fulfilling experience. Everett swam and played with the kids as well as doing odd jobs, fixing the pumps and tinkering with the jeep. When it was almost over they had an awards dinner and Kearney stood up to pay tribute to Everett.

"Here's a boy who's shown a lot of spirit, and not only in track," he told the assembly. "Everett wants to be an engineer. You can be sure he's going to be as good as he is in track. He's going to be an outstanding engineer."

But the summer ended on a downer with a rejection letter from Cal: he fell short on the required courses. The admissions office at Cal recommended he pick them up at a junior college and apply again later. For two years, Everett slogged through Hartnell College, while Lalo and Chole watched with glowing satisfaction. He was finally accepted at Cal, but the notification came too late. He had already been accepted as an electrical engineering student at the prestigious University of Santa Clara, a Jesuit institution with formidable standards and an all-male student body of only one thousand.

Lalo's chest swelled with pride whenever he recalled Everett's academic achievements. He himself had only completed eighth grade. There was nothing he admired more than a man who put everything into his work to better himself. His boy had worked hard and earned his laurels. Surely, Lalo reminded himself, a man who had done so well, who had shown such self-discipline and determination, would be able to take anything they threw at him in captivity. After all, what was Everett's early life if not a constant struggle against the odds?

The press burst in behind Tangee. There was no restraining them when the unofficial report broke that Everett was alive in captivity.

Lalo reluctantly positioned himself as the spokesman for a family now virtually cowering under the glare of the overpowering media lights. "We're all hopeful for his early return," he told them as he clutched a photograph of his son, resplendent in dress uniform. "He always told me, 'Dad, don't worry. We've got the best equipment they can furnish.' " Fighting back tears, his voice cracked when he said he had never lost hope and was proud of his son. And then, echoing the sentiments of the entire family, he said they were still hoping and praying for the other downed pilot and his family.

Chole, overwrought and feeling helplessly cornered by the crush of reporters, nodded nervously and smiled faintly. She still harbored memories of incidents from Everett's early childhood when she feared for his life. He was about four years old when they took him to the amusement park and sat him on a ferris wheel with three other children. Every time the wheel came down to ground level little Everett, visibly frightened, had stuck his foot out and tried to get off. Chole had pleaded with the operator to stop the ferris wheel but he apparently didn't hear her amid the din of the fairgrounds and she had watched helplessly as that little foot came out every time the car descended. That same year the family had gone picnicking at Pacific Grove, then a secluded beach on the southern curve of Monterey Bay, when Everett saw a man dive off the rocks. The little boy waded out in the direction of the rocks and suddenly found himself out of his depth and swallowing salt water. Terror-stricken, he hollered for help. Chole, who could not swim, responded with the raw instinct of a mother, racing towards her son and scooping him out. Her heart beat wildly as he coughed and sputtered and when it was all over she held him tight. Now, try as she might, Chole could not blot out those flashes of horror.

The photographers swarmed around Tangee. Even in her distress she looked comely in a fetching brown suit. With evident fond memories, she wore the Navy wings Everett had given her during their courtship. A newsman handed her a message torn from his office teleprinter: *Radio Hanoi today identified Lt. (j.g.) Everett Alvarez, Jr., of Santa Clara, California, as the U.S. pilot the North Vietnamese say they captured.* The North Vietnamese had also given his correct birth date. Tangee felt lucky. They bombarded the family with questions and asked her what she thought of the air raids. "It's worth it, even with my husband in danger," she replied as the cameras flashed and reporters scribbled down her words.

When they asked Delia to comment, she told them of Everett's letter arriving in the morning mail. "It was painful to read while we still thought Everett was dead," she said thoughtfully and softly. "It is enough right now to know that he is alive."

But they could not be one hundred per cent sure, even when they learned, almost a week after the air raids, that Hanoi radio had broadcast an account of Everett being led "staggering through the streets of Hon Gai, pale, weary and awe-stricken." At the same time, a Navy official drove them to an airbase and produced a poor quality wire service radiotelephoto, purportedly of Everett, which had been published in a Chinese Communist newspaper. The family crowded around the officer, wanting desperately to confirm the picture—almost willing themselves into verifying it was their Everett. It would be the proof that he was alive. They looked hard at the grainy reproduction. The man in the picture looked downwards. He had a few days growth of beard and looked weary and sad. Shadows obscured parts of his face, neck and clothing. It might not be a good likeness, but Chole was sure: that man was her son. Others were not so certain. The Navy official cautioned Chole, preferring she would say she wasn't sure. "Well if that isn't Everett, it's his twin brother," she mused, keeping a steadfast gaze at the photograph. Al tried to lift up her spirits. "Don't feel bad, Tia. Look at it this way, he's walking. That means he's in one piece." She wasn't thinking of that. Her mind registered only the drawn, disconsolate look on the man's face. He looked so forlorn and utterly helpless.

In the days that followed, the media onslaught intensified and the barrage of questions from domestic and foreign reporters threw the huddled family into desperate confusion. They took turns answering the telephone, which rang at all hours of the day and night, but they didn't know what to say or how to respond. The Navy had inhibited them with so many broad instructions, not to comment on *this*, because it might mean more trouble for Everett, and not to answer *that*, because the North Vietnamese could use it against him. In spite of the turmoil, whoever answered the phone always had the presence of mind to turn the tables and ask if there was any update on Everett's condition or whereabouts. Finally a Naval officer intervened: "Mr. Alvarez, I don't want them bothering you anymore. From now on we'll make all the statements. We'll take care of it." He, however, was referring only to the throng of reporters camped outside the house on Bohannon Drive. There remained the problem of the telephone.

Even though they had identified him from the initial photograph, the family could never be sure from one day to the next whether Everett was still alive. The uncertainty was relieved only by infrequent fresh photographic evidence. Whenever the Navy thought it had something new, it asked the family to look it over. Madeleine dreaded the appearance of the Navy's tan-colored car outside their home. It meant that the officer was here again— the one who had brought them the awful news of Everett's shoot-down. His reappearance was always a summons to accompany him to the airbase to look over fresh slides and photographs that might be Everett. One time she saw him in his flight suit and her mind went back dreamily to that day several years before when he had flown into Lemoore Naval Air Station in California's central San Joaquin Valley and they had gone to meet him. Everett had climbed out of the plane and hugged her but she could not close her arms around him nor feel his body because the flight suit was so bulky. Her little body got lost in the many folds and stuffed pockets. When she stepped back and looked up at him she thought he looked so important, so distinguished. Ever since, she liked to see men in military uniforms. They looked so fine and upright, just like her brother.

One evening after a few weeks, Chole and Lalo drove down to San Clemente to escape the tension and pressures. They looked out over the beach. The ocean was black and the moon bright yellow. Chole wished she could ride the moon and glide west over North Vietnam. Then she would be able to see what was going on—and be so much closer to her firstborn.

5
ISOLATION
AND STARVATION

THE KEY RATTLED IN THE LOCK AND OWL ENTERED, MILI-
tarily erect.

"Did you sleep?"

I shrugged my shoulders noncommittally.

"How do you feel?"

"I'm hurting."

"We will bring the doctor again." He scanned the room. "At daytime we
will keep your door open. But you must stay in this room and use that over
there," he said, pointing to a toilet bucket in the corner. "We will lock the
door at night. If you want to use the latrine outside, the guard will take you,
but only in the early morning or in the evening."

Through the open door I could look across the porch to the yard outside
fenced with barbed wire. In a corner was a wooden outhouse. Rice paddies
stretched flat and tranquilly beyond, as far as the levee and dyke. Peasants
with wide-brimmed straw hats labored calf-deep in the paddies while small
children scampered and splashed around a docile water buffalo. I could not
see the river but guessed we were close to the coast because at sunrise the
masts of many sailboats glided past, and in the evenings, the masts, now
illuminated, crossed the serene landscape in the opposite direction.

Little by little over the next few days my body began to heal, due largely
to prolonged sleep and a diet of underdone fried eggs, bits of chicken, chunks
of French bread, bananas and an exotic but tasty round fruit, with a yellowish-
black skin that had to be peeled off. After I asked Owl for milk, a guard
brought in a can of sweetened condensed milk with the wrapping printed in
Chinese.

60

A doctor arrived. He listened to my heart, tapped my knees and belly, felt my shoulders, ran his hands over my back, then looked me up and down. He said something in Vietnamese and left abruptly. Later, Owl brought in some white pills for me to take at regular intervals.

"If you need anything, you tell the guard," he said.

"How do I talk to them? They don't understand English."

Owl took out a notebook and wrote down a column of Vietnamese words with their English equivalents opposite.

"Use this," he said, tearing out the page.

The list had many words I would be expected to use: sick, hungry, thirsty, water, food, bathroom, sleep, wash. I was overjoyed. At last I could communicate with any one of them, and if Owl went away I would not feel like I was held captive by a bunch of deaf men.

On the third day at the farmhouse a guard made me put on my pajamas over my shorts. He handcuffed me for the ten-foot walk past a roomful of sleeping guards to another room, unlocked the cuffs with difficulty, then ushered me in.

Owl was seated. He plied me with familiar questions of military significance. From where had I launched? What was the name of the ship? What kind of plane was I flying? How many planes had attacked Hon Gai? I kept silent, reasoning that I did not have to answer anything beyond what the Geneva Convention required of prisoners of war.

"You think you are prisoner of war," Owl snorted. "But there is no war."

This was a new and disturbing twist to my captivity, renewing fears that they might take me out and shoot me any time. Yet somehow I clung to the belief that a U.S. diplomat would soon walk in and say, "C'mon, let's go home now, Everett." And if it didn't happen that way, then surely the Vietnamese would take me to a ship or a plane and send me home.

"If you have thought about escaping you will not get very far," he warned, as if X-raying my thoughts. "The Vietnamese peasants are all around. You will not get away."

I had considered escaping once my strength returned. Perhaps I could wade or swim to the levee then snatch a small boat and drift down river to the sea. It couldn't be very far away because although I had been there less than a week I could not help noticing the volume of daily river traffic. It had to be ocean-going fishing craft. But the guards would be a problem. A dash for freedom would be almost suicidal in broad daylight, even though the daytime sentries were younger militiamen who bore themselves like simpletons and carried antiquated rifles. Night would offer the natural cover of darkness but the nocturnal guards were a different breed of military men. Owl called them "guerrillas," indicating they were battle-scarred from earlier clashes with French colonial troops, or from infiltration raids into South Vietnam. One night, I asked to go to the outhouse. Alerted, a guard leaning against the building instinctively swung his shoulder-slung submachine gun into firing position, finger on the trigger, without so much as moving a leg or his left arm. This supple display of weapon control made me cautious. My adversaries were obviously agile professionals. If I were to make a break, it would have to be planned with deft cunning and carried out with superior stealth.

A day later they led me again into Owl's room. A distinguished-looking Vietnamese, in his late fifties, sat next to him. The visitor had a broad, flattish face and forehead with thick greying hair cut short and swept back. He looked infinitely wise and weary, even mournful perhaps, because of the bags under his distant gaze and the wide upper lip protruding slightly over the lower lip.

"Sit down," said Owl. "This man is a high-ranking officer. He was touring the area and stopped here to visit you."

The visitor spoke to Owl, who translated.

"You're very young," said Owl. "Exactly how old are you?"

"Twenty-six."

"Do you have family?"

I didn't reply. The visitor nodded and looked pensively out the window behind me. He asked innocuous questions which I answered briefly. "How is your health? Has a doctor been to see you? How is the food?"

He spoke softly to Owl.

"You may go back," Owl ordered.

Many years later I learned that this one-time visitor was none other than Pham Van Dong, the prime minister of North Vietnam since the communists ousted the French a decade earlier.

I had been there almost a week, and settled into the spartan confinement with relatively relaxed rituals when Owl burst in past midnight.

"Get up! Get up! Get up!" he fumed. "You hide behind what you call *prisoner of war!* You have to answer questions! I have to report to my superiors! I have to go!"

I stood bleary-eyed, dressed only in shorts.

"You don't tell me, but I know! You are Everett Alvarez, Jr. You are twenty-six. We know you live in Santa Clara, California. And we know your parents live at 2168 Bohannon Drive, and your wife's name is Tangee. We know! We know! Now you tell me, where was your ship! Where was your ship! I must answer to my superiors!"

Owl was too impatient to await a reply. Shrilly, he continued: "You were on U.S.S. *Constellation.* Your commander's name was Bolsted. Your admiral was William Guest. You were member of attack squadron 144." He removed the leather case, which always hung by a strap from his shoulder, and pulled out a map of Vietnam, the Gulf of Tonkin, Hainan Island and the South China Sea. "Now, show me, where was *Constellation?* From where did you take off!"

Frantically, I wondered how much I was now expected to stick to the Code of Conduct. If he already knew so much about me, wouldn't it be unreasonable to deny what they had obviously learned from the American media? How much more did they know? How could I fabricate answers to questions when they might be able to trip me up by producing clippings from U.S. magazines and newspapers? And if there was no declared war, how could I be a prisoner of war? What was I then? What was my status? Was I still subject to the tight restrictions of the Code of Conduct? Did I have any rights? I looked at his open map and decided to play it by ear.

"Some place here," I said, pointing to the South China Sea, way off mark.

"Draw it on the map! Draw it!"

I drew a circle with a radius of about 100 miles. "Somewhere in there. I can't tell exactly."

He peered at the map intently.

"What was your mission?"

I made out I was flying unarmed reconnaissance to spot torpedo boats and radio back their positions.

"Show me your route! What was your route!"

"It must have been something like this," I said, drawing a circuitous line far off the actual course.

"Ah! Good! Very good!"

Owl folded the map, stuffed it in his bag and stalked off without comment. He was back early the next morning.

"We are going to another place. You must come now."

We got in the back of a canvas-covered tender with benches facing each other. Instead of blindfolding me they attached a canvas cloth behind the driver's seat and papered over the rear window. But I could see well because the cloth slipped as we headed south over many bumpy roads and ruts, which often slowed us down to 5 m.p.h. I was handcuffed and holding a bunch of bananas, yet felt confident we were on our way to a rendezvous with American diplomats and my transfer into their custody. Suddenly we drove through a massive gate cut into a sturdy wall.

"You come out now. We will rest."

I tried vainly to sleep on a mat on the floor of the building. Through the window I saw a large emblem on the wall. It seemed familiar. Yes! It was the emblem of the French Foreign Legion. They must have billeted behind these fortified walls during their campaigns to rid the countryside of insurgent communists.

The guard in the back of the tender was still sleepy when we resumed the trip half an hour later, and did not notice when I pulled the canvas screen down a fraction to peek out. The gravel road teemed with pedestrians and bicyclists. All the while I began to sense the strangeness of the environment and the awkwardness of my presence. Compared to the routes I had traveled in Japan, the Philippines and Hong Kong, these people seemed more alien and distinctly backward. Among the mass of humanity, we often passed groups of people hammering at rocks with small hand tools to break them up into more manageable pieces.

It was stifling hot as we drew up to board a ferry boat. I was looking at a mass of shrubbery when all at once it rose up and moved towards the ferry. Only then did I see the hordes of Vietnamese troops camouflaged with boughs stripped from trees. One of them hopped in the vehicle and sat down across from me. From his grinning salutation I gathered he was enjoying himself. Later on, as we crossed a bridge, the guard looked straight ahead while the newcomer pulled the canvas cloth aside. As soon as we drove onto land, I saw with despair a large sign: HANOI. Oh, no! I thought. This isn't the way home! I'm not on my way to freedom! At that moment they caught me looking out, raised the canvas again and eyed me warily for the few remaining minutes of the journey.

We pulled up with a jerk. Heavy double doors opened and clanged shut with metallic echoes as we drove into a darkened tunnel, over a rough bricked path, and through another set of double doors. I was led out into an open courtyard surrounded by two-story reddish-hued buildings, except for the single-story section ahead of us. It was about 2 P.M. on August 11th. Though it would be several weeks before I realized it, I had arrived at Hoa Lo prison, built by the colonial French a few miles from downtown Hanoi. It would later be remembered by American POWs as the infamous Hanoi Hilton.

Owl walked me over with a jailor to the dark green double doors of room 24.

"You will stay here," said Owl. "This is your jailor," he said, turning towards the man with a sepulchral face who was removing my handcuffs.

Statistically, the gray and forbidding cell was larger than any room I had ever had to myself throughout childhood. But I had never before been caged, forced to live alone in a primitive trap, at the mercy of shrewd and calculating captors. The tan-colored walls of smoothed mortar over brick formed an enclosure twenty-one feet long and twelve feet across at its widest point. Six-inch square tiles, alternating red with a sickly yellow color covered the floor. The small ante chamber was only three feet deep and eight feet across. It led into the main room, fourteen feet deep by twelve feet wide. To my left was a metal frame bed with wooden slats, seven feet long and two-and-one-half-feet wide. An old, simple table and two chairs stood on my right. Close to the ten foot high ceiling, in the center of the room, was a small naked light bulb. At the far end of the main room were two paneled swing doors identical to the front doors. They were eight feet high with wooden shutters above that could be latched closed. Beyond these doors was the third section of room 24 measuring four feet deep and six feet wide. A rusty bucket stood in a corner. The rear of the third section was closed by two more eight foot high doors with the upper portion topped by two foot high vertical rows of iron bars. Above these bars, where shutters would normally be, was a wooden beam and more vertical iron bars through which I could see the sky. Owl said, "These back doors will be open to you only during the daytime. They will be closed during the night and during the lunch siesta. The front doors will be closed all the time."

The back doors opened into an angled courtyard with a solid concrete floor, eight feet deep on the left and narrowing to a few feet deep on my right. It was about fourteen feet wide, and enclosed by double, reddish brick walls, each fifteen feet high and topped with jagged glass and rolls of barbed wire.

Facing the courtyard and attached to the outer wall of room 24, was a foul-smelling vat, stained dark with moss and algae, and alive with enormous roaches. Though a cold water pipe came out above the vat, like a little spigot, there was no rubber stopper. A drain sloped down under the vat and into an open hole leading to the subterranean sewer system.

In the extreme right hand corner of the courtyard, enclosed by a brick wall, and raised a few steps, was the basic oriental latrine, with a hole in the ground separating two slightly raised cement foot-blocks on which to squat.

"You will stay here," said Owl, preparing to leave. "This man will bring you your food and water."

Like a foxhound sniffing around for the scent of its quarry, I looked high and low, probing for outlets and searching for hidden advantages. It did not take long to find a peephole to the main courtyard. The hole was concealed behind a three-inch diameter disk, pegged to the outside of the door so that they could peek in on me. Though it was latched from the outside I managed to work it loose and edge the cover open as secretively as a poker player squeezing his cards apart. I saw some Vietnamese walking across the courtyard to wash themselves and their clothes at the central water faucet. Nobody looked my way. There was some secret satisfaction in being a voyeur and turning the tables on those who thought they knew about my every movement. I felt a swell of relief, having so quickly discovered this link to the world outside my walls.

The lone light bulb glowed all through the night, too small and weak to light up the entire room, but bright enough to cast ominous shadows. It was a sultry summer night and I was perspiring and dozing uncomfortably in shorts, when I caught a shuffling movement of a vague shape lurking in a corner. Now alert and tense, I waited, motionless. Something darted across the floor. As it ran past my bed I recoiled in horror and disbelief. It was a long-tailed brown rat, so plump, and set with such a massive jaw, that for a fleeting moment I thought it must be a cat. Its jaw was locked around the half loaf of French bread left on the table for me on my arrival, and which now blocked the rat's exit through a hole under the front door.

There was barely any light at either end of the room but I felt the base of the doors puckered with holes large enough to admit the rats. With a sense of revulsion it dawned on me that the rats themselves must have gnawed through all the doors. Frantically, I stuffed my spare set of shorts and shirt into the gaps. Then I realized it would be to no avail. There were no shutters behind the bars at the top of the back doors. I opened the front door peephole and, incredulously, drew in a breath. By the light of the moon I saw the courtyard teeming with rats! In their frenzied scurrying they swarmed over the bushes and low trees, giving an animated profile to the silhouetted courtyard. There were so many of them that their movements sounded a collective hum.

The terror never abated, knowing that these monstrous rats used my cell as a thoroughfare between the main courtyard and the entrance to the sewers near the vat. In the months ahead it was difficult to sleep as they removed all my makeshift efforts to block the floor-level holes. They never attacked me in this cell but I often waited in the shadows to ambush them with whacks of my straw broom. And I was overly protective of any scraps of food lying around, making sure they were covered well to outwit the foraging rodents.

Late that first night, as I lay face up waiting for sleep to rescue me from the rats, my eyes fell on something scaling the wall near the ceiling. I sat bolt upright. It moved in fits and starts and as it closed in on a swarm of insects near the light bulb I saw it spring forward and devour its prey. It resembled a lizard but was light-skinned, almost translucent. I tried to shoo it further away and in the days to come, when more appeared, I'd even try and kill them. Later, I learned from my captors that these geckoes were harmless and something of a godsend because they fed on mosquitoes. Relieved, I would sit for hours, watching them at play and listening to them make their high-pitched sounds like *ki-ki-ki-ki-ki-ki*.

Ironically, my closest link with the outside world was the least communicative of the turnkeys—the one with the funereal face who had removed my handcuffs on arrival. In the years to come, when we gave appropriate nicknames to leading characters in the cast of Vietnamese turnkeys, interrogators and torturors, we dubbed this lugubrious man Stoneface. He reminded me of the caveman cartoon character, Alley Oop. He was about fifty years old and looked as if he had been born into middle age. His severe expression was held fast by a square jaw and a tight mouth that rarely opened. He communicated in grunts and hums. Once I saw his open mouth and he looked ugly in a repulsive sense because most of his teeth were missing. Of average height but darker than most Vietnamese, Stoneface always walked with a list, leaning over with an expression of such fixed concentration that it seemed he would forget where he was going if he were to relax. If he had to read or write, he would reach into his light khaki shirt pocket and bring out wire-rimmed spectacles. At moments like this he looked profoundly academic. He was never without his rubber-tire sandals.

I was able to keep track of the daytime hours by a combination of the gong reverberating in the courtyard just before sunrise, the punctuality of Stoneface's chores, and the positions of the sun beyond the back walls. Stoneface came in twice a day with food. At 10 A.M. he unlocked the front doors, placed the food and thermos of warm water on the table, then opened the back doors. As he left he relocked the front doors. By the time he returned to latch the back doors at noon, I had washed my plate, spoon and tin cup which he took away, after again locking all the doors. The back door was opened two hours later, until 5 P.M., when he brought me the evening meal and sealed me in for the long nights with the rats.

I successfully fought off an early attempt by the authorities to make me rise at the sound of the gong to clean my room. When Stoneface walked in I turned over contemptuously. He returned with an English-speaking interpreter.

"Your attitude is bad!" the interpreter admonished. "You have violated regulations! You must get up when the door is opened in the morning!"

I didn't bother to reply. There was no point in getting up that early. Time was so abundant in my bleak confines, that very soon I was banging on the rough walls. "Is there anybody next door!" I screamed. "Somebody answer me!" I kicked at the green doors with my sandals, venting spasms of outrage, visceral fury, and raw frustration. I was a twenty-six-year-old aviator, accustomed to the thrill of soaring high at subsonic speeds, not in being penned close within such cheerless limits of filth and privation.

The starvation diet rapidly drained my strength and sapped my will. Sometimes I lifted the cover off a plate and found a chicken head floating in grease, or in a slimy stew or soup smelling of drainwater. At other times an animal hoof, perhaps of a cow or a pig, with the hair still attached, came mixed with pieces of carrots or turnips. Six-inch long prawns, complete with eyes, were served floating in a dirty, brackish liquid. More than once a blackbird lay feet up on the plate, its head and feathers intact and the eyes open. I dug through the feathers and pulled the skin apart to pry off the small portions of meat. Often this meant chewing the meat off the attached skin. Then I'd take the few chunks of dry bread and soak up the greasy liquid. My insides churned and my body shook. This was always the prelude to fits of vomiting. Sometimes it happened so quickly that I heaved all over the plate. But extreme hunger led me to try again and I often ate the serving, splattered with my own vomit, to satisfy the craving for any kind of sustenance.

"I can't eat this food," I groaned to the interpreter.

He played the innocent: "We are very poor people. We do not have much. We are giving you the best we can."

Feverish and wasted, I hunched over the table and sobbed long and loud. "I've got to eat something!" I repeated over and over to myself, trying once more to down something from the plate. Most often I would puke again, aiming, when I had the strength, at my slop bucket. They gave me a mop to clean up my own mess, but they never brought any disinfectant.

I was sick with diarrhea and dysentery, passing blood in my vomit and stool for the first six weeks. One day as I squatted in the unfamiliar position in the latrine, the crap splashed all over my feet. From then on I took to using the jagged-edged bucket in the corner of my room. Even though I swilled it daily in the vat outside, the stench lingered pervasively in my cell and on myself.

Several times Stoneface came in while I lay down, unable to eat. Expressionless, he looked at the food and then back at me.

"Toi ohm, (I'm sick)" I whispered.

"Ohm?"

"Mmm."

Occasionally they served chicken soup with rice and just as infrequently I'd get a fresh banana. This would settle my stomach, but only until the next meal, which would be a reversion to the regular filth.

Even though it would be years before I saw myself again in a mirror, I felt wretched and squalid. I had matted hair, a stubbly beard, and such a malodorous body that it was offensive even to my own nostrils. Before the shootdown

I had taken good care of my fingernails and toenails but now, denied scissors, I took to peeling them off with the aid of the safety razor given me twice weekly to shave, or with the piece of glass I found in the back courtyard.

A number of medics visited me during those six weeks. They tapped and listened with their stethoscopes. Routinely, they gave me the same white sulphur tablets, and instructed me to make sure I lay under the mosquito net at night, or else I would catch some other illness.

"Malaria?"

"No, but something like it," the interpreter said.

What a far cry this was from the three-day survival course I'd gone through during pre-flight training, four years back. Our instructors had trucked us to a pine forest at Eglin Air Force Reservation, Florida, and taught us how to erect makeshift shelters and search for anything edible. We ate roots and made pine-needle tea with boiled stream water. We even caught a large black snake, beat it with sticks, and roasted it. Snake meat is tough and tasteless but I did not feel the slightest bit queasy. Through all this, we still retained a link with civilization by popping purification tablets into our drinking water. Finally, with the aid of compasses, we made it back to a rendezvous point where instructors "rescued" us with transportation buses home. We were all dead-beat but as soon as the instructors tossed out K-ration kits, it was every man for himself in a wild stampede to grab a share.

"Give me one!"

"How about me!"

"Hey, get out of my way!"

The instructors stood back and laughed. They'd done this so many times before and the cadets' reaction never varied: they always scrambled primitively with fierce disregard for their colleagues. We sat down in shame, aware that everything we'd been taught in the forest about finding and sharing, had vaporized within seconds.

The lessons of the survival course were irrelevant to my plight in the Hanoi Hilton because I did not have the basic freedom to roam in search of alternative food. If my captors kept this up much longer I would not make it out of room 24 alive—even though I already knew the points of the compass beyond the courtyard walls.

A new official, later nicknamed Chihuahua, came in about twice a week to spell out the law and gauge my thoughts. He had the pointy ears and beady eyes of the miniature Mexican dog and a volatile manner that could flash from pleasantly conversational to tersely authoritarian. Thin and darker than most Vietnamese, he had short-cropped black hair that stood up like a crew cut. He did not seem to be puffed up with a sense of rank, and I seldom saw him wearing the four stars and single bar of a major.

"Sit," he motioned, having already seated himself at my table.

Chihuahua had a pleasant, almost built-in smile which masked a keen mind.

"How is your health?"

"It could be better."

"Do you have everything you need?"

"I need something to write with and some paper."

"Why?"

"So I can write down more words."

"Ah, so you can build a dictionary?"

"Yeah."

"Yes, yes, we will see. Perhaps soon. But for now there are two words you must know: *Bao Cao*. They mean you wish to call our attention. You must use them whenever you want to speak to any of us here."

My Vietnamese vocabulary was improving but it was a great relief to speak again with someone who understood English.

"Your wife is very beautiful," he said, watching my reaction closely.

"How do you know?"

"I have seen a picture of her."

"Can I see this picture!" I asked, ready to plead and implore.

Again he smiled, but this time it turned to a smirk because he knew how easy it was to humble and degrade me.

"I will see if I can get it for you."

The following day he brought in the grainy picture, which had been transmitted over a teleprinter. Poor Tangee. She was seated in a white chair in the living room of her father's house, looking forlorn and tearful while clutching a handkerchief.

"She looks very sad," said Chihuahua. "It was taken the day we shot you down."

I held the picture close, wanting to comfort and caress her and hungering for the touch of her flesh and the sound of her voice. When she spoke she had such an appealing lilt at the end of her sentences. Even though the picture was of poor quality I was once again enchanted by her feminine allure, remembering well her large brown eyes and coal-black hair falling loosely over her shoulders.

Chihuahua roused me from my reverie.

"Do you have any children?"

"No."

"I saw a picture where she is with a little girl."

"Well we don't have any children." Hesitantly, almost fearful of his answer, I asked, "Can I see it?"

"I will see."

On his next visit he handed me the picture. Tangee was sitting on the couch in my parents' house holding Denise Sanchez, my three-year-old goddaughter.

"This little girl is my cousin's daughter," I told Chihuahua.

"Ah."

He let me keep the two precious pictures and as I gazed at them long and wistfully I relived over and over our wedding just ten days before the previous Christmas. The church ceremony was brief because we had opted out of having a wedding mass. Tangee was slightly overcome by the momentous event and shed a few tears. It worked like a cue for others in the wedding party because they, too, began to rub their eyes. Finally we intoned the sacred vows and pledged ourselves to each other "till death do us part." Only when we posed for formal photographs by the altar did we notice that we'd forgotten to let out the train from her white silk wedding gown. Tangee, who looked so stunning with her long hair done up, laughed it off as a minor mishap.

My mother-in-law was hospitalized but no one confided in us that she had terminal cancer because in those days the disease was a taboo subject. Tangee and I drove from the church to the nursing home. The curtains were drawn and the light was subdued in the room her mother occupied alone. She retained a wan dignity even though dark circles ringed her eyes. Her greying black hair, pulled back in a bun, somehow preserved a matronly appearance. We kissed her cheek and she managed a faint smile. Her tired eyes languidly scanned her daughter's fitted wedding gown and the nuptial bands we had bought each other.

"You look so nice, both of you," she whispered.

She had always treated me with genuine warmth, civility and affection. It was heart-rending to see her bedridden in this moment of joy. Had they not shielded us from the real magnitude of her condition, we would have done without the reception and other festive trappings. Poignantly, she gave us her blessing and we left. She did not live to see the spring.

We invited about two hundred guests to the reception. Our hearts were full and my cup ran over. In no time at all, it seemed, we had ceremoniously cut the cake and Tangee had thrown out her bouquet with a flourish. They showered us with rice, then we found ourselves driving down the coast to the historic Highlands Inn on the cliffs at Carmel, where we would stay a few days before moving on to Las Vegas for a week. Our car was festooned with flowers made of crepe paper, and a message on the trunk proclaimed to the world at large what Mr. and Mrs. Everett Alvarez, Jr., themselves could scarcely believe: JUST MARRIED!

We had no hint that something was wrong with the luggage until Tangee opened her suitcase. Everything she had packed was missing, except for a single change of clothes. In its place was a pair of panties, a pair of slippers and a rock to make up for the weight loss. Attached was a note from her sisters: "This is all you're going to need!"

My own eyes and ears were better informants than Chihuahua, even though we spoke the same language. Through the peephole I saw the daily arrival of long lines of men and women, chained together by their ankles. Some of the women were scraggly, others, clearly young prostitutes, flirted brazenly with the guards, seductively making eyes and swishing their long black hair. The processing took hours near the water faucet in the main courtyard, and when they were finished with individuals, the women were led off in one direction and the men in another.

Curious to know the nature of the complex where I was confined, I asked Chihuahua, "Are other people held here?"

"This is a prison," he said severely. "We have some thieves and prostitutes. They must be punished!"

Knowing that it was a jail, I decided to explore the surroundings more thoroughly. My cell was like a steam bath that summer so one evening I climbed up to the two-foot high space above the double front doors. I discovered I could open the shutters. It was an eight foot drop to the court-yard below. I heard voices to my left but nobody was in sight. Gingerly, I squeezed a leg out of the cramped space and was maneuvering to lower myself for the jump down when a turnkey looked up. Sheepishly, I greeted him. He grinned and shouted to his comrades. They ran out in a bunch and looked up to where he was pointing. As they jabbered among themselves I slunk back in.

Chihuahua bristled with outrage.

"What were you trying to do!"

"I wanted to get some water over there."

"You were trying to escape!"

"No, no. I was just trying to get out there and get some water."

"How did you know the water was there!"

"The door was open one time. I saw the water faucet. I tell you, I was thirsty. I only wanted a drink."

"You cannot drink that water! You must only drink the boiled water. Do not drink anything else!"

"Yeah, but I was thirsty."

"Don't forget, you're in a prison! This is not a hotel! That is why you must follow our rules!"

I paid a stiff price for that escapade. They nailed the wooden shutters closed, effectively blocking all ventilation from that end of room 24.

I prayed fervently, drawing deeply upon cherished memories of ceremonial rituals and chanted Latin when I was an altar boy at the church of St. Mary's of the Nativity in Salinas. It was comforting merely to remember our neighborhood's old, bespectacled, white-haired priest, Father Buckley, leaning over to pat me and intoning in a strong Irish brogue, "Ah, Everett. . . ." I loved him for the goodness that padded his stern, upright frame. Delia and I went regularly to confession on Saturday nights. She did not share my fondness for Father Buckley because she thought he was insensitive towards kids. But her opinion may have been colored by an incident one night when she flubbed the formal structure of her confession and he bawled her out in the confessional. Crying, she ran out to Dad, who was waiting for us in the car. I trembled because Dad, being angry and quick to explode, instinctively wanted to go in and settle accounts with Father Buckley. Mercifully, though, he calmed down and took us home. The church was two miles from home and after I got my first bicycle on my tenth birthday, I'd ride over for early Sunday morning Mass, either with my best friend and fellow altar boy, Joe Kapp, or with Delia perched precariously on the handlebars and grumping whenever we hit a pothole. St. Mary's was a beacon in our neighborhood and an anchor in my early years. Even before dressing in my black robe and white surplice, I felt enveloped by the purity within the simple wood-framed church, with its white stucco walls and dark beams, and I yielded blissfully to the serene aura of the visibly faithful.

I prayed in my own make-believe church in the back courtyard of the Hanoi Hilton from the very first Sunday after my arrival. When Stoneface opened the doors I walked around, looking closely at the walls and finding inscriptions of dates going back to 1950. The most recent date was 1960. How long had they languished here? I could not see myself surviving long if my captors persisted in serving up the foul diet. My only hope and comfort lay in prayer. Clutching a rusty nail found on the ground, I balanced on the edge of the topmost step outside the back door and reached up to a section of the wall immediately to my right. It jutted out about two inches and, shaped like an upright pillar, was as high as my back door. Laboriously, I scratched about a quarter of an inch through the tinted mortar until I reached the white base. Then I nicked at the wall, straining to keep my foothold as I drew the outline of a cross. After several hours I stood down and looked up approvingly from the courtyard. The cross was a foot high and eight inches wide.

Over successive days I busied myself scratching below the cross a statement of my presence:

> Lt. j.g. Everett Alvarez, Jr., United States Navy. Shot down 5 August 1964, arrived Hanoi 11 August 1964.

Below this, beginning with Labor Day 1964, I scratched the names of every significant holiday, as each arrived.

I now held my daily church services before my cross, which I pretended to be above the altar of St. Mary's. My memory of the form and wording of the Mass had dimmed but I went through every recollected motion of an altar boy. As a child I had never learned Latin. Like others, I had followed the service and recited the passages from a printed hand card. But what little I remembered filled me with warm memories and reminded me of the strength that came from faith.

I struck my breast and bowed in front of the altar, as I had done so often during the Confession:

Mea culpa, mea culpa. . . . mea maxima culpa. . . .

When memory failed me, I play-acted, pretending to give the ritual responses. I held up my imaginary hand bell and recalled its tinkle as the priest intoned, Sanctus, Sanctus, Sanctus. . . .

Sometimes, frustrated with this choppy, truncated Mass, I recited the Lord's Prayer, the Hail Mary's and the Apostles' Creed out of context but with comfortable fluency. Prayer, I discovered, gave me the vision to accept my misfortune with a measure of understanding. It also gave me the resilience to get through the long days and nights.

"Don't you have anything I can read?" I asked Chihuahua. "I am used to reading a lot."

"What do you read?"

"Magazines, newspapers, books."

"I will check."

He brought in a sheaf of 8 × 10-inch English-language typed translations of daily bulletins from the Vietnamese News Agency. Later he gave me translations of the four-page weekly Vietnam Courier tabloids and a stack of propaganda booklets with communist newspeak such as, "We, the women of

South Vietnam, protest against the crimes of the U.S. imperialist-backed stooges in the puppet regime. . . ."

"Is this all you have?" I asked despondently.

"We do not have many English publications in our libraries. We are a poor country. But we do have our independence," he added pointedly. Then he said matter-of-factly, "I read some stories in the paper about you and your family."

I perked up. "Can I see them?"

"Maybe. We shall see." He was about to leave when he turned and asked, "What do you think of your situation?"

"Well, I'm just a prisoner of war, I guess."

That gleeful smile rippled across his face again.

"There is no war here."

"Has there been any more action by our forces against North Vietnam?"

"No. There is no war. You will have to be tried by a court for your crimes against our people!"

"But I'm in the military," I reminded him. "It was a military action."

"You will be tried for your crimes!" he repeated. "The more difficult it gets with us, the more difficult we will make it for you!"

Chihuahua returned the next day.

"No, you cannot read your newspapers," he said, handing me a batch of recent *Vietnam News Agency* bulletins. "You will read ours."

From then on they gave me daily bulletins, all composed with the same repetitive words from the sparse communist lexicon. However, my eyes riveted on one article. A Navy captain aboard the *Ticonderoga* was quoted as saying that nobody had seen my parachute open, even though they had heard my beeper signal. The U.S. Navy assumed I was lost at sea. Further down in the story, Dad was quoted: "We'll pray for my son."

My God! Maybe they don't know I'm alive! Maybe nobody knows I'm here! What if they kill me—perhaps no one back home would be any the wiser! The prospect filled me with dread. I was without protection. In my ignorance, I had drawn strength from the belief that the Geneva Convention on the treatment of prisoners of war would shield me from brutalities or even death. Now I knew this was mere fantasy. I was already a corpse in the eyes of the world. How could the Vietnamese be restrained if their captive was nothing more than a phantom? No matter what my fate, the Vietnamese would never have to account to world opinion because nobody knew I was in their hands!

Stoneface unlocked the door, motioned me to put on my shirt and sandals and follow him. We entered the room immediately to the left of mine. A

large picture of Ho Chi Minh hung on the wall behind the table facing the
door. Three young men and a woman were seated. I sat down on the lone
stool facing them. They said they worked for the *Voice of Vietnam* radio and
wanted to interview me.

"What kind of questions?"

"How do you feel? How are you? What do you think of the Vietnamese
people? Are you married?"

I shook my head negatively. As a prisoner of war I was forbidden by the
Code of Conduct from making tapes for the enemy. They could so easily be
used for propaganda. The Vietnamese persisted, and while they redoubled
their efforts to persuade me, it dawned on me that I could use them to let
the folks back home, and the U.S. government and Navy, know that I was
alive. Chances were good that if the program aired it would be monitored
by U.S. intelligence. All they had to do was hear my voice to realize my
parachute had opened and I had been captured alive. So I answered their
harmless questions. "I feel well; I don't know anything about the Vietnamese
people; Yes, I am married."

When it was over they took turns in reciting lengthy statements on their
history and culture, glorifying the socialist ideals of their revolutionary struggle and denouncing the evils of capitalism and imperialism. They read in
monotones, as if they had lost the fervor of their own beliefs.

"Do you wish to send a message home? We will broadcast it over the *Voice
of Vietnam.*"

This was my big chance! I had to make it short and to the point and pray
that someone friendly would pick it up and get the message home to Tangee
and Mom and Dad.

"I am Lt. j.g. Everett Alvarez, Jr., United States Navy, 644124. I want to
tell my wife and my folks and friends at home that I am alive and well, and
that I have been well treated so far."

"Is that all?"

"Yes."

Back in the cell, Chihuahua asked if I would like to write a letter home.
I jumped at the opportunity. If the *Voice of Vietnam* tape didn't get through,
then maybe the letter would.

Though miserable, I did not want my wife or family to know the truth
about the harsh conditions. It would only add to their concerns. When I
wrote to Tangee I told her not to worry because I was alive and well.

Up to now I have been well treated. I am adequately clothed and sheltered.
My most precious wife, I am sorry for the grief and sorrow you have suffered.

*I know that my mother and father have gone through much anxiety also. For this
I am truly sorry, Tangee. Lead a good life, Tangee, be that it may be without
me.*

I signed off with a brief mention that my captors had advised they would
try me for crimes against the Vietnamese people.

Chihuahua returned with the letter.

"You do not have to write about your trial. You must take it out."

When Stoneface appeared a day or two later with my flight suit, helmet and
boots, and told me to put them on, I tried hard to contain the tingling
excitement that rushed through my body. Several times already I had grasped
naively at imagined hints of imminent release, only to suffer the nauseous
letdown of reality. I was bewildered. Could it be that the long nightmare was
approaching its end? I had been a POW for less than three weeks but they
had so debased my spirits and ravaged my body that I already felt like a
veteran inmate. But at last the pains I had felt since bailing out over the
Tonkin Gulf were easing off. I could walk without an agonizing stiffness and
sharp hurt in my limbs.

Chihuahua sat mute as we drove in a jeep over railroad tracks and on for
about ten miles. We pulled up to the side of the road and they unlocked my
handcuffs. A two-story white colonial building with verandah and red-tiled
roof rose out of the field three hundred yards down. Nearby were military
barracks.

"You must put on your helmet and walk down that road," Chihuahua
ordered.

"I only wear this helmet when I fly."

"You will wear it now!"

Oh, geez! Damn SOB! Grudgingly, I ambled down the road followed by
a guard with a rifle. Then the knots of people I'd taken for farm workers came
into sharper focus. They were cameramen—hordes of them! This was a
put-up job so they could film a downed U.S. pilot at the moment of capture.
Enraged but helpless, I flipped my visor down and picked up speed. The
guard had a hard time keeping up with my brisk march. When I looked back
his large pith helmet was bobbing loosely up and down and he snapped at
me to slow down. The pack of photographers kept pace, swarming around
me. Someone pointed for me to climb the stairs and they ushered me into
a room and sat me down on a stool. I immediately took the helmet off. An
immaculately dressed officer, self-assured in his pressed uniform and shining
boots, sat facing me behind the table. Through an interpreter he asked a

number of basic questions from my name to my age, merely to keep a semblance of conversation going while the cameras clicked and whirred. I was fuming, mad as hell that I had to sit there like some clown dressed up in a flight suit for a carnival.

"How much money do you make?"

I thought, "What the hell is it to you. See what you make of this figure!"

"$400 a month."

He converted it into his own currency and uttered the equivalent of "Wow!" It was a fortune to the average Vietnamese. But the show had to go on so he calmed down and offered me a cigarette. I was an occasional smoker, maybe one or two a day, but I took one just to draw deep puffs and exhale it in clouds to obscure my face from the photographers. After about five minutes he said I could leave. With my visor down, I ran the gauntlet of photographers back up the road again. The return drive was uneventful, but inside I was steaming.

The degradation took many forms. Once I had innocently shrugged my shoulders and opened the palms of my hands in a gesture of incomprehension at something Stoneface had said. He had no sooner left the room than Chihuahua stormed in.

"You have been disrespectful!"

I was non-plussed.

"It is very bad manners to open your hands like this to people and to shrug. We have our customs. What you have done is very improper!"

Another time, Stoneface reported me for looking out of the peephole. He'd been standing in the courtyard when I opened it too wide. A shaft of light probably shone through the open hole and caught his attention. Chihuahua chided me as if disciplining a young boy.

"You are not allowed to look out. You show bad attitude. You do not behave well!"

"What do you mean?"

"You were looking out of the hole in the door."

"I can't look out?"

He scowled. "No! You must learn to respect the people. You must obey the prison rules!"

Stoneface nailed the disk shut but within a few days I had worked it loose. From then on I was much more cautious, sliding the cover back only fractionally and even then with slow movements that required infinite patience.

One afternoon I was eyeing a building overlooking the courtyard when a female nurse came and stood by her open doorway and combed her long black hair. She had accompanied Stoneface to my room a few times to distribute pills. Though young, she was not a pretty sight. Her teeth were discolored a pale green and yellow and it was evident she seldom washed. She wore a long stained white blouse like an apron over her black slacks.

I slid the peep-hole shut and backed away when I saw her approach my room, carrying a small covered basket. She unlocked the door. I sat on the bed, surprised to see her enter alone for the first time.

"Ohm? Ohm?" she asked solicitously.

Yes, I was visibly sick. Almost six weeks before I had come in at 165 lbs. I probably weighed no more than 135 lbs. now. It showed in my boney body and I guessed I had hollow eyes. However dirty she looked, I knew I was a good deal more unkempt and unsightly. But she was unmoved by this outward squalor as she gently pressed me down so that I lay face up. She took a tube of cream from the basket, dabbed it on her palm and slowly spread it over my bare chest. At the moment her hand touched my flesh she rubbed with an unbecoming sensuousness, caressing rather than massaging and averting her eyes from mine.

Without warning, Stoneface burst through the unlocked dark green double doors. In the split second it took for him to pass through the ante room into the main chamber, the nurse jumped up, gathered her basket and, despite apparent jitters, made out that she had just finished administering medicine. Her smile disappeared and she tried to look composed and proper. For once, his normally severe facial expression suited the disciplinary message. He ordered her out with clipped commands and she never again came in by herself, but when she did visit, it was strictly in fulfillment of her duties.

The peep-hole provided a daily dose of comic relief, distracting me from despair over my failing physical condition. Regularly, before the rigors of another day set in, I got my fill of laughs. I had a peep-hole perspective on the dawn assembly of jailors, gathered together for their physical exercises. Most of the turnkeys were either elderly and out of condition, or slightly built middle-aged dopes.

At the beat of the gong they mustered, yawning and slovenly, dressed only in their underwear. The weirdest music, without form or melody, blared out of the loudspeakers. At intervals it faded out and a man's voice took over, sounding almost like someone yawning or exhaling loudly: "Aahhhh! Mahhhh! Oohhhh!" The voice alternated in volume with the music as the turnkeys stretched and whirled in the most bizarre of uncoordinated acrobatics. They pranced around, stood stock still in new positions, and giggled as they tried to catch each other. It was the Keystone Cops reincarnated in a courtyard of Southeast Asia. They were so hilarious that even in my weakened state, I regularly slid off the bed at the sound of the gong so that I wouldn't miss another comedy session (looking back, I realize that what they were probably doing was tai-chi.)

I thought long and hard for a suitable stage name for this crowd. Eventually I hit on it: *Magruder's Army!* Linked, these two words sounded like they were invented for slapstick. I could imagine this dawn patrol marching, not to the beat of drums, but to the helter-skelter of a musician gone berserk on a xylophone!

I made it as hard as I could for the rats by keeping the room as clean as possible. Every day I swept up and scrubbed with a damp rag and the mop. But there was no way I could remove the stench of vomit. As the days passed and I bled and strained more frequently from dysentery and diarrhea, it took more intense will-power to begin my chores and longer to complete them.

Weak and faint I lay down and let my mind drift effortlessly to memories of my maternal grandmother and my parents. All three had missed out on so many of the joys of childhood due to the rigors of poverty. To make ends meet they had all been compelled prematurely to take on the responsibilities of adults. And yet they had pulled through and survived.

Family stories of the adversities they faced had shaped my character and given me backbone. The bedrock was my maternal grandmother, whom we nicknamed MaMona—after a contraction of her real name, Simona. She was the stuff of which legends are made. The mere recollection of her wise and brooding presence shored up my flagging spirits. I had stopped by at the Salinas nursing home to bid her farewell shortly before boarding the *Constellation* that last time. She had been bedridden for three years due to a stroke. My grandmother lay propped up in a bed next to the window and was staring out. I gazed upon the same profile I had loved so much since early childhood. Aztec Indian blood coursed proudly through her dark-skinned, sinewy body. Though withered, she looked stately and serene with her silver-gray hair combed back. Rimless glasses helped her focus on a world whose every hazard and severity she seemed to know well. She was dressed in a pink nightgown. A knitted quilt of many colors lay spread over her legs.

As soon as she saw me she lifted her hands, the same caressing hands that had blessed me so often and made the sign of the cross when I joined the Navy. She began to cry.

"Don't worry," I said soothingly. "I'll be back in seven months. I'll be fine."

It was to no avail. She was sobbing uncontrollably, something I had never witnessed before. I had seen her prior to sailing on my first tour of duty a year earlier, when she had given me a quiet, ritual blessing. But now she was wracked by some unspoken concern that manifested itself in convulsive weeping. I believed she knew it would be the last time we would ever see each other. I fought hard to contain myself as so many memories spilled over. Aside from her love and affection she had been immensely influential, prodding me from boyhood to "get out there and study, and work, and earn." I had never questioned her wisdom because she was the source of our family pride—our matriarch who had pulled through the worst of times.

Gently I clasped her frail hands and kissed her softly. I was misty-eyed and aching deep inside. The painful parting was a chastening experience for one so much younger and less intuitive. In retrospect I marveled at her character. Maternal yet tough, she did not question the cruel twists of life. According to her, the world was spun with deep mysteries and dark secrets and only some of its paths could be divined or its spirits placated. Not surprisingly, she believed in the supernatural and earthly magic, even swearing that people had the power to cast spells with an evil eye. When Dad suffered from recurrent belly cramps she took him to her friend and together they rubbed a raw egg over his bare stomach to draw out the evil. Dad laughed at her superstitious ways, especially when her ritual failed to cure him. But it did not shake her own deep-seated beliefs.

She was born in the Mexican village of Huanimaro, about two hundred miles northwest of Mexico City. Her father, a reckless gambler and adventurer nicknamed *El Capitan*, was married to the beauteous Regina, so coveted by others that *El Capitan* once staked both her and their daughter, my grandmother, in a card game. He lost and the winner, another villager named Bernardino Mejia, took his prize and raised my grandmother as his own child. When she was twelve my grandmother tried to elope with a fifteen-year-old villager, Jesus Rivera, but the elders unceremoniously brought them back and watched over her until her thirteenth birthday in 1900 when they allowed the teenagers to marry. For years, my grandmother lived like a young widow while her husband worked on railroads in the U.S., returning to the village only to sire his children. But after a decade he took my grandmother north. They lived wherever railroads were built, shunting from one location to another like freight cars and bedding down in narrow boxcars or tumbledown shacks. Only three of grandma's dozen children survived—Joe, Mom and Cecilia. Mom, the eleventh, was born at Colton near San Bernardino. They christened her Soledad but everyone called her by a nickname, Chole. She was barely four when Jesus Rivera died of pneumonia. The family lived basically on money brought in by Mom's only surviving brother, Joe, until the factory where he worked in Lompoc shut down during the Great Depression.

The constant moving took its toll. Every time Mom entered a new school she was far behind the other kids. She was still a pre-teen when she learned of the thin line between poverty and destitution and it seemed entirely natural when she dropped out of school in the sixth grade to work full-time in the fields and orchards.

Mom was sixteen when they moved to Castroville, a cluster of wooden dwellings close to the railroad tracks and fields of artichokes, and then to Salinas, some eight miles southwest, where the girls found work in one of the canneries. It was in Castroville that my parents met. Cecilia's boyfriend, whom she later married, was Albert Sanchez, and his mother was my Dad's aunt. When they thought about who could partner Mom to the annual Mexican Independence Day dance, they naturally asked Dad, an orphan, who was then staying with Albert's mother.

Dad was born in the tail-end of World War I, in the copper mining town of Jerome, Arizona, where his mother died less than a year later in a flu epidemic. He was raised by his maternal grandfather, Felipe, who seized the boy after hearing a rumor that Dad's stepmother tied him to a second floor porch railing while Dad's own father was away at work. Felipe owned a pair of work horses and a cart to haul firewood within the mining community. He lived in a cramped bedroom and kitchen behind his tiny store, where miners came to buy bread and pies.

Dad was only twelve years old and already known to everyone by his nickname, Lalo, when the Great Depression struck. He saw the miners stream out of the pits like a colony of army ants on the move. They converged on the bank, but when they got there it had already gone bust and closed its doors for good.

Later, Dad moved down to San Pedro, California, to stay with relatives. He rose daily at 5 A.M. to sell newspapers at street corners and in diners to pay for his school lunch. On weekends he unloaded fresh fish at the market. Compelled to earn his own living, he dropped out of school at fourteen and cleaned and painted freighters in the shipyards.

When Dad learned there was good money to be made three hundred miles north, in the packing sheds of Salinas, he stowed away on a freight train, narrowly escaping suffocation by smoke in a tunnel. Just outside Salinas he jumped off, hit the ground hard and rolled over. Dusting himself off, he walked the short distance to his aunt's house.

"Lalo!" she screamed when she saw his clothing smeared with blood.

"It's nothing," he shrugged. "I just got off the train!"

Just before Christmas 1936, while he was still courting Mom, they were almost killed, together with my grandmother, when a drunk driver slammed his milk truck into their borrowed Model A Ford. Dad suffered a broken pelvis and Mom a fractured nose and shattered collar bone. My grandmother remained in a coma for almost a week and never regained normal hearing in her right ear. Her speech was also impaired. The doctors sent Mom home after three weeks but held Dad for a month. None of them was smart enough to handle the representative from the insurance company who closed the file with a one-time handout of $2500. My grandmother used her share to buy a small plot of dusty land with two humble dwellings on Pearl Street in Salinas, a few miles away from Main Street. She moved into the wood-framed house measuring no more than about thirty feet by twenty-five feet. The other adjacent building was a garage topped with a couple of rooms the size of nooks.

Four months after the accident, Mom and Dad married in the courthouse of neighboring Santa Cruz County and they moved into the space atop the garage, where dividers separated the little bedroom, kitchen and tiny bathroom. Nine months later I was born, just two days before Christmas 1937.

As I grew up, I began to sense the values that austerity had taught my grandmother and parents. Their collective legacy would never be measured in material worth. Instead it would be defined in terms of human endurance and the need to survive. Our lot was to struggle and to overcome. That was best done through hard work and education. The alternative meant yet another generation of vulnerability to low pay for unskilled labor.

I was still a young boy when they began to talk about the importance of good, honest work and the need to stand up to hardships. "You've got to learn what work is," they'd say. Mom encouraged me to keep the yard clean and to weed and plant years before I was a teenager. Then she spoke to my Dad's cousin, Uncle Phillip, who was the foreman in charge of the vegetable fields on a ranch outside Salinas. She asked him to take me with him in the summer after I finished sixth grade.

"Don't pay him. Just teach him to work," she told him.

Mom packed my lunches and saw me off every day before sunup. I walked the block and a half to his house, joined him and his sons for breakfast and then piled into his flatbed truck headed for the ranch. Most of the time I'd help carry irrigation pipes or hoe the fertile earth. I did this for a number of weeks.

At other times I'd go some forty miles south of Salinas to the labor camp in the Arroyo Seco run by Uncle Phillip's sister, Consuelo, and her husband. Their crew of laborers hoed, weeded and harvested. These were the brass-eros—men brought up on seasonal contracts after which they had to return to their homes in Mexico. I hoed a row in tandem with one of my cousins to keep pace with these adults. Overall, the experience was invaluable. Working the land was exacting and sometimes even punishing. But at the end of the day, when the setting sun softened the edges of the landscape, and the truck chugged through the cooling fields for home, we had that contented feeling known to all who have earned their Sabbath rest.

Mom and Dad never let up on their message that the only sure way to a good job and a better life was through hard work and higher education. They drummed it in even when we drove through the valley for occasional picnics. Pointing to the Japanese laborers, one or other of them would say, "See those Japanese. It's Sunday and they're still working. They're the ones whose children are going to be successful because they're working to send their kids to school. One day they're going to have a lot of money because they work so hard." Then balefully, they'd compare them with some of the Mexican laborers, who partied so wildly on Saturday nights that they couldn't do anything but nurse hangovers on Sundays.

Pocket money brought in from my work on the fields and from cutting neighborhood lawns went towards the purchase of clothes. I had only one pair of jeans but I was lucky to be the sole scout in our raggedly outfitted troop to have a complete uniform. The other boys just couldn't afford it.

Even at that young age I knew that nobody was going to hand me something for nothing—especially in the area where we lived. The railroad tracks divided our town both socially and economically. Everything east of the Southern Pacific railway tracks, as far as the airfield, was known as *Little Oklahoma*. The name had stuck for our poor Alisal district ever since migrant workers from the dust bowls of Oklahoma, Arkansas and Texas settled it during the Great Depression. Anyone who grew up there knew the value of money and the necessity for thrift. Survival depended on having sharp wits, a strong back and a thick skin.

Most of these simple, tested values came down to me from my family. But I also owed a lot to Joe Kapp, my closest friend from sixth grade. Even at that tender age he represented a role model for me. It did not surprise me years later when he quarterbacked the Golden Bears at the Rose Bowl and later led the NFL's Minnesota Vikings in the Super Bowl. He had fire in his heart and did not seem to know the meaning of quitting. Together we played a lot of basketball and were forever throwing footballs. He practiced relentlessly. I remember once we were out shooting basketballs when it started to rain.

"It's coming down too hard, Joe. I'm going in," I shouted.

"I'll catch up with you later," he replied, refusing to call it a day as he played on alone through the driving rain.

That was typical of his attitude—to practice and perfect what he was doing regardless of the obstacles. These traits marked him early on for excellence and a lot of the example rubbed off on me. We were inseparable, whether riding together at six o'clock in the morning to serve as altar boys or, more often, to play sports. When the municipal pool opened across town we hitchhiked together, thinking nothing in those calmer days of thumbing rides with strangers.

Joe and I saw our neighborhood from a fresh perspective the year our junior high school received an invitation to a dance from students at Washington Junior High across the railroad tracks. I got all spiffed up in my freshly laundered jeans and clean shirt and anxiously cycled across town. The grass there was so much greener and the homes spacious and fancy. We couldn't help noticing that all the streets had sidewalks! Then we looked over their junior high girls. They looked different, no doubt snobbish, and I got the feeling that if we had asked them to dance we would have been flouting a sacred taboo, trespassing on forbidden territory, courting trouble. It was an odd but inescapable sensation. Not long after, a rivalry developed between the schools and grew more intense as the numbers swelled at our junior high.

When it came time for us to go to high school, Joe and I both believed we were going to be All-Stars. That confidence drained the moment we sized up our small, skinny bodies with the other boys competing for places on the football team. They used to knock us on our tails. I was about 128 lbs. and Joe was not much more. It was the first time I had seen football uniforms close up. I had never gotten a really good look at shoulder pads and helmets. Our dreams seemed to be shattered and we both ended up as last string ends. But we gave it everything we had, enjoying the competition and knowing, after a while, that we were gaining on the others.

There was not much difference in our height until some months later when Joe sprang up like a beanstalk. All of a sudden he was gangly and awkward. His joints and knees seemed uncoordinated and he moved like a newborn giraffe struggling to find its feet. The kids laughed and called him "Daddy-Long-Legs." But Joe had guts and hung in there. His perseverance paid off in basketball when he made the team. Meanwhile I was getting involved in track, discovering that, compared to most of the kids, I was a good middle distance runner. Joe was always cheering and pushing me on to greater efforts. Combined with prodding from my coach, in my senior year I made it all the way to the northern California track meet where I did well.

Sadly, at the end of the first year of high school, Joe moved with his family to Los Angeles. It was as if we had been Siamese twins who were now surgically parted. But Joe left me with a lifelong legacy: he had toughed it out with the kids and earned their respect. I had seen him strive and I had watched him succeed. It was an inspiring lesson in willpower. It was also the stuff from which character is built. I remembered it well as I crouched in the isolation of my dismal cell.

In my lowest moments in room 24, Dad's words of encouragement echoed vigorously down the years: "Keep your chin up, son!"

But it was not enough merely to daydream of the past. I had to hear the sound of a human voice to break the monotonous silence. I began talking aloud to myself, often assuming a dual role so I could create a dialogue between myself and my friends. Sometimes, when I talked to myself or prayed aloud in the back courtyard, a turnkey leaned out of the window above and yelled at me to shut up. Any westerner looking in or listening to me would have concluded very quickly that I had flipped.

On September 15th Chihuahua told me I could write home to my parents. He gave me a quill pen and a bottle of ink, some sheets of thin writing paper and an envelope printed with a picture of a Vietnamese farmer plowing his field with a modern tractor. I wrote to Mom and Dad, telling them I had no way of knowing whether Tangee had received my letter written a month earlier, nor whether anyone had heard my tape-recorded voice saying I was alive and well. It was important to try and ease their burden by confirming I was not only alive, but well. The rest would have to be pure fabrication, though I had to establish that the letter was genuinely from me and not forged. I asked how my avocado tree was doing. They would remember the sapling I'd planted six years earlier.

> *I suppose all it will give is a lot of shade. I have not been hurt nor injured in any way. I feel fine and my health seems to be good. I have been treated well by my captors. I have a big room in which I live. I am given food and water, clothing and books and papers to read. There is medical aid available in case I may need it. I sleep on a flat bed with a straw mat, I assume just like everyone else in Vietnam; and there is a mosquito net to cover me at night. There is also a table and chairs where I eat and read. Outside the room there is a water faucet where I wash and bathe, and there is a water closet nearby. I do get fresh air daily and plenty of sleep. . . . I pray every day that all of you will remain healthy and well. Take special care of yourselves. . . ."*

The consistent lack of nourishment left me with headaches and dizzy spells. I moved listlessly, spending more time curled up on the springless bed, unable to exercise and unwilling to eat. I had not even consumed enough to vomit, so that I retched and heaved painfully, without finding relief by spewing out unwanted food. At the time I wrote to Mom and Dad, I believed I was close to death by starvation. Huddling in the grim cell, I did not have the strength to panic. My body burned with fever and I stared with the blankness of the doomed. My mind was still and passive, and my breathing ominously slower.

Stoneface entered, put the food down and stared at me. His face registered neither the triumph of the victor nor the compassion of the stronger. I knew I was going to vomit again. I felt nauseous and had that telltale queasiness with stomach cramps.

"Toi ohm," I said.

Stoneface unlocked the back doors then left. When he returned, he pointed to his watch, wrote down the time, 5 P.M., and said "Chao teat (chicken in rice soup)." But it was not to be. The evening meal was greasy food which I didn't even touch.

The following morning he brought in the flattish plates stacked, as usual, one atop the other. Out of habit, but also to break the monotony of the long day, I lifted the top plate. A large pancake-sized omelette almost filled the dish like a bar of gold! I felt a rush of excitement! Quickly I uncovered the next plate. Fried potatoes! And the next—sliced pieces of thick, fresh, white bread! And the next—a tomato! It smelled so good that tears welled in my eyes from the surge of joy. Stoneface grunted as I yanked out the chair and sat down to feast. I took a huge bite of the omelette and looked gratefully at him as I wolfed it down.

"Good! Okay!" I said with a wide grin.

Expressionless, he snorted and shuffled out, closing the doors behind him. I howled loudly, crying uncontrollably as the tears streamed down my face and onto my plate. "Thank God!" I said aloud. "THANK GOD!" I reeled with the ecstasy of every mouthful, trying to prolong each chew, yet gulping it down as fast as my gullet could cope. I savored every morsel, licking the plates clean and running my tongue between my teeth to free and swallow every speck of trapped food. I stared at the empty plates, entranced by the magic they had borne. My mouth still held the warm taste of home-cooked food and my belly settled with an after glow of fullness. "Amen! Amen!"

When Stoneface returned in the evening I was still crying. This time I uncovered a piece of ground beef in the shape of a hamburger, a slice of lettuce and tomato, some mashed potatoes and again, slices of fresh bread.

"Tot (good)?"

"Tot," I acknowledged.

I devoured it all, like a stray dog thrown scraps by a butcher. And again I sobbed with immense relief. As I sat alone, with no one to talk to nor anyone to listen, I thought to myself, "They knew. . . . They knew all along what the putrid food would do to me. They knew what I would be able to take and what would debilitate me."

From then on the food remained edible. There was not always enough, but the quality never again regressed to the putrid waste they'd served for six weeks. Through the peep-hole I saw Stoneface cycle out of the courtyard and return some five minutes later holding the handle of stacked dishes. I figured this new diet was prepared outside the prison, which was no surprise.

A day later Chihuahua again berated the U.S. for refusing to admit it had lost eight planes in the raids against North Vietnamese PT boats.

"We have shot down many planes but your government does not admit it."

"What do you mean?"

"They refuse to admit that they lost those planes. How do they tell those families of the pilots that were lost?"

"I don't know. What does my government say?"

"They admit only to your capture and one pilot killed."

"Really?"

"Yes. But it is in the news."

"Can I see it?"

"I will bring it to you."

He returned with one of the yellowish transcripts from the *Voice of Vietnam*. It reported that the U.S. Government admitted only that Everett Alvarez was missing and Richard Sather had been killed. Dick Sather piloted a Spad in another squadron on the *Constellation*. Though his stateroom was next to mine I did not know him well.

Chihuahua repeated: "How does your government tell the families of the dead pilots?"

"I believe them. You must be mistaken. We lost one pilot and I was captured."

"We do not make mistakes! We do not lie to the people!"

"In this case I believe my government."

"Would you like to see the wreckage? We have it."

He seemed so sure of his facts that I did not know what to make of it.

"Let me see it," I said.

The following night he came in with a turnkey.

"We come to show you The People's Revolutionary Museum."

They led me, handcuffed and blindfolded, to a jeep. One of the guards in the back asked if I knew where we were going.

"No. Where are we going?"

"We go to Hanoi!" he said and they all laughed.

None of them knew that I had seen the city of Hanoi sign the day they brought me in from the farm house. We drove for about an hour, making turn after turn in their ploy to simulate a long drive to the capital. When we stopped they removed the blindfold. As we walked under a covered walkway, a bunch of photographers had a field day, filming me as if I was a celebrity, though I was dressed humbly in a blue shirt, khaki trousers and wooden-heeled shoes that my captors had recently provided me with.

Sections of plane wreckage lay illuminated by floodlight in eight distinct piles, each ringed with a low wooden enclosure. Signs indicated whether the aircraft was a Skyhawk or Skyraider. I noticed pieces of my fuselage with familiar markings. The entire section in front of the cockpit was intact, complete with boom. I worried that they might have found my empty rocket pods because I had consistently denied firing rockets.

"Here is another plane," said Chihuahua, eager to prove his point. I surveyed the wreckage closely then looked at pieces of a Spad nearby. Something didn't seem right. I moved over to the rest of the wreckage then looked back. One pile had a piece of fuselage with part of a name: Lt. James Cru. . . . The remainder of the name, . . . mmer, was on a separate strip of fuselage in another display. Both pieces were from the same fuselage marked 505, which was from Sather's squadron! I realized that Sather must have been flying Crummer's Spad when he was shot down. I turned to another heap and compared it with parts I'd already seen. Then it hit me! I rolled my eyes.

"You didn't shoot down eight planes!" I said.

"Yes, it is true! What do you mean!"

"See that. It fits next to that piece. And this piece from here is part of that piece over there!"

Chihuahua picked up the wreckage of a seat pan from the pile of scrap purporting to come from a Skyhawk.

"This is not your seat! If it was your seat you wouldn't be here!"

I held the pan. Something had torn through the middle with brutal force, peeling the metal outwards like a blossoming flower. But it was from a Skyraider and did not belong where they had dumped it.

"You have only two planes here! You have one Skyhawk and one Sky-raider!" I shouted.

They talked at breakneck speed among themselves. Damn the consequences! I was boiling, not through anger but because I was irritated at their naivety as I went from one heap to the other pointing out the obvious connection between the separated parts.

"I've seen enough! You're trying to pull something off but this is just garbage!" I fumed, heading contemptuously towards the jeep. Now I knew what kind of people they were and what mode of government they lived under. It was a revelation because now I knew how they operated. Exposing their lies and deceit boosted my self-confidence.

"Our workmen mixed some pieces up," Chihuahua said, battling to explain the obvious discrepancies. "They did not know. Our workmen made some mistakes. They are not very technical. But it is true! It must be true! We shot down eight planes."

"You shot down two—one Skyhawk and one Skyraider!" I answered defiantly.

The "return" journey to Hanoi took only twenty minutes.

6
INTERROGATION

STONEFACE GAVE A HINT THAT SOMETHING UNUSUAL WAS
about to happen when he came in about an hour after sunrise on September
21st and made the gestures for me to shave and look smart.

He led me into the room where I had been interviewed by the reporters
from the *Voice of Vietnam* Radio. Owl and Chihuahua flanked a man older
by ten years, dressed in a starched off-white shirt, khaki trousers and gleaming
brown polished boots. Above his expansive forehead was a neatly-coiffed
wave. All three sat on raised chairs so that they peered down on my lowly
stool.

"How are you?" asked the newcomer, with a gracious smile that showed
off his perfectly white, straight teeth. Though he talked *to* me, he looked
beyond as if addressing the door behind.

"I want you to understand," he said in impeccable English, "that we have
come to interrogate you. You were captured attacking our territory and we
have come to find out all you know."

"Oh God!" I thought, chilled with foreboding.

"You have good food now. Your conditions are better. But they could get
much worse. Do you understand? We could go back to the food that was not
as good."

I shifted anxiously, fearful of the threat. Only forty-eight hours had passed
since the first good meal.

"Do you like sports? Football?" he asked, throwing me off guard.

"Sure."

"Tell me about football. We call it soccer."

"No, no. Our football is something else."

"How do you play football? What is it?"

I gave a brief explanation as he nodded and smiled while Owl took notes.

He said he was sports-minded, with a particular liking for track events. This
is what he would follow closely in the Olympic Games, scheduled to open

at Tokyo in three weeks. While he talked I tried frantically to come up with a game plan to handle the questions. Nothing in survival training had taught me how to react to a quiz in these circumstances. There was obviously no formal state of war between our countries. Was I supposed to clam up completely—even on discussions about sports? How would I handle questions about my family and personal background, and even about my ship and my plane when they already knew so much from published reports in the American media? If I refused to answer anything, they might try other means of forcing me to talk. Perhaps drugs or torture. Then I might be compelled to say things that I didn't want to, and maybe I could have misled them if I'd spoken out in the first place.

I paced anxiously in my back courtyard when we broke for lunch. And I prayed before my altar, imploring divine help in seeing me through this quandary. Suddenly the sound of voices filtered out of the back window of the quiz room facing the courtyard near the corner latrine. Slowly and quietly I stood on the topmost step at the entrance to the latrine and hoisted myself up the drainpipe. A partition stood between the window and the table where we'd faced each other. I cocked my ear and heard the three of them repeating the word *football* over and over. In an instant it clicked. The interrogator wanted me to loosen up and talk about anything, the more innocuous the better, so that he could get a good reading of my natural demeanor in normal conversation. This would make it easier for him to spot shifts in my tone and attitude under pressure, when I would most likely be lying.

I had little time to devise a strategy. One thing I knew for sure: it would be foolish to act humble and subservient. Once before I'd tried that with a turnkey and it had the opposite effect; he'd popped his chest out and pushed me around more than usual, enjoying his dominance and watching me jump to his orders. Likewise, I knew that it paid dividends to act with reasonable civility. Every time I'd blown my stack with a guard I'd been cut down to size with a lecture: "You must keep good attitude!" I figured my best hope was to play it by ear. I would lie and invent where I thought I could get away with it. But I'd also plead ignorance and play the naive junior officer, green, inexperienced and too far down on the pecking order to be of any use to them.

"Tell me about your wife," he began.

"Well, she's young and stays at home."

"Where does she live?"

"With her father. Sometimes with my parents."

"How do you write to her?"

"I address it to the same place I send mail to my parents."

"What is she doing?"

"I don't know. I haven't heard from her."

"That's all? You could tell us much more. Look at this, for instance."

He held up a copy of *Time* magazine, with a cover picture of the *Constellation*. He flipped the pages to pictures of myself and the family.

"Look! It's a good picture of you!" he said, brandishing the magazine close to my face. "Now, what does your father do? What is his occupation? He is not a Congressman or a Senator."

"He's a working man."

"Ah! He's one of the people!"

"Yes! One of the people! Yes!"

"Who does he work for? It says here in the magazine that he works for FMC. What does FMC stand for?"

FMC made military equipment and was the biggest producer of armored vehicles. Quickly I came up with a substitute title: "Foot Machinery Corporation."

"Foot Machinery? What is that?"

"FMC."

"Like a foot? F-O-O-T?"

"Yeah, like a foot."

"Ah! What do they do?"

"They make machinery for the feet."

"Like what?"

"Oh, they make machinery for companies that make shoes and socks."

"Ah! So he is a laborer! He is a real working person!"

"Yes."

"What does he do?"

"He makes parts for the machines."

He flipped through a sheaf of cuttings.

"But I see here from this newspaper that your father is a draftsman."

I could just see Dad trying to describe to some reporter that he worked with blueprints and the newsman getting the wrong end of the stick! "Well, he makes machinery parts by looking at plans."

"I understand that you said your father was a postmaster?"

"No, he's not a postmaster."

"How is it we have this information?"

I had already told Owl at the farm house that my father was moving and that I could reach him by writing to the postmaster.

"My family is going to move and I don't know whether they've moved or not, so I can reach them through a friend of ours, the postmaster."

"What is his name?"

"John Sanchez."

It was clear that the sum total of their knowledge about me came from magazines and newspapers—and whatever else I would tell them.

One morning the interrogator startled me.

"I have a letter from your wife."

"You do! Where is it?"

"Here."

I handled it as if it were fragile. Every handwritten word conveyed an image, a memory, a scent. It was my link back to the purer world and to the one I had dreamed of so much during the past few months. Tangee wrote, *I'm happy to hear you're alive and well and being taken care of. Don't worry about me, I'm fine.* But then she asked, *Tell me, now that I'm going to have to be making the car payments, what day are they due?*

Immediately I understood why the wording was so stilted and the contents superficially coded. Tangee still didn't know whether I was dead or alive. She knew the date the car installments were due because she'd been paying them regularly ever since I'd sailed out of San Diego in May. Obviously she had not received any letters from me. This was her way of confirming that I was alive.

"I want to write to my wife," I said.

"You may write as much as you want," he replied.

I wrote about twice a week, even though I had no way of knowing if she would get any of my letters. (Later, I found out that some—but not all—did get through.) But this was no time to daydream about Tangee. If I did not keep my wits about me they could trip me up during a quiz.

"What do you know about our country? About our history and our war of independence?" the interrogator asked.

"Not much."

It soon became apparent that this was his favorite topic, and it made him vulnerable. Whenever the questions became too compromising, or if there was a pause, I was able to sidetrack him by asking a question and getting a lengthy discourse on the war against the French. It didn't take much to wind him up for a history lesson.

"I remember when I was a teenager I saw newsreels of Dien Bien Phu," I said.

"Ah! Dien Bien Phu! Quelle victoire! What a victory against the French!"

Owl rolled his eyes in exasperation and put his pencil down. He knew what was coming.

"When you were fighting against the French, did you have medics and supplies?"

"I was imprisoned by the French," he continued, animated by the opportunity to relive the glory of his past.

"Were you put in solitary confinement?"

"I used to have my men around me."

"How did you communicate when you were in different areas?"

"It was difficult. Very hard. But there were trails over the mountains, and we had help from the villagers."

Sometimes he spoke for days, his eyes lighting up with the zeal of an aging revolutionary as he harked back to the time when they'd eluded the French along mountain paths, carrying huge quantities of food and equipment over great distances.

"If your President Roosevelt had lived longer we would have been good friends. He was our hero during World War II. Did you know that our President Ho Chi Minh copied your Declaration of Independence for our country."

I was surprised.

"It is true. Ours also begins *All men are created equal.* . . . But then, after the war, the French and the neo-colonialists tried to get back in and your country supported them."

Back in room 24 I thought about his diatribes against the French and colonialism. Maybe he was right but I was absolutely determined not to be taken in by such simplistic talk. The issues could not have been that black and white. The next time he began his tirade against colonialism I interjected.

"Everything you say sounds like it has a true ring to it. And I may have done the same as you under those circumstances. But it can't be that simple. There must be another side to it."

"Do you believe us?"

"In principle, perhaps, but not totally. There's got to be some other part. I'd like to hear what the other part is. Why we didn't do this and that. I mean, you're dealing with something that happened a long time ago."

Sternly, he said: "When you go home someday you're going to spend all day in the library reading about that. But for now you must know our part."

"Okay. But I can't be convinced until I do."

"We don't want to brainwash you. We want you just to know our side. You must change yourself."

He arranged for propaganda books to be sent to my cell. Some of them were about the Franco-Indochinese War and its conclusion with the Geneva Agreements. Others were elementary history primers written with communist jargon. The literature included the slavishly pro-Hanoi writings of the Australian communist, Wilfred Burchett.

They were almost childlike in refusing to acknowledge that we were in Hanoi.

"When you go to Hanoi. . . ." said the interrogator.

"Where's Hanoi?" I asked.

Owl pointed one way and the interrogator the other so that their arms crossed.

"Where?" I asked.

They'd look at each other and smile.

"Do you know where you are?" asked the interrogator.

"Sure, I'm in Hanoi."

"What makes you think that?"

"Because I saw the sign near the bridge when you brought me here."

They exchanged looks of amazement.

"What did the sign say?"

"Hanoi. That's how I know I'm in Hanoi."

"No, no. Hanoi is far. Very far away."

They held to this fiction, pointedly remarking at the end of the day, "We have to go now. Our driver is coming. We have to drive back to Hanoi to our offices. We have lots of work to do there."

Back in room 24, I'd look through the peephole and see them wheeling their bicycles out of the courtyard. When Stoneface let me out to the back courtyard I waited for him to depart then scratched Columbus Day below the cross.

Many times during those six straight weeks of quizzing the interrogator sat alone with me. The sessions began about 7 A.M. and ran through 5:30 P.M., with the break for lunch. When Owl and Chihuahua were absent, he confided that he was not a good interrogator. But I kept my guard up because this admission could so easily be part of a subtle attempt to win me over. Alone, he also reminisced about his childhood, when his father had been a wealthy landowner. He himself had attended a French school and had had to salute the French flag and sing the French national anthem.

"What happened to your father after the revolution?"

"He knew things were changing. He had to give up most of his lands—but they left him a small piece."

Neither Owl nor Chihuahua dared show insubordination. Though the interrogator never wore military insignia, he obviously outranked them because they referred to him as "our senior officer," and he alone gave orders.

Often he told me, "I am a teacher, but my government has asked me to do this. It is my duty. When we are given a task to do, we do it."

Though knowledgeable on history, the interrogator was woefully ignorant about naval aviation, even those basics that school kids would be expected to know.

"How do you land on an aircraft carrier?" he asked. "Do you stop?"

"No, no. You don't have to stop."

"You don't have to stop? It just lands?"

He exchanged puzzled glances with Owl.

"The deck, does it expand to make it bigger?"

Holy smokes! These guys really don't know anything about flying! Here's one topic I can safely talk about and make up what I want. And I don't even have to worry about feeding them straight replies because answers like this can be found in any illustrated book on naval aviation. Nevertheless, I was careful not to show any signs of relief or relaxation.

"Do you have a swimming pool on the ship?"

"Oh yes, we have a nice swimming pool."

"What did you like best about your ship?"

"The popcorn machine."

"Popcorn? What is popcorn?"

They were as woefully ignorant of the fabric of our political system.

"Where do you get your political lectures?" the interrogator asked.

"We don't get political lectures."

"So what does the chaplain do? Does he give you political lectures? What does a commanding officer do? Where do you learn about your politics?"

"We read the newspapers. We watch television. We read books. We have public meetings. We know what our government's doing. We're well aware."

"Yes, but. . . ."

They could not comprehend, nor even conceive of, a system without indoctrination by political cadres and commissars.

I had to be wary at all times, especially on minute details and names. Sometimes he'd ask me apparently harmless questions and then, two weeks later, lead me through a minefield when I couldn't remember what I'd fabricated in the earlier session.

"Who was the commanding officer of your squadron?"

"Er . . . Commander Bolsted."

"But you said it was Commander Sellers."

"Oh yeah, but he just left a week before and we had this new commanding officer come in."

"Who was the captain of your ship?"

"Gosh, I don't remember."

"Try! Try to remember!"

"Let me see. Bradshaw? Something like that. I didn't know him too well."

"Bardshaw?" he suggested, reading from a newspaper clipping.

"Yes, yes. That's it! Frederick G. Bardshaw," I answered.

"And the commanding officer of your air group?"

"I didn't get to know them too well. I was only a lieutenant, junior grade. I think his name was Don. . . ."

"Donald B. Edge?"

"That's it!" I said, trying to keep up the act but troubled about how much they really knew from those press clippings. He held up a kneeboard card, marked confidential. They must have retrieved it from Dick Sather's wreck.

"What does this mean—tower frequency?"

"That's what you call the tower."

"What do you mean."

"You dial that frequency."

"All towers?"

"No. Every tower's a different frequency."

"Oh. What does this mean—CCA?"

"That's when you're approaching the aircraft carrier."

"Every carrier?"

"No, no. They change it all the time."

"That's secret, right?"

"Yeah, that's secret. I shouldn't be telling you this."

"Yes," he said with a smile, "we have our secrets, too. What does this mean? Crow's Landing?"

"I don't know."

He looked at Owl. Apparently they thought they had latched onto something significant. Actually, Crow's Landing, where we practiced touch-and-go landings, was a small auxiliary field, just over the hills east of Moffet Naval Air Station, which lay at the southern edge of the San Francisco Bay. It also had a seldom used range for firing practice.

"How do you spell it," I asked.

They spelled it out.

"I really don't know," I shrugged.

Feeling somewhat smug, I was not prepared for his sudden verbal lunge. He executed it like a matador lining up his sword for the kill, having done with the preliminary twirls of the cape.

"You know that we pulled your plane out of the sea?"

I nodded, because I'd seen the wreckage at the People's Revolutionary Museum.

"Our military experts have recovered your guns. They found rounds of ammunition inside because the guns were jammed."

He looked directly at me, watching my demeanor and awaiting my response. I was trapped! I did not know whether to avert my eyes or meet his head on. Since my capture I'd held fast to the story that I'd been a scout plane and hadn't fired any of my guns. Now there was incontrovertible evidence that I had lied—and they knew it.

"You have been lying! You must tell us the truth!" He stared hard at me. "Go back to your room and think about it!"

I paced the courtyard nervously talking to God. "Things don't look too good right now. They want me to answer and I don't know what to say. What do you think I should tell them?" I wasn't expecting a divine solution or answer but my prayers were comforting, and gave me the strength to face the open threats and hidden terrors.

I didn't get much sleep that night. I worried more about what to say the next day than about keeping vigil against the rats. At the sound of the pre-dawn gong I knew there was only one way to wriggle out of his trap.

"You don't look well this morning," the interrogator remarked.

"No," I agreed, playing the contrite liar for all I was worth.

"Well," he demanded, "have you thought about it?"

I lowered my head in shame. I forced the tears and looked up.

"I have to admit something. I lied to you."

"Yes! Yes!"

"I didn't tell you the truth about this."

"But why did you lie?" the interrogator asked with fatherly concern. Owl nudged him and Chihuahua stirred. Everyone sensed an imminent confession. "What is the truth?"

"I did fire my 20 mm. rounds at your boats."

"Yes! Yes! Go ahead! Yes!"

"I lied to you about that."

"Did you fire rockets and bombs?"

"No. No rockets and bombs. I didn't have any. Just guns." I said softly. I was confident they had not picked up the pods I'd jettisoned shortly before ditching because they weren't on display with the wreckage in the museum.

"Why did you lie?"

"Because I thought if I told you I'd shot at you, you would kill me."

"Oh, no, no! Don't think that! We will not kill you!"

I looked long and hard at all three. And then I knew, for the first time, that they had never intended to kill me. My God! Here I was, four weeks into interrogation and all the time I could have played it the other way and refused to answer anything. They really weren't going to kill me! What a relief!

"I'm sorry. I hope I didn't hurt anyone."

"We don't know if it was you or the others."

"I didn't tell you the truth but. . . ."

"Is this the truth?"

"Yes."

If they believed me now, it would validate the role I had played all through the quiz, of the hopelessly green aviator who didn't even know the carrier's chain of command, and who had an open mind on their reading of history. If they bought my confession, it was unlikely they would press me further. I was not far wrong. The pressure eased. Now he seemed more eager to smear the United States with hackneyed slogans, even as he spared no effort to advance his own intense nationalistic pride.

"America is no longer the big power it used to be," he said. "What can the United States do for you here? This is Vietnam. They cannot do anything for you here. The paper tiger is dead. It is just a harmless little bag of wind."

"Is that a Vietnamese pen you've got," I asked, trying to throw him off balance.

He'd seize on questions like this to brag about their fledgling industries. They didn't have much, he admitted, but they had defeated the French and, above all, they were independent. He and the others seemed driven to prove their nationalism. It was not sufficient to believe in it. They had to proclaim it. Nationalistic songs blared interminably over the speakers and sometimes I heard crowds of Vietnamese chanting collectively in the street parallel to the courtyard. There could be no doubting the herd mentality and the lathering of public opinion through the grinding propaganda machine. Even this interrogator, a learned man without malice or bombast, who at times spoke nostalgically of his privileged youth, marched to the drum beat of the slogans.

At about this time I read with dismay an article in a *Vietnamese News Agency* handout about Jim Thompson, a U.S. Army special forces captain, held captive in South Vietnam since March. Oh my God, I thought to myself, he's been held down there for six months! I wonder how he's surviving! Is it as hard for him as it has been for me? Did they also bring him to the brink of starvation? Though I could not even guess at the conditions of his captivity, I thought he was probably being held in the mountains because in the article he described the beauty of looking out over ridges foliated with the overgrowth of a jungle. At least he was moved to speak somewhat wistfully of nature. It was more than I could say of my confinement.

The article made me fretful about the foreseeable future. If Thompson had been held for so long down south there was no reason to expect that the North Vietnamese would release me any time soon. I began to fear that I might indeed be trapped for weeks or even months to come. If they were not going to kill me then my fate might well be prolonged incarceration. Why had it taken my government so long to secure my release? Months had already passed since my capture. How much longer would it take for my government to get me out of this hellhole? There had been no visits from Red Cross or other intermediaries. Already I felt burdened by the weight of this alien, structured culture. Initially, I had the single-minded goal of staying alive. Now I had to fight the mental strictures of a bigoted, controlled society, so unsure of itself that it could only survive by feeding on its own excesses.

When next I appeared before the interrogator I seized on our common love of sports to brighten the days. As he had told me he listened daily to BBC summaries of the Tokyo Olympics, I asked if he could give me some results. It did not surprise me when he complied.

"Valeri Brumel of the USSR won the high jump, clearing 7 ft. 1¾ in." he crowed. "But your Robert Hayes, he won the 100 meters in 10 sec."

There was still another world out there—healthily competitive, civil and free. It brought home more painfully my isolation and dependency on the Vietnamese for any news beyond the walls of room 24.

At the beginning of November the interrogator was brief.

"Today is the last day of this interrogation."

A feeling of relief washed over my body.

"Are you sure you have told me everything you know?"

"I know many things I haven't told you."

"Like what?"

"Well, I know that the sun rises in the east and sets in the west, and that there are 365 days in a year. . . ."

"No, no. I mean military things."

"Oh! Military! No. I don't know anything else!"

What he said next made me feel proud of my performance and completely vindicated.

"You're just a young, innocent victim," said the interrogator. "You don't really know anything important. You were used." But he warned, with a grave countenance, "Maybe you'll be here a long time. Maybe you won't. It depends on you."

Back in room 24 I sat down and wrote to Mom. I had finally received a letter from her confirming that my first letter of mid-September had arrived exactly a month later.

Don't worry about me here. I lost some weight at first. The diet here is not what one is accustomed to eating at home. But in the past month the food has changed and I am able to eat much better. I may even gain back the few pounds I lost. The people here are making an effort to give me what I am used to eating—more meat and vegetables for example."

The bitter winter chill seemed to swirl and settle in my dank cell even though I closed the inner swing doors and the shutters above them. I made the most of every chance to get warm. Cupping a lighted cigarette warmed my palms while the deeply-inhaled smoke lined my insides like insulation padding. Mercifully, the wooden-soled shoes protected my feet from the icy floor tiles. My persistent pleas for a hot water bath paid off when they finally brought in a metal tub large enough to sit in. I even had to pour in some cold water to make it cooler. I immersed myself and closed my eyes to the surrounding gloom. In those fleeting moments I remembered soaking languorously in the steaming hot tub of the hotsie baths at Yokosuka, Japan, during my carefree days as a bachelor aviator. It seemed that eons had passed since the petite Japanese attendant drifted into the cubicle from beyond the vapors to give me the sublimest massage with her sensitized palms and fingertips. These nostalgic reveries recurred every fortnight for the remainder of the winter when my captors brought in the tin tub and allowed me to wash and wallow.

Dear Mom,

the other day I was able to bathe with hot water. Boy, it really felt good. I was also able to wash my hair real good. It is longer now than I wore it before.
It was so good to get your letter, Mom. It really is lonesome for me here.

As uplifting to my spirits as the letters at that time were two books they gave me. I hungered to read anything apart from propaganda, and the two novels, translated from Russian into English, were stirring epics of heroism and endurance. One was about a Russian pilot who lost his legs in World War II yet survived to fly again with artificial limbs. The other was a saga of a Russian exiled to Siberia, who made his way back to his family after several decades only to find his wife remarried and his children scattered. The force of the literature worked a powerful spell, momentarily whisking me out of my dingy quarters and onto the grand sweep of the Soviet steppes. It was mentally liberating but when I got to the end I came crashing down to the cramped reality of my own captivity.

In mid-December Chihuahua told me three Americans were attending an international conference in Hanoi on *Peoples of the World against U.S. Imperialist Aggression in Indochina.*

"They have asked to see you. Would you like to go?"

I had not spoken with any of my countrymen since the last radio contact in the Skyhawk. I was also intrigued. What kind of Americans would attend a conference whose very title foretold the virulence of its anti-Americanism.

"Okay," I said.

First thing the next day they gave me a haircut, told me to shave, and brought in a pan of warm water for me to dip my sponge in and dab myself clean. And finally, after weeks of protestations, they gave back my underwear and socks which were taken away the day I was captured. With winter closing in fast, they also gave me a quilted blue jacket.

That evening we drove for half an hour to an area near the Lake of the Restored Sword. By the light of the moon, the house lamps and our vehicle lights, I saw widespread neglect of the residential acres. They were run down and overgrown with weeds though it was obvious the area had once been a showpiece, spread with embassies and spacious, whitewashed French-colonial-styled homes, roofed with red tiles, ringed with verandahs, and circled by wrought iron fences.

We drove into the grounds of one of the residences and a large black man in a black suit, with a thinly-spread beard and a low, booming voice, introduced himself as Robert Williams. I didn't catch the name of his wife.

"Sit down," he said with a gruffness sounding almost like an order.

He sat forward, elbows on his knees, and chomped on a cigar. My eyes fixed on the coffee table between us, laden with apples, oranges, bananas, vanilla wafers, candy, cookies and coffee.

"Would you like something to eat?" his wife asked.

"Thanks," I grinned, grabbing a handful of cookies and eating ravenously as she excused herself because she wasn't feeling well.

"I was at the museum and saw the wreckage of your plane," Williams droned. "I asked them, 'My God! Did anyone survive this crash?' They told me you had. So I asked to see you. They must be treating you well. You look good."

My mouth was full. I nodded.

"I'm from the States. They call it 'the land of the free' but there ain't no freedom there. That's why I live in Cuba. I have a radio program there called *The Voice of Free Dixie.*"

He seemed so full of biases and flowing with such rotten juices that if he was not for real he could only have come from central casting. While he vented his coiled spleen for more than an hour against racism, capitalism, imperialism and every other objectionable "ism," I dug into the candy and stuffed my pockets with oranges and apples.

"These people here, they wouldn't hurt anybody. How could we be doing what we did to them?" he asked as several adults popped their heads in the door while others peered in through the windows. "The imperialists who are responsible for bombing and killing women and children in Vietnam are the same ones who are responsible for killing and bombing blue-black babies in Birmingham."

The coffee was like an opiate. I poured myself a second, and a third cup. At length, he asked if I would like him to do something to help win my release.

"I know Ho Chi Minh. I can talk to him. Would you like me to do that?"

"Fine. Go ahead," I said.

"Well, wait a minute! You gotta do something yourself, too. You gotta ask Ho for your release. Write to him. Tell him how wrong the U.S. is and how sorry you are for what you did."

"Forget it. I'm not writing anything."

"I can't help you then."

I had eaten well but now I had a gut-full of this renegade.

"It's time for me to go. It's getting late," I said, rising.

"Here, you can read this later," he said, handing over a newspaper. "It's got an article on what I said at the conference. Incidentally, how'd you like to make a tape for my radio program? Your folks may hear it."

"No thanks."

I wanted no part of his act. He left me with a sense of loathing. I could not tolerate him knocking his own country for supposed lack of freedom and then settling, of all places, in *Cuba!*

Unknown to me, the U.S. media reported in early January that Williams had returned to Cuba, announcing that I had "recovered nicely" from my injuries, though he found me depressed and homesick. He also disclosed that I was confined in a Hanoi prison, though I would not have to stand trial.

Chihuahua kept up the pressure for me to write to Ho Chi Minh, coming into room 24 once or twice a week.

"You must write to President Ho Chi Minh and ask him for your release. If you say you were wrong and that you are sorry, you will see what he will do. He is a good man."

There was no doubt in my mind that they would have freed me forthwith if I had written the apology they wanted. But the price was too high. They were looking for servile submission. It would be unconscionable. Rather than walking out a free man, I would be covered in guilt and shame, branded for life, stigmatized in my own mind as a sunshine patriot and ostracized by society as a turncoat. Stripped of integrity and honor, I could never have faced my family, nor held my head high among my naval colleagues. I would have had to sell out everything I held dear, my very gut beliefs in the goodness of America. And to whom! To the breast-beating despots of a cruelly regimented society, who had the audacity to preach the virtues of freedom to the most democratically sensitive nation the world had ever known.

Chihuahua pressed harder and more persistently. To get him off my back I decided to write a short note, neither confessing nor pleading. And it would not be to Ho Chi Minh.

To Whom It May Concern:

I am Everett Alvarez, Jr., Lt. j.g., U.S. Navy, 644124. Captured August 5, 1964, at Hon Gai. I feel that during my captivity I have shown a good attitude and good behavior, and feel that you should review my case for release. Thank You.

Chihuahua was apoplectic with rage.

"What is this! What is this!" he screamed, thrusting the paper before me so that I could see the splash of red pencil markings. "You have written *To Whom It May Concern!* You have been told, you must write to 'Honorable President Ho Chi Minh of the Democratic Republic of Vietnam'! You have not understood anything!"

His face was flushed with anger, his eyes wild and scornful. Chihuahua almost spat out the words.

"You say nothing about your good treatment! You say nothing about the aggressive war in the South! You say nothing about how the United States violated the Geneva Accords! You say nothing about our history! You say nothing about our war against the French! And here, at the end, you sign it Lieutenant, junior grade! You *know* we have been telling you that your rank means nothing here! Nothing! Here all men are equal! You are not to use your rank!"

Taken aback by the fury of his outburst, I replied calmly.

"I am not going to say all that. I will not write what you want."

"Then it is hopeless for you," he said and left abruptly.

Dejected and lonely, I marked off the days on my handwritten calendar. Christmas was coming, with neither good will nor eager anticipation. One barren day followed another, without the seasonal caroling, gift wrapping, or decoration of the Christmas tree. I ached for the warmth and festive spirit of our extended family. We had always gathered together for the traditional tamale dinner on Christmas Eve, then expectantly, and with much merriment, unwrapped the gifts. Condemned to pass this special holiday in isolation, far from home, and alone for the first time, I could not help but brood on the memories of Christmases past. I remembered vividly the route Joe Kapp and I had taken to Christmas Mass, past the homes of everyone we knew and over landscape so familiar that we could have covered the distance with our eyes closed.

It was numbingly cold on Christmas Eve. The sun had hardly shone that month and I was more vulnerable to the cold because of the spartan diet. My cell was wide open above the back doors to the chilling night air, and it scarcely helped when I closed the shutters above the inner doors. The tiled floors retained the cold like a refrigerator. They had recently given me back the woolen Navy watch cap taken from my survival vest, and I pulled it protectively over my head and down to my neck. I curled up in two of the thin gray blankets, rolling them over like a sleeping bag. Fortunately, I had another blanket to wrap around my feet and keep them from turning into frozen blocks of meat.

When the evening meal came later than usual, it took me by surprise. Chihuahua had told me I would receive a special Christmas treat but I didn't believe him. Now I felt rescued from total oblivion, and even somewhat merry as I lifted the dishes and tucked into turkey and clean, tasty rice. Another dish was laden with little pastries and cookies. The coffee was as thick as molasses and I had to thin it out with warm water and some of the concentrated sweet milk.

At a random moment when I guessed it might be midnight, I recited those parts of the mass I was able to recall.

Domine non sum dignus . . . sed tantum dic verbo et sanubito anima mea. . . .

The only sound in the desolate cell came from the rats pushing free the pieces of brick I'd plugged into the holes to delay their passage through my quarters.

I realized how detached I was from my culture when Stoneface entered with the regular morning food and I could not even wish him a merry Christmas.

Out in the back courtyard I nicked at the wall again, adding Christmas Day, 1964, to the list of dates. But I felt the need to inscribe something else, to remind myself of my own mortality and insignificant passage in the grand scheme of divine will. I wanted to read some words of sacred wisdom daily, so that I could humble myself in the eyes of the Lord. Well to the left of

the "pillar," above a ledge on the wall space between the cross and the latrine,
I etched a partially remembered passage from the communion:

Lord I am not worthy . . . but only say the word and my soul shall be healed.

I wondered how Tangee and Mom and Dad and my sisters had spent this
day. They must have prayed long and hard. I sat down at the table and wrote
them a card:

> *I am thinking of you. I had a very big meal last night. Hope you enjoyed
> Christmas dinner. I don't believe I told you that the government here allowed
> a N. Vietnamese Catholic priest to come see me. He was a very elderly priest,
> said his church was nearby and he asked me if I heard the church bells real early
> each morning. I do hear them around 4 each morning when I happen to wake
> up early, and again before noon and on Sunday mornings. We talked for a while,
> through an interpreter. When he left he gave me his rosary to help me with my
> prayers. I use it daily now.*

For the first time ever, the family across the Pacific let Christmas come
and go like any other day. They did not even buy a Christmas tree, which
for decades had been the festooned beacon around which they shared their
joy. Madeleine felt cheated and robbed, wondering how anything could
justify gutting the festivities of this happiest of holidays. How could anyone
be expected to enjoy the seasonal celebrations without the trappings that
always went with the holiday? It seemed to her just like there had been a
death in the family. But she did not protest. Instead, she cried in the safe
haven of her room and wondered how long this drought of happiness would
last in her home.

7
IN A CONCRETE STRAIGHTJACKET

IN THE FIRST WEEK OF JANUARY, STONEFACE, WITH ACCUS-
tomed glumness, walked in with three letters from Tangee and one from
Mom. He also had a large cardboard carton which he set down on the table.
I thought it was from home until I saw the Geneva stickers and labels printed
in French. It must have come from the International Red Cross in Switzerland. I opened it like a child impatient to see a surprise. What a bonanza it
turned out to be! That little box was a cornucopia of delights which I
rummaged through deliriously.

I brought out two huge bars of Swiss milk chocolate, each a foot long
and three inches thick, wrapped so meticulously they seemed packed for
gourmets. Tremulously, I brought out more luxuries, each with a label
printed in French, German, Italian, Spanish or English. I almost purred
handling the jar of Nescafé instant coffee labeled *café solubile*. But there
was more: a package of cookies, a big pack of sugar cubes marked *zucker*,
five packs of Swiss filter cigarettes, a toothbrush and toothpaste, a jar of
vitamins and a tube of *creme sandwich truffee*. Wide-eyed and palpitating,
I grasped two huge blocks of green, sweet-smelling Sunbeam soap, two
packs of dried prunes, apricots and peaches, a can of corned beef from
Paraguay, two undershirts and two large bath towels. I hovered over my
windfall. Everything was stacked neatly, as if a croupier had just pushed
across my jackpot winnings.

Dear Mom, Dad, Delia and Mad,

*One of the guards here walked in and really surprised me. He gave me another
of your letters, Mom, dated 6 December, with Del's included, and three more*

from Tangee (numbers 19, 20, and 21). He also had a large package for me—has a lot of goodies in it. I'm sure I will enjoy them very much. It is very comforting to me also to receive and read mail from home. It really raises my spirits.

Madeleine, Mom said you were doing well in school and now I see you have made the Honor Roll. That's good, Mad. Keep it up.

And Del, so you finally bought a new car for yourself. Have you sent out any bulletins to warn all the other motorists in California? Hmmm? Just kidding of course.

I will keep writing you often, but you know, nothing much happens here. Big events are when I get your letters, and days like today are rare. I don't know how long this will go on.

I decided immediately to ration the food, to make it last as long as possible. But I couldn't resist digging into the chocolate. It was so good that it taxed my will-power to the full not to reach for the remainder and gobble it down. But if I were to preserve the delicacies for future feasts, I would have to protect them well against the rats. It became more a battle of wits than simply blocking them physically. I had to stuff the chocolate, with its own wrapping, inside other possessions, and even then keep a watchful eye on the scavengers.

The jailers often brought their young children on the rounds. One Sunday some kids popped their heads inside as a turnkey walked in. I broke off a piece of chocolate and held it out to him, motioning at the same time that he should give it to the children. He shook his head negatively and handed it back to me. It appeared they were under strict orders not to fraternize at all, for fear, perhaps, that they might begin to treat me more leniently.

I wondered how the jailors raised their children. What expectation could these coarse and uneducated men have for their own offspring? Would they want them to remain peasants or would they have loftier dreams? Would they brag to their children that they had responsible jobs because they were guarding the enemies of the state? Or would their dreams be so base that they would hope only for tough children to succeed them in their prison work? It didn't even occur to me to ask the guards these types of questions because they obviously lacked the basic knowledge to carry on thoughtful conversations. Besides, we were separated by the language barrier.

After the improvement in diet, I had sufficient strength to exercise and did push-ups, though neither regularly nor rigorously. For the moment I had to battle the inclemencies of winter rather than the deprivations of captivity. I felt more relaxed, convinced now that they were not out to kill me, and confident that they had backed off on their threats to try me for criminal acts.

Dear Mom and Dad,

I have been here just about six months now. My captors here say that six months isn't a long time. But for me, here, it is a long time. I know it is for you also. I guess for a Vietnamese, or an Asian, it wouldn't be a long time. They certainly do think differently.

There was a new edginess to the Vietnamese which I sensed in their collective mood and in the normal sounds filtering into room 24. They appeared more watchful and disciplined yet irascible and touchy. "We know there's going to be a war," they'd tell me. "The planes will be back some day." Under cover of darkness, they practiced air raid emergency defense procedures. The habitual quiet of the night was punctured by the chugs of river traffic and accelerations of heavy trucks starting up and moving off.

"If war does break out," I said aloud to myself, "it won't last long. That means I might be out soon."

But I felt neither elation nor hope. I was under the numbing grip of winter. And anyway, wars never had clean, clear-cut solutions. Maybe my captors would just become more savage and wreak vengeance on me, the only enemy they had close enough to bash around.

It was during this period that Stoneface made one of his infrequent inspections of the back courtyard to check that I was not hiding anything. By chance, he happened to look up at the inscription from the communion service. He took out his wire-rimmed glasses from his shirt pocket and edged closer to the wall, studying each word like an archaeologist deciphering hieroglyphics. I did not give the incident much thought after he grunted and left, but later that day Chihuahua burst in.

"It is bad! Bad! You must not write on the walls! You will be severely punished if you do it again!"

Fortunately they did not erase anything and I continued over the months to scratch in the festivals and national holidays.

One night in the second week of February, 1965, the prison's loudspeaker systems bristled with unintelligible shrieks and shouts, indicating bulletins of major significance. Even Stoneface broke his granite silence, squawking in a high-pitched, equally incomprehensible voice.

The following night the key rattled in my door about 8 P.M. This was almost unprecedented. Once Stoneface locked me in at dusk I would be left alone with the rats until morning. I looked apprehensively as four Vietnamese military officers walked in. They were brisk, efficient and in no mood to linger.

As they looked around Stoneface gestured to me to greet them in Vietnamese.

"Chao Ong (hello)," I said.

One of them spoke through an interpreter I had not seen before.

"Do you know what happened yesterday?"

"No."

"We shot down many more planes. Then we captured an American pilot."

"Yesterday?"

"Yes."

"Where? In South Vietnam?"

"In south-central Vietnam."

"Where's that?"

"It is not too far."

I had no idea whether we had bombed in the north or the south until a few days later I read in a *Vietnam News Agency* report that the activity was over Quan Bien Province in North Vietnam. One pilot was reported killed. I remembered him, as soon as I learned his identity from the story and saw the picture reproduced from his ID card. I felt a pang of grief. Ed Dickson had been with me at Lemoore and we had gone through replacement air group training about the same time. He was in a different squadron and though we were not close friends, we had once been in the same ski party. Our orders had been to separate carriers. The report also claimed the Vietnamese had shot down an F8 Crusader and captured Lt. Cmdr. Robert Shumaker. "At last I'm not alone!" I thought to myself.

There was a war going on. No question about it. From now on I would not give my captors anything. Nothing. I was no longer plagued by doubts and dilemmas. Now there was a clear-cut case for sticking rigidly to the U.S. military Code of Conduct. From this moment on they would get only my name, rank, service number and date of birth.

A day later Stoneface delivered a handwritten note to room 24. It listed a number of ranks in their abbreviated form. "What do these letters mean?" the note asked. I did not reply.

Stoneface led me into the quiz room again. I was surprised to see Owl, whom I had not seen since the lengthy interrogation.

Looking sincere, he pleaded, uncharacteristically. "I want you to help me. Please help us. You helped us before. We don't understand. We need your help."

He held up a handful of kneeboard cards carried by pilots. They contained information on ordnance load and capabilities, fuel specifics, dive angles, setting for bombs.

"There are many things here that we do not understand."

"No, no. I cannot answer questions. I've never seen those. I don't know what they are."

"And what about the list of letters we sent you. What are they? What do they mean?"

I did not answer. Owl was visibly irritated at my stubborn refusal to help but dismissed me without further ado.

A couple of days later I was pacing my locked cell during the normally quiet midday siesta break when the clanking noise of the metal gates reverberated through the prison precincts. I rushed to the peep-hole and saw a sedan pull up in the courtyard. Shouting and gesticulating guards dashed from the buildings on my left to the vehicle parked on my right. Obviously someone of significance had been brought in. I assumed immediately that it was Shumaker though I couldn't see beyond the front of the car. Whoever it was, they took him to the adjoining buildings on my right, which we later dubbed New Guy Village.

Over the days I tried to make contact by shouting in my back yard. "Hey, Shumaker! Are you there?" There was never any reply.

Then I noticed, through my peep-hole, that the Vietnamese who regularly bicycled through the main gates, holding the handle of my single tray of food, now came through daily with two trays. Stoneface continued to bring me mine but the other was always taken off by another turnkey in the direction of New Guy Village.

About mid-March there was another commotion in the courtyard and I caught a vague glimpse of a Caucasian walking over to New Guy Village. The next day the bicyclist came in through the main gates holding the handles of three trays of food. This could only be Hayden Lockhart, whose capture was reported in one of the *Vietnam News Agency* handouts.

Vainly, I tried to make contact. Sometimes I'd go to the peep-hole, at other times stand in the back yard, and whistle *California Here I Come* and *Mexican Hat Dance*.

I was hauled off to quiz sessions again, this time before three new interrogators. Though the information sought was basically military, the questions themselves were inane.

They asked, "What kind of training do you have to have to be a pilot?"

I kept absolutely silent.

"What kind of airplane were you flying?"

Again I stared blankly ahead. I had not even said "Good morning." By the afternoon they tired of my silence and ordered me back to room 24. I felt good, gritting my teeth and vowing to myself, "Now we'll play the game the way it's played during war time."

The penalty was swift. They withdrew all my cigarettes and told me I would not be allowed to receive mail nor write any more letters.

It was during this mid-March period that I first met Rabbit, so named because of his large, protruding ears. But that was his only resemblance to a bunny. Mercilessly sadistic, his name later became synonymous with torture and terror. Though only a warrant officer, he looked no older than nineteen, Rabbit conducted himself as if invested with the authority of a senior officer. He had a cruel and haughty expression, with the corners of his mouth pulled down disdainfully. His eyes darted and moved furtively, though they were more often hooded beneath lowered lids.

Rabbit sat down in room 24 and in his high-pitched voice, asked in fluent English, "What do you know of the Vietnamese people? What do you know about our history?"

I shrugged and sighed, signaling my distaste for propaganda.

"Look, you're wasting your time," I said. "I've heard this many, many times before. You're not doing any good, neither did your superiors, the officers. I don't believe your stories and you are not going to convince me."

Rabbit rebounded savagely.

"You don't believe!" he screamed. "You think I'm not doing any good! You've heard this many times before!" He was almost salivating. "Get up! Walk over there! You go and stand in the corner! You stand there!"

"What the hell," I thought. "Is this for real?" I walked slowly to the corner, unable to fathom this new personality and unwilling to buck him during a spasm of outrage.

"Turn around!" he yelled. "You stay there! You don't move!"

He slammed the door behind him. I ran my fingers through my hair. That guy has got to be a little looney! And if he's not, he's going to be deadly dangerous. I'll have to learn how to handle him.

Three days later he came in again.

"Sit," he ordered.

"Do you still think I can't do you any good? Do you still think you've heard it all before and I'm wasting my time?"

Diffident, but refusing to be cowed by this teenage thug, I replied, "Yes."

Again he shrieked as if prodded with a red-hot branding iron. He cursed and shouted, raging on about my stupidity and criminality. His anger subsided as suddenly, but he scowled menacingly.

"We believe. . . ." His sentence trailed off as his whole body shook with anger. He paused to regain some composure then began again. "We believe that the mind of the capitalist man is like an old brick from the wall of a water closet. It takes one hundred years to get rid of the smell," he sneered.

With that, Rabbit got up and left the room. I sat rigid, like a waxwork, unused to this firecracker personality and taken aback by his hatred.

My "bad attitude" did not prevent me from receiving the second and final package from the International Red Cross in Switzerland. Stoneface brought it in, accompanied by Rabbit, a few days after the encounter. Obviously, Mom had received another letter from me because my request to her for thick winter socks and vitamin pills was fulfilled. Apart from this, the contents were identical to the first package. This time Rabbit handed me a written list of the contents and asked me to sign an acknowledgment of receipt. I checked the list and saw no reason to refuse because every item was given to me.

The only edible item left over from the first package was the can of corned beef, with its little opener attached to the top. I put it aside with the new can, resolving to keep them for a special occasion or an emergency. Bombs might wipe out the kitchen one day. Or the moment might come when I could escape. I already knew many Vietnamese words and was dressed like a peasant. Perhaps the opportunity might arise where I could get out of room 24, steal a bicycle and head down the road to the coast. The corned beef would certainly come in handy then.

The Red Cross would have been surprised to learn that the cardboard box proved to be as indispensable as the items inside. During May I ran out of toilet paper but the guards and turnkeys turned a deaf ear to my pleas for more. Forced to improvise, I tore pieces of the box and stripped off layers from the thickly padded cardboard. It was better than the only other alternatives—using washable rags or my hand.

Through the peep-hole, I saw a vehicle pull up on June 20th. The guards led a tall, blond guy in black pajamas to the building on my left, which we later named Heartbreak Hotel. I calculated the Vietnamese now held about four Americans in the Hanoi Hilton. Perhaps I would soon get a roommate. For ten months I had lived alone within the forbidding walls of room 24. By nature I was not a solitary type. I liked company, especially people with a sense of humor, so the thought of sharing a cell with another American aviator, someone from my own country, who spoke my language, filled me with a thrilling sense of expectancy.

The very next day, Stoneface signaled me to roll up all my possessions in my straw mat and follow him. "This is it! I'm going to be moved in with Americans! I can hardly believe it!" He led me across the courtyard, veering left at the water fountain, and into a building facing room 24. He opened a door and ushered me in. It was a ten foot by twelve foot cell! I felt winded. What a hell of a let-down! How could I have raised my hopes so stupidly! They locked me in for three weeks. Room 24, by comparison, was luxurious because there, at least, I had the freedom to roam the back yard for several hours a day.

The food got worse and I had to subsist on a diet, served twice a day, of half a bowl of tasteless, dirty soup and a piece of dry bread about the size of a round of butter. They let me shave once but never came around to cut my hair. I braced myself for a return to the medieval horrors forced on me during my earliest weeks in the prison, when they had almost starved me to death and left me weak from diarrhea and dysentery. Though fearful, I reasoned that if I had weathered it once, at a time when I was green and innocent, I could probably survive again because my wits were sharper and my honor still intact.

Early in July they moved me to another cell in a complex of buildings along the prison's northern wall. My cell space had now contracted to a mere seven feet by seven feet. Though I was the sole occupant, the only space to walk in was a two foot by seven foot area between the two concrete slab beds.

It was not difficult to find the pinhole in the door because the outside light shone through it like a glimmering shaft into the shadow-darkened cell. When I peeped through it I had an undisturbed view across the four feet width of the cell-lined corridor, through the iron bars of open windows in the opposite wall, and out to the tiny courtyard with a vat below a high wall. Suddenly someone whistled in the courtyard outside, as if calling a pet dog. Then, incongruously for this southeast Asian prison, the whistler gave a rousing rendition of the Marine Corps Hymn—*From the halls of Montezuma to the shores of Tripoli!* I leaped up, put my right eye to the peep-hole and strained to focus. A Vietnamese man stood in the courtyard, several yards away from me and directly in line with the pinhole. The man looked squarely at my cell door. He was of average height, round-faced and lean, and his hair stuck out like a porcupine's. Like me, he wore blue summer shorts. This was my first view of the man who was *"dinky-dow"* in Vietnamese slang. Translated into English it meant crazy. I called him Crazy Guy.

I coughed to acknowledge my presence. He must have been in my cell at one time because no one could possibly see the tiny hole from the outside. Crazy Guy looked up and around, checking to see that no one was watching. Then he trilled, *Yoo hoo, yoo hoo!* His eyes widened and he laughed. It was the long, loud, unhinged cackle of a wild man. When he was done, he whistled *Cherry Pink and Apple Blossom White.*

Over the course of the next few days, Crazy Guy and I established a rapport. As soon as he finished whistling those well-known American tunes I would answer him with a whistled refrain. He stood at a short distance from the pinhole so I could see him clearly, and he indicated by gesture and words that he had been imprisoned for five years. Then he pointed to his head and laughed as meaninglessly as an hyena. He was an expert mime and it was not difficult to read out of his act that he had pushed down on a detonator and caused a huge explosion. That was why they had him incarcerated. On another occasion he pointed to his rags and showed me the saddest eyes, making him look like a clown at a funeral. Those expressive eyes had begged for a gift of clothing so the next time I was out in the courtyard washing clothes, I left some of my accumulated rags and a frayed undershirt for him to pick up.

Crazy Guy and I were never allowed out in the courtyard together. When I was outside, however, I took several chances by sneaking past the two cells between ours, in the covered passageway, and slipping scraps of bread under his door. I also got a chance to hoist myself up a wall and look over. It was another courtyard, even more depressing and somber than mine. I ducked and slid back as soon as I saw guards manning a nearby watchtower.

It took me some weeks to click that the prisoner in the cell next to mine was concerned for my well-being. I could never understand why he bumped our common wall lightly every so often on a daily basis. Only after I paid more attention to his timing did I realize that he bumped a few seconds before a turnkey came down to open my peep-hole. It was his way of warning me of approaching prison staff. I wanted to see what my neighbor looked like so at the first opportunity outside I slid open the cover of his peep-hole. He was an aged Vietnamese, very distinguished looking with silver-gray hair. Impetuously, I decided to look into the cell between his and Crazy Guy's. It held two Vietnamese men but I didn't get a good look because I hurried back.

Chihuahua, whom I had not seen for some time, came into my cell the next day.

"You have very bad attitude! You look in the other cells! You did it twice!"

"No. I only did it one time."

"You must not look in other cells! If you do it again you will be punished!"

I figured that the two inmates had betrayed me because no one else had seen me open their peep-holes. My immediate neighbor was above suspicion because of the solidarity he had proven with the warning knocks. Later, when he continued to knock on the wall, they overheard him and immediately clamped him in irons. I would have to be more cautious in future.

The constant banging and hammering in an adjacent metal shop took a toll on my nerves. It went on day after day, week after week, with no daytime respite from the clash of tools against metallic objects. There was not even the relief of a rhythm to the cacophony, only the dull thud of countless tools driving inharmoniously against the sheets of metal. I felt like I had cluster headaches, pounding from sunrise to sunset. I beat the walls of my cell and kicked at the door, shrieking for peace and quiet and some cessation of the interminable drum beat. "AGHHHHH!!! STOP IT! SOMEBODY STOP IT!" I tried plugging my ears with shredded pieces of rags, holding my hands over my ears, and winding the towels around my head. Nothing helped.

The sounds of the night were even less welcome. From nearby came the lash of whips and the cries and screams of female prisoners. Unfortunately, the prison's acoustics were even sharper at night and try as I might, I could not erase from my mind a graphic picture of the downward swish of whips, followed at the lacerating moment of impact by full-throated shrieks. It seemed, from the night-long lashing and wailing, that the torturers were moved neither by the gender nor by the pain of their victims. Were these the hordes of young, shackled women, brought into the courtyard daily, whom Chihuahua had testily identified as prostitutes? If so, it said something about the severity of the regime if this was its method of correction.

I felt entombed in this seven foot by seven foot vault and began to fear for my sanity. Maybe Crazy Guy had originally flipped right here in this concrete straightjacket, unable any longer to withstand the crush of the walls. Mentally, I had to escape. I watched the ants and found myself entranced by their comings and goings. Day after day I played tricks with them to watch their reactions. If I squashed a single ant, those behind promptly made a detour around it. Then I became fascinated by diverting them from their new trail by placing random obstacles in their path. The tireless ants brought motion and purpose into my lifeless cell. Their drive and energy contrasted so much with my own enforced idleness. As such, I welcomed them as the best substitute for the throngs of humanity from whom I had been removed.

Solving complex math problems and playing both sides of a makeshift chess board also helped me through the long days and nights, not only in this cell but in other locations for many years to come. I fashioned my chess board from the cardboard backing of a writing pad and cut pieces of paper into different shapes to represent pawns and the other pieces. The letter K stood for king while Q denoted queen.

For much of the time I relived in my own mind events and incidents from earliest childhood through capture in the Gulf of Tonkin. People and places reappeared on the screen of my mind's eye as I reconstructed exchanges of dialogue. I replayed these scenarios so often over the years that my past became a series of vivid memories. It was almost as if I had taped the segments of my life and stored them like video cassettes in the folds of my brain. And just as often I would fantasize, casting myself in scenarios with real people I had known, then working all of us into imaginery situations with fictional outcomes. The more fanciful the plot, the more engrossed I became. To stave off madness I had somehow to remove myself mentally from the awful sterility of my day-to-day existence.

But even my daydreams were peopled by the mentally unstable. I remembered how, as a young boy, I had seen others a little bit like Crazy Guy. They were in a hospital for the mentally ill, where I went to visit my uncle Joe, Mom's older brother. He'd come to our home in San Francisco, where we lived during World War II, unshaven and begging for money. Dad offered him food instead, but uncle Joe shook his head and somewhat surly, turned around and went away. He became a derelict, shuffling around San Francisco's skid row. It was something of an adventure accompanying Dad in the car when we explored that area of down-and-outs, trying to locate Joe. Then he was in and out of the mental institution. One day, when we were living again in Salinas, I spotted uncle Joe walking towards our house carrying a paper bag. Unkempt and dazed, he looked like a tramp holding all his worldly possessions. I ran to Mom. "Uncle Joe's coming towards our house!" Mom and MaMona looked startled, but he stayed a couple of months. Then there was a howling ruckus and the police were called in because he had threatened my grandmother. He was out back and acted really cool, saying he'd be with them shortly as he just wanted to clean up. They were just as casual and took him away without difficulty.

After he was transferred back to the mental hospital we visited occasionally. I felt a little bit scared and intimidated at the sight of demented men shadow boxing and talking to themselves, but I felt safe because I was always with my parents. Dad would ask him, "Who are you, Joe?" and he would reply, "I'm Joe Rivers the boxer and I had a fight with this guy." Then he'd stare at us with a curious smile. It was difficult to know if he was putting us on or if he was completely crazed. Another time we'd ask him where he'd been and, gesturing to the orchard fields around the hospital, he'd say, "Those are my acres over there. I've had a good harvest this year." Again he would flash that enigmatic smile. He was still hospitalized at the time I was shot down.

8
AMERICANS!

I HAD BEEN IN THE HANOI HILTON EXACTLY A YEAR WHEN
the banging suddenly stopped. It was such a relief I started exercising again,
running in place and doing a few push-ups in the two-foot width between the
beds. My weight was down to about 110 lbs., my hair stood out dry and
matted, and my moustache was so long I used to twirl it. In the absence of
toilet paper, I had used leaves and then more layers of cardboard from the
Red Cross box. Finally they gave me a limited supply of paper.

A new guard had replaced Stoneface. He always had a finger up his red,
bulbous nose so it was inevitable we would later call him Rudolph the
Red-Nosed Guard. He was a homosexual, and on the few occasions they let
me shower in another room, he sat down, staring at me unabashedly. One
day he came into my cell with my food, put it down and stared for a while
with a finger up his nostril.

"Whoosh! Whoosh, you!" he said suddenly, waving his arms like a floundering swimmer.

I couldn't understand what he was getting at so I ignored him and ate my
rations. Like most guards, Rudolph was a simpleton, but fortunately he lacked
the meanness that characterized so many of them.

September, 1965, dawned with a bright, clear sky. A year of captivity had
passed and I was still alive! I was so thankful and so surprised at my own
staying power that I burst out into song for the first time. As I exercised by
pacing up and down the courtyard I lustily sang the words to *Oh What A
Beautiful Morning!* Suddenly I heard a voice from the other side of the wall
say, "Oh my God!"

I stopped dead in my tracks as if paralyzed by a ray gun.

"Who are you?" I asked breathlessly.

"Geronimo," came the reply. "Who are you?" he asked.

"Al."

"Al?" the voice queried.

"Yeah!"

My God! Geronimo! The paratroopers have arrived! Fearful of being caught by a guard, I looked around. It was too late. A guard approached. He hadn't seen me communicating but ordered me back to my cell and gave Crazy Guy time out in the courtyard. I stared out the peep-hole. Crazy Guy started whistling the Marine Corps Hymn. Then he pointed over the wall, and at me, and started sobbing. It took me a while to figure out the mime. Crazy Guy was trying to tell me there was another American over there, like me, and that he was in a pitiful condition. The next time the guard came in I held out one of my Red Cross towels and pointed in Geronimo's direction. "Take, over there," I urged. He took the towel and closed the door. It was my way of signaling I knew a fellow American was there and I was hanging in there with him.

During the next few days I was still speculating on the American's identity as I prepared to wash my empty food bowl. By chance I spotted some script written on the base of the bowl with a burned matchstick: *Is there a Wop in Hanoi?—Percy*

That could only be an American. But who? And where? Days later I turned over another bowl. The message was written in a different handwriting: *Alone in the pigsty, near to God—G*

That must be Geronimo! I took out the nail clipper I'd received in the Red Cross package and scratched my initials. The next time the bowls came around I read a list of names: Storz, Shumaker, Morgan, Lockhart, Vohden. Contact! At last! I wondered if that was the same Ray Vohden who'd been a catapult officer on the *Constellation* during my first cruise in 1963. I didn't have any matches but their next message read: *Hi, EA, the score is Navy-7, Air Force-7.* "Why," I wondered, "would they give the football score?" Then it dawned on me—there were seven Navy POWs and seven Air Force POWs!

Another message followed later: *We're doing good work, hitting bridges, roads, communication lines. Doing good work in south—Storz.* All these communications took place within a two-week period. It was warm and already dark on September 13th, 1965, when Stoneface came in somewhat agitated. He gave me the signal to roll up my straw mat with all my belongings and follow him. I folded my blankets and wrapped in my two cans of corned beef, spare socks, underwear, wooden-heeled shoes, toothbrush, soap, towels, notebook and the two pictures of Tangee given me by Chihuahua the year before. Stoneface checked to see it was rolled tight then handcuffed and blindfolded me. He led me to the waiting jeep.

"Keep quiet! Do not talk!" Rabbit announced firmly.

I clung to my bed roll as they sat me down. Immediately I felt someone nudge my leg.

"Hey! Guarino!" he whispered.

So this was Geronimo!

"Al!" I murmured.

There was a pause, then, "Al who?"

"Alvarez!" I said, scarcely able to talk I was so excited.

"Oh God! Oh God! Where you been! You been here all this time?"

"Shhh! Don't talk!" Rabbit snapped.

Another person clambered in and sat down. I felt his careful, deliberate pressure against my arm. I edged my elbow into his ribs.

"Butler," he mumbled.

"Alvarez," I said in a hushed voice.

He stiffened.

"Alvarez!" I repeated.

"Yeah, yeah! Rog! Wow!"

"Guarino is across from me," I whispered.

I felt him reach across and the two exchanged names in low voices.

"Alvarez is in here!"

"Yeah, I know. He just talked to me!"

"Where've you been?" asked Butler.

"Here."

"Jeez, all along!"

"No talk! No talk!" a guard hollered.

Another person got in the back of the jeep.

"Lockhart," he murmured.

"Yeah."

"How you doin'? Alvarez is across from you!"

"Holy cow!"

We drove for about an hour and a half to a compound we later named the Briar Patch. It must have been about forty kilometers west of Hanoi. The guards removed our handcuffs then led us off. They removed my blindfold as I stood in front of an open cell door. Guarino was already inside the darkened cell.

"Hey, where's the head here? Ask the guy. I gotta take a leak," said Guarino, wide-eyed. "And where's the lights? No lights here!"

"Do not talk! Keep silent!" Rabbit interjected.

"You see that SOB," I said loudly to Guarino, as I pointed to Rabbit, "I hate him. I hate that jerk!"

It was rash but I didn't give a hoot what Rabbit thought.

He reacted vengefully. "Out! You, out!"

Jeez! It was more than a year since I had shared a cell with Mr. Sea and Mr. Blue, my last roommates. Now I was separated from Guarino within seconds of pairing up. They took me to another equal-sized cell in the same hut. It measured eight feet by seven feet. There was only one bed, of wooden slats on concrete posts, and no electricity. The ground-brick walls were so rough that parts of them protruded like spikes several inches long. Four-foot-high metal bars blocked the window forming almost an entire wall. At night its shutters were closed from the outside.

As soon as I lay down on the bed, I heard someone tapping on a wall. It was similar to the tapping made by the aged Vietnamese prisoner to warn me of impending danger in the Hanoi Hilton. I tried tapping back but no one responded.

The following morning a guard pulled my shutters back. About fifteen feet beyond the barred window was a ten-foot-high wall. I walked to the window and greeted the guard. He gave me a cigarette. As I stood there, grunting in my pigeon Vietnamese, I couldn't believe my eyes. A tall, blond guy, with a reddish beard and the figure of a classical Greek warrior, walked up the hill to my left, carrying a slop bucket. For a while he disappeared from view but came back down the same path at a slow pace. The guard had his back to the Caucasian, who looked at me as he returned. I continued my monosyllabic conversation to distract the guard, while darting my eyes in the direction of the prisoner. With my dark skin, long hair and moustache, and nondescript clothes, I must have looked like a genuine Vietnamese. The blond guy was now behind the eight-foot-high wall on my right and I heard him washing dishes.

"Hey guard," I heard him say, "ask him if he's a bijee or a changee." This was Vietnamese military slang for captain or major.

I continued to look at the guard, so he wouldn't think I was communicating with someone else.

"How about a lieutenant, j.g." I said, taking a nonchalant puff of my cigarette as I waited for his reply. The dishwashing stopped briefly, then resumed.

"Sounds like a Yank talking," said the dishwasher.

"It is," I replied casually while the guard continued to talk and I nodded my head.

"What's his name?"

I took another puff.

"Alvarez."

The dishwashing stopped again. A head poked around the corner, then disappeared as quickly.

"Alvarez! Where in the hell have you been! You could pass for a V anytime."

"What's your name?"

"Ron Storz."

By now the guard had put two and two together. He motioned me to be quiet and locked the shutters. Our hut contained four cells under a common roof. The single window in each cell faced a different direction, as did the heavy wooden doors. However, by standing at the shuttered windows we could hear each other, and some of the other POWs in identical huts, also fifteen feet beyond the common dividing wall.

Irrepressible, Larry Guarino shouted to another hut visible through his window. I didn't catch it all but I didn't mind because it felt so good just to hear the sound of American accents.

"Hey you guys!" Guarino kidded, "you got television? There's an antenna on your roof!" he ribbed, referring to the lightning rod. "Who's in there, anyway?"

"Butler, Lockhart, Shumaker, Harris" someone replied. "Who's over there with you?"

"Guarino, Storz, Morgan. Alvarez was here for a minute last night, then they ran his ass out."

"Hey, Alvarez!" someone yelled.

"Yuh."

"Where are you?"

"Right here next to you."

"Where were you? How'd they keep you? How've you been?"

I heard a lot of whispering.

"Say, Alvarez, what name do you go by?"

"Ev," I replied.

There was more suspicious whispering. Maybe they thought I was a Vietnamese plant.

"What squadron were you in?"

"VA 144."

Someone asked if I knew a particular individual in my squadron. I told him he had the name right but the wrong squadron. I also corrected him on the guy's job description.

"What did your friends call you? Wasn't there another name you went by? Another name they had for you in the squadron?"

"Yeah," I sighed to myself. "Alvie."

Here we go again, I thought. I never liked the nickname Alvie but it had stuck with me right after I got my wings. I had reported to Lemoore Station for six months of training in the Navy's front line carrier aircraft with the fleet replacement air group. Our senior officer, Cmdr. Pat Cunningham, a crusty veteran of World War II and the Korean War, was nuts about giving nicknames to pilots. He automatically gave the nickname "Smokey" to anyone with the family name of Burgess. Men with the surname Dawson were instantly dubbed "Red."

We had barely reported to the base when he asked, "Ensign Alvarez, what do your friends call you?"

"Ev."

"Nah, that's no good. We have a couple of pilots' wives named Ev. You need something catchy, something like, let's see . . . Al . . . Alv . . . Alvie! That's it! From now on, Ensign Alvarez, you're Alvie!" He was delighted with the choice. "Hey, everyone! Listen up! From now on Ensign Alvarez is Alvie! Got that?"

There was nothing I could do to reverse it. As time went by everyone called me Alvie. Casual acquaintances didn't even know my real name. It was one of those things I just had to live with.

Ironically, it was now the best proof of identity I could offer my fellow POWs at the Briar Patch.

"Alvie! That's it!" exclaimed one of the captive Americans. "Your friend, Dick Cherba, was in my squadron!"

I was cleared!

"How's it feel, Alvie, to be part of the gang again!"

"I feel like I've been liberated!"

"Must seem like Coney Island, huh."

"You bet."

"Alvie, where were you all this time?"

"Hanoi."

"Was that you whistling *California Here I Come* and *Mexican Hat Dance?*"

"Yeah."

"We figured it might have been you. We called that place *The Hanoi Hilton.* You remember that guard with the bubbly nose and queer as could be?"

"Yeah."

"That was Rudolph the Red-Nosed Guard. We didn't know where you were so we showed him a magazine with your picture and made swimming motions, telling him 'wetback.' "

I laughed. That explained why Rudolph had come in saying "Whoosh, whoosh you!" accompanied by the thrashing arm movements of a floundering swimmer.

"Alvie, do you know the tap code?"

"No."

"When you want to raise someone, you raise them with a shave and a haircut. Two bits. Got it?"

"Okay."

"We use a five by five square. Five rows, five columns. First row is A, B, C, D, E. One tap for first row. Pause. Then one tap for A, two taps for B, three taps for C, etc. Two taps for second row. One tap for F, two taps for G, etc. There's no K. Instead of K use C. Now here's a message."

He tapped out a brief greeting. I figured it out immediately because it was short. Then I slowly tapped one back. It took me a few days before I could read every message comfortably and tap my own with ease. In time, all of us became so proficient, using a shorthand by tapping initials to abbreviate frequently used words, that we were able to send messages as fast as verbal communications. Good night, for example, would be G-N. But our knuckles were chaffed raw from constantly tapping on the rough-surfaced walls.

That first morning Herschel "Scotty" Morgan, an Air Force Captain born in Candler, N.C., spoke to me from one of the neighboring cells. Shot down in April, 1965, while flying an RF 101 photo reconnaisance plane on his 94th combat mission, he told me what to expect about 10 A.M. "We've got an air show. They come in every day and hit the target just over the hills to the west of us. You're going to see it from where you are. You'll see them again about 2 P.M."

About ten o'clock a Vietnamese beat the gong repeatedly, as if panic-stricken. No one ran to close our window shutters, though they regularly shut these during the midday siesta and at night.

"You've got a good view, Al," said Scotty. "You'll see them pop up right from where you are at your window."

I had a clear view of the blue sky above the wall separating us from Shumaker's hut. The reverberating sound of the gong was blotted out by the whoosh of four F105s. They climbed to several thousand feet in the pop-up maneuver as they readied to dive in on a power plant on the Black River, a few miles away on the other side of the hills from where we were. Now they were out of sight, but the AAA cracked distinctly before the thump and rumble of exploding bombs drowned it out. The aerial activity aroused the naval aviator in me from a year-long dormancy. My adrenaline pumped wildly. Cheers erupted from the huts as the planes dove in.

"Did you see them, Al?"

"Yeah! It's beautiful!"

"Number 4 looked like he had a satchel full of kids. He sure didn't dive in very close. He just sort of dropped the bombs and took off."

A short break in the action was followed by blasts of anti-aircraft artillery. An F101 reconnaissance plane streaked across the horizon photographing results of the strikes.

"That's it for now, Al, until this afternoon."

The last of the tactical attack aircraft shrieked away, leaving behind clouds of smoke and the shouted pandemonium of people in the fields. Sure enough, at 2 P.M. they were back, with the air defenses peppering the skies with popping flak. Down below, in our barred and locked cells, we watched like chained eagles, cheered by the sight of our guys socking it to them, but sobered by our own collective grounding.

Ron Storz, an Air Force Captain, had told me what to expect that first Sunday morning. About 8 A.M., with our shutters still closed, and with everyone under orders from our captors not to talk, all fifteen POWs stood up in their scattered huts at the sound of pre-arranged taps on the walls. With one low voice, hushed and barely audible but proud and declarative, we recited the Lord's Prayer:

> *Our Father, who art in heaven, hallowed be Thy name. . . . for thine is the kingdom, the power and the glory. . . .*

At its conclusion every man turned east towards the United States, stood militarily erect, placed his hand over his heart and said with defiant vigor:

> *I pledge allegiance to the flag of the United States of America and to the Republic for which it stands, one Nation under God, indivisible, with liberty and justice for all.*

As I spoke, tears welled up and rolled down my cheeks. This was a glorious moment of bonding. So long ago, at kindergarten, we had learned to recite the *Pledge of Allegiance* as the clearest expression of our common heritage. At the Briar Patch we reaffirmed that the *Pledge* represented all that united us and everything that we cherished. It was the indissoluble glue of our shared culture.

When it was over I sang *The Star Spangled Banner* very quietly as tears streaked down my face.

It was a momentous day in my life, standing there once more among fellow Americans. Though far from home, wretched, tired, hungry, dissheveled, unwashed, and caged, we were solidly united as one.

The gong sounded with unwelcome regularity at 5:30 every morning though we weren't fed until 10 A.M. and then again at about 5 P.M. As we weren't allowed outdoors, except to empty the slop buckets and wash our hands, we communicated guardedly out the windows or by tapping on the walls.

"How long do you think we'll be here?" I asked, knowing the recent shoot-downs had a better idea of how the war was going.

"Don't worry, Al, we won't be here very long. It won't take long at all. Matter of fact, they might be talking now at Geneva or someplace."

That figured, because we hadn't seen the F105s for a few days since their consecutive daily strikes near the Briar Patch. POWs began to interpret these signs, depending on whether they were optimists or pessimists.

"It's been pretty quiet the last few days. Must be something going on," mused Scotty Morgan, a stubborn optimist. "We've done good work bombing railroads, rail points, highways, bridges, and hitting convoys and supply dumps."

"Yeah, and women and children and hospitals and schools," I jested, echoing the Vietnamese propaganda line I'd been fed for so long.

"Don't believe that crap! That's a bunch of lies!" someone interjected.

"Hey fellas, I was only kidding," I said, surprised that anyone would take me so seriously.

On a late September evening, a week or two after our arrival at the Briar Patch, the guards went from one cell to another ordering POWs to exchange their clothes for new issues of green pajamas. I was the sole exception. Nobody explained why they left me with my khaki pants and blue shirts.

"What are these for? We goin' home?" asked Scotty, again looking at the bright side.

The Vietnamese guard mumbled something in the vernacular.

"Geneva? Peace?" Scotty queried.

I imagined the guard may have nodded his head unwittingly, or else Scotty's spirits refused to be dampened.

"I think we're going home, Al!" he said.

Later, in the thick of night, the guards blindfolded and handcuffed us and loaded everyone into hard-benched buses.

"What's this? I'm in a cracker box," said Ron Storz, miffed, as he tried to edge his big physique into one of the tight-fitting seats.

"All of you, keep quiet!" Rabbit reprimanded. "You are not allowed to talk."

Storz and Morgan began to cough deliberately, each cough corresponding to a hand tap on the cell walls.

Rabbit jumped aboard.

"Quiet! No noise! No talk! No cough! You must be silent!"

The bus chugged off and I began to think the optimists might be right. Perhaps we were on our way home. But there had been so many let-downs in the past that I did not feel exhilarated.

We drove back to Hanoi and off-loaded at our new camp, apparently a disused former film studio with single-story, flimsy, barrack-type buildings. The concrete floors were carpeted in thick dust and sprinkled with shattered glass. An Olympic-size swimming pool was filled with junk, garbage and countless reels of discarded, exposed film. The site must have had its heyday during the French colonial period. Since then it had been abandoned, along with most reminders of the ousted bourgeoisie.

For a few weeks they shuffled us between rooms in a number of barracks while they brought in laborers to block up the windows and build dividing walls for smaller cells in other empty buildings. I remained in solitary confinement in a barracks we called the Stable, while others shared rooms. Again, they released us only to go outside to empty our buckets, wash our dishes and dab ourselves with cold water from the slimy vats. When the builders finished working on the adjacent barracks, dubbed the Pigsty, they moved on to another building we named the Pool Hall, to seal more windows and contract the size of its rooms.

"It looks like they're getting ready to receive more guys," the pessimists concluded.

"Nah," one of the optimists parried, "all it means is they're going to make a BOQ (Bachelor Officers' Quarters) out of this place when we leave."

"I don't know. It doesn't look good. They're making this more permanent."

"You're wrong, fella. They're building a hospital. They need it for their own people."

The door slammed behind me in my new ten-by-ten foot cell in the Pigsty. The window had been bricked up and the room was bleak and damp from the fresh cement. I stood on my bed, a flat board resting on sawhorses, and peeked out of the tiny slits facing the Stable. Quickly, I made voice contact with some of the men still there.

The Vietnamese raised a makeshift shower stall outside where we washed ourselves and our clothes in the icy water for ten minutes twice a week. But the wet clothing hanging up to dry in our dark cells, merely added to the damp and cold. All through the night, my cell was lit by the harsh, unblinking light bulb on the ceiling.

Winter approached and they issued us two thin blankets and two pairs of green pajamas.

"What we gonna call this place?" someone asked.

"Go ahead, Al, you name it," said Larry Guarino.

Uninspired, I called out, "Okay, let's call it Camp America."

"Hear that, guys," said Larry. "It's Camp America."

Someone down the line objected.

"Why call it that?"

" 'Cause Alvarez called it that, that's why," Larry answered.

"Aw, we've got a better name."

"What's that?"

"We'll call it the Zoo."

It sounded good and it rang a bell. When we'd moved in and were talking through the spaces under the cell doors, Bob Purcell had remarked, "You know what this place is? It's a zoo. The other kind of zoo. It's the first kind of place where the animals come to look at the people!" In time, many civilians came to peer at us, photographers, peasants and even adults with children. If some of us didn't see them, we knew they were around just by listening to the uproariously funny animal impersonations made by guys locked up in their cells. All at once the Zoo seemed to be lined with pig pens and cow sheds, dog kennels, stables and chicken coops as POWs snorted, mooed, barked, neighed and clucked like Old McDonald's regular farmyard animals.

"Hey, Al, pick an animal!" someone shouted. "Here come the animals to look at us!"

"Kill 'em with fil . . . um!" yelled Purcell, a photo reconnaissance pilot.

Our food rations were usually left on the floor of the porch surrounding the Pigsty. Guards would open the door and occasionally get a laugh out of upbraiding us for trivial reasons.

"Stand properly!" they'd order, and then giggle as the POW straightened up.

We had been at the Zoo less than a month when I heard a commotion at the other end of the Pigsty.

"*What* do you want?" a POW asked dumbfounded. "You're not going to let me have my food unless I *bow!* Bow? No, no! I'm not going to bow! No bow! No bow!"

The guard slammed the door and moved to the next cell.

"No bow! No bow!"

The refrain was taken up at every cell in the Pigsty as guards went back and forth banging doors shut. As a result, no one got any food. But a little later the guards returned, opened a few doors and pulled the inmates' hair to force them down into bowing positions. Only then did they deliver the food. Soon the POWs were tapping away like woodpeckers, passing word down the line that guys were getting beaten up for not bowing. Cmdr. Bill Franke, two doors away from me and senior ranking officer in the building, decided that in this case discretion was the better part of valor.

"Hey, guys, go ahead and bow. This is ridiculous," the SRO ordered.

With our hands by our sides, we bowed quickly, but like automatons. In succeeding months they demanded that we bow to every Vietnamese, not merely to guards bringing food. And we had to bow with obvious respect. They became so demanding that the slightest detection of casualness brought a swift rebuke. If we failed to bow we were slapped around and beaten up. Even if a guard walked by while we were washing, we had to bow. It got so ludicrous; we were like serfs humbling ourselves before an endless procession of mandarins.

I passed many hours playing chess with the POW in an adjoining cell. He had tiles on his floor and we tapped out the numbers of the squares in the eight rows and columns. Our chess pieces were stones, sticks, wire, glass and any other small portable object. I had become quite adept at scavenging, after fourteen months in captivity, and had even collected several glass jars during my brief forays outdoors to wash. I urinated in them whenever my guards refused to let me out to empty my overflowing slop bucket.

9
A CELL MATE

IN NOVEMBER, THE GUARDS SWOOPED THROUGH ALL THE
cells, confiscating almost everything other than blankets, clothes and tooth-
brushes. They seized my glass jars, notebook with Vietnamese vocabulary,
bits of wire and pieces of glass. They even took the sawhorses on which I
rested my bed board. Mercifully, they let me keep the two grainy photographs
of Tangee and the two cans of Paraguayan corned beef. The explanation was
tapped through to everyone: the guards had discovered we were communicating through drops in the shower stall. They'd found handwritten notes,
instructions passed down from the overall SRO, Lt. Col. Robbie Risner, and
an unsigned map of the Zoo, which I had drawn. They discovered the map
on a new shoot-down, Tom Barrett, who was living in the Stable. Word came
through the walls that Barrett had been worked over, but information was
sparse because he was in solitary confinement, with no one to communicate
with in the empty cell adjacent to his.

On November 18th, 1965, the key rattled in my door. Towering over the
guard was a 200 lb., six-foot, red-bearded American clad in loose, baggy green
pajamas, and clutching his rolled-up gear.

"You allowed to live together," the guard announced, then slammed the
door.

I could not contain my joy, thinking to myself, "At last, a roommate for
me!"

Wide-eyed and registering shock and surprise with an open, dropped jaw,
I held out my hand.

"Everett Alvarez!"

"Tom Barrett."

He looked stunned and stood motionless, as if trying to recollect something
about me.

"My name's Alvarez. Everett Alvarez!" I repeated.

"Yuh, I know. I heard you. I heard you," he said, still dazed.

"God you look heavy," I said, looking over his fatty flesh that was the telltale sign of all new shootdowns.

"How long you been here?" he asked.

"Fifteen-and-a-half months."

His jaw sagged.

"How long?"

"Hey, I'm Alvarez. Everett Alvarez! First guy shot down!"

"Yeah, yeah. I remember now. I'm surprised you're still alive," he said, utterly flabbergasted.

I was so excited. My neighbor had tapped over recently, "Hey, I got me a roommate!" So here's one for me, too! I felt so happy I wanted to jump up and click my heels.

"You haven't been here very long, have you?" I asked.

"Shot down October 5th."

That first night we hardly slept as we traded bits and pieces of our life stories. Like me, he was a Catholic. But he was an only child, born and raised in Chicago's south side near Comiskey Park, though the family moved back and forth several times to Lombard in the western suburbs. The son of a factory laborer, Tom had graduated with a B.A. in mathematics and an Air Force ROTC commission from Bradley University in Peoria. A year later he had graduated from pilot training.

Late into that night we laughed uproariously as we swapped information about the antics of the guards. We both found it weirdly comical that the English-speaking interrogators called us *air pirates, criminals, arrogant and aggressors.* He buckled up laughing about Rabbit, who reminded him of Howdy Doody. And it cracked us up when we compared incidents of guards stamping their feet and yelling "Eet! Eet! (shut up!)" at POWs. It was invigorating to laugh and giggle again on the same wavelength as a fellow American. I was so hungry for the company of others that we talked and snickered for hours, like a pair of schoolgirls wrapped up in boy-talk.

Tom was an Air Force 1st lieutenant backseater pilot in an F4C, shot down on a bombing run over an ammunition dump about thirty-five miles north of Hanoi. Two years younger than me, he had spent the first twelve days in Heartbreak Hotel at the Hanoi Hilton. Since then he had been in solitary at the Zoo. He had been more or less left alone until the day someone anonymously slipped my map under his cell door. Being a new guy, he wasn't prepared for the flash, unannounced room searches. When the guards found the map they wanted to know where he got it. He clung to the line that he had picked it up outside his cell. But they weren't satisfied and began withdrawing his food and water, putting him on half rations and cold food. They handcuffed him and clamped the kind of leg irons on that still enabled him to shuffle around his cell.

Tom got his first taste of violence about ten days after they found the map. He had laughed at the non-English-speaking interrogator who was badgering him about the map. The interrogator, who out-ranked Rabbit, lunged across the table and swiped Tom with a blow to the head, knocking him off his stool. Handcuffed, he had to kneel on the floor for about an hour before they took him back to his cell. There they handcuffed his hands tightly behind his back and tied his arms with rope. They left him there for about thirty hours while his arms swelled up painfully through lack of circulation. Then they led him back to the interrogation room, where they dropped all questions about the map, insisting only that he answer routine biographical questions and write a short note of apology to the camp commander for laughing at the interrogator. Tom figured this was harmless, since they already knew the type of plane he flew and other insignificant data about himself. But he still felt bad about having technically breached the Code of Conduct. Two days later, they told him to roll up his gear and moved him in with me.

I did not realize how green he was until the next day when the guards let us out to shower.

"We've got to hustle, Tom, 'cause we have to get our clothes washed and we don't have much time."

"Oh, no, no," he said avuncularly. "Don't wash your clothes. They'll take them and give you new ones."

I stared at him hung-jawed. Then I realized. He was a recent shoot-down and had been issued new clothes at the Hanoi Hilton, and again at the Zoo. Now Tom figured he was due for another change of clothing. He thought we had a laundry service!

"Tom, you're crazy," I said. "I had my last set of clothes for over a year!"

He blanched. Oh, boy, I thought, he's going to have trouble with *new-guy-itis*, the breaking-in stage of overcoming the frustration and boredom of being locked up and packed tight in a small space, smelling of human excreta, with nothing to do and no mental stimulus. It wasn't long before he occasionally threw tantrums, pulled his mosquito net down, hurled objects and beat against the walls. Temperamental and irritable in those early days, he was also short on sleep, complaining that my snoring kept him awake. Head down and moving his mouth idiosyncratically, as if chewing his tongue or aligning his teeth, Tom paced back and forth, a few steps in one direction before he had to make an about turn at the edge of the wall. With the onset of winter he paced up and down, a blanket draped over his shoulders.

"Look at you! Look how skinny you are!" he sneered one time. I dismissed all this as the inevitable rantings of *new-guy-itis*. He'd cuss and shout and even complain about my bad breath. He was not yet inured to the sharp stench of urine and the foul smell from the open slop bucket we shared. Watching him grapple helplessly with the crush of confinement, the lack of sunlight, and the total absence of privacy, made me feel like a village elder in some primitive community, wiser than the green newcomers because I had long since fought the battles they were now up against.

Tom was somewhat narrow-shouldered, barrel-chested and spindly-legged. And he seemed destined to develop a paunch in middle age. But he was smart, an attentive listener and a deep thinker. Often he would say, "I'm not sure if that's right. I want to think this out logically." Once he told me he wanted to take advantage of his time as a POW, thinking things out, so that when he finally got home he would never have to think again.

One of the first things I taught Tom was the tap code. At the Hanoi Hilton he'd been in voice contact with other POWs and had little need to use it, though the code's basic features were explained by a cell neighbor. On one of the rare occasions he tried tapping, a guard caught him and as a punishment and deterrent, he was placed in leg irons. In the Zoo he had no cell neighbor with whom to communicate until he moved in with me. Soon he was proficient and "talking" with others in the Pigsty.

As Thanksgiving approached, I decided that the moment had arrived to open the two cans of Paraguayan corned beef. It was the kind of very special occasion I had been waiting for, and Tom's presence perked me up no end.

"Thanksgiving's coming up, Tom. Look what I've got for us!"

"No, no," he demurred. "You have it. Go ahead."

"C'mon, Tom! I've been holding this almost a year for the right occasion. I want to share it."

Fortuitously, we had bread on Thanksgiving Day so we made corned beef sandwiches. It was a feast, and I daydreamed from the memory of it for years to come. It meant much more to me than the gourmet dinner I'd treated myself to at Hong Kong's swank Mandarin Hotel, two days before my ill-fated flight.

In December, the guards brought in sweatshirts and installed radio speakers so that we could listen to the *Voice of Vietnam* broadcasts.

"How long do you think we'll be here?" I asked Tom.

"Oh, not more than a couple of months at the most," he guessed, still blindly optimistic.

He'd been on the outside as recently as October and was more in tune with moods and currents of opinion at home. But somehow I could not share his optimism.

Knowing that I was more familiar with camp conditions, he asked, "When they release us, how are they going to send us home?"

"The first thing they're going to do is give us a shave and a haircut. Then they'll issue us clean clothes and put us on a bus to an airport or to the port of Haiphong. Or maybe they'll even take us down to the DMZ. But that's how we're going to know. They'll come and give us shaves and haircuts."

Thoughtfully, Tom twirled the hairs of his red beard. As he stood, a thin shaft of sunlight pierced through a ventilation hole high up near the ceiling and lit up his face.

"You look just like Charlton Heston playing Moses in the Ten Commandments," I remarked.

He smiled boyishly, evidently flattered, and strode around a bit.

A few days before Christmas the Vietnamese moved us to the reconstructed Pool Hall, which we'd all believed was being prepared to receive a lot more POWs. Our captors easily achieved their goal of providing many more small cells by raising a ceiling-high wall down the middle of the length of the barracks. As a result, one complete row of cells was without windows. We moved into one of these dark and gloomy rooms, where the only glimpse of sunlight came from the two ventilation slits, each five inches wide and six inches high, near the ceiling. By daylight we could make out people moving outside by watching their shadows cross the inch-and-a-half open space under our locked door. The only improvements over our old cell were the permanent beds of wooden slats on concrete blocks.

One morning we were singing carols in low voices, each of us lost in memories of Christmas at home as we tried hard to put some cheer into the words and melody. We were in the middle of *Silver Bells* when Tom choked up. He started to sob. It was a particularly meaningful carol to him and it was his first Christmas away from home.

"Don't worry, Tom, we'll stop. We won't sing for a while."

I remembered how hard it had been for me the previous year to be alone at Christmas, so far from home.

Tom and I had been saying the rosary at night, using the one given me by the Vietnamese priest the previous year. The same cleric visited us fleetingly close to Christmas and as we sat and talked I noticed how this elderly, hunched priest was wary of the watchful guards. Looking over the top of his semi-circular lenses, he asked, "Do you pray?" I nodded affirmatively. "That's good," he said, blessing me even as he glanced suspiciously at the guards.

On Christmas Eve, 1966, a turnkey took me out to the camp commander we called the Fox. He was a three-star officer, about fifty years old with a ruddy complexion and tough, thick hair cropped short like a clipped porcupine. Though he, too, had been vicious on occasion, Fox was now more at ease with himself. Months later he would tell me how he hoped U.S.–Vietnamese relations would be better after the war. He even wanted to visit the U.S. to get first-hand impressions. Taking advantage of his new mood, I had asked him, a few weeks back, why the guards kept calling me *Ao*, a word I had not paid much attention to until other POWs arrived It seemed to be used only when guards spoke to me. Fox told me every POW was given a random name in Vietnamese. "Ao" was their word for shirt. It had no particular significance. Tom Barrett was *Bang*. In time, many of us called each other by these names.

At this moment, as Fox drew deeply on his cigarette, he had a Christmas surprise.

"Today you have a letter from your wife."

I gasped, taken off guard and unprepared for evidence that I had another life beyond this hell-hole. I hadn't heard from home in about eleven months and had last been allowed to write in February. Many months ago, I had consciously blocked my family out of my mind. If I daydreamed about them, it brought on a heavy and obsessive depression. So I just erased them from my mind. And if their images intruded, or if memories stirred of everyday luxuries, of plentiful food, or of warm beds with clean sheets and sprung mattresses, I snapped back doggedly to reality. Caged and debased for seventeen months like a vassal, I could not endure the lean present if I allowed myself to luxuriate mentally in the abundance of the past.

I reached out with a hand that had once caressed her face but which was now rough from harsh captivity. The letter was delicately scripted in her familiar feminine hand, with all the letters sloping neatly to the right. It had been written four months earlier. Tangee said they had all been advised months before to stop writing. But now she was trying again, hoping that I was safe and well. It was obvious: they hadn't heard from me since February and had assumed that either our letters were being blocked or that the worst had happened.

As soon as I finished reading it Fox took back the letter immediately, for I was never allowed to keep them.

Reverting to terse commands that reinforced his role as top dog in the camp, Fox declared, "Today you are allowed to write a letter home." But he warned me not to mention conditions in the camp nor anything about Tom Barrett. I reverted to a simple code, telling her, "My roommate and I do a lot of talking. We're both sports fans. My favorite team is the San Francisco Giants and his is the Chicago Cubs. We both say our rosaries."

Unsettled by the sudden impact of news from home, I was led back to the

Pool Hall. Tom, who had shed all his fat and now had the rib cage look, was sitting on the porch getting a haircut and a shave.

"Aren't you excited! We're going home!" he said, beaming and hardly able to contain himself. "You remember what you said? 'The first thing they're going to do, before they release us, is give us a shave and a haircut.' "

"Jeez, Tom," I said gently, aware what a letdown my words would be, "they're only doing it because it's Christmas Eve."

He slumped visibly but kept a stoic silence.

It was cold on Christmas Day. Bundled up in our thin blankets we wished each other season's greetings and lapsed into silent personal reminiscences. It was impossible to blot out recollections of loved ones on the single day of the Christian calendar devoted so exceptionally to family. Their faces were vividly impressed in my mind's eye. My own face felt awkwardly smooth after the shave and haircut. Two days earlier I had turned twenty-eight. I wondered what I looked like now and how they would react if they could see me. I had not been allowed near a mirror since the first month of captivity.

A shadow fell across the space under the door and metal plates rattled on the concrete step. Tom and I knelt on either side of the door and peeked under. A turnkey ladled some hot food on each plate and moved down the row. When the door wasn't opened immediately we knew we had to wait up to an hour before another turnkey came down the line, dishing out something else on the same plate. In the interim, we had to watch helplessly as ants, rats and chickens sometimes had their fill. But this was Christmas and we knew from the warm aroma wafting our way that my prediction had been fulfilled and that the meal was, like the year before, seasonably special.

In no time at all a column of ants marched determinedly towards our plates. We huffed and puffed, blowing many of them off track but they quickly fell back into line and pressed on single-mindedly towards the food. Desperately, Tom and I blew more rapidly under the door. Other bugs and insects crawled towards the prize. Our gusts of breath upended some and steered others off course. But enough of them assailed the plates to make us fret that we might actually witness the drawn-out theft of our holiday meal. We were even more fearful that the chickens and rats would appear. Our blows and curses would be no match for them.

Suddenly, a shadow darkened the porch and a key rattled in the door. We backed away. The door opened and the camp commander, held up the plates.

"Merry Christmas!" he said with a smile.

As soon as he left, we split up the food and devoured it, flicking off some of the ants and other insects and ingesting the rest. This time there were real potatoes in the soup. There were also hot turkey slices, round rice balls and something tasty wrapped in palm leaves. To top it all, we each had coffee and half a cup of beer. We toasted our families and sipped slowly. It made us light-headed and giddy but not loose-tongued. Tom and I sat quietly in the gloom of the chilled cell, our bodies warmed somewhat by the food. But again we were reminded disconcertingly of how much of the earth's bounty was being withheld from us.

Later that day, a guard opened the door and without explanation flung in my woollen seaman's watch cap. Camp officials had taken it away during a flash confiscation of personal belongings four months previously and I didn't expect to see it again. It was a godsend in the bitterly cold winters. In successive years it even came to identify me among my colleagues, so much so that many would jest, "Here he comes again, the old seaman!"

In February, they moved Tom and me back to the Pigsty. We had gotten along pretty well but now we seemed to have run out of things to say to each other. We'd exhausted ourselves narrating the highlights of our own lives. Both Tom and I seemed to be more interested in tapping on the walls with neighbors to learn more about them and news of the Zoo and other POW camps. He was still having problems adjusting to close confinement and the wretched conditions. He got his days and nights switched around, sleeping a lot from the noon siesta and on until the late afternoon, so that he was wide awake at night when he sang softly to himself. The guards didn't hear him, but it was loud enough to keep me awake.

One day we were talking idly about Vietnam when I related what my Hanoi Hilton interrogator had told me about French colonialist practices. I sympathized with some of the interrogator's views, remembering how he had rankled at having to attend a French school, salute the French flag and sing the French national anthem.

"Huh," Tom sniffed, "you've been brainwashed!"

I got mad, slipped off my wooden-heeled shoe and threw it down as hard as I could against the floor. As I watched it come to rest I wondered whether I might indeed have been brainwashed. I turned to Tom.

"Maybe I am brainwashed," I said, adding an apology for my behavior.

"Forget it," he consoled, quickly regretting his remark and obviously not wanting to pursue the matter further.

It marked the high point of tension between us.

Perhaps the frugal diet and our constant hunger exacerbated the friction. We had a craving for salt, sugar and fruit but instead were consistently fed a small hunk of dry bread and lukewarm slop with a chunk of animal flesh that might have been horsemeat. Drinking water came lukewarm off the boiler but we used some of this to rinse our hands after defecating.

While we were back in the Pigsty, the Vietnamese introduced a new procedure for feeding us. They set up a table in front of the building to serve the prisoners. But the food didn't all come at once. A guard would place some on the table and it might be half an hour before another guard came along with the rest of the meal. In the meantime the rats would race in from a nearby polluted pond, scale the wall, scurry across the grass and zoom up the table legs to snatch whatever they could latch their jaws onto. We set up a rat watch to scan their movements by peering through the slits of our louvered shutters. Whoever sighted the rats immediately alerted the others and we would scream and shout to try and frighten them off.

"Get away from there!"

"Shoo!"

"Scram!"

Sometimes the guards ambled onto the scene, found bread on the ground and replaced it on the table. The rats had often bitten off chunks. The Vietnamese never made up the losses, nor provided innoculations against the possibility of disease carried by the rats.

A lot of the captives were falling ill and all of us were skinny waifs. But it surprised us that winter when a huge contingent of medical staff appeared to put all the POWs through what they called "thorough medical examination." The routine included blood pressure checks and urine samples. One Vietnamese officer appeared at each cell with specimen bottles, loudly declaring, "You must make stool! You must make stool in this bottle! Do you understand?"

The walls reverberated with taps. "Hey, whatta we gonna call this guy?" Someone suggested *Dum-Dum*. It fit him admirably.

No sooner had they left than our rations were doubled. One of our neighbors, Larry Guarino, tapped through his optimism about our early release.

"Don't worry guys, it's all downhill now. We'll be out of here in a few months. These guys are beat."

He was way off mark. By early spring, recent arrivals from the Hanoi Hilton informed us that POWs there, including SRO Robbie Risner, were being beaten up and tortured to induce them to write autobiographical sketches. The word from Robbie himself, communicated through our walls by guys shuffled in from other camps, was laconic: resist if anything could be used for Vietnamese propaganda. Resistance would let them know they would have to apply pressure each time they wanted something from any of us.

One Sunday, as I sat on the bucket feeling particularly downcast with a fever, chills and diarrhea, Tom tapped light conversation through the wall to Air Force Captain Lester "Smitty" Harris and Bob Shumaker.

"How's Ev?" Smitty asked.

"Not too well," Tom replied.

"What's wrong with him?"

"It's that time of the month. He's got his period."

"Tell him I'll play him a tune," said Smitty.

That evening Smitty tapped on the wall again.

"How'd you like my tune?"

Tom and I brushed it off as a meaningless remark. We knew Smitty and Bob had fashioned a "piano," but we just didn't connect it with the comment he made about whether we liked his tune. For months our neighbors had secretively stashed away pieces of their rationed sheets of toilet paper and glued them together in a roll with a paste made from rice and water. Meanwhile they had passed the word around for POWs to scrounge the grounds for matchsticks on our daily walk down to the wash area. When the guards weren't looking we'd pick up the matchsticks and leave them at a pre-determined place near where we dumped our bowls. Smitty and Bob made ink from the burned tips and used the rest of the matchsticks as pens. Ingeniously, they drew an entire piano keyboard on their scroll of glued toilet sheets. The multi-talented Bob, who had been selected for the astronaut program shortly before his shootdown, was also an accomplished pianist and he managed to teach the basic chords to Smitty, using their paper piano.

Only years later did I learn that when Smitty heard I was sick he had unrolled the piano and played me his favorite melodies and tunes all day long. He was unconcerned about the guards making a snap appearance because, it being a Sunday, they left us alone from the time they let us out to dump our bowls in the morning until they returned with our food in the evening. The very next morning, however, the guards broke in unexpectedly on one of their surprise inspections. The doors swung open and two guards rushed in, pinning Smitty and Bob to the wall and aiming fixed bayonets perilously close to their abdomens. Simultaneously, other guards searched for contraband, classified as anything we were not supposed to have in our rooms. They found the piano and took it away.

At the same time, more guards swooped in on my room and on Larry Guarino's on the other adjoining side. One of the guards picked up my porcelain mug, turned it upside down and saw some scratches. They were nothing more than cracks from wear and tear but he thought otherwise.

"Look! This is evidence! This is evidence! You have been communicating! You will be punished!"

He stalked out with my cup, leaving me hung-jawed and flabbergasted.

"What the hell is he talking about?" I mused.

Mercifully, he did not follow up on his threat and I was not punished.

The confiscation of our neighbors' piano, though depressing, served only to recharge their spirits. The day after the raid they were again hoarding toilet sheets and scavenging for matchsticks.

Not long after that, the guards began hauling POWs out of the Zoo and taking them off to unknown destinations. Food rations were again reduced and the authorities tightened their control. In mid-May they drove Tom and me back to the Briar Patch and shoved us into a cell. None of us queried why they periodically moved us between the various camps. There was speculation it might be to prevent us becoming too familiar with one location, which would make escape easier. It was obvious that the rural holding camps were less secure than the more permanent structures making up the Hanoi Hilton, which had the additional advantage of being in a heavily-populated and well-guarded area. Moving us around also lessened the opportunity for would-be rescuers to get a fix on our location and routines. Our captors, we reminded ourselves, must have learned a lot about the mentality of imprisoned combatants from their own experiences in French colonial prisons.

The Briar Patch was still without electricity, but changes to the interior reflected the escalation of the U.S. air raids. They had dug about four-and-a-half feet through the concrete floor, under each bed, and scooped out foxholes two-and-a-half feet wide. We were ordered to jump in and remain there whenever U.S. bombs fell nearby.

Through the tap code we quickly established that this was where they had brought the other POWs who had disappeared from the Zoo. They were determined to elicit written bios and had been brutal in extracting them from some Americans. Ron Storz had sat defiantly on a stool for ten days refusing to write anything. Every time he had slumped towards the table or collapsed on the floor from fatigue, guards had beaten him up and set him upright again. Finally, they had even used the ropes on him. Our whispering walls narrated how Bob Purcell had actually humored his tormentors, inviting them to hit him on the other cheek, "Because this side is getting awful sore!"

When my turn came in June, I was led down the hill to an 8-by-10 foot room in the office complex near the kitchen. A short, plump, pompous official we nicknamed Mr. B., short for Mr. Blue because he always wore a blue shirt, ordered me to sit down on the stool in front of a table. Mr. B. had a round, smiling face and large eyes that reminded me of Crazy Guy at the Hanoi Hilton, but his hair was combed to one side.

"How are you?" he asked ingratiatingly. "You got food? You got water?"

"Yeah."

"Good. Now you write your biography."

"But you know my biography."

"You must write! You must write now!" he shouted with a swift change of mood as his eyes curled menacingly.

"I can't. I'm not allowed to write."

"You must write! You must sit there and think about it! There is a pen!"

I sat tight-lipped and motionless.

"You will sit there! You will sit there until you write!" he screamed, then stormed out and locked the door.

A guard poked his head in through the open-screened window to look me over, then patrolled outside. It was easy enough getting through the daylight hours and even the early part of the warm night. I watched the moon rise and, intrigued by its changing size and color, began to calculate its phases. I determined the dates of the full moon and theorized about its appearance on specific holidays. It kept me mentally alert. But late into the night, as I began to slump forward drowsily, guards came in and beat me on the head and face, shrieking, "No sleep! No sleep!"

Feelings of fright, confusion, anger and fatigue overlapped. It maddened me that they were doing this to break my will and extract propaganda. Obviously it was their way of asserting control but I still felt indecisive, wondering how far I should take my resistance. There was no knowing where compliance with their demands might lead. If I gave them the bio what else might they demand? And if I held steadfast would it make sense to court death just because I was withholding a few trivial facts about my life? At this time POWs had no general guidelines to follow. Only later that year did a succession of these crises force the issue. Then help came in the form of directives from senior ranking officers. The word was to resist as far as possible to let the enemy know they would not come by information easily. But individual POWs would have to make judgment calls in each case, weighing whether and when to submit, or to hold out tenaciously and risk death by attrition.

The following day they brought me a few bananas and some water. I was allowed to urinate in a bowl in a corner. But every time I sank forward or slipped sideways off the stool, they screamed through the window or charged in and slapped me around. At the end of two days, I could scarcely think coherently. By this stage I was numb to the blows. The pain hardly registered. But I craved sleep.

Mr. B. strode in haughtily. "Look, you must write! Here are some others that have been written."

I skimmed over a few pages. Al Brudno had written a marvelously sensitive piece on childhood among the snowflakes of Christmas. Robbie Risner had written reams of utter garbage. Their bios held the key to the only way out of my dilemma: fictionalize. A lot was already known about me from the media but I was free to flesh this out with careful imagination.

Groggily I looked over the list of guideline questions. *Who are your squadron mates? Who were your best friends in the squadron? Who were your best friends at home? What are they doing now?* Friends? Let's see, my closest friends, since childhood, were Joe Kapp, the professional football player, Johnny Nardone, a dentist, and Charlie Besman, an engineer. Okay, "Joe Crapper, Johnny Cornhole and Charlie Bestcan have been my closest friends since childhood. Joe Crapper washes and dries football clothes. Johnny Cornhole makes false teeth, and Charlie Bestcan is a farmer." I wrote pages of gibberish, running wild with imaginative job descriptions and inventing personalities. For friendly squadron mates I seized on *McHale's Navy* and wrote about Navy Lt. McHale and the World War II fictional comic strip character, Don Winslow.

"Ah! very good, very good!" said Mr. B., who was evidently so impressed with the length of my manuscript that he ordered me back to my cell.

But the conclusion of that incident was no guarantee of a respite from their crackdown. And they didn't need much of a provocation to make life more wretched than it was already. One day, as Tom paced back and forth, he paused yet again to read the camp regulations displayed on the door. Sneeringly he read: *Do not talk loud!* "Humph! It doesn't say you can't sing!" he said. At that he sang lustily in his rich, baritone voice, *Oh Marcia, oh Marcia* . . . the name of his fiancee, fitting it to the tune of "Donna," a popular song of the fifties. He had sung no more than a few bars when Pig, the guard who always walked around in a pith helmet topped with camouflage leaves, stuck his head in the window.

"Shhhh! Silence! You have violated camp regulations! You two will be punished! You will have your window closed for one week!"

He slammed the shutters closed.

In the darkness Tom mumbled, "I guess I blew that one."

"What do we sing now, Tom?"

"Aw, shaddup!"

10
HANOI PARADE

THE RADIO SPEAKERS IN OUR CELLS SQUAWKED NOISILY IN
the final days of June, 1966. *Hanoi Hannah* was more shrill than usual in
condemning the latest U.S. air raids over North Vietnam. It stiffened our
morale, knowing that our guys were really putting the pressure on. The
optimists among us took to the walls and tapped out a flurry of upbeat
opinions.

"Should be over pretty quick!"

"We'll be out of here soon if they keep this up!"

In these moments of heightened suspense we tracked every open sign and
veiled signal to back up our hopes. We didn't have to wait long. There was
a stir of expectation when they fed us early on the morning of July 6. Then
they took away a set of green pajamas from eighteen POWs and told us to
roll up our mosquito nets and straw mats. They marched us down to a gate,
where our pajamas lay in a pile, and handed the sets back to us. Each article
of clothing was now stamped conspicuously with a stenciled number. I was
handed clothing stamped 206 though there were only fifty-three POWs at
the Briar Patch. Without comment, the guards blindfolded all of us, roped
us in pairs by our wrists and loaded us onto two trucks.

As the engines started someone whispered, "We're going home!"

"They're sending us down to the DMZ!" another voice volunteered.

Tom, handcuffed to me, nudged to signify agreement.

"No talk! No talk!" a guard commanded.

We stopped briefly several times along the road and heard beating gongs
herald the imminent overflight of U.S. bombers. Several hours after leaving
the Briar Patch, we drove into a large city, identifiable by the volume of traffic
and the street cries and shouts of vendors and pedestrians. When they took
us out and down to the dressing rooms of a sports stadium, they removed the
blindfolds and we knew we had to be in Hanoi. They took off the handcuffs,
ordered us to sit silently on straw mats, and fed us rice balls rolled around

144

pieces of meat, bananas and chunks of bread. Uniformed Vietnamese men and women moved to and fro, each of them smart and self-assured, in sharp contrast to the riff-raff and trash who made up the ranks of our turnkeys and guards.

It was getting dark when they blindfolded and handcuffed us once again before driving us out of the stadium. Tom's blindfold slipped a fraction as we pulled up. "We're in front of a big building," he murmured.

They hauled us off and removed the handcuffs. A guard pulled me forward a few steps then roped my left wrist to someone else's right wrist.

"Who are you?" I mumbled.

"Robbie Risner. Who're you?"

"Hi, Robbie! Ev Alvarez."

"Rog! Got you! Where are you?"

"Briar Patch. They brought eighteen of us. There are fifty-three of us out there."

"How're your spirits?"

"Shit hot," I replied, using an expression popular in our squadron.

"Do not talk!" a guard snapped.

I continued whispering, barely opening my lips. "Jim Bell's senior officer."

"Rog! Rog! I thought you were still at the Zoo."

"We moved out in mid-May. Where are you now?" I asked.

"Heartbreak Hotel. Rough treatment."

"How do you feel?"

"Good," he replied vigorously.

I moved my head, as if craning my neck to relieve a stiffness. As I looked skywards, I peeked under the blindfold and saw Robbie. He, too, was blindfolded but stood imposingly erect. His sharp nose stood out and he reminded me of the movie actor, Van Heflin. Both had strong jaws, firm mouths and crew cuts with V-shaped hair lines.

Robbie and I had last spoken at the Zoo the year before when I had exercised briefly outside his cell. He was an Air Force colonel and a highly respected air ace in the Korean War. Raised in Arkansas and Oklahoma, where he became a passionate horseman, he was married with five sons, the eldest of whom was only seventeen when Robbie was shot down just over a year after me. As senior ranking officer, he had passed down the word to conduct ourselves with pride and to show the Vietnamese our mettle. It was not macho talk. Robbie was a highly principled officer who stood up to the most savage torture with enviable fortitude. Because of his status, the authorities singled him out for particularly sadistic treatment. Within weeks of his capture they lay him down on a cold cement block, manacled his legs, and kept him there for thirty-two straight days and nights. Unable to turn over, he lay in his own filth, trying to eat scraps of bread and sip water even as they continued to beat him. After that they had trussed him up with ropes, almost broke his neck and back while working him over again, and very nearly suffocated him by stuffing paper down his throat.

When the guards removed our blindfolds they warned us not to look around, nor to talk to each other. We stood in pairs under trees on a grassy square island. The road appeared to curve a bit before leading down to a broad traffic thoroughfare. On both sides of the curve, almost obscuring the thoroughfare, we saw, under floodlights, prefabricated grandstands packed to capacity with people. Though it was dark, the road was eerily devoid of traffic.

"I think this is all for show, for propaganda," said Robbie.

"Do not talk!"

I looked ahead.

"That's Butler and Lockhart," I said.

"Where?"

"Right in front of us."

Robbie had a faraway look, as if trying to recall names and faces.

"Who?" he asked.

"Phil Butler and Hayden Lockhart."

I turned to see who was behind us.

"Do not look back!" a guard bellowed, at the same time prodding us with his fixed bayonet to continue forward. Guarded on both sides, we walked in handcuffed pairs towards the grandstands. But because of the mobs of people, we didn't see, nor realize until we got close to the grandstands, that we were being pressed to walk down the thoroughfare lined with crowds. We had suspected that we would parade only around the grassy island.

"Obey the orders of the guards!" an officer thundered. "Bow your heads! You must bow your heads when you march!"

As we neared the corner I saw Rabbit. He looked directly at me then put the bullhorn to his mouth and boomed, "Alvarez! Alvarez! Son-of-a-bitch! Son-of-a-bitch!"

The crowd took up his lines in a full-throated chant: "Alvarez! Alvarez! Son-of-a-bitch! Son-of-a-bitch!"

The citizens were massed ten deep on either side of the main road. They, too, reacted on cue, egged on by marshalls screaming insults and cursing us through bullhorns. The noise built to a crescendo, as if the aroused spectators were at a heavyweight prize fight, witnessing savage, bloodletting blows and hoping for the knockout punch. They shook their fists and surged forward, trying to reach past the guards to flay at us. Rocks, bottles, shoes and sticks flew overhead, striking us on our heads, backs and faces. I held my head down protectively but outstretched arms flashed out of the seething mass and crashed down on my face. It did not matter that they spit in my face and tore at my clothes and hair, even though I tried to fend them off with my free right arm. I was more sensitive to their wild kicks and I buckled reflexively to deflect the blows from striking my groin.

The further we walked, the more agitated and frenzied the mobs became. By now there were thousands of flailing arms. Everyone was whipped up and given official sanction to brutalize and perhaps murder the hapless line of tethered Americans. I was seized by a real fear that we would be torn apart, limb from limb, and stomped to death.

We approached a big flat-bed truck, illuminated by harsh photographers' floodlights. About fifty Caucasian cameramen stood atop the truck. On a building beyond them I caught sight of an advertisement for Seiko watches. It was almost 9 P.M. Suddenly, from out of the pandemonium, a short, fat, grubby man broke through and stepped alongside as I stumbled on.

"Cubano, eh?" he shouted.

I glanced at him. He was holding a large camera by its outsize handle.

"You're a Cuban!" he screamed in Spanish. "A dirty Cuban traitor! You lousy traitor!"

Undoubtedly he was Cuban himself. He paced beside me for one block, shrieking obscenities above the din of the howling mob. Then, without warning, he whacked me ferociously with the camera behind my right ear. I blacked out momentarily, oblivious to the bedlam. I sank to my knees but Robbie crouched over and pulled me up. Immobile for those fleeting seconds, we became easier targets for the vengeful pack of Vietnamese. The hysterical mob closed in, swinging blindly and landing punches from both sides. We seemed doomed. The guards, our only protective barrier, were themselves pummelled as they attempted to hold back the assailants. Just as I found my feet again, someone struck Robbie below his rib cage. He gasped, drew his hands to his belly and doubled up.

"C'mon Robbie! You have to get up!"

I helped him up and he stumbled forward. Ahead of us I saw the crazed mob savagely beating and kicking Butler and Lockhart. I turned quickly. The same was happening to the two aviators some fifteen feet behind. The thrashing, roaring mob was so dense that I could not see further back. A guard poked me with his bayonet to move on. Another marshall raised a bullhorn and bellowed, "Kill the Yankee sons-of-bitches!" Faces dripping sweat were mere inches away, their eyes dilated, almost popping, and their mouths stretched wide to release the torrent of abuse.

Rabbit appeared from out of the heaving mass and screamed at the two guys ahead of us. "Bow to the people! Bow to the people! You must bow!" he shouted as he struck them furiously with clenched fists. But Butler and Lockhart stood stoically, refusing to bow. Rabbit grabbed their hair and yanked, forcing them down while continuing to shriek commands. Then he repeated the scenario with Robbie and I, swinging at us with his fists before he forced us down by our hair. Adult women of all ages reached out to beat us with sticks and strike us with shoes. We inched our way forward with no apparent goal other than to escape the mob. It seemed interminable. We stumbled and staggered through the gauntlet for perhaps an hour. I started to pray.

Hail Mary, full of grace, the Lord is with Thee. Blessed art Thou . . . Holy Mary, Mother of God, pray for us sinners . . .

Almost immediately, I ceased to feel the impact of the blows. But still fearful and terrorized, I wondered how much longer this could endure. Soon we would drop from exhaustion and succumb like weary prey to snapping wild dogs. The guards behind each of us, who had been prodding us forward with fixed bayonets, now turned their attention to the unruly hordes. With their rifles slung over their shoulders, they tried desperately to push the masses back.

Suddenly, a file of young men and women linking hands emerged miraculously from behind us, fanning out on either side of our straggling line. They were easily identifiable by their white shirts and blouses, dark trousers and conspicuous red armbands. Prancing forward while the crowds backed off slightly, they seemed to dance to a playful choreography as they came between the lunging masses and the guards. When the leaders of both rows ahead closed hands they formed a tight barrier between us and the mobs, clearing a narrow opening ahead. Our new protectors moved along with us, keeping the tormentors at bay. Then they shouted at us to run towards the soccer stadium on the far side of another grassy island ahead. The only light came from a few shop windows and neon lights on the side streets. The massively high stadium doors were almost shut by the crush of people furiously beating Butler and Lockhart ahead of us. When the two POWs finally slipped through the doors we still had about twenty-five yards to cover.

"Go! Run!" screamed one of the red-armbanded men next to us.

Robbie and I gave it all we had, out of step with each other and stumbling over spectators shoved flat in our path. But we had seen the light at the end of the tunnel and raw fear propelled us to that sanctuary.

As our saviors in red armbands struggled to keep back the swaying masses, we ran past a mound of twisting bodies and I thought they must be mauling a POW underneath. Now within a final spurt of the stadium doors, a uniformed soldier held it ajar and we squeezed through, sustaining more blows from people trying to block the entrance. Just as I thought we were clear, someone struck me viciously on the back of the head with a heavy instrument and I reeled. But we slipped through and the doors blocked the enemy.

Our trucks were lined up on the far side of the stadium but the guards ordered us to sit on the grass by the tracks. I put my hand up to where the Cuban had struck me with his camera. It throbbed painfully. Then I saw blood on my hand from touching the head wound. My nose was also bleeding and my eyes felt swollen and puffed. Dazed, sweating and palpitating, I looked at Robbie. He, too, was out of breath, disheveled, bruised and bleeding about the face. He sat deep in thought.

"Holy cow! What was that! What happened!" I asked myself, practically in shock. I turned to Robbie. "You okay?"

"Yeah. How about you?"

"I guess so."

"God bless you," he said, as if offering words of comfort for the horrors he foresaw for the future.

"Don't talk! Don't talk!"

Furtively, I looked around. The few pairs of POWs who'd made it into the stadium sat like punch-drunk boxers. Everyone's clothes were torn. Some had lost sandals in the melee. Fortunately I still had mine.

The last of the POWs made it to the trucks in the stadium about thirty minutes after my arrival. Nobody talked as we tried to recover our composure. We were all exhausted. Our emaciated bodies, lacking nutrition, sunlight and exercise for so long, were ill-equipped to withstand this kind of ordeal. And we were not quite sure whether they had brought us to the stadium by design. Perhaps they had wanted to have us killed by the same breed of bloodthirsty spectators who had enjoyed seeing defenseless men pitted against wild beasts in Roman times.

A guard bent down to undo the ropes binding our wrists while another held the blindfolds to our eyes and knotted them tight. Before I had time to rub the chaffed skin on my wrist, I was tied to someone.

"Who is it?" I queried.

"Tom Barrett."

"Tom, it's Ev! You okay?"

"Yeah. Do you think all the guys made it back."

"I don't know. Hope so."

Rabbit's mocking voice cut in. "Now you have seen the determination and vengeance of the Vietnamese people. Now you know," he said.

We climbed aboard the truck, wondering what might lie ahead and alert for every hint of renewed violence. But as the truck picked up speed outside the stadium, we lowered our guard and relaxed. The crowds must have gone home because the raucous din had given way to the familiar quiet of the night. We had set out in such high spirits, anticipating release from captivity at the end of the journey. Now, as we nursed our cuts and bruises, someone wisecracked, "That was one hell of a trip home, wasn't it guys!" I could not restrain a smile. Much later we all chuckled about Lt. Cmdr. Jerry Coffee's quip. He had been shot down five months earlier and was brought into Hanoi only one day before the infamous parade. When it was over he deadpanned, "Hey, does this happen every Saturday night?"

All of us were exhausted by the time we got back to our cells after midnight. Moonlight shone in through the open shutters as I drifted quickly and thankfully into a deep sleep.

My head and body ached with a throbbing pain the following morning. There was no way I could see the damage to my face but if Tom's was any indication, I was black and blue, mauled, puffy and swollen. Tom was still cut and bleeding inside his mouth and, like me, had bumps on his head. The walls came alive early that morning as we hastened to find out if all eighteen had made it back to the Briar Patch safely. Incredibly, we had.

At low points like this I vividly recalled the ominous overtones of two incidents in Hawaii shortly before I was shot down and captured. We were sitting around in the carrier's ready room after completing day and night flight maneuvers when Nick Nicholson reflected aloud what many of us had been thinking.

"What do you think the commies would do if they ever captured us?"

"Oh God," the skipper interjected, "don't even think of it."

Not long after, I had gone with some pilots from our squadron to Fort De Russey, an officers' club on prime property at Waikiki Beach. It was a popular place for R 'n' R because you could get drinks, have dinner and see Hawaiian dancers perform on the little stage in the middle of the outdoor courtyard. A section of the courtyard was surrounded by old single-story wooden barracks, palms, and lush, potted tropical plants. When the floor show was over the band would strike up and couples would cram onto the cement dance

At the age of four and a half, wearing a sailor's suit.

Circa 1946 in front of our house on Pearl Street, Salinas, California: me (above) and Delia (left).

In front of our house on Williams Road in Salinas: Delia (age fifteen), me (age eighteen) and Madeleine (age three).

In flight training at Whiting Field, Milton, Florida, February 1961, with a T-28 in the background.

Flying an F-9F jet trainer at Kingsville, Summer, 1961; at the time, I scrawled on the back of the photo: "You wouldn't look too good at 35,000 feet either."

Capt. R.H. Mathew pins on my
aviator's wings (above) in
November, 1961 at Kingsville
Naval Air Station, Texas. Lt.
(j.g.) Everett Alvarez, Jr.
U.S.N. (left), 1963.
(Official U.S. Navy Photos)

Cutting the cake during a party for the crew while I was officer-in-charge of a detachment of pilots, Cubi Point, Philippines, July, 1964.

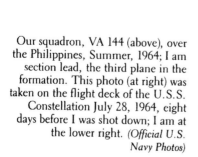

Our squadron, VA 144 (above), over the Philippines, Summer, 1964; I am section lead, the third plane in the formation. This photo (at right) was taken on the flight deck of the U.S.S. Constellation July 28, 1964, eight days before I was shot down; I am at the lower right. *(Official U.S. Navy Photos)*

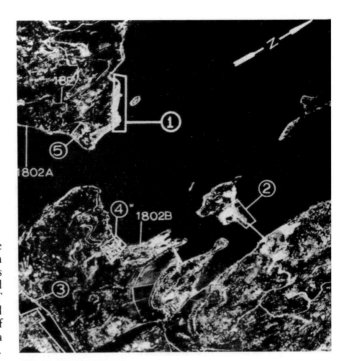

An aerial reconnaissance photo of the Hon Gai area taken after our raid; I was heading North and did two strafing runs on PT boats lined up at the naval docks (1), then pulled off to the right, maintaining a very low altitude.

After firing on target PT boats (upper left), I pulled off to the right and crossed over the town of Hon Gai (to the right of 3 in this photo), was hit and bailed out, just clearing the cliffs (lower right) and landing in the Gulf of Tonkin, where I was picked up.

I was driven from "The Zoo" to downtown Hanoi in July, 1967 for this photo, which was taken by a Soviet photographer; the guard we called "Elf" is at right.

NGAY VIẾT (Dated) 19 September 1970

Hi Sweetheart! I love you. Hope you are OK, also Mom, Dad & family. It sure has been a long time since we were together. I look at your picture every day. Try to include long underwear in your next package. I have been fine—don't worry. I am planning for our future. Take good care of yourself honey. Your husband, Everett.

GHI CHÚ (N.B.):
1. Phải viết rõ và chỉ được viết trên những dòng kẻ sẵn (Write legibly and only on the lines).
2. Gia đình gửi đến cũng phải theo đúng mẫu, khuôn khổ và quy định [...]om families should also conform to this proforma).

NGÀY VIẾT (Dated) 28 March 1972

Here's hoping that everyone at home is ok. as for myself, I'm fine.
I just want to thank you about Tang. at last I know. Mom, I'm sure
that it was hard on you also. It's sure difficult when you're doing
what we all are - living a dream; when just out of the clear sky, your dream
is shattered and you find that your world has vanished. The reality
is hard to face - but you must; then pick yourself up, and go on.
Someday, I will return home. Love to all - your Son, Everett

GHI CHÚ (N.B.):

1. Phải viết rõ và chỉ được viết trên những dòng kẻ sẵn (Write legibly
   and only on the lines).
2. Gia đình gửi đến cũng phải theo đúng mẫu, khuôn khổ và quy định
   này (Notes from families should also conform to this proforma).

Beginning in 1968, our letters generally had to
conform to this restrictive seven-line format; this (left) was
written to Tangee after she'd left me but before I knew about it. This (above) is
the first letter I wrote to my family after learning, via a letter from my mother,
that Tangee had left me.

24 November 1972

Hello everybody! I hope you are all well. It's Christmas time once again and I'm taking this chance to send my holiday wishes for a happy, joyful, but safe holiday season. I guarantee you my greatest wish at this time is for a speedy return for all of us. It's at this time of the year that all usually think mostly of home. I suppose that's natural - everyone usually likes to spend Christmas with their relatives or close friends. Anyway, I want to let you know that I am fine and hoping this won't last much longer.

Mom, when this war finally ends, and I'm released; be sure to remain calm. I feel that you and Dad will want to meet me somewhere. I think it may work out more suitably if you did not. I'll get in touch with you and instruct you on what's best. I don't have any idea what our schedule will be but I'm anticipating a thorough medical examination which may involve being assigned to a hospital, just until our records, uniforms, and other necessary paperwork is straightened out. Unless something else comes up, I plan on taking a nice long vacation. Since my health is good, I don't expect any delay. I guess I have many things to straighten out at home, after that I probably will visit Europe. Please give my regards to my uncle & aunt, my cousins, and everyone at home. May God be with you all on this Christmas - hopefully next year I'll be home eating some good 'tamales'. Happy Birthday to Madeleine. Love, your son, Everett Jr.

As our release neared, we were again allowed to write somewhat longer letters such as this one.

GUI MAY BAY
PAR AVION

Aerial recon photo of the Hanoi Hilton (Ha Lo Prison) with the main gate (1), Room 24 and its courtyard (2), Camp Unity (3) and the tiny cell where my hall-mate was Crazy Guy (4).

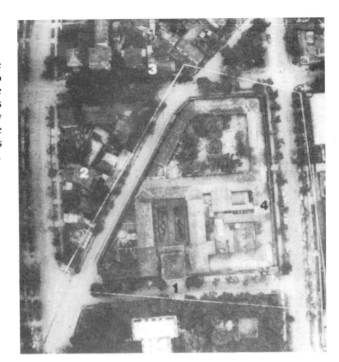

"The Zoo" from above with main gate (1), Pigsty (2), Office (3) and Annex (4).

"BAO CAO"

From 1965 until 1970, we had to bow to everyone; if we didn't—or if we didn't do it politely enough—we were beaten by the guards. These sketches are from Lt. Cmdr. John McGrath's *Prisoner of War: Six Years in Hanoi.* (Naval Institute Press)

These were the type of manacles used; if you spread your elbows they cut into your wrists and the guards were very inept with the locks.

Stress positions were a favorite torture method; this one (and at far right) we called the "rope trick" and it was often combined with the application of cuffs on the arms, which cut off all circulation and caused unbearable pain.

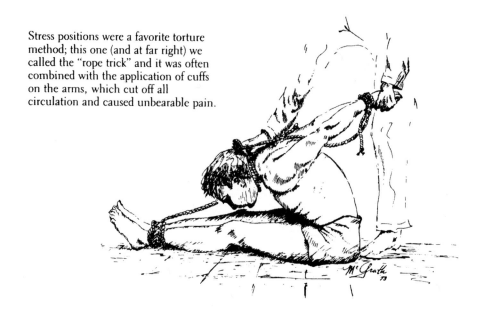

Sign language was the primary means of communicating from one building to another; I would usually stand on the shoulders of my cell-mate to look out through the air vents.

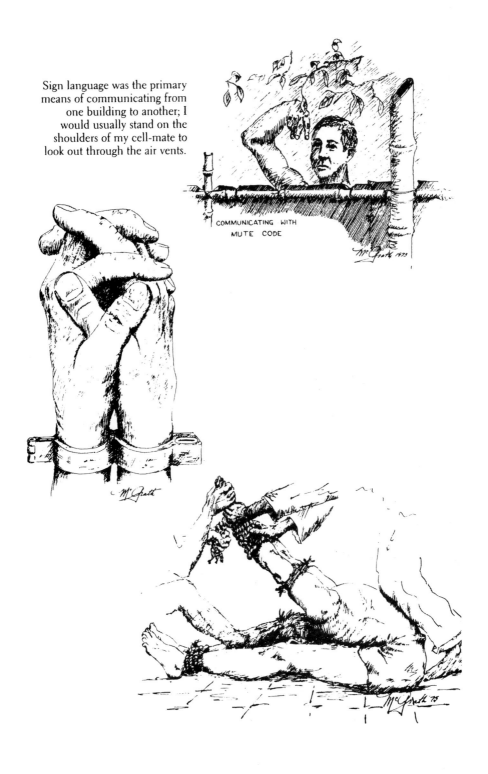

COMMUNICATING WITH
MUTE CODE

Fall, 1970—we played basketball at "The Zoo," prior to the Son Tay Raid and our transfer back to "The Hanoi Hilton"; that's me behind the tree.

Christmas, 1970—we sang carols (I'm in the middle), unaware that the photo would be used for propaganda purposes.

February 12, 1973; I headed the line as we were released and prepared to board the transport plane to freedom. (*Official U.S. Navy Photo*)

Robbie Risner and I posed for this photo at Clark Air Force base on February 15, 1973, shortly after our release.

February 16, 1973; the family is reunited at Oak Knoll Naval Hospital in Oakland; Mom and Dad are on either side of me; Delia (right) and Madeleine (left) behind us. *(Official U.S. Navy Photo)*

February 19, 1973; I answered questions at a press conference at the Oak Knoll Naval Hospital. *(Official U.S. Navy Photo)*

I borrowed Delia's guitar (left) to play "Cielito Lindo" during my stay at the Oak Knoll Naval Hospital, February, 1973. I spoke to the hometown crowd in Santa Clara (above) on March 25, 1973, when a city park was named after me; quite an honor! Life-long friend Joe Kapp, who quarterbacked the Minnesota Vikings in the Super Bowl, presented me with an award at my homecoming ceremony the same day (below) in Santa Clara. *(All official U.S. Navy Photos)*

Tammy and I on our first date (above), the White House dinner for returning POW's, May, 1973. Our wedding (right), October 27, 1973, St. George Antiochian Eastern Orthodox Church, Pittsburgh, Pa. At home with the boys (below), Bryan, 12, left, and Marc, 14, right, May, 1989.

I spoke in my capacity as Deputy Administrator of the Veterans Administration at the dedication of the Vietnam Veterans Memorial, November 11, 1982 (Veterans Day). *(Official Veterans Administration Photo)*

floor, surrounded by grass. The dining tables were always bathed in subdued lighting and faces flickered in the candlelight.

That night the club was thronged with military officers from all the services. Everyone was jovial, and, loosened by liquor, struck up conversations with strangers packed in the courtyard.

Someone clasped my wrist.

"Let me see your hand," said a middle aged woman, whose nondescript features were difficult to register in the outdoor light. She held both my palms face up and turned them slightly for a better look in the pale light.

"You're going to have a very hard time," she foretold.

"You mean my lifeline's not long?" I asked flippantly.

"No, no," she answered, still holding my right hand close. "You have a very long lifeline. But you see how this crosses your lifeline early? Something's going to happen in your life. You're going to have some difficulty. But you're going to come through. You're going to be fine."

"Aw, c'mon," I laughed.

"Your right hand shows conflict," she said undeterred. "Now this one doesn't," she said of my left hand. "It also points to a long life ahead. And it shows you're going to have an accumulation of wealth later on. This hand shows you're going to be very wealthy."

"I can't wait till I'm rich!" I quipped, trying to lighten the mood.

I never saw her again in the crush of merrymakers. It had all happened so quickly, almost as if I'd been riding a bus and a stranger had said, "Hey, let me look at your hand," seconds before disembarking.

11
ANGUISH ON THE HOME FRONT

TIPPED OFF IN ADVANCE BY THE NETWORKS, THE FAMILY
bunched expectantly around the TV in Chole and Lalo's home on Bohannon
Drive, Santa Clara, to watch the film of the Hanoi parade. They were
unprepared for the fury of the crowds and the physical threat to the Americans. They could barely distinguish Everett in the melee of flailing arms and
kicking legs. Unwilling to watch him beaten yet unable to avert their eyes,
the family watched transfixed.

It was the first live-action film they had seen of him in almost a year-and-a-
half, when NBC had shown clips from a propaganda movie prepared by
North Vietnamese and Japanese photographers. Then they had seen Everett
prodded along a road by an armed Vietnamese until he was later "interro-
gated" by a military officer. They could not have known that this was staged
by the Vietnamese, nor that Everett had lost his temper during the charade
and tried to outdistance himself from the armed man in a pith helmet.
Nevertheless, the family was cheered by Everett's photographic image because it showed him alert and uninjured.

Now, however, as they watched the throngs of crazed Vietnamese chanting and bashing the straggling line of captive pilots, their spirits plummeted.
An ocean apart, they could only pray for his safety. Their delight in seeing
him living and breathing was so brief that it left no feeling of joy. When the
black and white clip was through, they were again left on the outside of their
aviator's tomb of silence. Only this time their dread was heightened because
of what they had just witnessed.

Two full years of waiting and hoping had gradually changed all of them.
It was as if they had been seasoned by the years. They had steeped themselves

in the history of that distant land, scouring the public libraries and seizing on any recommended book or magazine article. There was not much in print but it was enough to advance them far beyond their initial concept of Indochina as just another geographical blip somewhere in the East. Neither of Everett's parents was handicapped by their lack of formal education. The material had such compelling relevance. They turned the pages of Vietnamese history not so much out of curiosity as from a compulsion to learn. It taught them about the ancient land of their son's captivity and its strange natives who could so easily snuff out his young life. In time, their new knowledge gave them the confidence to articulate uncommon views. But they weren't ready yet to express them outside the home. Forever conscious of the boundaries between private license and public constraints, they dared not expose the family free-for-alls to the watchful and critical eye of the public.

Chole had always been the most curious about the broad sweep of historical events. Her romance with history began in childhood when she played among the ruins of a Christian mission at Lompoc, California. The faded glory of her surroundings made her think about her roots and her ancestors. Where did they come from? Why were some in her family light-complected and blue-eyed while others resembled burnished, copper-colored Aztecs? The more Chole researched the more she wanted to get out and see the legacy of Mexico in California. She took the initiative when Everett was still in high school and by the time of his capture had visited all but one of the twenty-one Christian missions.

Chole brought the same keen inquiry to her studies of Vietnamese history. Though eager to learn, she was a slow, plodding reader who dimmed her bedside lamp with a newspaper so her husband could sleep undisturbed while she held her book open late into the night. As she read about the millenium of subjugation by the Chinese, followed by a century of French colonial rule, she began to doubt the wisdom of the American presence in Vietnam. No people of another culture had ever triumphed permanently over the Vietnamese. How, then, did Americans believe they could influence or squelch what other empires, with closer links and historical ties had failed to do? The politicians said they were containing communism. They spoke of a domino theory: if South Vietnam fell then neighboring countries would follow suit. Chole began to ask herself why, if the battle was against communism, the fight was not taken to the heart of the conspiracy, to Russia itself. Why not hit the snake on the head? In the privacy of her own home, she even began to wonder how she would react if an enemy parachuted down in her backyard. She developed the idea that God had put the Vietnamese over there, in their own continent, in their own area, to live the way that was best for them. He had likewise given Americans their portion of the world. There was even something comparable in her mind between the poorly armed Mexicans who fought for their sovereignty against a much better equipped army, and the out-gunned Vietnamese who appeared night after night on her television screen. Force would never change them, so let them believe in whatever they wanted. And if they killed each other, well, so be it. That was their country. In the privacy of her own home, she began to wonder aloud whether America should not rather stay on its side of the world and manage its own affairs. It was a view she did not hold when her son was shot down and captured. But that had been two long years ago.

Lalo was a much more earthy observer. Not for him this muddling, slow process of arriving at a conclusion. He had always held that there were only two causes for all wars: economics and religion. Wasn't this the case in Vietnam? Hadn't Ike sent Cardinal Spellman over on some kind of mission? And hadn't the cardinal returned recommending Americans get involved there, otherwise all those Catholics were going to be overrun by communists? Clearly, thought Lalo, the cardinal really cared only about saving his religion. And economics? Why, the Vietnamese had manganese, didn't they? And America would go down the tubes if it didn't have the raw materials needed to keep its factories going. What angered him was why they had to go to war for these necessary resources. Why couldn't they apply a little bit of good old American ingenuity and build up a healthy trade relationship?

And yet Lalo felt it was the duty of citizens to support the government and respect the president's decisions. What a man said in the confines of his own home was his own business, but he'd better watch his tongue in public, particularly if, like himself, he worked in a defense-related industry, with a son serving in the military and the country at war.

So he kept his peace, whenever possible. It wasn't easy to avoid the mounting provocations as Everett's captivity stretched into a third year. Once, an ex-marine and World War II veteran Lalo worked with mouthed-off about how wrong he felt the war was, with all the bombing and the killing. Lalo took exception and the two narrowly avoided getting into a fist-fight, the former marine eventually growling that he had fought for his country once before and would gladly go again if called, then storming off, not wanting to escalate this fruitless exchange of insults. The war was becoming a divisive issue at home for just about everyone. And Lalo found it increasingly difficult to stand aside from the ugly squabbling.

Two years back, he had assigned Delia the job of family spokesperson. A graduate in social work from San Jose State University, she articulated with ease what her parents struggled to express. In time, Delia inevitably assumed the mantle of leadership, tugging her reluctant family into a more confident role, unafraid to speak out and take issue with officialdom. Her abundant self-assurance and vigor were the very lifesaving qualities needed to pull the dejected family through its travail. With her dynamism they might somehow salvage Everett from the war without end.

But the transformation was slow even for her. She, too, had clung to the view that the military and the government must know best because they were in charge and had access to all the facts. In the beginning she was a staunch supporter of the war, so much so that when Everett was captured she had cursed her gender for disqualifying her from a combat role. But six months after his capture the bombing had begun, with the U.S. aerial armada blitzing Vietnamese targets. Delia knew then that it would be a long time before her brother came home. This was a hot war and Everett was trapped behind enemy lines.

Defense Department officials apologized for not being able to divulge the nature of ongoing secret negotiations and offered reassurances that they were doing their best. But even if this were true it did not assuage the family's frustrations and Delia, like the others, felt it increasingly hard to hold fast and keep faith with the bureaucrats.

Delia had long since canceled plans to enroll in the Peace Corps for community development work among Chile's poor. She had been scheduled to go at the end of 1964, but by then it was clear that Everett would not be coming home as soon as they expected. Now she worked full-time for the Santa Clara welfare department among the same under privileged Spanish-speaking families she would have served in Chile. In the community's eyes she was the good Samaritan, an educated young woman who called on the elderly, brought hope to the unemployed and comfort to those in the throes of emotional breakdowns. While she checked their eligibility for financial assistance, applicants took note of how she always insisted upon every child remaining in school. As one of the country's handful of Hispanic female college graduates, Delia had become even more deeply attached to the community through volunteer calls on the schools. Her message never varied: they *must* continue their studies because education was the proven key to better jobs and advancement.

Familiar as she was with so many of these families, it became apparent how the war in Vietnam was spawning even more injustices against her ethnic group. A disproportionate number of its young men were being sent to fight in Vietnam. They all knew it was only because they lacked the educational opportunities to enroll in college, and earn an automatic deferment like countless young men across the country from more fortunate backgrounds.

Frustration about the course of the war grew more intense, and the bickering at home turned nastier. Delia felt the family should become more outspoken and take a stand publicly against the war. Her father would not hear of it, even though he agreed that the war had dragged on for long enough and there seemed to be no end in sight, nor hope of Everett's early repatriation. What they had all accepted as gospel in the early days of the war was now dismissed with varying degrees of anger and cynicism as false and misleading. They had been told they were at war to save democracy in South Vietnam. But television brought them images of South Vietnamese holy men burning themselves alive to protest government injustices. They had watched with dismay as one government coup followed another in Saigon's swirl of political intrigue, and how the corruption had spread to the South Vietnamese armed forces and to the civilian population. Why should America help prop up a regime that showed no signs of wanting to help itself? Delia and her parents began to ask themselves how the communists of the North could really be worse than their enemies in the South. At least the despots in the North were disciplined and dedicated. The family's doubts mounted as every day seemed to bring greater military escalation with nothing to show for it. The rain of bombs did not staunch the flow of men and materiel from North to South Vietnam. The enemy showed no sign of giving up nor any readiness to negotiate, even under the enormous pressure of more than 300,000 U.S. military personnel who had moved into Vietnam within two years of Everett's shootdown.

Vietnam consumed their lives. It was in the morning papers and on the portable transistors. In the evenings they saw it on television. And when the family sat down to relax the talk invariably turned to the war.

The tension was palpable and Madeleine, now in her teens, consciously kept out of the way. Much earlier, she had tried to discuss the routine concerns of a normal teenager with her mother but her father had snapped, "Be a good girl and don't make waves or cause any trouble. Your mother's going through enough tension." So Madeleine turned inward and grew up a quieter adolescent than she might have been, keeping her questions to herself and crying quietly in her room. She had trouble sleeping. There was no one at school to whom she could turn. Even her two best friends had no inkling of what was going on in Southeast Asia and how this had touched her so personally. She talked to them about boys and clothes and movies but never about Vietnam and Everett. Once she had tried but they had looked at her curiously, with blank faces. Their brothers were not involved, so they had no way of feeling her anguish. Her peers knew she was different because Madeleine's name was in the news so often, but they just had no way of relating to her loneliness. The other students didn't shun her but they did set her apart, in a way, because they were over-protective and condescending, giving her the feeling that they knew something was terribly wrong and that they were going to be especially nice to her. How she wished things could be normal like they used to be.

12
TORTURE

THERE WAS NO LET-UP IN THE BRUTALITY OF THE GUARDS
after the Hanoi parade. The excesses of that public frenzy seemed to have
whet their appetites and now they came at us more often. They demanded
we bow whenever in their presence, just as they had done back at the Zoo.
It infuriated all of us and we decided to ignore them.

A few days after we got back from Hanoi, Tom and I were talking in
subdued voices, as always, when a guard sneaked up to our window.

"Bow!" he ordered.

I looked out and saw it was the guard we called J.C., because he strutted
around as if he were Johnny Cool or Jesus Christ himself. A wiry, nasty
thirty-year-old, who spat through moss-colored teeth, J.C. was always dressed
in dirty khakis with rolled-up sleeves.

"No bow! No bow!" I shouted back.

He turned and left, but moments later came back armed with a branch and
thrashed at us through the window. I grabbed the branch and yanked it away
from him. J.C. screamed and cursed before stalking off. It was a dangerous
move on my part; I had acted on impulse without weighing the consequences.

All night long I waited for the repercussions, but nothing happened until
the following morning when the keys rattled in our door lock. There was
nothing we could do but brace ourselves for a beating. J.C. flung the door
open and, accompanied by other guards holding rifles and fixed bayonets,
stormed in. While some of them held Tom at bay, J.C. motioned me outside
and quickly set upon me, lashing out with clenched fists and pounding my
head and body with wild swings. A succession of blows slammed into my jaw
and I felt it give as I tried shielding my face with open hands.

To have struck back or tried to block his attacks would have invited a
punishment far worse than the pain he was inflicting. It would have done no
good pleading for leniency. Most camp guards, like J.C., were thugs with little
or no education. After he had spent himself, he stood over me, a little out

of breath but mean and wild-eyed. He and his cohorts let loose a torrent of insults then hauled me back into the cell and pulled Tom out to work him over. While I nursed my own wounds my heart went out to Tom as I heard the fury of his attackers and the crack of their fists. After they pushed him back in they eyed us furiously then slammed the door shut. At times like this it was good to hear the key turn. It meant we were locked out of their reach and safe again.

My head spun and my ears hummed. With my fingertips, I gently touched my face, trying to dull the stabbing sensations of pain. It felt like an unskilled acupuncturist had skewered my jaw with sharp needles. My jaw in particular was so sensitive that for several weeks I could open my mouth only a fraction, to sip liquid or slowly swallow rice. The blows had dislocated my jaw bone and I was slurring my speech. In the years ahead it occasionally popped out of place, sometimes slipping back of its own accord, failing which, I had to open my mouth as wide as possible, like a snake after devouring its prey, to align the jaw so that I could close my mouth.

A week later they walked me down to a quiz room and Mr. Blue told me to write a letter to the American soldiers in the South, emphasizing the receipt of mail and Red Cross packages and reporting favorably on my treatment. I steadfastly refused to budge. They left me alone throughout the day, denying me food and drink, but made no threats. In the evening they led me back to my room. It took me a few days to connect this attempt at eliciting a propaganda letter with the faint but distinct sound of screams which broke the silence of the nights. It was difficult to pinpoint its source, for every one of the six huts in my area of the Briar Patch was surrounded by its own wall, which deflected sound, and each hut had four rooms, all of whose doors faced different directions. More likely, the gut-wrenching shrieks came from the larger buildings which could have housed many POWs but which our captors used to quiz us one at a time.

On August 5, exactly two years after my capture, they took Paul Kari out of the room next to ours. Days passed before he returned to beat out a loud tap on the dividing wall: "Those-rotten-bastards!"

"What happened?"

"I-couldn't-take-it-any-longer."

He could not tap out anything more that night but over the next few days managed to convey that they had tortured him to extract a confession of crimes and an apology to the Vietnamese people. They had tightened ropes high up on his arms, cutting deep into his skin and blocking circulation so that he had lost much of the feeling in his hands, which were discolored and swollen.

Now we understood the screams in the middle of the nights.

They came for me the next day. I had to roll up my gear and carry it over to the quiz room. I stood in the doorway, dressed in green pajamas and rubber sandles, and bowed.

"You will write apology to peace-loving people of the Democratic Republic of Vietnam. Confess your crimes. Promise never to bomb Vietnam again."

I shrugged. "Heck, no."

Mr. Blue snarled. "You have bad attitude! Do not forget you are air pirate and capitalist warmonger! You are criminal aggressor who has bombed and killed peaceful Vietnamese! You will sit and think about it and you will write confession and apology! If you refuse you will be punished!"

Night fell and I had not written a word. They took me back to my room. Later I heard a tap on the wall. Kari's roommate, J.B. McKamey, had been brought back from his torture session while I was in the quiz room. I acknowledged his signal.

"What's up?" he asked.

I told him.

"God bless."

I asked how he had made out.

Laconically, he replied, "I gave in."

August 9 was my day of infamy. They came in early and again took me to the quiz room. They eyed the blank piece of paper. I tried to make light of it, nervously remarking, "See, I haven't written anything."

"You want me to punish you?"

"Well . . . I guess. . . ."

"That's the only way you're going to get anything."

To help him put on the cuffs, he summoned J.C. I knew what was ahead and prayed I would be able to withstand it. They held my hands behind my back and closed the ratchet cuffs around my wrists, squeezing the metal to the last notch. But my wrists are smallish and they could see that the cuffs were not biting in hard enough. They opened them up, bent my arms as close together as they could and fastened the cuffs tightly a few inches below my elbows. The pain was excruciating. It felt like a hacksaw had stuck deep in my flesh. The cuffs seemed to cut through to the bone. My head was pushed far forward and all I could do was yell and scream to ride with the pain. They left me alone for quarter-hour spells and then returned, yanking my arms up and squeezing the cuffs tighter yet. The worse it got the louder I shrieked. The more I howled the more they slapped and punched. J.C. preferred to strike from behind but when he came from in front it was always with the underside of his closed fist. My eyes felt like popping. My veins wanted to explode in a gush of boiling blood. J.C. was joined by "Ichabod Crane," a spindly 6′ 2″ turnkey with a drooping head, blazing dragonian eyes and clothes that were too short and tight-fitting. Together they worked me over heartlessly, like a couple of kids pulling wings off flies. "Write!" they shouted as they struck with their fists and feet, knocking me off the stool, hoisting me up again and using me as a punching bag.

In the intervals when they left me alone to change my mind and confess, I heard them working over Tom Barrett and Scotty Morgan. Their cries carried full-throated across the gaps between our buildings. I wanted to die, but not even in these extreme circumstances, battered and trussed by metal, could I ever have ended my own life. Somehow I had to ride it out or submit. Desperately I prayed and moaned. I was drenched in my own sweat but felt more acutely the pounding pressure from the blocked blood circulation. I had expected pain of a limited duration, something I could grit my teeth against and endure, not this unrelenting squeeze. Just when I figured they must surely have had their fill, the two sadists returned to their business. They were not going to let up until I had broken or passed out.

By mid-day I knew I had reached the end of my tether. There was no fight left in me. My resistance had been bludgeoned down. I barely had the strength to call an end to it.

"OKAY! TAKE 'EM OFF! STOP IT!"

When they unlocked the cuffs my hands were numb. I saw them attached to the ends of my arms but they looked like frozen gloves. I could not bend the fingers nor cup the palms. They felt like dead-weights. For the first time in my life I felt sheer hatred. What my captors had done was not only unnecessary but barbaric. There was no military advantage to be gained from extracting a "confession." They would use it strictly for internal dissemination, to justify planned tribunals against the U.S. "war criminals."

It took a few hours before I could hold the pencil and when I did, my writing looked like a drunkard's scrawl. What they told me to write was essentially what they dictated to virtually every other tortured POW. The sum total was a confession of war crimes against the peace-loving people of the Democratic Republic of Vietnam. This was coupled with an expression of guilt for raining bombs on their land and a promise never to engage in such high crimes again. I took pains to misspell words to make the confession as phony as possible. But it was the low point of my misery. I felt I had let down the folks at home, betrayed my country. I had vowed to die rather than confess lies yet when the time came I chose not to die. I had been tested and found wanting. I hollered for them to save my skin and this was the price I had agreed to pay. I capitulated during a single morning of torture.

When they took me back to my room that evening, Tom was already there. We looked glumly at each other. He had been through the same torture. They had broken him, too, and he had also sold out.

"August 9," he lamented, "the day we became traitors."

We tried to excuse our treachery, wondering who, back in the U.S.A., would possibly believe the confessions anyway. But it didn't help to think this way because we knew there would always be some people who would be fooled. Worse, still, we could not fool ourselves. We had acted against our basic values and no amount of self-deception would ever convince us otherwise. In the midst of all the soul-searching we promised ourselves that we *would* die rather than submit to anything harmful to a fellow POW. Fortunately we were never put to that test.

Jim Bell, the SRO until Larry Guarino came to the Briar Patch, tapped out a pep talk to bring us out of our black moods. He tried to make us see things in perspective. "You did your best. That's all the Navy or anyone can expect of you." But it didn't really console me, even though I stared helplessly at the effects of the arm torture. The skin on the back of my hands had deadened and turned black. It would be about two years before the natural color returned. I asked myself how much was expected of me, even taking into account that I had been locked up for two years and treated like a subhuman. I still felt lousy. There was no way my head could tell my heart how I felt.

I was uncommunicative during this deep depression and it wasn't fair to Tom. He tried to keep my spirits up.

"C'mon, Ev, let's make a chess set," he said, slipping down into the foxhole beneath his bed board to get some more pebbles.

"Tom, I don't feel like playing chess."

"You want to talk?"

"No."

To make matters worse, the day after we signed our confessions they woke us up before sunrise, fed us and made us put on our long pajamas, even though it was the hottest month of the summer. They handcuffed our wrists behind our backs, closed the shutters and locked the doors. In the evening, during his routine harangue over the camp radio against U.S. air pirates and aggressors, the camp commander announced we would remain handcuffed on a daily basis. It was a precaution against bombing raids and the need to have us fully dressed and secure in the event they had to evacuate us swiftly. After a few days, they substituted ropes for handcuffs.

We sat in the darkened gloom of our sweat boxes for three weeks, with nothing to do but nurse our injuries and brood over our betrayal. Fortunately we managed to work the ropes loose from a single wrist, but we always remained alert to the guards' appearances so we could quickly retie them before the door opened. One day they moved Jim Bell to another location and transferred Tom and me into his cell. From then on until we left the Briar Patch, they allowed us to remove the rope from one wrist but we had to have the other wrist tied at all times. This meant having the rope dangle from one wrist for five consecutive months, and being at the ready to secure the loose end to the other wrist during a hasty evacuation.

They used the empty room next to ours as a torture chamber. Ed Davis, a Navy lieutenant, j.g., was brought in and worked over for almost a week merely because he was overheard talking too loudly with his roommate. They clamped the cuffs high up on his arms and gave him the same brutal working-over they'd given us. It was pitiful listening to his torment. The dividing wall did little to dull the sound of his deafening cries. They accused him of plotting with his roommate. What was the plot? What were his plans? As Ed shrieked his innocence, we could only hope that he would have the will to hold out. Late at night, when we guessed they had left him alone until dawn, we tapped out messages of support. Our strength lay in our unity. Our survival depended on our solidarity.

"Hang in there, buddy. We're with you all the way."

"Goodnight, Ed. God bless."

But his long silences unnerved us. We wondered whether he had passed out, or worse. Hesitantly, we tapped and waited. We tapped again. We had to strain to hear the faint response but it was unmistakably a tap on the wall.

"Ed, you okay?"

"Yeah. I just got the cuffs loose."

"What! How in the hell did you do that?"

"There's a straw broom here. I pulled a piece of straw, bent it over and made it work like a key."

If he was *that* smart he must be holding up okay!

Others had been experimenting with the locks on the cuffs but Ed's success was upbeat news. Like earnest woodpeckers, we sent it out on the wall telegraph to every POW within earshot. Ed's luck, however, was short-lived. While turning over during the night, he accidentally tightened the cuffs and couldn't loosen them because he mislaid his "key". It was harrowing listening to him writhe in such pain.

"We're with you, Ed."

"It's okay," he tapped later. "Sometimes a little pain is good for you."

I marveled at his spirit. That sentence was of great comfort to me down the years.

Septembers had been good to me. It was in that month in my first year that they broke the starvation diet, and exactly a year later that they ended my thirteen months of isolation. I was wondering what this third September would bring when the door opened and the turnkey gestured for Tom to roll up his gear and clear out. A smile broke over Tom's face. There was no doubt he was relieved and even happy to be going. I had been miserable, churlish and grumpy ever since "confessing" on August 9. He could not be blamed for wanting out after ten months in the same rat-hole with me.

Five minutes later Kyle "Red" Dag Berg moved in. My cloistered world was so dismal that it was a tonic to have someone new to talk to and exchange life histories. An Air Force Captain a year younger than me, Red had been shot down in the summer of 1965, the day the Air Force lost seven 105s. Unknown to him, he had been reported missing in action because his wingman didn't see the parachute and the plane went down in a fireball. His year in captivity had been rough. Just before moving in with me, he had been beaten so viciously by the guards, that he was still shaken up. "I'm scared of these people," he whispered. "I don't know what I'll do if they come after me again."

The son of a mathematics professor at Redlands College near San Bernardino, California, Red had moved with his mother, brother and older, deaf stepsister to a little rural community outside of Seattle after his father died. His childhood was idyllic among the farms and wildlife of the sparsely populated countryside, where he lodged with an uncle who made wood shingles. Red often lapsed into daydreams of his youth in the open landscape of the Pacific Northwest, trying to escape the walled reality of our cramped prison quarters where shadows were more plentiful than sunlight. When we reminisced he frequently spoke about flying. He loved planes and talked about every flight being the fulfillment of a passion first felt when he was barely a teenager. If we ever got out of our hellhole he wanted to study business administration so he could run his own airfield for light aircraft.

His easygoing personality was a godsend. In the two years of confinement we spent together he taught me much, from sign language, which he'd learned to communicate with his stepsister, to ribald Air Force lyrics he had sung between swigs of liquor so many eons ago. On a more practical level, he surprised me, the veteran POW, by demonstrating the most effective way to use our shared, jagged-edged tin toilet bucket. The first time he saw me squatting he looked puzzled.

"What's wrong with your shoes?" he asked.

"What do you mean?"

"Why don't you use your sandals?"

I didn't understand.

"Sit on them."

It had never occurred to me to squat comfortably on the rubber sandals placed over the saw-toothed tin edges. What a revelation!

"Jeez! And for two years I've been sitting on the can, thinking about the good old days of a porcelain bowl! What made you think of it?"

"I was doing the same thing you were doing—until someone showed me how to protect my ass!"

The stench was with us all the time. We had long since accepted as normal having to sit a few feet away from each other when one of us had a bowel movement, which was often because we always seemed to come down with diarrhea. There was never enough water to wash the odor off our hands. And though we took daily turns dumping the bucket and swishing the inside with sticks and straw brushes at the well near the bottom of a hill, they never supplied us with any disinfectant. As the tin buckets were not replaced, they developed a hard coating of crap that no amount of cleaning could remove. Though it was the source of the interminable smell, we had to live with the bucket in our sealed quarters day in and day out. The odor was just as bad immediately outside our doors because cows, pigs and chickens drank from the concrete vats and rats frequently drowned and floated in the slimy water where we shaved and washed out cups and plates.

Just as routine were the bugs and insects we ingested with the rice and water. The last meal of the day frequently came when it was already dark, particularly in the winter, and while we ate we would hear the telltale crunch as our teeth bit through the hard outer coverings of live roaches. Sometimes a guard close by would respond to our cussing and shine a light in our direction. That was when we got close-up looks of the insect-infested rice and the live bugs struggling to crawl out of the cups of water. In those brief moments of illumination we had a chance to flick some of the invaders away. Most often, though, the rice was not brought into our cells but left outside for us to retrieve on command. By then the foraging insects of the night had already tracked down the scent and were having themselves a feast.

Most of us came down with diarrhea and then beri-beri through lack of vitamins, fruit, sunshine and exercise. We were also throwing up because the only solid food fed to us for seven straight months was rice, and it was either lukewarm or cold. Like most of the POWs at the Briar Patch, I did not have much of an appetite. But the camp officials instituted a campaign to see that we ate what they gave us. It was not easy to buck them. It was the year we lived on the edge of fear, not knowing what each day would bring. Failure to show respect and servility, bowing the moment they opened the doors, invited a swift, on-the-spot roughing-up. Discretion, in those dark days of terror, was by far the better part of valor.

But there were moments for grins and even belly laughs. We were often caught eating just as U.S. bombers struck close by and the Vietnamese air defenses opened up, their sharp spurts of fire blotted out by the thuds and rumbling of exploding bombs. We continued eating as we stood in the bomb shelter pit below the bed, our arms resting on the concrete floor as the ceiling shook and dust and wood particles fell down. This was what we called our stand-up diner, where we played make-believe.

"Hey, Red, pass the salt, please."

"Salt and pepper coming up. Got any sugar?"

"Sure. You want tea or coffee?"

One day the key rattled in the door and we scrambled to rise to the bowing position. In the rush and confusion I shuffled backwards and accidentally fell into the bomb shelter. J.C. opened the door and looked aghast, unable to believe his eyes. I lay flat on my back, half in the shelter, looking for all the world like I was taking a nap, except that I still held my plate and my head poked quizzically up towards him.

"See, fini! Fini!" I blurted out, at a loss to explain why I seemed to be taking an after-dinner snooze instead of standing up and bowing.

"Ah, eat, sleep," he replied, also caught off balance and unrehearsed.

Phew! It was a close call! When he left Red and I laughed so hard we had tears in our eyes.

Periodically Red and I were hauled off to quiz for a few hours at a time, mostly to answer innocuous questions. They thrust my written confession before me and asked, "Do you really believe this?"

"Hell, no. I don't believe it."

"Why did you write it?"

"Are you kidding me? Why did I write it? Because you damn guys made me write it!"

"What do you believe of this?"

"Well, to be honest I don't believe anything, except my name, rank and serial number."

"You don't believe any of this!"

"No."

So far so good. There was no retribution. But the overwhelming feeling in that year was one of stark terror whenever we heard the guard approaching and jangling his keys. We did not know where he was going nor even his intentions. Primed for trouble, we sat alert as his keys rattled in someone's cell door. At such moments we all tensed up with conflicting emotions. There was pure relief at having been spared one more time, but there was also the sorrow and sympathy felt for the targeted POW whose door had just been opened. These mixed feelings washed through me less than a month after Red moved in, when J.C. ordered him off to quiz. As Red left the room he turned and faced me with the most sorrowful expression. It was the look of a condemned man submitting to his fate. I waited all day and then ominously they came that night for his tin cup and blanket.

Two days later they led me off to quiz. I sat on the stool.

"How are you?"

"Where's Berg?"

"Ah, Berg? He is okay. You are worried about him?"

"Well, I want to know where he is."

He held out a book. "Have you ever seen this?"

It was a book on Ho Chi Minh, one of the pile of propaganda books they'd brought to our room a few days earlier.

"Yeah, I've seen this book before."

He flicked a few pages then held it open.

"What's this?" he asked.

"The flag of the Democratic Republic of Vietnam."

"Good."

He turned more pages.

"And this?"

I smiled. It was a photograph of Ho Chi Minh, but since I'd seen the photograph someone had given him a huge penciled-in black eye.

"Look!" he shouted, quivering as he held it in front of my nose. "You did it!"

"No."

"Yes! You did it! We know you did it! We have tracked it down to you! Berg has confessed! He told us you did this!"

"That's not true! He knows I didn't do it! I didn't even read the book! I didn't touch it!"

"Not so! You did it! You did it! You will confess! You will apologize!"

He set a pen and paper on the table.

"There's nothing to confess. I didn't do it!"

"You will sit and think about it!"

"There's nothing to think about! I didn't do it!" I shouted.

"You will apologize!"

"I'm not going to apologize for something I didn't do!"

I was so angry I got up and started to walk out. Then I threw caution to the winds. "Do anything you want to me, but I didn't do it!"

He paused. "I will talk to the camp commander."

An hour later he returned. "The camp commander is not here. He has gone to Hanoi. But you will go to another room and think about it."

For the following two days I languished in another cramped room with only two feet of walking space at the end of the bed. Through my neighbors' tapping I learned that Red had been held here while they accused him of defacing the picture of their president. They were also pressuring him to write some propaganda letters.

I had no protection against the multitude of mosquitoes though I tried zapping them with open palms to allay my very real fear of contracting malaria. But tiring of this, I lay down at night wrapped in a single blanket like a shrouded mummy, hoping the mosquitoes would not penetrate the small opening left to breathe. They turned out to be the least of my concerns during a restless night of fearful alarm because the room was a main thoroughfare for rats. They scampered over me, their massed shifting weight seemingly unaffected by my rolling movements to try and dislodge them. I lay curled up in the fetal position but the pressure of their prickly feet chilled my skin, sending wave upon wave of goose pimples up my legs and arms. The blanket shielded me from having to witness the frightening sight.

Back in the quiz room, they got straight to the point. "You will write a letter to American pilots flying missions in the south. You will tell them it is wrong and they are criminals. You will tell them to protest to their government."

They herded me into the notorious Blue Room and locked the door. In this small enclosure of blue-painted walls, the feeble bodies of American pilots confronted the simple instruments of betrayal: the stick pen, the bottle of ink, the blank paper—all placed neatly on the plain wooden table. Here was where principles and valor buckled under to limitless physical strain. Here was where honor was measured by days of endurance.

It was November 5. Through the grapevine I knew Tom Barrett was locked up in the adjacent room. I tapped out four words: "Hi, Tom. Happy Birthday!"

"Who are you?"

"Ev."

"Why?"

I told him they wanted letters to the U.S. pilots. He said a lot of the guys had been hauled through this room for confessions. Ron Storz had held out for ten days.

"They let you sit for a while. Then, if they want it bad enough, they put the cuffs on."

It gave me no advantage to be forewarned but the encouragement and support of friends listening in on the other side of the blue walls were as good as double shots of whiskey.

"Hang in there, Ev. Be tough. If you want to sleep during the day, we'll keep watch for you. We'll bang on the wall and wake you up. Try and get naps."

No amount of encouragement could ward off the drowsiness. In the beginning I spent a lot of time concentrating on the changing phases of the moon. My concentration broke when I fell victim to the chill nights. I had no socks and my feet swelled up and felt as if pins were stuck into the soles and toes. As the hours stretched into days I slowly eased into a state of numbed paralysis, seated on the stool like a zombie, too groggy to stand upright and walk, too tired to keep my head from nodding and drooping lower.

"What was that noise?" someone tapped in consternation.

"I fell off the stool," I replied.

The more I dozed off, the more regularly the guards came in to bat me around, slapping and kicking at random and vainly demanding I write. They brought in the regular swill of soup but fatigue left me with less of an appetite. Forbidden to get up and use even the primitive toilet facilities, I managed to contain my bowel movement for some days but I could not hold in my urine. The damp and soiled clothing added to my discomfort, particularly in the cold night hours. After four days of nothing but stolen catnaps I was almost immune to their physical and verbal abuse. They had weakened me to the brink of insensitivity. My mind was clogged and my body heavy with sleeplessness. A guard warned, "If you do not write by tomorrow we will take away all your food!"

The fifth day they withheld both food and drink.

"Let me sleep . . . let me get some sleep," I mumbled.

"First you will write."

"O . . . kay."

I used their garbled, dictated English, mangling it even more by inserting a torrent of extra adjectives. The more grammatically incorrect, the less chance it had of being accepted as authentic by western analysts.

To the Navy pilots flying over Vietnam. Protest against this long, involved, lengthy, durable, expanding, extenuated combat action. . . .

"Ah! It is good!" they beamed.

"Now, can I sleep?"

"No, no. Now you will write letters to the Bertrand Russell Tribunal, to

Senator Fulbright, the U.S. government, the American people, the American students. You will tell them you are against this criminal war."

Bertrand Russell, the British pacifist, was one of the most militant western critics of the war. William Fulbright was the chairman of the powerful Senate Foreign Relations committee.

I sputtered some protests but my resistance had crumbled. "How can I write. I can hardly see straight!"

"You will write the letters!"

They confined me for a sixth night in the Blue Room. When they returned their letters were ready—in comic English.

I protest against the long, involved, costly, controversial, violation war against the gallant, heroic, liberated, freedom-loving, independent-loving Vietnamese people. . . . . . .

Just when I thought the ordeal would end and I could drop off into a mercifully deep slumber, they walked me back to the rat-infested room for another night of snatched catnaps and manhandling. In the morning there was a new demand. "You will read a news article on the camp radio."

"No."

They shoved me out of the room and beyond the camp walls, to a building on top of the hill where I had never been before. From this vantage point I looked down on the hillside, slit with the trenches where they had taken so many of our pilots for punishment, leaving them bound and exposed to the elements, the rats and even the occasional snake.

They had set up a small tape recorder inside the building and told me to read an article about Americans using chemical warfare in South Vietnam. Again, I had to butcher pronunciation, ignore punctuation marks and vary the pace of the story to discredit its content and my belief in it.

"No, no. You must try again. You do not read very well."

"I never could read aloud," I said. "It is difficult."

"You Americans all have the same problem."

They gave me some tea and I cleared my throat for another attempt. This time I tried not to distort so obviously and they accepted it approvingly. The ordeal was over. I was free to go back and sleep.

They never told me to read again but some of the best laughs we ever had in captivity came from Bob Lilly and Dick Bolstad who played with the phonetics of foreign names in their taped news bulletins over the camp radio. They were hilarious. Cambodian Prince Norodom Sihanouk became "Prince No-Good Shnook." They pronounced President Ho Chi Minh as "President Horse-Shit Men." We picked up these mispronunciations and used them when taken to quiz, so that when we said, "Now your President Horse-Shit Men. . . . ." they would correct us and tell us we Americans obviously had great difficulty in pronouncing their names.

Red figured they had called him to quiz primarily to let him see the envelope on the interrogator's desk. It was a letter to me from my wife. I had neither received nor been allowed to send a letter in the previous six months. "They wanted me to see that letter," he said. "There was no other reason for the quiz. All they kept asking me about was my attitude."

The next time they marched him out I had a queasy feeling. There was no way we could forecast how long a quiz might take. He might be back in an hour, a day or weeks. There was always the unspoken fear that he might never return. When we heard the turnkey approach, jangling his keys, every nerve was alert. Cold terror filled our hearts. Which door would he open? Whom would he take? Where would they go? When would they return—if ever?

This time Red was gone for several hours. It was long enough to fear the worst. Then suddenly I saw him walking back along the path to our hut. Unbelievably, he had a smirk on his face, which widened into a huge grin the minute we were alone. He said they had quizzed him about Batman and Robin because they had opened up a letter sent by Red's wife and inside found a membership card for the Batman/Robin Fan Club. His wife had wanted him to know that their two boys, Kim and Kelly, were dressing up as Batman and Robin. Red recounted how the Vietnamese had wanted to know all about Batman. It had not been enough for him to describe them as the forces of good against crime and corruption. The camp officials also wanted to know Batman's political affiliation, the strength of his support, and the cost of club membership. It had taken Red hours to spin out the yarn and satisfy his interrogators!

We were careful not to lower our guards just because of the harmless interlude with Batman. One of the best ways to be prepared for the sudden summons to quiz was to be overdressed. This meant wearing both shirts and trousers for extra insulation against the numbing cold of sleepless nights in the quiz room. As we were not supposed to take socks with us, we tried hiding them under out belts or in our clothing, because, worn over our hands, they were the best protection against mosquitoes. I was baggy with this double layer of clothing when the door opened in early December and the guard motioned me out. Gravely, I turned to Red.

"Take care," he said.

"Yeah."

This time they wanted me to write a letter to the soldiers in South Vietnam, telling them about the "humane and lenient treatment" I was getting. They locked me in the Blue Room and all my shame washed over me anew when I saw the inkwell, the stick pen and the blank paper waiting almost mockingly on the otherwise bare table.

I made immediate contact with Tom.

"Hi, Tom."

"Who is it?"

"Ev."

"Why?"

After I told him, I heard him tap out this information to a POW confined beyond another wall. Our survival depended so much on sharing intelligence. The more informed we were, the less they took us by surprise and the easier it was to prepare common defenses. We had to make it as hard as possible for our captors to isolate us from one another. Knowing what was happening to fellow POWs made it easier to foil attempts to pick us off one by one, or even to play us off against each other. Trying to keep one step ahead of the enemy meant tracking the movements of POWs and flashing news of ups and downs in both physical and verbal abuse. With this rapid exchange of intelligence, we developed a keen sense of their maneuverings. It gave us a fairly accurate reading of their mood swings—a kind of barometer of brutality.

The interrogator came in twice a day, glanced at the blank paper then sternly admonished, "You must write something! You must write to the soldiers in South Vietnam!"

I was physically in better shape and much more alert than on my previous stay in the Blue Room, because I had learned to take catnaps. It was an acquired skill. The trick was to rest and relax but always with an ear cocked for the sound of a key in the door. It also helped that I was doubly wrapped against the cold and that the guards did not slap me around as violently nor as often as they had done before. This time around they seemed to rough me up just to keep me awake. Perhaps it was the approach of Christmas, a time of the year when they were generally more lenient.

I felt the cold creeping up because I did not have a blanket, and then I set to thinking of how harsh they had been with us that year. Ruthless and pitiless, they had escalated their punishments and demands. If they sustained this terror, we very likely would not survive. Who could tell one way or the other whether they would bus us to another parade in Hanoi? The number of pilots captured that year bore witness to the intensity of the bombing and the ferocity of the air defenses. We knew from recent arrivals that there were now almost 350,000 American military personnel in Vietnam. It was a formidable commitment, something absolutely unthinkable twenty-nine months earlier when I had flown in the first reprisal raids against North Vietnam. We POWs could not hope for repatriation in the foreseeable future. That meant hanging in much longer than anyone would have dared predict. It was going to require so much more iron will.

On the fifth day in the Blue Room I realized I was a participant in a contest of wills. They did not really care what I wrote just so long as I gave them a sheet of paper with something on it. I held the pen and wrote, *To the soldiers of South Vietnam. This is what Christmas means to me: Silent night, holy night.* . . . I filled the rest of the paper with the words of the Christmas carol. Happily, it was adequate for the camp official. He scanned it carefully and exclaimed "Good! This is good!"

But he surprised me when, in the next breath he invited me to make a Christmas tape for the family back home. We walked to the building atop the hill and, to my amazement, they gave me a cup of tea before recording my seasonal greetings to Tangee and the whole family. No sooner had I finished than they put me back in the room teeming with rats. What now? I readied myself for the cuffs and the blows but they left me alone. And then, just as unpredictably, they shoved me back in with Red. They told me the tape had malfunctioned and would have to be recorded again. But I had changed my mind, feeling now that it might be used for propaganda to deceive the outside world into thinking we were treated humanely, so I refused to comply. It did not become an issue because they did not insist.

The Christmas spirit brought a measure of sanity to the camp administration and it filtered down even to the lowliest of the guards. Torture sessions came to an abrupt halt. There were no more beatings or kickings. Though still surly, the guards held themselves in check. They cut small branches from the trees, sliced off rounds half an inch thick, and gave us the wooden pieces to scrape off the bark and smooth them out to use in games of checkers.

Christmas cheer permeated the Briar Patch as they handed out paper and cotton so we could decorate the Christmas tree in the quiz room. There was some dissension among the POWs when the camp authorities offered to tape record some of the guys' songs and entertainment for broadcast over the Briar Patch speakers on Christmas Eve. Those who objected felt the tapes might be played elsewhere, lending credibility to the claims of our captors that they were treating us well. Others, however, thought the Christmas tapes would be good for our morale and our unity. We were quickly vindicated as a hush fell over the camp and the speakers crackled with the familiar, albeit nostalgic bounce of *Jingle Bells, Puff The Magic Dragon* and *Amazing Grace,* sung with such deep emotion by fellow captives. We laughed uproariously at one of the entertainers, Master Sergeant Art Black, during his solo performance banging a drum like a kindergartener. It was, he announced tongue-in-cheek, a family tradition at Christmas. Another of the POWs had recorded *Malagueña* on a guitar. It was the first time we had heard our own instrumental music in captivity and it was heartwarming. The songs took effect, particularly the carols. Fleetingly, we forgot about the stench and the rot as we shared remembrances. In those jaunty sounds we heard America again, sprightly, young and fresh. The tunes seemed to waft over the camp like a playful wind, dispelling the gloom and cleansing the squalor. It was a tonic, a refreshing close to an horrendous year.

But the warmth of this festive season was short-lived. The biting cold of January struck remorselessly. Perched at a high elevation, the camp grounds were frosted over at dawn and we were thankful to have the shutters closed most of the day. By 5 P.M. the gray skies had already blackened for the mournfully short winter days. Red and I shivered in our misery. We huddled close to each other on a single bed board. Each of us had two ultra-thin blankets and we spread a mosquito net over us for added insulation. Knowing that the chill had weakened us to the bone, we lived in constant dread of another summons to the Blue Room or to the chamber of rats.

Our luck held out. We escaped further quizzing through the end of January, when a guard made the rounds of all the rooms, thrusting before the inmates a handwritten note in English. *Prepare to wrap all your gear tightly. Tonight you will be REMOVED.* We chortled, like the rest of the POWs, at the misuse of the English language. It was dark when they blindfolded and handcuffed us in pairs then squeezed us aboard a bus already brimming with household goods, pots and pans and caged chickens and pigs.

Was this it! Were we going home at last! Is that why they stopped the torture and softened up at Christmas? Perhaps, but I did not let myself get carried away. Experience had taught me to keep a tight rein on expectation to avoid the pain of letdowns. Besides, we had not got word of any breakthrough towards a cease-fire or peace. It seemed unlikely our repatriation would be so sudden and unheralded.

When the bus driver finally cut the engine we knew we were not in a city or a port. There were no sounds of traffic nor the bustle of pedestrians. Clearly we had been brought to an isolated area. They walked us into a building and removed our blindfolds. At once I knew our location. We were back in the Zoo, just a couple of miles south of the Hanoi Hilton.

19th February, 1967

My Dearest Tangee,

Hi Sweetheart! Boy it was sure good to hear from you again. . . . I received your letter on the Vietnamese Tet or Lunar New Year. We had a big meal that day, with coffee and extra cigarettes. This is the big annual celebration in this country and the people had 7 or 8 days of celebration. . . . Winter is almost over. I made it through catching one cold which lasted only a few days. I suppose I have sort of become used to the climate. . . . The rain you describe is just how I remember the usual winter rain showers at home; the way the drops of rain cling to the colorful leaves and bushes, usually giving everything a fresh and unusually bright appearance. . . . I only wish I were there with you to enjoy all this once again. I too hope and pray for the day we can be together once again. Like you said Tang, it can't be too soon. . . . I know what I have when you say that you are waiting for me. I love you very much, and I always will. You can be sure of that. . . .

All my love, Your husband, Everett.

Tom, Red and I were living in the same room when we ate our first bread in eight months. It was laid out for us on a rickety table on the porch not long after our arrival back at the Zoo. Also, there was the first salt given to me since captivity two-and-a-half years earlier. However, the staple diet at the Zoo remained rice, with sewer greens in the winter and pumpkin soup in the summer. The sewer greens were the leafy wild plants with the texture of spinach, that flourished among the slime and algae in the ponds around the camp. Peasant girls and women, who carried the water around the camp in buckets at the ends of long poles, used to wade into the ponds and scoop up the plants. They boiled the green weeds, and chopped them up before depositing the shriveled mass on our plates outside our rooms. Though probably rich in iron, it tasted foul.

We still craved the sweetness of something with sugar, a delicacy they had never given any of us, and though we pleaded with them incessantly, we never expected them to yield. Then suddenly, in mid-1967 they brought us the regular bowl of rice with a surprise plate of white sugar and a spoon for each POW. We mixed the rice and sugar and it tasted magnificent. There wasn't a man among us who didn't gobble it down. But a plate of sugar was often the only food served for dinner and after a while it lost its appeal, unless eaten with bread or some other compatible solid.

Though we were all thin and frail from the putrid diet, they did not let up on the physical torture and indiscriminate harassment. At random, POWs were driven to the Pool Hall, bound with ropes and violently abused to extract information on our chain-of-command and details of our camp communications system.

However childish the rules, they were enforced rigorously. A U.S. bombing raid was so close to our camp that we heard the rumblings and felt the vibrations. The planes struck what appeared to be a truck depot and an ammunition dump. When they finally got the blaze under control they took Red Berg to quiz and shortly afterwards returned, ordering Tom and I to roll up our gear and follow them to the Shed, a darkened utility shack in the southeast corner of the Zoo, which was lit up only at night.

Red was already there and after they locked our ankles into leg-irons so we couldn't roll over, and handcuffed our hands behind our backs, he told us we were all being punished because of the way he had answered a question at quiz. They had asked him what he thought of the air raid and he had replied that a motor pool was an obvious target. It was not the answer they had expected or encouraged so they yanked Red off to see bomb fragments lodged in some of the camp's wooden shutters, then scolded him for the way he had answered them. The upshot was that the three of us were collectively punished, cursed persistently for our "bad attitude" and immobilized for a week in the Shed. Fortunately it did not rain because two POWs who were there shortly before us had yelled frantically for help when a large poisonous snake slithered under the door during a storm. Luckily for them it had happened at night, when the light was on, and a guard was able to find it and beat it to death.

We were allowed out of the Shed for only ten minutes a day to dump our waste bowls and wash up. For a solid week we could neither roll over on our bellies because our feet were locked in position, nor lie down on our backs for fear of tightening the handcuffs. The answer was to turn our torsos slightly to try and rest on our sides. But there was no solution to the greater problem of Tom's diarrhea. By sitting up and painstakingly working the bowl upwards, I tried to edge it closer to him.

"How's it going? Can you make it, Tom?"

"Can't see very well," he strained. "Try moving the bowl a little over here. . . ."

"Okay now?"

"No," he grunted, feeling the iron biting into his legs. "Wait . . . agh . . . oh, forget it," he sighed.

And then, unable to contain himself, he had to let the excrement splash out. Unable to wipe himself because his arms were handcuffed, Tom lay covered in his own filth. He started to snigger. Then Red and I giggled. Before long we were all convulsed with laughter, whooping at the absurdity of our ridiculous misfortune.

At the end of the week they freed us from the leg irons and the handcuffs and took us back to our room, warning, "In future, you must have correct attitude!"

That summer they moved Tom and me to a small room created by bricking up a portion of the hallway in the Auditorium. We constantly spied through the narrow slits of our louvered door. It provided a good view of the camp, enabling us to keep tabs on everyone walking by, especially those we knew were on their way to quiz. As I pressed my face close to the door and squeezed my eyes like a sniper taking aim, I drew in my breath.

"Holy smokes, Tom. I just saw two guys walk by and one of them was Ev Southwick!"

"There's nobody called Ev Southwick here," Tom replied.

"That was Ev Southwick!" I said firmly. "I got to know him when his squadron flew onto the *Constellation* four years ago."

We took turns watching even more intently and several hours later, I saw Southwick return.

"That's him! That's Ev Southwick."

"Nah," Tom said. "There's no one by that name here."

But a couple of days later, as we communicated with other POWs, they reported one of the new guys in the camp was a Charles Southwick.

"You see," said Tom, "You said his name was Ev Southwick. It's not. It's Charles Southwick. It's not the same guy."

I shook my head. "That was Ev Southwick. I'm sure!"

We sent a message to the men who had originally given us his name. "Confirm Southwick's first name or nickname."

It took about a month for the reply to get back. "Charles Everett Southwick."

"You see, Tom, I don't forget faces!"

Not long after, as Tom and I sat on our tiny beds set head-to-head against the wall, the guards ordered us outside and detailed us to sweep the roads and paths with brooms. It did not keep us outdoors for long but it gave us a new advantage. Freed from the dulling shadows of our bolted cells, we were sharp and alert in the open sunlight, our eyes and ears acutely sensitive to every stir and sound. Compared to monitoring movements through the louvered door, this was sleuthing on a grand scale. We fed every scrap of information into the invisible POW network, especially the movements of those we monitored coming in and out of the camp. And by scraping our brooms against the ground, using the same code tapped against walls, we secretly made contact with men locked up in other rooms.

One morning while Tom was away at quiz, I was alone in the cramped quarters and perspiring in the tropical heat. Quite suddenly I thought I had crapped in my shorts. I took them off and something plopped to the floor. It was an eight inch pinkish worm. Startled, then horrified, I screamed for the guard. "Bao Cao! Bao Cao!"

When he came in I pointed to the worm and told him to call the medic. Instead, an exceptionally thin interrogator we called the Weasel, appeared.

"Uh, huh," he said anti-climactically.

"What's wrong?" I demanded. "Tell me! What's wrong!"

"You have parasite," he said.

"That's bad!" I said, filled with alarm.

"No, no. It is good," said the Weasel, turning to leave. "In Vietnam everyone has parasites. It is good if you have parasites. If you do not, then you bloat."

I was dumbfounded. But as with everything else at the camps, I soon got used to having them. About every three months they came out on schedule, preceeded always by three or four days of severe stomach cramps that left me doubled up as if I had swallowed poison. On one occasion, while I was living in the Barn, I passed a whopper some fifteen inches long. I named it Wilbur and left it where the guys dumped their bowls so they could see it. Though some of the other POWs also passed worms, I was among the few who never suffered from the more common and equally painful boils.

Punishment was meted out almost capriciously. On one occasion they told me I would have to meet with an unspecified delegation. When I refused to go, guessing it was another propaganda stunt, they again took me to the Carriage Shed, so named because it had swing doors through which they used to haul a wagon. There they made me kneel with my arms extended straight up. I must have knelt for four hours, during which the guard beat me persistently, especially when I had to drop my arms through sheer fatigue. Then they roped my ankles together and bound my arms behind my back. For two days I lay on the concrete, defenseless against the guard who burst in half a dozen times each day to punch me around.

Only when they untied me was I able to make contact with J.J. Connell, a uniquely brave Navy lieutenant, who faked the incapacitation of his hands and arms because of the torture a year before. He was being held in solitary confinement in the Gatehouse, a building opposite mine on the other side of the camp entrance. Before his incarceration there, we had seen him shuffling around the camp. Though he had once had a muscular body and had even wrestled while at the Naval Academy, J.J. let his arms dangle uselessly like a marionette's and if he had to use them, like picking up a bowl, he fumbled with the palms of his hands, feigning difficulty in holding onto anything. He looked like a pathetic Sad Sack, lopping his deformed body across to the wash area, his arms dreadfully scarred, his neck bent down and his shaven head tipped sideways and up.

It was all done to avoid being called on to write propaganda statements.

With crippled arms he could not be expected to hold a pen, much less write with it. But his deadly gambit was a double-edged sword. Having made out that he had lost the use of those limbs he could never reverse his role. When the guards beat him and even wired him for electric shock treatment to put him to the test, he had no option but to play the part to the hilt. If they pushed him from behind he could not break the fall with his hands so he would land flat on his face. This remarkable hoax lasted for the four years that we knew of his whereabouts. Even though the Vietnamese suspected he was having them on, he never once confessed. It was a classic lesson in courage and a testament to the lengths to which a patriot would go in refusing to compromise his country.

J.J. was holed up alone in a dark sweat box no more than eight feet long by six feet wide. His window on the world was through a peephole in the door and, higher up, through the single ventilation space no bigger than a regular brick. Despite these handicaps, he triumphed as the self-appointed nerve center of our communications network, partly because the Gatehouse was closest to the camp's main entrance, and also because he was a talented spy. J.J. was like a sentry, keeping a watchful eye on all movements in and out of the Zoo. He fed back the information furtively, using the one-handed American Sign Language Manual Alphabet for the hearing-impaired which Red Berg had taught me the year before, and which had then spread throughout the camp for use whenever POWs were in visual contact with one another.

He was particularly adept at relaying information from prisoners held for torture in the Carriage Shed. This way we knew who was being worked over, how badly, and for what purpose. During my spell in the Carriage Shed I had to hoist myself up to the top of the door before signaling through the wooden latticework above it. I could see J.J.'s hand very clearly, sometimes behind his four-by-four-inch square peep-hole and at other times motioning from the ventilation space higher up. He assured me he was feeling okay but he cautioned me to be very careful when communicating with him.

"Don't let them see you communicating with me because I don't want them to catch on," he signaled.

J.J. said his squadron had been on the *Constellation* the year after I was shot down. Before that he had been at Lemoore Naval Air base with his wife and child. We exchanged information on mutual acquaintances. He seemed to know the whereabouts of just about everyone in the camp and filled me in on the comings and goings of POWs and Vietnamese officials in and out of the camp. His faith throughout remained strong and he invariably signed off with the words, *God Bless*.

A few days after the guards took me out of the Carriage Shed, they handcuffed and blindfolded me and took me by truck to Hanoi, where they led me up some stairs to the rooftop of a building. The guard indicated during the swift photo session that the cameraman was a Russian. He was apparently the unspecified delegation I had earlier refused to meet with and the reason they had thrown me into the Carriage Shed.

13
FIDEL

DESPITE OUR BEST EFFORTS TO KEEP INFORMED, NOT ONE of us picked up any hint of why they worked us so hard outdoors in mid-August, 1967. For two weeks we collected litter and removed trash, trimmed bushes, cut the grass, tidied up flower beds and swept the grounds. The turnkeys and guards who watched over us walked around at dusk, surveying the neat landscape and looking for flaws to be corrected the following day.

Instead of going home in the evenings, as was usual, the camp commander stayed overnight. We nicknamed him Lumpy because of the large lump on his forehead, and because he was fatter and rounder than the other Vietnamese and resembled the cartoon character of the same name. Lumpy regularly dressed in a khaki-colored Mao-tse-Tung tunic buttoned up to his neck below his bulging Adam's Apple. While he sat on his porch talking animatedly with subordinates, we speculated that he must be preparing for the arrival of a Vietnamese big shot. Or perhaps the beautification project was designed to deceive an inspector from the International Red Cross. We could only guess because none of us had picked up any firm intelligence.

At the end of August, the object of our curiosity drove up unannounced in a green sedan just after the guards sealed us in at dusk. Lumpy led the camp staff in a thunderous roar of welcome. Before anyone could glimpse the VIP, however, he was swallowed up in the crush of Vietnamese moving towards the headquarters building. Not long after, we heard them singing and partying. We wondered whether the Vietnamese had not felt cheated because the visitor had slipped in at night and not seen the results of the beautification.

The following dusk Tom was peeking through the slits in our door when he exclaimed excitedly, "Ev! It's the same sedan that came in last night!"

Before long the doors of the Garage slammed and we saw a POW taken off to quiz. Another followed soon after. Then a turnkey we called Pimples pushed open our door, pointed in my direction and ordered me to follow.

I stood at the door of the quiz room, surprised to see what looked like a

181

foreign delegation of two seated on either side of Lumpy. On one side of the camp commander sat a tall, bulky man with thick jet black hair rising straight up. Of fair complexion, he looked like a slightly less rugged version of the movie star, Anthony Quinn. His white shirt was unbuttoned and I could see his blue pants were neatly pressed above pointy-toed shoes. The other visitor, also Caucasian, was much smaller and older with graying hair. He wore a white T-shirt. Even though a fan revolved behind them, the room remained stiflingly hot. I bowed to Lumpy but it was the large visitor who spoke.

"Sit down!" he ordered with a commanding tone to his voice.

It surprised me that he showed no deference to Lumpy, who looked detached as he sucked on a pencil.

"What's your name?" the heavy visitor growled in an accent I couldn't place.

I was still sizing him up, wondering where he could have come from and what his purpose was when he snapped, "I asked what your name was!" He stood up so that his bulk now loomed much more intimidatingly. "Don't you hear well?"

"My name is Alvarez."

"Ah, Alvarez. Alvarez. What's your first name?"

"Everett," I replied, wondering what was happening and beginning to feel threatened.

"You speak Spanish?"

"Yeah."

"You a Mexican?"

"No."

"C'mon! Your mama and your papa?"

"They were born in the U.S.A."

"And their mamas and papas?"

"From Mexico."

"Uh-huh!"

He sat down and as he did so, I felt the fear of imminent terror recede somewhat, even though he held me fast in a riveting glare.

"Here, have a cigarette," he said, offering an open pack of a Vietnamese brand.

I shook my head.

"What's your rank?"

"Lieutenant, junior grade."

"When were you shot down?"

"August 5, 1964."

He paused but betrayed no emotion.

"What were you flying?"

I wasn't about to oblige him with military information. The Vietnamese had not had such an easy time forcing me to sign their fictional confessions. They'd had to beat it out of me.

"Well," he demanded, "what were you flying?"

"I was flying an airplane."

He turned sharply to Lumpy and the other visitor then back at me. His face flushed and the skin above the bridge of his nose furrowed.

"AN AIRPLANE! AN AIRPLANE! HE'S FLYING AN AIRPLANE!" he boomed. "Wise guy, uh! So you're a f---ing wise guy!"

Again he stood up and towered over me, his eyes straining to pop and his hands curling into ominously clenched fists.

"You're looking for trouble, eh, wise guy! You want trouble, you got it right here!"

I hoped Lumpy would temper the visitor's outrage but the camp commander continued to look cooly up at the ceiling, indicating a hands-off attitude.

"You a wise guy, eh?" the monster asked, daring me to answer affirmatively.

"No," I replied.

"Okay, okay."

He stood low to whisper to the little guy in the white T-shirt who, like Lumpy, chewed on a pencil.

"He's a pretty wise guy, isn't he," the hulk said to the older visitor.

"Yeah, he sure is," came the reply in better-accented English.

Then, to my relief the bulkier man sat down.

"Look Everett," he continued in a mollifying tone, "I don't want to give you any trouble. I don't want any trouble from you. I'm just asking a few questions like a decent human being. Why can't you answer my questions?"

"Well, I don't know who you are."

"It doesn't make any difference who I am," he replied, still trying to be amiable.

"I don't know who you are or what you are," I said.

"Okay, Everett. Here, have a cigarette. Go on. You're not very cooperative. I offered you a cigarette and you wouldn't take it. What's wrong?"

"I don't smoke very much."

"You don't *smoke* very much! C'mon. Have a cigarette! They're much better than those shitty little perfumed Chesterfields!"

"Okay."

He inhaled deeply and blew the smoke out towards the ceiling.

"You married?"

"Yes."

"What's her name?"

"Tangee."

"What does she do? She got a hobby?"

"She's an artist."

"Ah! Very good! An artist!"

"Yeah."

"So you're married, eh? Well you better start showing a good attitude. You ought to think about your position. You know, realize where you are."

He launched into a long diatribe, swearing like a drill sergeant against the United States, and getting most heated up in cussing Americans for their treatment of minorities, especially blacks and Hispanics. Then he bellowed against the U.S.A. for its "criminal aggression" against the people of Vietnam.

"You guys really think you're hot, don't you! Hot Yanks! But all you sons-of-bitches do is take the best from everyone else and give them your crap in return. You're all full of shit! Look what you did in Cuba! You bastards took sugar! And what do you give back? You sell them Coca-Cola! You take bananas from other countries! And what do you teach them? You teach them how to make milk shakes! Yanks, eh! And what do you do when you move into foreign countries? You screw their women! Their girls! Yankees make whores out of everyone's women—wherever you go! You screw up every place you move into! Then you wonder why they shout 'Yankee, go home!' "

He leaned over to whisper to Lumpy. The camp commander opened his mouth for the first time that evening to speak a few words of English.

"You want to put him in there?" Lumpy asked, pointing to the Chicken Coop where I knew they clamped leg irons on POWs before torturing them.

"No, no, no," said the visitor. He looked me over as if I were scum. "Go on back to your room. Maybe I'll see you again."

I stood up to leave but he held me in his withering stare as if asking, "Well, aren't you going to bow?"

I bowed deeply and slowly, as we had been instructed, then left the room.

Back in the cell I was almost speechless, still stunned by the confrontation. I warned Tom, "if they come for you, don't piss the guy off. For Chrissake be nice to him!"

I was still troubled by his accent and it didn't hit me until the next morning when a guard left Larry Spencer to wash up in the area between us and the guys in the Pool Hall. We overheard Larry say the VIP had ordered him placed in leg irons in the Chicken Coop. "He's a Caucasian!" Larry whispered.

Of course!

"Tom! The guy's a Cuban! I swear he is! He talked to me like 'your mama and your papa.' Things like that. I'm sure of it now!"

Pretty soon we were all referring to him as Fidel.

They came for Tom that night. And then it was my turn again, before Tom returned.

I bowed at the door.

"Sit down," Fidel ordered. "How are you?"

"Fine, sir."

"How are you feeling today?"

"Fine."

He paused. "I see you have reconsidered. You are much more pleasant tonight. Much more pleasant. That's good. Better attitude. Much better attitude. Now you are maybe worthwhile to be treated better. You must remember always where you are and why you are here."

Again, as he chain-smoked, he lectured me on the evils of Yankee imperialism and greed, reminding me that I did not deserve to be kept so well by the victims of U.S. crimes.

"Last night I asked you what you were flying and you gave me a wise-ass answer! You told me you were flying an airplane! An airplane!"

I shifted uncomfortably as he eyed me thoroughly, looking for hidden weak spots.

"What kind of car did you drive?"

"A '64 Buick Skylark."

"How much did it cost?"

"$3200."

"You didn't give me the right answer! You are lying!"

"I'm telling the truth. It was brand new."

"Nah. . . ."

He turned to his older colleague, whom we nicknamed Chip.

"Is that a good figure?"

"Yes," said Chip.

"Umph!"

He looked me square in the eye. Then he spoke paternally, as if he cared what happened to me.

"Look, Everett, you have to take care of yourself. You've got a wife. You want to go home. You don't know how long you're going to be here. You have to think about these things, Everett. We don't want to hurt you."

Reunited, Tom and I found we had been through identical quizzes. And he, too, had been warned to keep a good attitude at all times. But then reports filtered in through the tap code that Fidel was sending more guys to be placed in leg irons. One day he walked around the camp in daylight, looking over the buildings like some lordly overseer. He towered over the short, spindly Vietnamese, making them look like a tribe of lowly pygmies. And when he lounged on Lumpy's porch, sipping tea with the camp's top administrative officers, Fidel looked to all intents and purposes like Gulliver in an oriental Lilliput.

Three weeks after Fidel's first appearance, they separated Tom and me. He was taken over to the Stable and I moved in with Red Berg and George Hall in the Garage, located just in front of the Carriage Shed. Of the eleven guys Fidel had called to quiz, I was the only one he left more or less alone after that initial grilling. Some of us speculated much later that he left me alone on orders from the Vietnamese, who may have considered me "their own."

Fidel was given a quarter of the camp's acreage to carry out what we called his Cuban program. Within his domain he was an absolute dictator, not responsible to any higher authority. Every time his torture broke a man, the victim was placed in a room with those who had already submitted. By Christmas of that year he finally had all ten, including Tom, in the same room. They were close to being automatons, broken by the repetitive assault on their exhausted bodies.

The towering Cuban enjoyed the unequal test of wills and the painful binding of his victims into certain capitulation. He had one end in mind: to assert his dominance. He did this by crushing their independence and getting them to do his will, no matter what it took. We sensed that he was dissatisfied with the previous policy of the Vietnamese, which included bouts of torture, but which also acknowledged that we always seemed to bounce back with our communications and organizational structure intact. Fidel apparently wanted to savage us to such an extent that no man would dare buck the system. He wanted us to be totally compliant, and that meant bashing our brains into putty. He may even have hoped to institute a release program, using his broken captives for maximum propaganda effect, through broadcasts and other means, culminating in POWs expressing gratitude on being released. This theory gained credence much later in Fidel's program when Tom Barrett turned down an offer of early release, contingent on his making a propaganda tape against the U.S. and apologizing to the Vietnamese people for "war crimes."

Shortly after Christmas, Fidel quizzed three new arrivals from the Hanoi Hilton and threatened them with a taste of his brutality. Ens. Chuck Rice, who'd been captured three months earlier, didn't believe Fidel until the Cuban moved him into the room with those who had already submitted. Immediately, Rice's morale plummeted when he learned that some of the

men had been held POW for as long as two years. Then he heard first-hand
how Fidel had broken each of them. At that point, the veterans urged Rice
to try another tactic. Sooner or later Fidel would get him anyway. He was
sure to buckle, just as all the others had. Why not try and outwit the Cuban
with some new ploy? So when Fidel confronted Rice, asking him what he was
going to do, the newcomer said, "What do you want me to write? Tell me
where I have to sign." It so surprised the big Cuban that he asked, "What
do you mean? Will you write what I say?"

"I'll write anything," said Rice, taking a calculated risk.

"Will you do what I say?"

"I'll do anything," said Rice, calling Fidel's bluff as he picked up a pen.
"Give me that paper. I'll sign anything."

Fidel balked. "Well, that's okay. That's all I want to know. Go back to your
room."

It was almost as if Rice had played possum and the Cuban had backed off.
Like the coyote, Fidel needed first to toss his prey into the air and paw it
playfully before feasting on it.

Ironically, his ruthless cruelty caused his own downfall. For reasons known
only to himself, he singled out two Air Force officers, Capt. Earl Cobeil and
Maj. James Kasler, for intensive beatings. Day after day, for weeks on end,
Fidel whipped them mercilessly with rubber hoses. The two men held out
in a remarkable display of courage, refusing to break. Cobeil was so limp that
he could no longer feed himself. When electric shock treatment failed to
bring him out of his physical slump, Fidel ordered him thrown back in with
the other men in the program. Cobeil's roommates force-fed him in a desperate attempt to keep him alive. He was a pitiful, skeletal figure when the guards
came one day to take him away, and we never saw him again. Everyone
assumed, as we did when other men vanished over the years after torture
sessions, that Cobeil was dead. Sadly, this was confirmed after our release.

It was a hollow victory for Fidel. Cobeil's fate marked the point at which
even the camp officials became disenchanted with him. Up until then, the
Vietnamese appeared to have given Fidel a free rein. They watched him
guardedly, however, because they were somewhat sensitive to the currents of
world public opinion. The camp officials must have told Fidel to back off after
Cobeil's murder because he never again worked over the POWs so sadisti-
cally.

We knew his claws had been pulled when we sensed his loss of standing
among camp officials. Emboldened, those who were in the program changed
their attitude towards him, becoming cocky and irreverent. They swore at
him and he cussed back, treating them differently now, having taken their

measure and found them extraordinarily brave. While Fidel considered himself a jack-of-all-trades, the guys regarded him as a jerk and many times told him so. "You're full of shit," Glen Perkins frequently told him. Fidel, who now acknowledged our chain of command, would turn on Jack Bomar, the senior ranking officer, and sneer, "Jack, that Glen Perkins doesn't have a good attitude!" But Bomar, who was nutty about cars, was just as critical of Fidel, who prided himself on his own expertise when it came to automobiles. One of the old cars in the camp was forever breaking down and Fidel would shove the ignorant Vietnamese driver aside, raise the hood and try to fix it. "You don't know anything about cars," Jack said scornfully. "That's not the way to do it!"

The macho Cuban was even more of a bumbler in dreaming up absurd construction projects. When he assembled the POWs to explain how to make an adobe oven he was woefully ignorant and Perkins again told him he was full of shit.

"What do you mean!" Fidel thundered. "You assholes never made adobe in your lives!"

Fidel's views prevailed because he was too proud to learn, but the adobe oven never materialized. It ended up almost pure mud and they tore it down without ever using it. The same fate befell the fish ponds which Fidel tried to build within the camp grounds. It was obvious to all that they would not hold water and besides, the banks were too soft. One day Fidel grasped a tree branch overhanging a bank by the side of a pool. Suddenly the branch snapped, the bank subsided and he tumbled into the pool. The men who witnessed it could not contain themselves and his humiliation was complete.

For his part, Fidel could not hide his low opinion of the Vietnamese. He considered them imbecilic because they were so inept when it came to anything mechanical. His frustration mounted, especially if he ordered the POWs to do something and the Vietnamese countermanded, insisting it be done their way. Bomar would complain, "Fidel, you told us what to do, we started it your way, now the Vietnamese come along and tell us to do it their way!"

"Jack, I know," said Fidel irascibly, "Just go along with it for now!"

The more familiar the POWs were with Fidel the more they seemed to ridicule him. After one heavy bombing raid by U.S. aircraft, Fidel grasped Bomar's arm and made him stand on a table to look at the smoke rising in the distance.

"Look what your pilots are doing! Look at that damage where the smoke is! Did you see how the brave Vietnamese people fought back?"

Just then a rooster crowed.

"And listen to that valiant cock crow!" said Fidel, carried overboard in the enthusiasm of the moment.

The remark flashed around the camp and wherever it was repeated it had the guys in stitches. We had not laughed so much in years.

But we were careful not to push him too far. He still had authority, even though he reeked of alcohol and looked haggard, tired and hung over. One morning I was sweeping a roadway when he stopped and stared at me from little more than a yard away. I was so startled that I returned his stare. Fidel scowled. His face was mean and contorted and he was daring me to stand up to him. I blinked and got on with my road sweeping work.

Towards the end, this misfit from the Caribbean was the very model of a loner. The expatriate had clearly lost all ardor for his tasks. He roamed sluggishly, like a castrated bull.

Raucous sounds of partying broke the quiet of the camp grounds exactly a year after Fidel's arrival. We figured it might be his going-away party because he had not been around for some time. It turned out we were right. No one ever saw the Cuban again and the relief was unanimous.

Throughout the time Fidel was at the Zoo, and for six months after his departure, we also had to put up with what we dubbed the "Kiddy Program." Haughty boys who looked like they were fresh out of high school hauled us in to quiz, making us sit for hours on end, in the mornings and again in the afternoons, answering inane questions in broken English about our way of life and Vietnam. We figured it was a training program, with us as live dummies, for them to improve their English and see what real Americans looked like. The sessions degenerated into silliness, sorely testing our patience.

"What you have in house? What clothes you wear?"

"What you know about Vietnam? Do you understand?"

"What? What did you say?"

It was difficult concentrating for any length of time and in the summer they made it additionally hard by making us dress in long-sleeved shirts and trousers despite the humidity.

Alternating with the Kiddy Program in early 1968 were the propaganda tapes aired over the camp radio, also for several hours in the morning and afternoon. Again, we had to dress in winter wear and sit attentively on our bed boards as the squawk boxes emitted a stream of vitriol against colonialism, imperialism and capitalism while extolling the virtues of Vietnam. The guards held spot checks, eyeing us through the peepholes in the door. If they caught us walking around, lying down, or dressed improperly, they meted out immediate punishment. Some of these tapes were made by POWs who gave their names and begged forgiveness of the government and people of Vietnam. Though some said they were treated well, we never heard from them again and no one ever saw them in the camps. The quality of their recordings was never good, but we always assumed they had broadcast under duress.

The threat of violence never diminished. It was always there, whether open and undisguised or indirect and roundabout. One day, a Vietnamese we called Spot because of the white birthmark on his chin, summoned me to quiz.

"Alvarez," he said, "you were the first criminal shot down."

"What of it?"

"Do you want to be the last one to go home?"

"That's not up to me," I replied.

"Yes, it is. It depends on your attitude. What will you do?"

"I'm not going to do anything special to get out first," I told him.

"Look, Alvarez, you must realize something. Your attitude is very bad. Understand one thing. We have you like this." He cupped his hand as if holding my testicles. "We can make you do anything we want."

"You can make me do it. But not of my own free will."

"We can make you do anything!" he repeated tersely.

These unpromising circumstances were not peculiar to me. But they made all of us keenly aware of the need to hold onto our organizational structure and group unity.

We held together through the communications system. It became our lifeline and by the summer of 1968, when I moved into Dick Ratzlaff's room in a building we called the Office, we were using the mute sign language of the deaf as often as the tap codes. To reach up to the air vent and maintain hand signals with those outside our Office building, I would often stand on the shoulders of Dick, a newly-married Navy lieutenant j.g., when shot down in March, 1966. In this manner information frequently passed between Red Berg and myself while he was inside the Pigsty or when he came to wash up by the well behind our building. Contact with one another was as essential as a deep-sea diver drawing on a reserve tank of oxygen. Without it, we were doomed. We could not permit our coded links to be silenced nor our invisible bonds to be sabotaged. POWs withstood all measure of painful torture to preserve the secrecy of our intelligence network. This commitment to unity saw many a lame and hobbled individual through the darkest days and the most perilous moments. It fueled our morale and stiffened our backbone. Above all, it kept us informed of what had happened to others and what we could expect. To be forewarned was to be forearmed. We all knew how doubly important it was to try and keep in touch with those manacled and roped in solitary confinement. It was vital to keep up their spirits. As long as a man had his hearing he could still receive messages beaten on the wall and decipher the persistent coughing beyond his cell. And if he had unimpaired vision he was equipped to read the silent language transmitted by another's moving fingers. We peeked out of every tiny crack or hole in the doors to try and keep abreast of the comings and goings in the camp. Like the deaf and the blind, we sharpened our remaining senses. Inevitably, we became nimble spies and artful communicators.

There was no let-up in the glut of propaganda over the air waves. Perhaps in our weakened condition they hoped we would be more susceptible to their doctrinaire thinking. Every evening they relayed the *Voice of Vietnam* and if we listened closely we could extract some nuggets of news stuffed deep inside the thicket of communist platitudes. That was how we first got wind of the peace talks in Paris. Briefly, it galvanized all of us, and when we heard about the bombing halt, some speculated we might even be out within three months. But the veterans among us had experienced too many false alarms. We were careful not to be swept up in the initial headiness because the downside was always so bitter. Once again, we were proved right when the two sides squandered time arguing over the shape of the conference table.

I remained convinced that the only way we were going to get out of there was to bomb the hell out of the Vietnamese. We had to force their hand. The on-again/off-again occasional precision strikes didn't hurt. They were nothing but pinpricks. All of us had been shot down conducting limited warfare. POWs shot down just before the bombing halt in the spring of that year reported the U.S. was attacking the same roads and bridges over and over. It proved the ineffectiveness of the bombing and the resilience of the enemy. A change of policy was needed. We had to remove all restrictions and send the planes in to hit rail lines and shipping, anything that kept them going. We had to catch their attention and finally let them know the gloves were off.

However, all we got from the *Voice of Vietnam* was criticism of the U.S. for its continued stubborness at the peace talks. With deadlock apparent, and the bombing halted, we seemed set for indefinite confinement.

14
EASING UP

AN INQUISITOR NICKNAMED GOLD TOOTH STOOD BEHIND
the table in the quiz room, a stern look on his face. It was January 17, 1969,
and I expected the familiar harangue about keeping a good attitude and being
thankful for lenient treatment.

"Today, due to the goodness and humane treatment of the Vietnamese
people and government, you are allowed to receive a package from your
home."

A PACKAGE FROM HOME! Holy mackerel! Almost five long years had passed
since the arrival of the last package. This was too much to expect! Too good
to be true! It was manna from heaven! My heart thumped loud and fast. I
could not repress a look of wonder and excitement.

"But first you must sign this statement," he said with a meticulously slow
delivery.

I glanced over it. As expected, it was a load of propaganda, an acknowledgment of their peaceful intentions and concern for our humane treatment.

"No," I said, looking him full in the face.

"You will sign this! You forget you are criminal air pirate!"

It was a painful refusal. Who knew what might be in the package. Maybe
winter wear, toothpaste, sweet-smelling soap, chocolate, or perhaps even
photographs. As I looked at Gold Tooth, it was obvious he would dangle the
package until I relented.

"You have bad attitude, again!" he snapped.

"No."

"We will see," he smirked.

There were packages for many of the POWs but not one of them agreed
to trade their treasure for enemy propaganda. It cost us severely. Again they
roughed us up and once more our will sagged under sustained atrocities. But
fortunately, before we crossed the threshold, they gave us a mimeographed,
watered-down version of the statement, more like an acknowledgment of

receipt of the packages, and word came down from the SRO to go ahead and sign.

I watched eagerly as Gold Tooth emptied the contents of my package: toothpaste, soap, packs of powdered milk and drinking chocolate, candy and bottles of aspirins and vitamins, all so rare and almost mythical that in my ecstasy they seemed to glitter like polished gold nuggets. And how good they smelled! Such a whiff of the old familiar PX and neighborhood supermarket. The only fly in the ointment was having him handle my gifts before I got to touch them, and the patronizing remark he made as he handed over each item: "You are allowed to have this." It was as if he had waylaid the package and now masqueraded as the donor. To me, it felt like he stood between my family and me, robbing me of that special intimacy in opening a surprise package.

We did not get to keep everything sent to us. They took away my deck of cards and confiscated all games, pipes and tobacco. But we felt high enough with our grand new possessions and the walls resounded with rapid hand-taps, like muffled bursts of automatic submachine gun fire, as we relayed news of our gifts.

"I got a comb!" someone exulted. "A plastic comb!"

"And I got instant coffee! Real coffee!" said another.

A few supremely lucky guys hit the jackpot. They got photographs.

That same month, they gave me a letter from Tangee. It was the tone rather than the brevity that disturbed me. As I read and re-read it there seemed to be something amiss, something unfamiliar. Perhaps it lacked closeness and warmth. It was disquieting. Try as I might, I could not pinpoint the source of my uneasiness. It was as if she had written to a stranger. But then again, maybe it was only my winter blues and the depressing realization that I had now entered my sixth calendar year of captivity. Januaries were crueler than other months because they trumpeted the beginning of another year of detention. It was a reality made bleaker by the cold and damp of mid-winter.

Since the Hanoi parade, I had dreamed frequently of Mom, Tangee and MaMona but now the dreams recurred more regularly and persisted throughout the remainder of my captivity. The setting was always inside our new home in Salinas, where I lived when I was in high school. Mom was predictably busy by the stove in the kitchen. MaMona sat by the door leading to the dining room. She was always eating the big, black Concord grapes from which the very dark wines were made.

In my dream, I would talk to MaMona about my mother and ask, "Grandma, why is my mother so dark and my aunt Cecilia so fair?"

MaMona would momentarily stop eating, hold a grape in her hand and fix me with that serious expression through her rimless glasses. Then, with the utmost profundity that bore the wisdom of her age, she declared, "The year your mother was born was a good year for the grapes."

Just as often, I dreamed I was walking back and forth between the kitchen at the back of the house and the dining room facing the driveway. But whenever I looked out onto the street no one was there.

"What's wrong?" my grandmother asked in Spanish.

"Where's Tangee? I can't find her. Where is she?" I kept asking.

MaMona said nothing. But she made me even more flustered by riveting me with her immobile gaze.

When next I wrote to Tangee I realized how much duller my letters must have seemed to her. I was allowed no more than six lines of handwritten text. Short as it was, I never had anything new to write. If I sought encouragement, like asking her to keep hoping or praying, the Vietnamese censored it out. My life had no ups and downs of any magnitude to report, just the cheerless routine of incarceration. How could I convey anything different from the stale cliches of past letters? A combination of the censors and my wretched conditions left me with little to write about but the changing seasons, assurances of my well-being and expressions of enduring love. How flat they must have read, each sent from Camp of Detention of U.S. Pilots Captured in the Democratic Republic of Vietnam, c/o Hanoi Post Office, D.R.V. All things considered, I felt bad about even imagining a coldness in Tangee's most recent letter.

The spring of 1969 marked a frenzied renewal of torture, matching the worst the guards had previously meted out. The Zoo resounded with the victims' cries following the recapture of two POWs who had made a break from the Annex, outside the walls of the main camp. Two Air Force captains, Edwin Atterberry and John Dramesi, made their bid for freedom in defiance of policy laid down by senior officers. There were sound reasons for putting the lid on any thoughts of escape at that particular time: the odds of pulling it off were zilch because we were in a densely-populated area; the Paris Peace Talks, begun the year before, might lead to our repatriation; and we did not know what repercussions might stem from attempted escapes. As it turned out, retribution was savage and deadly and I shared the general opinion of all who suffered in the aftermath that it had been foolish to try to escape at that time and in those particular circumstances.

We first got wind of the prison break when we heard truck engines roaring and guards running around, shouting to each other. The would-be escapees were tortured with a vengeance. The physically stronger of the two, Dramesi, survived. Atterberry did not, and word of his fate spread throughout the camp from witnesses who saw his corpse placed in a truck and driven away. Our captors then turned on the senior officers, convinced that the escapees had acted under orders. Navy Capt. Eugene "Red" McDaniel, senior officer in the Annex, suffered mercilessly before senior officers in the main camp were similarly singled out. Guards turned on everyone sharing the same building as the captured pair, moving from cell to cell as they whipped the inmates with straps and rubber hoses and beat them with clenched fists. The beatings continued until the guards cracked some secrets of our elaborate communications system and command structure. Hurting physically and weakened organizationally, we had to lie low before gradually rebuilding our links with each other.

Whenever they started a new program, they invariably came to me first, probably because I had been there longest, and they could test how it might pan out with everyone else by observing my reactions. So it had been when Fidel arrived and then the English-speaking "kiddies." Now they pulled me to the quiz room and told me I would have to record a tape of news items from the Vietnamese media for broadcast over the camp radio.

"No, I will not do that," I said flatly.

This was one of those times when I got mad because I had been a captive so long. My patience frequently wore thin because there seemed to be no end to being pushed around by these sadistic imbeciles. I was going to make it hard for them to get what they wanted. Perhaps they would not waste their time with me if I made it tough enough. Though I could not know when my breaking point would come I obviously would not hold out to the point where they would kill me. I would not lay my life on the line to prevent a tame radio broadcast. And even if I gave in, it could not compare with outright treachery, such as immediately agreeing to broadcast in return for release back to the States. In any case, I was determined I would not broadcast without a fight.

"So you will not make the tape?" the interrogator repeated.

"Here we go again," I thought to myself. As with previous instances where they turned on the pressure, I knew I just had to hang in there and give it my best shot.

"No! I will not make the tape!"

"You *must* do it! You *must*!" the new interrogator shrieked.

"No."

"You forget, you are an air pirate! You must do as I say! You will read it in English!"

"No."

Shoved to the concrete floor, I was forced to kneel and hold my arms rigidly upwards, my hands open and taut. When I tired and my arms bent at the elbow, a guard slammed my face with the side of the butt of his rifle, knocking me to the floor. Then he yanked me by the hair and hoisted me back up again.

"You will read the news!"

"Do what you want! I will not say anything!"

"We will see!"

The assault went on for about six hours. When he didn't smack me with his rifle butt, he punched me with his fists. My face puffed up and, falling to the cold floor, I felt like Humpty Dumpty. My head seemed to be cracking and blood spattered my clothing.

As the evening approached, the interrogator returned with Lumpy, the camp commander.

"You have been here so long and still you do not know!"

He ordered me back to my room to think about my attitude overnight. The threat was implicit. Either I complied or they would be just as savage the following day. I stumbled out, groggy and weak. My eyelids must have swollen, because I could barely see where I was going. As I stumbled by the wash area I heard some guys whispering sympathies. Dick was furious when he saw me.

"The bastards! Why did they do this!"

Curiously I didn't feel so bad. I told him what happened.

"But you didn't have to take it!" he said. "How are you going to keep it up?"

"Dick, this doesn't really hurt any more than a football game hurts. It didn't hurt playing football, did it?"

"No," said Dick, who had also played high school football.

"Look," I continued, "I'm just not going to give in without a fight."

"Okay."

He tapped the wall, feeding details of my punishment into the camp intelligence system. Our neighbor, Galand Kramer, transmitted it down the line until it got to Fred Cherry, the SRO in our building.

"Just-do-your-best," Cherry tapped back.

Galand, who was living alone at the time, tapped out his own bugle blast.

"When-the-going-gets-tough-the-tough-get-tougher!"

Coming from Galand, it was a particularly stirring line because for more than a year Dick and I had heard him wheezing and coughing so badly that we thought he would surely choke to death.

The next day they pulled me out again.

"You have changed your mind? You will make the broadcast tape?"

"No!"

He nodded to the guard who walked over and, holding his rifle like a broomstick, struck me in the back of the head with a resonating crack. For the next few hours I had to kneel again. I tried holding my arms up high but it was as difficult as keeping a jaw wide open for hours of prolonged dental work. Subconsciously, I relaxed my arms and as soon as the guard saw them sag he was on me. My knee caps ached from the contact with the hard concrete floor but if I moved slightly to adjust my position, the guard took it as another invitation to strike. After about four hours my strength ebbed drastically and I could barely lift my arms. The more the guard struck, the more painful it was to hold them up high or to stretch out my fingers to keep open palms. Pulped and exhausted, I could not hold out much longer.

"Why don't you just read a little bit?" the interrogator asked in a tone so ambiguous that I did not know if he was mocking or trying to be compassionate.

I was in no condition to quibble. Bloodied, bruised and aching to drop my arms, I nodded. The outcome was never in doubt and I felt like a wrestler caught in a full nelson and forced to submit. But when I read the propaganda I drew on the experiences of previous forced recordings and mispronounced names, stumbled over words, slowed my diction and ignored punctuation. The quality was so bad that they did not use it. It was the last time they tried to get me to broadcast. I chalked it up as a significant victory.

In the weeks that followed I became more aware of the strange skin growth enlarging over the heart of my roommate. It had first appeared as a small spot the year before but Dick dismissed the darkish dime-sized circle as nothing more than a mole or a birthmark. He did not show any concern, probably because he claimed it did not cause him any discomfort or pain. My concerns lessened somewhat when the discoloration appeared to have stopped spreading. But it left me with a disquieting feeling although I could not speak of it for fear of alarming him more than might have been necessary. Dick did not seek medical attention and it is doubtful that the camp medical personnel would have measured up to diagnosing the problem. The discoloration was actually a sign of melanoma, a malignant cancer, but Dick would learn this only upon arrival back home four years later.

Sometimes there were sweet diversions from the marathon war. That hot, clammy summer opened sensationally when a naked woman took an outdoor shower in full view of a select few. Her strikingly beautiful features, long, light brown hair and tall, willowy figure had already made her deliciously conspicuous among the female peasants who criss-crossed the camp preparing food and doing menial chores. This one had tight thighs and whispering hips and walked like a woman, every step reaffirming her mystique. We figured she must have French blood so we called her Frenchie.

I was dozing in the back room of the Office with Dick during a siesta when a furiously loud wall tap startled us into bolt upright positions.

"That's Fred's wall!" said Dick. Fred Cherry's shoulder was smashed so badly from physical torture that he could not communicate as often as he would have liked. If he did tap, it signified something of importance, particularly as his middle room in the Office was the only one with a clear view of the entrance to our compound.

We listened carefully and decoded the taps: "Frenchie-just-walked-into-the-bath-area! Tell-me-what's-happening!"

This was a call to Bill Metzger, Gary Anderson and Joe Milligan in the front room to give a graphic rundown as only they had a full view from their air vent near the ceiling over the brick wall surrounding the well.

The next thing we heard was a loud plea from Gary: "Let me up! Let me up!"

But Bill wasn't going to give up his coveted perch. Standing atop Gary's shoulders he had a bird's-eye-view of the sensuous apparition disrobing a mere ten yards away. Breathlessly, he reported the play-by-play to Gary and Joe, who immediately transmitted it to us for relay down to the others. Everyone in the building was now electrified with anticipation: "She's taking her clothes off! Oh my God, she's got nothing on! She's bathing herself!"

Messages flashed from everywhere as men in locked and darkened rooms communicated like blind men without tongues, using their knuckles to tap out an audible version of braille. "Describe it!" "C'mon guys, tell us what's happening!" The feedback was full of the minutest sensuous detail—a guess at her vital statistics, the tone of her breasts, the slope of her back, the shape of her buns, the swoop of her legs. We imagined her standing like a supple Venus, soaping her slender limbs and stretching her elegant neck skywards before bending down to draw up the bucket of well water and pour it over her bare body. All the while she was oblivious to the havoc of the caged aviators, who could only dream of what it was to touch the female form. But then it ended, as abruptly as a hazy mirage dissolving into thin air. Frenchie dried herself, slipped on her clothes and walked out of the camp. She never disrobed in front of us again but the memory lingered like a whiff of perfume. Not a man forgot that day when Frenchie bared her elongated body beneath the azure summer sky.

That same summer, when my cuts and bruises had already healed, I came down with a persistent fever and nausea. I was so drowsy that all I wanted to do was curl up and sleep. I didn't think twice about my condition because our bodies had taken twin beatings from the food and the torture. Diarrhea was so common that we would sit up and take note if we went without it for a long period. It was often followed by dysentery, with its accompanying fever and blood-stained stools. In such cases the lanky, unwashed camp medic, dressed in a filthy white smock and cap, distributed white and brown pills. Jokingly we assessed the severity of the diagnosis by the varying combination of the colored pills.

Once a year, the medic did his rounds carrying an enormously long hyperdermic needle to innoculate each of us against unspecified diseases. He used the same needle on all of us. Perhaps I picked up my infection from this needle but it occurred to me only later, long after I first noticed my darkened urine when the room was lit up at night.

"Holy smoke, Dick! Look here! There must be something wrong with me!"

"Yeah, your eyes are yellow and droopy!" said my roommate.

I thought I had yellow jaundice. The guards gave me some pills but they did no good. For a week I lay down on my bed—four strips of hardwood bolted to three concrete stanchions. I could not hold down any food and vomited even though there was nothing left inside to spew out. I felt so sluggish and feeble that it was an effort to get up. Inert and feverish, I thought I might drift into a long sleep from which I would not awake. Dick got them to call the medic. He told me I had hepatitis, and he gave me Vitamin B-1 pills and some injections. Thereafter they also gave me frequent plates of white sugar as a form of medication. They took no precautions to isolate me from the others, even though it was commonly known to be a highly contagious disease. About three weeks later I began to show signs of improvement and they moved me out and into a room with Tom Barrett, Bill Metzger and Chuck Rice. It took about four long months to shake off the effects. Fortunately, none of my roommates picked it up though others in the camp periodically came down with the same symptoms.

The company of my roommates was heartwarming. Until then, I had not shared a room with so many people. I could hardly believe my good fortune, even though there were only three beds in the cramped room so that one of us had to sleep on the floor. But being together again with so many people was exhilarating, like arriving at an oasis after a long stumble through the desert. Like me, Bill Metzger was a lieutenant, j.g. when shot down. A native of Wisconsin Rapids, Wisconsin, he had the body of a football player though he walked with a slight limp. A leg broken during shoot down had healed somewhat grotesquely without medical attention and ended up more than an inch shorter than the other. Chuck Rice, a muscular youngster from Long Island, New York, and a lowly Navy ensign when downed over North Vietnam, was the son of a commercial airline pilot.

On September 3, camp officials suddenly appeared wearing black arm bands and mournful music filtered out of the squawk boxes. We learned from the *Voice of Vietnam* that "the great leader" Ho Chi Minh had died.

"How fitting," Bill quipped. "I got shot down on his birthday. He died on mine. That's about right!"

Ho's passing was a milestone. It marked the beginning of a significant change for the better in our treatment. They had been at the negotiating table for more than a year and realized that we were going to be a key element in the final outcome. We gained a measure of security, knowing that our safe deliverance would be part and parcel of any final settlement. But none of us got over-excited, expecting a quick breakthrough in the absence of Ho. In Paris it was likely to be business as usual. For us at the Zoo there was a lot less brutality—and larger bowls of rice.

Better treatment and an improved diet gave us the strength to prolong our physical exercises and even to compete with one another. In the beginning I could barely manage five push-ups. But within seven or eight months I was able to do more than one hundred push-ups, an equal number of sit-ups and I could join them in doing twenty hand-stands, propping my feet against the wall and then doing push-ups with my hands so that my nose came to touch the floor. The contest to exceed the number done by the other roommates became more intense as the months rolled by. The stronger our bodies became the more driven we were to excel among our peers.

I was alone in the quiz room a few weeks later when the interrogator told me "you are allowed to receive this package from home." Without waiting for permission I stepped forward but he stopped me short and opened it himself. On top of the contents was a white envelope marked *photos.* I felt the goose pimples breaking out on my arms and legs. It had been five long years since last I had received a picture of Tangee and that was a newspaper clipping. I reached out and in my excitement fumbled the envelope. One of the two photographs showed Tangee sitting down in her living room and baring a lot of leg because she was dressed in tennis shorts. She looked spectacular, still so gracefully feminine and more beautiful than I ever re-membered her. The other picture was of Mom and Dad in the back garden of their home in Santa Clara. They had aged slightly but thankfully both looked well. Again, I looked at Tangee and in an instant my defenses cracked. Overcome by emotion, I could not prevent the tears from welling up in my eyes. The interrogator left the room, leaving me alone to cry for the lost years and frozen memories. For five years I had tried hard not to think too much of her because I always ended up more depressed by my surroundings. Over the years I came to believe that I had grown a hard protective shell against daydreaming of our times together. If I could not be with her, I would not brood about her. But all this theory was just so much poppycock when I held her photograph. The woman I loved really was out there and not just a fading dream. It made me howl inside for the memories and the future that might not be.

I was wiping my eyes when the interrogator came back in.

"You are ready to receive your package?" he asked.

I nodded.

This time they even let me keep the playing cards. What a godsend! We started playing bridge, poker, blackjack. Every night, as soon as they turned the lights on, out came the cards. However, I would have been grateful just for the photographs. It was the tonic that I was most desperately in need of.

As he pulled out each item, I wrote it down. The list had to be signed by me as an official receipt. There was dried and canned food, a big plastic container of instant coffee, underwear, towels and almost the same goods received in the package nine months earlier. I carried it back to the room, impatient to share my food and my joy.

"Hey, guys, look what I got! Photographs of Tangee and my folks!"

They crowded around.

"Wow!"

Bill looked me over as if to say, "How does a runt like you, skinny, dirty, unshaven and dressed in rags, get hold of such a good-lookin' wife like this!"

"Holy moley, Ev, that's a helluva short dress she's wearing!"

"Dress? What dress?"

"That's a mini-skirt, Ev. Betcha that's a mini-skirt!"

I looked closer. "I thought they were shorts, tennis shorts or something."

Everyone peered harder. It certainly looked like tennis shorts but on closer inspection I saw it was a dress. I couldn't believe it and we laughed, wondering what kind of fashion had hit the U.S.A.

I held the photograph close, as if it was a voucher to reclaim all the lost time we could have spent together. For days and weeks I held it, staring longingly, and then at night I put it next to me so that in the morning I woke up beside it. How long would it be before I saw her again? How many more years would have to pass before I could hold her and kiss her, cup her face in my hands and run my fingers through her long black hair. How long?

15
BETRAYED

THE WAITING AND WORRYING TOOK A HEAVY TOLL ON
Chole. Her blood pressure rose and her body tensed, leaving her edgy and
brittle. She felt helplessly locked in a trap, exposed and vulnerable to un-
relieved stress. The fruits of the earth no longer pleased her. She ate frugally
and without joy, always conscious of the hunger that she knew her son must
feel. If the Vietnamese themselves could not afford to eat well, why then
would they care for the nourishment of their prisoners? Thanksgiving and
Christmas were especially brutal reminders when she spread her table with
festive abundance and looked sadly at the place where her son should have
sat. Perhaps, Chole thought, he would die little by little. The Vietnamese
were so preoccupied with the war that if they gave him any attention it would
be scant. And yet, she reflected, if he had survived this long it could only have
been because he had adapted and was making do with a diet of rice. She was
thankful she had only one son to give up for this disastrous war.

Meanwhile the foundations of her own life were crumbling. MaMona died
on the last night of 1967, slipping quietly away as Chole and Cecilia flanked
the nursing home bed. The sisters had skirted talk of Everett during their
regular weekend visits. Only once had they told her he was in the service and
stationed abroad. They could not say more because they themselves were in
the dark. But they never could tell if their mother had sensed the awful truth
because the stroke had robbed her of speech. They buried her in Salinas and
cried for the loss of a mother and the passing of a teacher. Tenacity was her
hallmark and courage her legacy. Everett, they knew, would be shattered. He
had loved her deeply and may even have been her secret favorite. The
bereaved sisters decided not to tell him that MaMona was no more.

The bottom had fallen out of Chole's marriage and Lalo stayed away from
the home more frequently. For a year she had gone to meetings of the
Alcoholics Anonymous family program, desperately hoping they would come
up with a magic solution to his problem. But he never accompanied her and

all she learned was that she herself would not be able to change his ways.

Sometimes, when Lalo was home and Chole sat quietly knitting, she saw her husband cry for his absent son. But she could not give him the consolation that she herself needed so desperately. However much she regretted the disintegration of her own marriage, she gave her husband credit where it was due. He had been a good father to their children, even though he had at times been as impatient as many others. And he had always been an exceptionally dependable worker. Whenever he returned from an absent weekend, merely to change clothes, he would be off to work on time to give an honest day's labor. But when they were together there was strife and she cowered if he raised his voice. At such moments she would rather clam up, if only to stop him shouting. Anything for peace and quiet in the home. Her doctor advised her to release the tension by crying and screaming or even throwing a few pots and pans, but she could not become what she had never been. So she suffered. And then, in a cruel twist of timing, she felt the hot flashes and melancholia of her change of life.

When Everett sent a note to his cousin Al saying he had been given a book to read called *The Story of a Real Man,* Chole had taken it out of the library and read it. When she was through, she wished she hadn't bothered. It was about a Russian pilot who survived the loss of both legs when shot down in World War II, and who flew again with the use of artificial limbs. Though heroic and inspiring, the tale left her even more fretful about his physical condition. Some of her friends suggested she go to a palm reader to divine the unknown and put her mind at ease. But this idea only made her more agitated. She explained that she did not want to be told her son was dead. Deep down she really believed Everett was pulling through. She had an inner confidence in his character. He had always been so quiet and resolute and content to be by himself. But, she asked herself, for how long could *anyone* survive such a long period of isolation?

His letters confirmed only that he was alive on the date each was written. They gave no real reassurance because months passed before each was received. By then he could be dead. Lalo let Chole write the letters because he knew what she was going through as a mother. Sometimes he appended tidbits of sports news. More often he would simply add the words he had used since early childhood to encourage Everett in moments of adversity: "Chin up!" Chole consciously wrote a sanitized version of the routines of home life, hoping it would give her son peace of mind to remember the bedrock of his being.

The irregularity of his letters posed wider problems. Not hearing from him for months created anxiety bordering on despair. Military and government officials in Washington, D.C., wrote to the family from time to time, updating scraps of intelligence about the POWs. But one particular letter horrified them for its inference that the cumulative effect of long periods of confinement, together with maltreatment, might have left some of the POWs slightly deranged. Tangee was more distraught than ever and Chole had to hide her own fears to soothe the wild concerns of the younger woman. This might be the last straw for Tangee. She might ask herself why she had to wait for a madman to come home and be institutionalized.

"Don't you believe it! It's not true!" Chole said, trying to show belief in the conviction of her own voice. "When I get those letters I don't feel like I'm reading them. I feel like he's talking to me. I can read between the lines. He's alright. So don't you believe that he's gone crazy!"

Tangee did not stop crying; Chole felt she had to be firmer.

"The day you see me crying because I think that something like this is happening, that Everett is losing his mind, then you can get worried about it! But if I don't cry, then don't you cry, because it is not true!"

After that Chole was careful to screen every letter from the government agencies. If another letter ever came bringing into question Everett's sanity, Chole would make sure Tangee did not see it. The young bride had suffered enough. She did not need the additional pain of some such remote, unprovable analysis.

Chole hoped that her young daughter-in-law could hold out longer. She tried hard not to doubt Tangee's staying power but too often was reminded of it by friends and acquaintances remarking, "Poor Tangee, she must be so lonely. She's been waiting so long."

She remembered all too well that Everett and Tangee had been married less than five months when he was shot down and much of that time Everett had spent on special training courses away from his wife. Their life together, thought Chole, had been no more than an extended honeymoon. Regardless of the passage of time they were still newlyweds. Nevertheless, she had faith that Tangee would hold on, no matter how long, because she came from the same cultural milieu. Mexican wives had lived at home and waited years for their husbands to return from jobs up north. MaMona herself had gone through this same separation from Jesus Rivera, and sat it out for year after desolate year.

Be that as it may, Chole tried to talk Tangee into going to college. Tangee had plenty of free time and wasn't forced to find work because she was getting Everett's paychecks. Chole tried to convince her of the advantages, but Tangee was unresponsive. No matter how many times Chole tried, Tangee rebuffed her.

Chole had felt very comfortable when Everett chose Tangee to be his wife. There had been other girls in Everett's life, several of whom Chole would have welcomed as a daughter-in-law, but Tangee seemed like a good choice. From the outset Chole had warmed to the attractive young woman because she could converse with her in Spanish. Notwithstanding her own failed marriage, she believed that a bride and groom would get off to a better start if they had the natural harmony of a common culture. She remembered how, in the earliest days of Everett's infatuation, he had come home and described what Tangee had prepared for dinner. "Mom, guess what, they eat like us! It's exactly like you fix dinner! Mexican dishes!"

Though the family thought Tangee was somewhat of a giggly air-head, unable to hold her own in a serious conversation and perhaps a let-down for Everett, they approved of her because she was cast so securely in the traditional Mexican mold. Shapely and feminine, she could be expected to raise a loving brood with solid virtues and values and be the warm-hearted center of the family. Even Delia, an astute observer, believed her conservative brother would be happy in spite of Tangee's occasional silly remarks that made Everett playfully shake his head or roll his eyes in exasperation.

Everett's father had been more cautious but for different reasons. When Everett was still a bachelor he had called his father one day to ask what he would think if he married Tangee.

Lalo warned him about what the long separations could do to a new marriage. "Don't you think it might be better if you wait until you finish your stint in the Navy and then get married? I've seen a lot of military marriages go on the rocks. I saw it all in San Francisco during the war. It's up to you, but my advice is to think it over. You don't have to rush into it."

Days later Lalo got another call from Everett.

"Dad, I've been thinking it over. I want to get married."

"I guess so, son. You're young and she's a very beautiful girl. But I know what you're thinking. You want to get into her pants. Listen, don't think it's all going to be sleeping with her. After you get married things will change. Think about it some more."

The next time Everett saw his Dad, he had made up his mind and neither of them had any qualms about it. Lalo knew that Everett was every bit a man and, so far along the line, had done the family proud.

Lalo did not care at all that Tangee happened to be of Mexican origin, but he would not deny that it voided some potential hazards. He flashed back to that nasty incident from Everett's high school years. Everett had borrowed the car for a double date with a high school beauty who'd been eyeing him. She and her friend lived on the other side of the tracks in Salinas. The daughter of a Scandinavian immigrant who was a successful local contractor, she was a bombshell and Everett fell for her that first night. They dated several times and he could hardly wait for Saturday nights to roll around. But the first time he picked up his date at her own home instead of at her friend's, everything soured.

"What's up, son?" Lalo asked when they were alone in the kitchen.

"My date says her Dad won't let her go out with me again because I'm Mexican."

It was the first time Everett had encountered serious prejudice on a personal level and it was clearly time for some solid paternal advice.

"Listen, son. Don't let it bother you; don't let it surprise you. You're a good, clean kid. Not a bum. This guy is ignorant. You know, sometimes people used to ask me, 'Everett, what are you?' I'd tell them I was a Mexican. They'd say 'You don't look like a Mexican.' So what's a Mexican supposed to look like? I've run into this plenty of times. Some Mexicans feel that way about blacks, and some Wasp types, well, they're the real bums. You've got to figure it out. There's something wrong with people, when they judge you on account of your color or your race or whatever. You're going to run into this the rest of your life, which is one reason I want you to get a good education. Be qualified whenever you apply for a job. If you are, they can't run you down because you're dumb. You're already as good as they are, and if you can, try to be better."

It was an early lesson in facing up to prejudice and thanks to Lalo's words, it didn't hurt Everett as much when he ran up against similar situations. He simply dismissed it as the other person's problem and moved on.

Tangee had been a good daughter-in-law and quickly became one of the family. But her visits to her in-laws became less frequent the longer Everett remained a POW. Lalo thought she came up with too many excuses to avoid regular contact. Once they invited her to take a short vacation with them in Oregon or Washington but she begged out, pleading too many other commitments. If he came home from work and saw her sitting with Chole he would invite her to stay over for dinner but again she'd make excuses, saying her sister was waiting for her. And something bugged him about the time she had sat in the kitchen waiting for him to return from work so she could ask him to take her unused sewing machine out of storage. She didn't sew and as far as he knew she wasn't interested in taking it up. What was she planning to do with it?

After Delia left for a European vacation in 1967, Tangee went to live up in the Bay Area, in Lafayette, and they saw even less of her. Lalo felt uneasy. Something didn't jibe. He told Chole he smelled a rat. He wanted to go up there and find out for himself, but what the hell could he do if he found her fooling around with someone else? He would only make matters worse. Better to let it ride, try not to let his suspicions get the better of him.

Delia extended her scheduled three-month European trip and by the time she returned twenty months later it was early 1969. In all that time she had kept in close touch with her family and even received correspondence from Tangee. When she visited her sister-in-law in Lafayette, she was surprised to find that, though Tangee lived alone, she was remarkably upbeat. She seemed rejuvenated. Some of her old frivolity had returned. She seemed to be more outgoing and independent, even enrolling on her own steam in a beautician's course. Though taken aback by this change of mood, Delia was happy to see her again and relieved to find her in such fine fettle considering the circumstances.

Through the network of relatives of career military pilots Tangee had kept in touch with the wives of other downed aviators and that same summer joined their newly formed National League of Families of American Prisoners in Southeast Asia. These were the same women Chole had earlier spurned because they did not dare take an anti-war stance. When the League campaigned for release of the POWs, it turned the spotlight not on the U.S. but solely on the communists, hoping the adverse publicity would force the North Vietnamese to change course and release the airmen. It gave Tangee an opening to break the five-year-long public silence recommended by the State Department and the Navy. "You'd think the communists would consider the time involved and let him go," she told a journalist as she looked wistfully out of her apartment over the rolling hills. "I guess our love for each other has kept me going. You have to have hope and faith. I have a lot of both. Sometimes my faith wavers. Then I remind myself my waiting is nothing compared to what my husband is going through. I'll never be that bad off. I'm free to move around."

Though Tangee had gone public, she was light years away from approaching the activism of her sister-in-law. Delia had come back a markedly changed person. Having quit her job to find out first-hand what made Europe tick, she had traveled widely, crossing Romania, Czechoslovakia, Bulgaria, Hungary, Yugoslavia, Greece, Turkey, Italy, France, Spain, Germany, Sweden and Britain. Wherever she went, she witnessed flaming passions against the U.S. for its perceived aggression in Vietnam. It shocked her to see the American flag torn, trampled on and burned at such widely spread anti-war demonstrations. It was a sobering experience to cross the European continent and feel the depth of rage against the American role in Vietnam. There were now more than 500,000 U.S. military personnel there.

As she stood on the sidelines, Delia's questioning of the war ran deeper. She heard the strongest opposition in France, and came to agree with the protestors that the U.S. was repeating the costly mistakes made a quarter-century earlier by that colonial power.

Shortly before leaving the U.S. for Europe she had gone to a rally in San Francisco honestly believing that the government should stop the war and bring back the troops. But she had not felt comfortable amongst the vocal crowd of 50,000. It was almost as if she had betrayed her brother just by being there.

Delia returned from Europe with a readiness to confront the issue. The clash with her father was inevitable and immediate. He didn't feel the troops should be brought back at *any* price. Delia didn't give a damn how it ended. She wanted them out and her brother back home—the sooner the better. He wanted to bomb their cities, pulverize them non-stop so they would roll over in the ashes and scream for mercy. She got mad, shrieking that the bombing had done no good and was getting them nowhere. They raised their voices until neither of them could be heard in the overlapping tirades. Madeleine bolted the room, unable to take the racket. In the quiet of her own room she wished they would not be so divided. It could only weaken their united desire to get her brother back home.

Deep down inside Lalo knew it was a bad war from every angle. They had to get it over with before it drove the country nutty and they had to do it without pussyfooting around. It ripped his guts apart every time Washington grounded the bombers for a special holiday or to coax the enemy into winding down the war. That was no way to win.

How could they ship half-a-million American boys over to run an obstacle course, telling them, "You can hit over there but not here. You can jump that fence, but not this one. You can fight weekdays but not on their holidays or ours."

Lalo sometimes yielded to the weight of his frustrations, signaling it might be time to call it quits and pull out. Delia overcame her own frustrations with a stiffened will. She was more determined than ever that the North and South Vietnamese should fight it out themselves seeing it was their civil war. If the country was destined to fall to the communists, so be it. It was their fight, not America's.

The remaining months closed in on the stormy decade and still there was no end in sight to the wrenching conflict.

"Dad," Delia warned, "I'm going to do anything I can to get him out! And if Ev doesn't want to talk to me when he comes back, at least I'll know that I did something for him!"

Lalo looked hard at her. She was telling him to stay out of her business. Yet still he tried to rein her in and reason with her before she went completely overboard and got the entire family into hot water.

"Look," he said, "if it were simple, we could do something. But when those big boys in Washington decide it's going to end, or whatever they're going to do, they'll make the decision. Not you or me."

"We can do something!" Delia screamed.

"We're going to get him out!" Chole chimed in.

"Okay, okay! Go ahead! I'll stay away from you!" said Lalo, his booming voice now broken and reflecting despair and impotence. The war had split the family and brought him down. He was no longer top dog, the final arbiter, in his own home. Delia and Chole had stood their ground. They were going to fight this war their own way.

Chole understood his plight, even though there was no longer any love lost between them. She knew better than anyone else that he was against the war but dared not speak out as she and Delia had done. It would be foolhardy for him to stick his neck out in public. He might lose his job at FMC. A man of his age could not afford to be thrown into the street to start all over again.

Chole's position was quite different. She was not the wife of a career Naval officer and therefore not bound by the unspoken rules guiding the behavior of military spouses. She had neither to conform nor agree to be muzzled. She would be governed only by her own common sense and protective, motherly instincts.

Traditionally, the clan got together for a Labor Day picnic in the country, driving from widely dispersed homes in Agoura, Monterey, Salinas, Ventura, Gilroy and Santa Clara. It was a time of intimacy among family who were in many cases close friends. They had much to talk about and it was fun frolicking in the open spaces with the new generation of growing young children. The activities made for a full day and in the heat of the afternoon they reclined, reminiscing and snoozing until it was time to fold the blankets and pack their gear.

In 1969, they gathered in Bolado Park, just east of the San Benito River and a few miles south of Tres Pinos. Tangee was among the absentees but it drew no special attention because she had for some time distanced herself from the clan.

Not all those picnicking saw eye to eye on U.S. aims in Vietnam. But they were united as one in wanting to do their damndest to get Everett back home. The misfortune of one was a blow felt by all. There was not one among them, neither an Alvarez, Sanchez, Espinosa, Zermeno or Bustamante who did not dream of the day they could hug and hold their Everett again.

Their sense of helplessness was deep, even more so when one of them recounted a conversation with a congressman who lamented the public's short memory. He saw the years going by and nobody giving much thought anymore to the downed pilots. The POWs were ghostly figures, long forgotten in the daily drumbeat of mounting body counts and bomb tonnage.

The hapless relatives were debating how best to catch the public eye when one of them, Mickie Sanchez, suddenly popped the question, "How about starting a petition to ask the president to do more to get Everett home? That way we'll all be able to help out by getting as many signatures as we can."

The idea took off like a dry grass fire. They all remembered how three years earlier worldwide public outrage had killed North Vietnam's plans to try the POWs as war criminals. If they let matters drift, the Vietnamese might misread American silence for indifference. Should that happen, the POWs were doomed. The family had to turn the spotlight on the POWs. At the very minimum the North Vietnamese would have to account for the physical well being of each man.

The wording of the petition did not come easily. They trashed a number of drafts considered intemperate, undiplomatic or too politically partisan. It had to satisfy the opposite extremes of the family and net the widest cross-section of the public. They finally came up with a compromise and it was addressed to President Nixon:

> *We, the undersigned, do respectfully request that more forceful, positive action be taken toward the release of Lt. Everett Alvarez, USN, and the other American prisoners held captive by the North Vietnamese.*
>
> *As you well know, Lt. Alvarez is the longest held prisoner of any war in the history of the United States. His plane was shot down over the Gulf of Tonkin and he was taken prisoner August 5, 1964.*
>
> *Sincerely*
> *The American People*

None of them expected the petition would speed Everett's return or bring him home. But the least they could do was shake up a forgetful populace and remind it of the special suffering of the POWs.

Publicity came quicker than anyone dared expect. Linda touched base with a reporter, mentioning offhand that the family was thinking of starting a

BETRAYED   211

petition. The following day it was the lead story in the *Salinas Californian,*
splashed across three columns under a banner heading *Petition to President,
Move to Free Alvarez.* The wire services picked it up and fed it to media
across the country. Television reporters and talk show hosts called. Nobody
was prepared. They had not even planned how or where they would circulate
the petition. But they scrambled, determined to make the most of this sudden
surge of publicity. They asked Tangee to boost the story photographically and
she came down to Salinas, posing solemnly while holding pictures of Everett
in full Navy dress uniform. She looked distant and contemplative, almost as
if, in looking once more upon his youthful face, she was asking herself what
he might look like now, five years after shootdown.

Somehow, the family found its feet through those early uncoordinated
efforts, enlisting the aid of influential local bodies and elected officials. Solicit-
ing thousands of signatures by going door to door and standing on street
corners and outside churches, banks and business centers was a very difficult
experience. They were unprepared for the insults and vulgar rejections. The
war had so polarized people that the family became a lightning rod for hate
and obscenities. Not content with declining to sign, some people shouted that
the POWs got what they deserved. A priest refused to sign and rebuked them
for inserting language urging *more forceful positive action.*

Madeleine tried to co-opt her friends and when they refused she felt let
down and angry. In the weekends, when she helped out, she was forced by
the very nature of the petition to come out of her shell and approach complete strangers. It was unnerving, even more so when she got her first rejection. To herself, she thought, "How dare you not wish my brother be brought
home!" She was too young and too shocked to express her outrage. But the
next time it happened she argued a little bit. As the weeks passed it became
a bit more bearable and Madeleine knew it was all worthwhile when she made
her first conversion and watched the man add his signature of support.

One of the signatories, Congressman Charles Teague (R.-Calif.), later
cabled the White House and got a reply from a presidential aide saying the
matter would be treated with "urgent priority" at the ongoing talks with the
North Vietnamese in Paris. The administration promised not to relax efforts
to ensure humanitarian treatment for all American POWs.

The Navy did not object to the petition but an official pointedly told the
family to remember to "place the blame where it most properly belongs,
namely the North Vietnamese government." Chole and Delia boiled over in
their quest to find out exactly what the government was doing to secure
Everett's release. The Pentagon had been in regular contact with the families
of POWs, mailing copies of identical letters addressed to *Dear Navy Wives*

and Parents. While the correspondence had been polite and official, it had nevertheless been cold and formal, bearing the imprint of the military and the mindset of the bureaucracy. The letters kept them up to date on regulations covering Everett's pay and taxes and advice on when and how to send him mail and packages. Occasionally they were tipped off to upcoming TV or print media news on POWs. And they were given guidance on other matters too, but there never seemed to be anything of substance that Chole or Delia could seize on and proclaim with satisfaction that yes, their government was doing everything it could to free the POWs. They tired of reading about the formation of even more government committees charged with looking after the interests of the POWs and their families. They grew weary of reading about Hanoi's violations of the Geneva Convention. What they wanted was more concrete evidence of moves to free the captured Americans.

Insisting they had been stonewalled for too long, they flew to Washington and met with legislators and government officials but came back empty-handed and none the wiser. They felt cheated. Mother and daughter went public, complaining to the media that they were tired of hearing government officials claim they could see the light at the end of the tunnel. "That's why we've started this petition drive—we've got nothing to lose," Delia told reporters. They heard clicks and static on their home telephone. If it was a government tap, as they believed, it did not intimidate them. They had nothing to hide. As far as they were concerned they were American citizens, exercising First Amendment rights in an effort to bring back their own flesh and blood.

Lalo was livid when they took their crusade to the media. One day he fumed at Linda and Mickie Sanchez, "You people are only helping the other side with all these outbursts in the papers! They love it over there! They're enjoying it! But the more you people do it, the worse it's going to get!"

They coolly ignored him, adding salt to the wounds of his waning influence. He felt cornered. Reluctantly, he took a petition to work but he had no stomach for this activism and was apprehensive how the men would react. His boss signed, but handed it back with a caveat: "It's not going to do a damn bit of good."

"I know," Lalo sighed.

When he got home he swore he would not do it again. He was not cut out to make waves. The congressmen who had been in Washington for decades were the guys running the country and they should be doing something. Not he, Everett Alvarez, Sr. His half-hearted attempt to join ranks with the family left him even more isolated and seething. All the fuss about the petition sickened him. A guy couldn't talk about basketball or baseball anymore. He felt better keeping his distance, trying to stay out of their way—and out of earshot.

But Californians climbed aboard by the thousands. Within two weeks of the Labor Day picnic, the family had garnered 13,000 signatures. Family volunteers sent in heavy batches of completed sheets to Delia, the campaign coordinator. Politicians, aware of its publicity value, signed up in front of cameramen. Some even suggested staging a parade, either in Washington or California, to give an extra boost to the cause. But for the meantime the family stuck to tentative plans to have Tangee deliver the petition to the president at the White House, sometime in the new year. The media chronicled every new success, and by December, reported 70,000 people had signed across the state.

This new sense of purpose electrified the family. For the first time in years they felt energized, able at last to do something to bring back their man. On Christmas Eve, they gathered in Salinas at Cecilia's home. Lalo sat apart in the living room while the others, animated by the holiday season, milled in the kitchen as Cecilia made tamales.

When someone said, "You have to be really nutty to be in the military," Lalo caught the remark as if his ears were satellite dishes. He took it as a personal provocation and cut in angrily.

"Wait a minute! All you guys do is worry about yourselves. All you're doing is cry about how bad you feel and all that crap. How about the guy over there? He's taking it. Right? Trouble with you is you can't take it!"

"You'd make a good military man, Unc," said his nephew, Al.

"I don't know! But I'll tell you one thing! Right now you guys probably don't like what I'm doing because I'm keeping quiet. But if Ev ever turned turncoat, and he got out, I'd back him up, just as much as I'm backing him up right now! I won't turn against him!"

"You'd make a good military man," Al teased again.

Lalo shot him a withering look and stormed out.

A Christmas card from Everett arrived in late January, 1970, addressed to Tangee and his parents.

Here I am again. Just like previous years. I am hopeful that this will be my last Xmas away from you.

It stiffened their resolve to push even harder for more support. The petition gained steam and it seemed they would soon top 100,000 signatures. The handful of exhausted novices had done well, but now they needed Tangee because she could soon go to the nation's capital to make the presentation.

Chole and Lalo had suspected for some time that Tangee had given up on Everett. She had not telephoned for months and no longer came down to Santa Clara to mail her letters and go over the procedures for checking the contents and size of Everett's packages. They had always posted them in Santa Clara because it was a familiar address and they knew the postal officials personally.

They buttonholed anyone who might know Tangee's whereabouts but drew a blank every time. Her family either did not want to or could not assist.

Though Delia tried, she could not make contact. Tangee was always out. It had been months since anyone had heard from her when, unsuspecting, Chole telephoned. She was surprised to hear a recording announce that the number had been disconnected. Tangee had apparently moved but they had to be sure before trying to track her down. Delia drove along the shorter route, up the east bank of the bay, oblivious to the scenic landscape as she felt a creeping sense of uneasiness, almost a foreboding of worse to come. She pulled up just off the main street, outside the same building she'd visited on her return from Europe, and her worst fears were confirmed. The apartment was vacant and shuttered. Tangee was gone.

Chole telephoned Tangee's sister, Mercedes, who lived in Walnut Creek, not far from Lafayette. The questioning was brief and blunt. Mercedes did not know how to explain and then she broke down and cried, confessing that yes, Tangee was involved with another man. It had been going on for about two years. The family had found out, but no one had the courage to spill the beans. They themselves had little to go on because Tangee had kept a cool distance for a long time, removing herself even from her own sisters. It had been months since they had last seen her. They were all so ashamed, embarrassed and upset that they wanted nothing more to do with their youngest sister. Mercedes could not even help with Tangee's whereabouts because she herself did not know where she might be.

The families of POWs had open access at any time to a designated official at the Pentagon. Lalo wasted no time in placing a call.

"What happens if you know a Naval officer's wife is fooling around. What would the Navy do regarding the pay?" he asked.

"We stop it if the marriage is over. But we need proof."

"What do you have to have?"

"Get me a signed statement from anyone who has first-hand knowledge it's over. Then we'll put a stop to the allotments."

Unexpectedly, Tangee herself wrote to Chole and Lalo. To the point, she announced she had met someone else. And by way of apology she confessed she had not expected events to turn out like they did. Now she wanted to write to Everett and tell him that it was over between them.

Chole read the letter with mixed feelings. Her thoughts were far off—with her son. After so many years, the dam had burst. She was not really surprised or shocked because they had already suspected the betrayal. But now she wondered how they would tell Everett. Would he have the strength to take it? She moaned for her firstborn, her only son. It was too bewildering. Why had he been singled out for so much tragedy? He was much too young and too good and too honest to lose both his freedom and his wife. She hurt, deep down in the depths of her maternal being, where no amount of balm could help. If she ached so much, how much more would Everett feel it? At best it would scar him for life. At worst? She feared for his sanity.

And yet, in her despair she had the purest grace of understanding. Her daughter-in-law had been expected to wait, but too many years had passed. It was too long for a young woman in the flowering of her life. Though she would never have admitted this, least of all to herself, not even Chole had expected Tangee to hold out forever. In the latter years, she had feared it would end disastrously, either with Everett's death or with Tangee finding someone else. To have hoped for any other conclusion would have been self-deceiving and, as it turned out, unrealistic.

There was minimal discussion between Chole, Delia and Lalo about what to do next. They quickly agreed that Tangee had to be dissuaded from writing a "Dear John" letter. Knowing how much Everett relied on the continuity of his marriage to pull him through captivity, they believed such a letter would break him and quite possibly drain him of all incentive to hold out. If they could not save his marriage, the least they could do was delay the blow until a more appropriate time. Let him cling meanwhile to the misconception that he would be coming home to the woman he thought was waiting for him.

They wrote to Tangee at her previous address in Lafayette, hoping it would somehow be picked up or forwarded. They asked her to transfer to them her privilege of being the sole consignor of packages to Everett. It seemed a natural enough request if she had voluntarily abdicated her right as his wife.

Obsessed with the survival of their son, yet helpless as they watched his marriage crumble like dead leaves, they waited for Tangee's response. It came in a letter dated July 20, 1970, and postmarked Hayward, California. Their relief was immense when they read of her agreement not to confess anything to Everett.

I've been thinking a lot about your wish for me not to tell Everett what has happened, and I have decided not to tell him after all. This is what you have asked of me, and because it is your wish, I will do this for you. I only hope it is the right decision. But, when Everett returns, please tell him I wanted to tell him but I was afraid for his well-being and that you had asked me to wait—and not to tell him while he was a POW. It's a hard decision either way because both ways will be hard for him. But, I feel very strongly, as you do. I would hate for him to give up hope after receiving a letter from me. So, I'll just wait until he returns, for then he'll find out. I just hope he understands why we didn't want him to know sooner. I hope to God.

One thing I cannot do tho, is continue my letters to him. I just cannot lead him on. Please try to understand my side, too, as I do yours. I pray for the best for Everett.

It bugged the hell out of Lalo that Tangee was still collecting Everett's monthly pay. God knows how long she might have been spending it getting dolled up for this other guy in her life. And yet the letter was not enough to stop her allotments. She was still married to Everett. She could shack up with any number of guys in town and still continue to receive his pay because she was his wife.

The first casualty was the petition. Buoyed by the statewide success of the drive for signatures, the enlarged family eagerly looked forward to the possibility of a televised presentation in the nation's capital. One of the California congressmen was pushing hard for a parade in Washington as the penultimate step before Tangee's hoped-for meeting with the president. But they were unaware of the grim new revelations about Tangee.

It fell to Chole to inform them. They had asked her to go down to Cecilia's house in Salinas to get her input on the parade. Though she herself was hurting, Chole knew what a comedown it would be for them when they realized why there could be neither a parade nor a visit to the Oval Office. As close as they were, she shrank from her obligation. She could not recall undertaking such a difficult duty before. When the moment arrived she made the disclosure in fits and starts, softly and self-consciously telling the hushed and stunned relatives what little she knew about Tangee's switch of affections. There was not a trace of anger or scorn in her voice, only the resignation of a tired and saddened mother.

They took the blow stoically even though they wanted to cry for Everett's loss and their own dashed hopes for a momentous finale. Without further ado, they quietly let the rest of the dispersed clan into the secret. Linda offered no explanation to her congressman, Burt Talcott (R.-Calif.), who had been pressing so hard for the parade and who would play a memorable role in shaping the course of Everett's life years later. She simply told him the family believed it would not, after all, be such a good idea. She didn't leak a word about Tangee for fear the media would seize on it and unwittingly expose everything to Everett. It was left to Delia to put an inglorious end to their exhaustive campaign. Alone and unannounced, she took the remaining reams of signed petitions to her congressman's office in San Jose. "These are the last," she told the staff. "I hope they do some good in Washington."

The weeks stretched into late summer and the family considered lobbying for special congressional legislation to stop the Pentagon from sending Everett's checks to Tangee. Delia's political contacts believed they had an excellent chance. Tangee had made no effort to stop any of the remittances, even though she had declared the marriage dead. Neither had she set aside any fraction of the payments for his eventual return.

Suddenly, like a windfall from providence, an envelope arrived in the mail for Chole and Lalo. There was no covering note, only a three page letter in Tangee's familiar handwriting. Written to her father and her sisters, someone had passed it on anonymously. In the first page and a half Tangee expressed surprise and excitement at getting birthday cards, especially when she admitted not expecting to receive any correspondence from them. Almost as an afterthought, Tangee continued:

Oh, we are married. See, first I got a Mexican divorce, later we got married in Tijuana. Andy and I felt it best if I also got a divorce here in the States to make it more legal. My lawyer says that as far as we are concerned, we are married, but it's wise to get a divorce here. So, I have already started legal procedures and he says I can get a divorce, but because of the unusual case for him, it may take from six months to a year, but I will get it eventually.

I think everyone should know. Oh, we were married June 22, in Tijuana, but will remarry in the States after my final divorce. The only thing I dread is that the file for divorce by me will have to come out in a section of the paper and when the news leaks out, that's something else! But I know it has to be done.

Love, Tangee.

It was precisely the proof they needed to put an end to her Pentagon payments.

16
DESOLATION

WHEN THE VIETNAMESE SUMMONED A BUNCH OF POWS
that winter of early 1970, we went willingly, thinking we were going to a quiz
session. Only when we were in the jeep and on our way to downtown Hanoi,
did we realize it was probably a propaganda stunt. They took us through the
War Museum, to impress upon us their victory against the French and their
resilience in the face of American military might. We passed through the
section with captured French war materiel. I remembered my last visit there
in 1964, when they had shown me parts of downed U.S. aircraft, trying to
convince me they had shot down eight planes on the day I bailed out. Then
they took us through the more recent display. I saw my helmet and uniform,
clearly labeled with my name. There were many blown-up photographs and
equipment of other captured pilots. Even though I did not see any cameramen, the message was not lost on us.

While looking at the exhibits I felt an urgent need to relieve myself. A
guard led me to the bathroom and waited outside. I stood and looked at the
urinal and regular seated toilet with amazement, unused to anything but the
crude jagged-edged slop bucket I had used for so long. Who would have
thought that squatting on a toilet seat could induce such a feeling of comfort
and well-being!

But then, as I went to wash up, I saw the mirror. It had been five-and-a-half
years since last I saw my face. I approached like a man entranced, as if
transfixed by the image of my own face growing larger with each step forward.
My God! Could that be me! Delicately, as if afraid my skin might crumble,
I touched my stubbly cheeks and felt my chin and then my eyes. I dragged
my fingers over the furrowed lines. Something inside of me recoiled from the
image in the mirror. Good God! I looked so old! With shock and astonishment I saw the flecks of gray in my hair. I could not believe it. I was only
thirty-two but the man in the mirror did not look a day younger than forty.

Inside I did not feel the weight of age, but I had only to look at that face staring back at me to see the ravages of time and the wear and tear of captivity. Though I still had the stout heart of a young man my outer casing was worn, cracked and middle-aged. I studied the drawn cheeks and looked deep into the lackluster eyes. They were drained and tired, colorless and empty. Gone were the flashes of youthful animation and the healthy tone of a younger skin. I let the tips of my fingers slowly stroke my jawline, trying to get a feel for my new face. But even as I struggled to adjust, my eyes balked and I felt my pulse register my inner agitation. I trembled much like any youth might have upon waking from a nightmare to find that the glimpse of his own aging face was not a dream but a reality.

When I rejoined my roommates I told them I had looked at myself in a mirror in the bathroom.

"Jeez," one of them sighed, "I wish I'd been able to do that."

I wondered whether he was not really better off, having been spared that shocking revelation.

The months went by and, in the spring, conditions took a marked turn for the better. One day the guards surprised us by going from one room to another announcing, "No more have to bow! Understand?" We were so astonished that we all bowed out of conditioned servility as they left. Bowing had become second nature in the presence of our captors. The habit was hard to break and in some instances immediately following the change of policy, the guards slapped around POWs who continued to bow. The irony of it all brought smiles to many faces.

That spring they also gave us a little bread and sweet milk in the mornings. Everyone's spirits shot up. They let us out of our rooms for about a quarter of an hour a day. Not long after we heard the unmistakable sound of bricks being knocked out of sealed windows. Every little change was regarded as a signal of better things to come. Improvement in the food augured well for the future. Perhaps they were fattening us up for eventual repatriation. We waited expectantly. Even die-hard pessimists declared the barometer was moving way up.

When the food rations reached an adequate level we were even able to put aside scraps of bread to make ashtrays, tubular cigarette holders and other useful objects. It became a popular pastime to eat the crust and then dip the soft leftover in water. This doughy mixture could be kneaded into a multitude of shapes.

During one of our forays outdoors someone discovered four tomato plants. They were quickly apportioned one to a room and a prize declared of an imaginary case of booze for the group which grew the largest tomato. We cultivated the surrounding soil, loosening it with our hands and weeding around the roots, then adding fertilizer in the form of our own excrement scooped out of the buckets with sticks. Everyone involved became obsessed with the growth of the plants, treating them with the overwhelming tenderness shown towards a new love. Even though one of us aired the soil and smoothed it down, another would come by and repeat the procedures, going through the same motions to strike up a personal concern for the welfare of the plant. The green vines represented life itself and each of us hovered around the frail shoots like concerned physicians. The plants had stickers attached with names like *Bloody Mary, Big Red* and *Cornucopia* and we did our light-hearted best to sabotage the growth of our competitors' plants by kicking dirt over them. As with so much else in that infamous perimeter, however, the plants wilted and died before the buds even opened. We mourned their shriveled remains with genuine sadness. For a few precious weeks we had actually nurtured new life in our sterile acreage. It was an uncommon distraction from the stark reality.

During this episode, a Christmas card arrived for me from the previous year. It was signed by everyone except Tangee. Momentarily it seemed strange, but then again, she may have sent a separate card which had got tied up in the bottleneck of what must have been a very circuitous mail delivery route. We could only assume that the Vietnamese or third party intermediaries were responsible for the long delays in the mail. The fault could not lie Stateside.

I wrote letter after letter, hoping that if just a single one got through it might elicit a reply. Finally, in July 1970, they handed me a reply from Tangee. Nine months had elapsed since she wrote it. But my excitement was short-lived, like a Fourth of July fireworks show suddenly rained out. For the first time in six years apart, Tangee sounded unhappy. Her letter was a weary lament about the length of the war. There was no need to read between the lines to feel the strain upon her. The war had become a burden of epic dimensions, exacting a terrible toll on a few, whose lives like hers, had been singled out from the norm. My protective instincts ached to reach out and comfort her, to relieve her from her lonely vigil. How I yearned to put the wretched enslavement behind me so that we could be together again in the fullness of our youth. But like a man chained to the oars of an ancient galley, I could only dream of eventual deliverance. It would not come easily nor out of compassion because my enemy was both pitiless and unsentimental.

July 7, 1970

Hi Sweetheart! . . .

I recently got your letter. Tangee, I miss you. It hurts me to know what you are going through, and our being separated all these years. I love you very much honey—you are still my sweetheart.

A few weeks later I wrote again. It was the seventh consecutive year I had been away for her birthday.

Happy Birthday, Sweetheart.

Looks like I missed another one. Buy yourself a nice gift from me. . . . Take care my love, I'll be home someday. I love you. . . .

The summer was bleak and hollow. Other POWs continued to receive packages and letters but, without explanation, nothing came for me. It had to be the fault of the Vietnamese. They must be testing or baiting me as part of some mischievous scheme. They had been heartless before and would be equally inhuman in the future. This time the pain went deep when I saw others opening their letters and packages prepared by wives and parents. I was always the outsider, the puzzled, luckless observer. All I could do was look at the glow on their faces and listen to them excitedly exchange news of loved ones. These infrequent contacts with home were the high points of our charred lives, sustaining us through most of those wasted years. If we did not hear from home then no amount of time outdoors nor unexpected treats of bread and sweet milk could raise the spirits.

September 19, 1970

Hi Sweetheart!

I love you. . . . It sure has been a long time since we were together. I look at your picture every day. I have been fine—don't worry. I am planning for our future. Take good care of yourself honey.

My roommates provided strong emotional support. All of us knew the intimate details of each other's lives. We had vivid knowledge of the cast of family characters who gave color and texture to each man's story. Those around me were as close to me as my family. They did not have to ask how I felt. They knew with the sureness of instinct. I was hurting and they talked gently, trying to find excuses for the delays and pressing me not to make too much of it.

When finally I did get a package in late summer of 1970, followed by others in November and December, they were from my mother. It seemed natural enough that, for a change, she should want to prepare the gifts. Vicarious contact was better than none at all. But then she sent some photographs and everyone was represented except Tangee. More troublesome were Mom's letters which made no mention of Tangee.

October 16, 1970

Tang,

> *I love you more than ever. Never forget how much I love you. Keep faith, my love. Keep writing. Remember that I need you, and I'll be coming home to you. . . .*

Why had my wife been so silent for so long? The answer came on Christmas that same year when they handed me her letter. It had been written thirteen months earlier, in November, 1969. So the Vietnamese were to blame after all! They had withheld and stockpiled her letters! How many more were stacked up somewhere in the Zoo, their delivery dependent upon the caprice of some anonymous official?

In mid-summer, 1970, they knocked more bricks out of the windows of another building. Their appearance in our room seemed imminent. How we looked forward to watching them unblock the window space to let unfamiliar light into those depressing quarters. But once again we were caught off guard as the unexpected happened. Harried guards appeared one night and briskly ordered everyone to roll up their gear. Simultaneously, trucks drew up noisily in the compound. The commotion portended something of great significance. Tense and alert we began to speculate. Could this be the big move we had prayed for? Could it be the prelude to freedom? Conditions had been improving dramatically. It would not be farfetched to suggest we were about to be sprung, to be trucked out to an embarkation point. A few weeks back we had seen the guys in the Annex move out, though no one knew where they had gone. In all likelihood, we were going to join them. Hopes rose to quivering highs as we sat impatiently for several hours in the lit room, awaiting further orders.

A guard motioned for my three roommates, Tom Barrett, Bill Metzger and Earl Lewis, to move out.

"Ao!" he snapped, using their Vietnamese name for me and roughly signaling me to wait.

The POWs looked sympathetically at me, knowing they were about to be driven out somewhere while I alone had to remain. I felt crushed and abandoned. Where were they going? Why was I being singled out from my colleagues once more? It was unsettling and slightly ominous. Each one shook hands with me, saying a few words of farewell and encouragement, like mourners offering condolences to a bereaved friend. I did not have to wait long, however, before they walked me across the camp to the Pigsty, where the windows were already unblocked. Jerry Coffee, a slender, dark-haired, heavy-bearded senior lieutenant was already there. Years before, when he was still a lieutenant j.g., he had been decorated with the Distinguished Flying Cross for a low-level reconnaissance mission over Cuba which provided damning photographic evidence of secret Soviet missile installations. I was followed into Jerry's room by Air Force Captains Norm McDaniel and Harry Johnson, Air Force Lt. Mike Lane, and Navy Lt. j.g. Brad Smith. In all my years of captivity I had never shared a room with so many POWs. Each of the Pigsty's other three rooms also held half a dozen captives. It was reason enough to feel jubilant and hopeful that we had turned the corner on the long road home.

Jerry would become one of my closest friends. We had much in common even though he was three years older than me. A fellow Californian, and a talented artist with a degree in advertising art from the University of California at Los Angeles, Jerry was from Modesto. I called him the *Modesto Flash*. He dubbed me the *Salinas Streak*. The junior colleges we had attended at Hartnell and Modesto were old rivals in the same athletic league though he preferred football, swimming and competitive skiing. We shared a special fondness for the Monterey peninsula and the giant Redwoods at Big Sur. He told me he remembered my shootdown well because he had been visiting his parents at Hanford, California at the time and the newspapers had given it big play. He thought the Tonkin Gulf incidents were nothing more than a small police action and he expected I would be repatriated in no time at all. Never in his wildest dreams did he imagine that eighteen months later he, too, would be a POW in Vietnam.

In those closing months of 1970, the Vietnamese relaxed their restrictions and provided us with a ping-pong table, volleyball, basketball nets and tennis shoes to wear during basketball. They even gave us a King James Bible which I, like the others, read once in a while. It would have been a far more popular read if it had been available in earlier years, when we were two or three to a cell and denied all the activities now permitted. No one really felt like reading in the sudden gush of liberties. The novelty of rooming with so many people was exciting and gave us the chance to indulge in long and animated conversations. Overall, the relaxation of camp regulations gave us a virtually open-door policy. We could now wash up anytime we wanted.

The combination of playing sports and being outdoors improved my physical condition. It also gave me a break from my sullen obsession with Tangee's silence. I did not know whether she was dead or alive. More and more I came to suspect that she had contracted some deadly disease. I remembered how her family had hushed up the sad but terrifying news when her mother was found to be terminally ill with cancer. What if Tangee had fallen victim to this same dread disease which no one dared speak of?

Though a lighter mood permeated the Zoo, reflecting relief and an easing of tension, it had to be seen in the context of other restrictions still enforced. They maintained the rule against communicating, and guards continued to lock us up during the siesta to prevent contact between the buildings. But their best efforts met with the same fate as before. Intelligence passed just as regularly through the walls and then across the open spaces by sign language.

Security tightened measurably in November and persisted through December. They unrolled coils of barbed wire around the camp but made no effort to curtail or interfere with our basketball games. We had no idea what prompted these moves and could not even hazard a reliable guess. On Christmas Eve, the Vietnamese caught us by surprise when cameramen suddenly appeared to film us playing basketball. It was so unexpected and inoffensive that we did not have time to consider the implications. As soon as the photographers got what they wanted, the guards dismantled the basketball stands, retrieved the balls and tennis shoes and led us off to the Christmas meal.

We were in for a greater shock later that night when at short notice they herded us into trucks and drove us over quiet roads into the bustle of the capital. We entered the familiar double gates which clanged shut with a ringing echo, and drove over the bumpy brick path and through more metallic-sounding gates before coming to a halt in the courtyard. I was back in the Hanoi Hilton. Room 24 was on my left. Heartbreak Hotel just ahead of me. They led us through a gap in the buildings, past Heartbreak Hotel, into a larger courtyard ringed with buildings. I moved in with nineteen others into one room. Most of the other POWs were ordered into rooms containing as many as forty men.

More than five years had elapsed since first they put me under lock and key in solitary confinement. How green I had been way back in 1964, expecting to be released within months, if not weeks. My memory swirled with ghosts of the past: Crazy Guy, Stoneface, Magruder's Army. So much had transpired since those early days that I felt like an old man returning to gaze at the scenes of his youth. I had to reach far back into the chronology of captivity to recall the time I had scratched humble words of faith in the brick wall of my altar:

Lord I am not worthy . . . but only say the word and my soul shall be healed.

And yet, through all those years of testing, my faith had held up. And my honor remained intact. They were the twin bulwarks with which I had resisted every blandishment to cave in and gain freedom in return for collaboration. It was a bittersweet reflection, but I would not have wanted it any other way—even with the benefit of hindsight.

Almost four hundred POWs had been brought together in the Hanoi Hilton. As they represented just about every known American captured in North Vietnam we called the ring of buildings around our courtyard Camp Unity. We nicknamed my twenty-five-by-thirty-foot room Buckeye, after our SRO, Air Force Captain Dick "Pop" Keirn, who was from Ohio. It had two long slabs of solid concrete, each two feet high and facing each other along opposite walls. Between the slabs was walking space. Ten men slept on each row, unrolling their straw mats and bedding down beneath two blankets and mosquito nets tied to string stretched along the length of the room.

Earlier arrivals explained why we had been herded into the brick prison in spite of the security clampdown at the Zoo. They told an astonishing tale of an elite force of American commandoes having made a daring rescue bid on Son Tay prison in November. Son Tay was a mere fifteen kilometers away from Camp Faith, where Tom, Bill and Earl had been taken when separated from me that summer. They had come tantalizingly close to being rescued by the Americans. The raiders had hoped to airlift POWs to safety. They were forced to go back empty-handed, even though they had penetrated North Vietnamese air space undetected and fanned out in search of imprisoned compatriots. By sheer chance, the Vietnamese had transferred the Son Tay inmates to Camp Faith only about a month before, leaving Son Tay abandoned. The luckless POWs at Camp Faith had actually witnessed the nocturnal raid, seeing the explosive flashes light up the dark sky and hearing the U.S. fighter cover scream right over their own nearby holding camp. There was little likelihood of a similar raid coming so soon after the abortive one but the Vietnamese were taking no chances. It would be much harder for the commandoes to scoop us out of enemy territory if we were kept under lock and key in populous Hanoi. It had the best air defenses and none of the rural isolation of Son Tay.

Our swollen ranks in each of the large rooms of the adjacent buildings of Camp Unity did wonders for our spirits and our camaraderie. The unity and solidarity that we had risked so much to preserve seemed to have paid off. Far from being isolated and lonely, we were all caught up in the new euphoria. Among such numbers it was impossible to feel the misery and sense of abandonment which came with solitary confinement or isolation. Confidence in our present strength and ultimate fate peaked on Christmas night, 1970. Until then, we had conducted our church services covertly because the camp authorities had never relaxed the rule against POWs communicating between rooms and buildings. But in our current mood no one gave a damn about the regulation. Christmas gave us the impetus to act. Suddenly the cold night air was filled with the sounds of a carol sung joyously and assertively by the men in one of the buildings. No sooner had they finished than the inmates of another building sang a different carol. Camp Unity soon resounded with the words and tunes of many a beloved carol, each time sung in a defiant *fortissimo*. Even though the wall in front of Buckeye prevented us from seeing the other buildings, we could hear our fellow carollers because none of the iron-barred windows had shutters. The guards scurried to quash our insubordination. Appearing at the windows of each of the buildings they shouted for silence and obedience. This only served to encourage even more POWs, who joined in singing *God Bless America* and the national anthem with such gusto that it became a challenge our captors could not ignore. Soon the riot squad appeared. Swiftly and forcefully the Vietnamese hauled senior officers over to Heartbreak Hotel and clamped them in irons. Other guards stood by with fire hoses, ready to turn on the flow if we escalated the unruliness.

But they had no need for them. We had made our point. We had acted spontaneously and in unison. And we suddenly realized our new potential. The camp commander appeared. "You are allowed to have church services," he said, "but you must not be disruptive. You must do it in your own rooms. And the senior officers are responsible."

From the following Sunday, the faithful in each room conducted church services, praying and singing hymns together. Individuals appointed by the senior ranking officer gave pep talks instead of sermons. With fear vanquished, and on the heels of such a significant victory, we no longer spoke in the hushed tones we had become accustomed to over the years. It was gratifying to reflect that the concession wrung from our captors had stemmed from our faith and our massed demand for the right to conduct religious services.

Later that winter, caged again in the gloomy darkness made worse by the chill, I could not shake off the mystery surrounding Tangee. It was a cold February day, the sky closing in like the lid of a pewter bowl, when I wrote to her again, squeezing each letter tight to cram as many words as possible into the permissable seven lines.

February 22, 1971

Honey, are you still using the big fur coat? Someday, my love, I'm going to buy you another one with a fur hat to match. I'm tired of our being separated for so many long years now. A few weeks more will make seven years since I hugged you. It's just as if it was all a dream. But darling, the memory of those precious few moments is what keeps me going on. I love you with all my heart.

Soon after, the camp authorities gave us permission to write letters longer than the standard seven lines. I used the extra space to pour out my feelings to Tangee, telling her that no matter what the reason for her silence, I still loved her dearly. I forgave her anything she had done which might have embarrassed her or hurt me. But none of the letters apparently went out as nothing came back from her and Mom made no mention of receiving any of them. I reverted to the shorter letters of seven lines each.

April 10, 1971

Are you working Tang? If you are, where and how much are you working? . . . Keep faith; I still love you very much Sweetheart. Just take real good care darling, until I return home to you . . . All the love I can send to you. . . .

Jerry Coffee and Dave Carey were my closest props. I bared my heart to them out of a need to talk. Jerry spoke with the concern of a friend and the wisdom patiently acquired from his own pitiful experience. He was happily married with a daughter, aged seven, and two sons, five and three. But his situation was especially poignant because his wife was pregnant at the time of his capture. Jerry, however, had such an optimistic nature that he refused to let me give up hope. It was difficult to turn a deaf ear to a man who was so manifestly solicitous for my well-being and who had such an engaging smile.

Dave was a red-haired, freckle-faced Skyhawk pilot four years younger than me. He had grown up just outside of Pittsburgh, the son of an interstate truck driver whose job kept him away from home for days on end. Dave had impressed football talent scouts whose recommendations won him entry to the prestigious U.S. Naval Academy at Annapolis. There he had graduated, like me, in electrical engineering, and captained the wrestling team. I had wrestled a bit at school but was no match for him when we locked arms. He taught me many maneuvers, though our principal aim was to keep in shape and pass the time doing something active.

Dave was going through a similar period of agonizing speculation about his father because for more than a year the letters he received from home were no longer signed "Love, Mom and Dad," but merely "Love, Mom." We wondered out loud what it could mean and even considered the dread possibility that he had died. It was only a suspicion but there seemed no other explanation. Our circumstances made us pragmatic and nothing, however hurtful, was a taboo subject. It made no sense to delude ourselves that all would remain well at home during our prolonged absence. Every passing year brought a sharper awareness that we might one day have to face up to unthinkable news. It was this sense of realism that prepared Dave for the sad confirmation on his release that his father had in fact died in 1969.

One day Dave told me he had written to his girlfriend, Karen, to whom he was all but engaged, to try to locate Tangee. Karen had gone to San Jose State; I believed Tangee was still living in San Jose, so in coded language he asked, "How's your aunt Hortensia (Tangee's given name) doing down at your old alma mater?" A letter came back saying both she and aunt Del were fine. It made her silence all the more enigmatic. What was wrong? Why didn't she write? I had to keep on writing, hoping I would eventually be rewarded with a reply.

May 31, 1971

Hi Sweetheart! . . .

Hope you don't get sunburned this year as you do every Spring. . . . Always remember—you will always be my Sweetheart.

By mid-1971, I could no longer bear the silence. It was like being trapped alive in a tomb with severed vocal chords. I could neither reach beyond nor cry out. Certainly no one seemed to hear me on the other side. All my hopes had centered around the fulfillment of being with her again. I dreamed of the family we would start and the house we would buy. Being together again would have to be sublime because of our yearning for each other in the years apart. And yet . . . her last letter had arrived seven months ago, though it was written thirteen months before that. That made it close to two years since she had last written to me.

Distraught and feeling like I'd been pushed to the brink, I had to find out one way or the other what had happened. I was not alone in wondering how long she could hold out. Maybe she had left me for someone else. Others, too, had gone through nightmarish moments of wondering whether they might be the victims of this ultimate rejection. The only people who could give me a straight answer were my parents. I had to write and ask them point blank. They would surely not mislead me. If Tangee had indeed died or lay ill with an incurable disease I had a right to know. If she had somehow got entangled in drug abuse, which we knew a little about, I wanted to know. Perhaps she was paralyzed and could not talk and no one had the courage to tell me. Whatever fate had befallen her should not be kept secret from me. The only anger I felt was knowing I would have to wait about six months for their reply.

I walked out of our large, twenty-man cell and through the gate separating our courtyard from the big compound area. The shack with the chair and table was just outside the gate. A guard who spoke crude English gave me the blank paper. Surprisingly, I did not have to steel myself for the moment. It was like being relieved of a monstrous burden. I held the stick pen. The words came easily because I had thought about nothing else for so long.

June 30, 1971

Hi Folks!

I'm sure something happened to Tang. No word from her or mention of her for a very long time. I want to know what happened to her. Don't worry, I'm prepared mentally and spiritually for whatever you can tell me. If she's not alive, or found it too hard to wait for me any longer—I want to know. I love her dearly. All I ask is a chance, if possible, to return to her, to continue our life, or start anew. Tell me if I have this chance. Don't worry, I'll be alright. The sadness is heavy in my heart, but I need to clear this doubt in my mind. I know it's been very hard for my wife.

Jerry and Dave prepared for the worst. Even though they knew Everett would bear misfortune with admirable stoicism, they stood ready to protect him from impending disaster. Both men had warmed to his likeable manner.

There was something attractive about his soft-spokenness and low-key strength. They shared a sense of being relaxed and secure in his company. He was always on an even keel. It would be totally out of character for him to act impulsively or speak off the top of his head. Living cheek by jowl, imprisoned men quietly got to scrutinize each other's true characters. There was not much they could hide in the closeness of their captivity. Jerry and Dave had ample opportunity to watch Everett under pressure and each time he had displayed the same calm level-headedness. This was the essence of his personality and perhaps the most compelling reason they liked to be in his company. The man had kept his frustrations in check and his sense of priorities in order. This unassuming Californian had real sensitivity and a generous spirit. It was unexpected and something to marvel at, coming from one who had taken it on the chin longer than any of them. They hoped the reply from his family would not be too severe. Good guys deserved better breaks.

Chole, Lalo and Delia had dreaded this moment ever since they discovered Tangee's divorce and remarriage. They had since gotten her lawyer to withdraw U.S. divorce proceedings filed on the scandalous grounds of desertion. By the time Everett's letter arrived, they had kept their secret for more than a year, convinced that no good could come out of volunteering the terrible truth. It was a tough decision but they felt convinced that no man could take the full force of such news and still hope to pull through years of captivity. Not even Everett with his exemplary composure. When he eventually found out, he might rage against them in his delirium, but they believed they had no other choice. They would bide their time and wait until he demanded answers, allowing him time to brace himself for a hammer blow that might knock him senseless. And even then they would hold back much of what they knew. To come clean with the whole tale of his wife's infidelity would be like driving a stake through his heart. The wiser course called for discretion to soften the blow and a certain blurring of detail to dab the wound.

They left it to Chole to write the regulation seven-line letter. It was the kind of news best conveyed by her. She had the matchless quality of a mother's instinct. She had given him life and would know best how to protect him from death. Not that any of them believed he might commit suicide, but that they feared he might lose the will to survive. Even though an ocean apart, they would try to shoulder him through the tough months ahead.

She told him Tangee had decided not to wait. No one had seen her. They all hoped and prayed that he would stay strong and well and that he would return home to them soon.

In the months that I knew would pass by before I received a reply from Mom and Dad, I tried to preoccupy myself with other pastimes, even though Tangee was uppermost in my mind. We had begun to formalize daily math and foreign language classes among ourselves. I taught Spanish, structuring the lessons along the lines of the French classes taught by Dave Carey. The instruction met the needs of many who craved any form of mental stimulus. Even more popular were the entertainers among us, the raconteurs, the born storytellers who could recite the screenplays of movies they had seen. Such performances called for a delight in verbal dramatization, an inventive and imaginative mind, a flair for the telling line, an eye for vivid color and a gift for embellishment. Sometimes the "soundtrack" of these movies stretched over several days of telling, heightening the suspense and exerting a powerful hold over the audience.

I spun a yarn I had developed over the previous six years to pass the time. Set in the years encompassing the Civil War, it was the saga of an Hispanic boy, whose epic struggles seemed to reflect my own constant challenges, though the untitled story was in no way autobiographical. My hero was orphaned as a child in Texas when bandits slew his parents. He came to be raised by an Indian until, as a teenager, he was smart enough to fend for himself. He joined a wagon train to Missouri, worked as a stable hand, then journeyed to the East Coast where a Navy captain became his surrogate father. Together they sailed the seven seas while the old salt taught the boy to read and write, then got him an appointment to West Point. Both men fought with the Union troops though the old sailor fell in combat. Disgusted by the slaughter, the young man stashed his inheritance into saddle bags and rode back to the wild Southwest, where other men were quick to discriminate against his ethnic group, calling him Pancho and telling he him could not drink in their bars. Goaded and insulted, he killed many of his taunters in gunfights. Only when he moved down to Mexico did he find peace of mind through a cultural identity. He married the daughter of a large landowner but his bride died during a cholera epidemic. Devastated again, the young man rode north, signed up as a military scout, then met a beautiful woman who, like him, had experienced life's ups and downs by roaming far and wide. For the final chapter I envisaged the couple riding off to California to fulfill their dreams in the booming new frontierland. It was little more than the outline for a novel but it seemed to hold the attention of all who listened in.

Perhaps the most challenging of our new activities was the Toastmasters' Club, formed to equip us to handle public speaking engagements we expected to be called upon to undertake on our return home. Americans were sure to be curious about our experiences in prolonged captivity so those among us who had learned the rudiments of public speaking agreed to be tutors. We were given little or no time at all to prepare and very often this made speakers flounder. But if the speech came from the heart little more was required than a confident delivery.

One day I was given thirty seconds to prepare a five-minute speech on any personal experience in my life. Without any need to embellish or dramatize, I recounted an incident from shortly after World War II, when I was barely eight years old. My parents had separated briefly and Mom took me down to live with my grandmother in the house on Pearl Street in Salinas while Dad remained in San Francisco. One day, my grandmother took me aside and reminded me in a whisper that it was Mom's birthday. I wanted to buy her something nice but I didn't have any money. There was only one way I could scrape together enough to buy her a gift. I would have to collect a lot of empty soda pop bottles and trade them in for a penny each at the corner grocery store on Alisal Street. I wheeled my little red wagon out of the yard and foraged for bottles among the neighborhood trash. Whenever I filled up my red wagon I trudged up to the store and exchanged them for a total of five or eight cents. By late afternoon I had covered several blocks and figured I had already pocketed enough pennies. I pulled my wagon up the hill to the drugstore and brought out a handful of coins. There were enough to pay for a birthday card and even something more with the surplus. I looked around and my eyes locked on a Babe Ruth candy bar. There was just enough money to buy it for Mom. I stuffed the candy bar in my pants pocket, tucked the card under my shirt and ran off home. By now I expected to get into trouble because it was already getting dark. As I rounded the corner to go up the road to the house I saw Mom looking out on the porch. I could tell she was angry.

"Where have you been?" she scolded, angrily emphasizing each word. "I've been looking all over for you! I've been so worried looking for you! Look how dark it is now!"

I was afraid of her mood and as she took me inside I started to cry.

"Tell me, where were you!" she shouted.

Still blubbering, I explained, "Mom, I was out with my wagon taking empty bottles to get some money for your birthday present."

I reached into my shirt and gave her the unsigned greeting card. My hands were dirty and they left a smudge mark where I would have signed it. As Mom looked at the card I pulled out the Babe Ruth bar. It had almost snapped in two inside my pocket. "Mom, I also got you this."

The anger vanished from her face; I watched her chin wobble as she began to cry. She reached out to hug me. I heard her sobbing as she held me tight and buried her face in my hair.

That night when the neighbors came over one of them asked her why there was a candy bar on the window ledge.

"My son gave that to me as a birthday present," she replied, proud and moist-eyed.

When I finished telling the story to the POWs they sat as if spellbound. There wasn't a dry eye among them.

"Damn you, Ev!" one of them exclaimed as he wiped away his tears.

Rabbit called me into quiz in the same month I asked Mom and Dad to tell me the truth about Tangee.

"Here, you are allowed to receive a letter," he snapped.

He drew the folded paper out of the envelope and flung it on the table like a butcher throwing scraps to an alley cat. It was an unusually long letter from Delia and it put me on guard immediately because she opened by saying she had been assured I would receive it.

I want you to know that I recently went to a conference in Canada and had the opportunity to meet many people who felt that the war should be stopped. . . . I met some people from North Vietnam and we both recognized that we have been the victims of this war and want it to stop. . . . We're all fine. We're praying for you.

It was so unexpected that I could scarcely believe it was genuine. But there was no question it was my sister's handwriting. My curiosity turned to quiet outrage. How could she stick her neck out like this, even if she didn't agree with U.S. government policy! How could she be so dumb as to meet with the North Vietnamese! Didn't she realize they would play it for all it was worth in the propaganda war! It was the kind of morale-booster the communists needed. They could not have wished for a better ally than the sister of a highly publicized POW.

"See, your own family disapproves of your criminal actions!" Rabbit said scornfully. "Now *you* must change your attitude!"

Though preoccupied with Tangee, I now worried about the family, wondering how far Delia might take her anti-war activism. My close friends who knew the extent of my worries were comforting. "When it rains it pours," said Dave sympathetically.

A few days later, I had one ear tuned to the news over the camp radio when the announcer startled me by stating, *Delia Alvarez, sister of the longest-held American POW, Lt. j.g. Everett Alvarez, Jr., has stated in a conference that she has taken action to do what she can to stop the war. She said the war is not in the best interests of the United States and her views differ from the policies of her government. She said the war is wrong and is hurting America more than anything else.*

I was shocked. As far as I was concerned this was playing directly into the hands of the communists. It could only harm the U.S. war effort and give comfort to our enemies.

Knowing the guys in the room would probably be talking behind my back, Pop Keirn did the sensible thing by suggesting we bring it out into the open. I welcomed the opportunity for frank discussion.

"Go ahead, Ev," said Pop, "you have your say first."

I was a little uncomfortable, since I knew Delia well enough to respect her motives even though I could not agree with her actions. "I don't agree with what she did or said but, darn it, you know, our families have had their ups and downs so many times. They want us home. I guess they've reached a point, after so many years of frustration and disappointment and loneliness, that they need us home badly. I guess they're all so tired they just want the war to end."

A couple of guys ripped into me, all talking at the same time so their opening remarks were lost. "I don't care who said it or what the situation is at home," said one antagonist. "They should never say things like she said!"

"But it must be really hard for them. I don't agree with what she did but it sure is understandable to me," said another POW.

"Yeah, but even so, they shouldn't say anything," someone else cut in. "They're just feeding propaganda to the enemy."

"Wait a minute," yet another interjected. "Be reasonable. She has a right to say what she did."

"The heck she has! She has a special responsibility not to say anything harmful to the U.S."

The discussion got nowhere. All of us basically knew she should not have been so outspoken. We differed only in the degree to which we felt she had compromised us. I did not worry too much because Delia's remarks were not at all inflammatory and it seemed to me she had done nothing more than voice a little impatience with the length of the conflict.

I could not be as forgiving of two American military officers among us, Marine Lt. Col. Edison Miller and Navy Capt. Walter Wilber, who, in my opinion, gave real aid and comfort to the communists. Many of us felt they broke ranks without shame and were the outstanding blots on our solidarity. We first heard of Miller during the black days of 1969, when the Vietnamese tortured us to broadcast propaganda tapes over the camp radio. Most prisoners gave tell-tale vocal signs of broadcasting under duress. Miller, together with another POW, Navy Lt. Cmdr. Robert Schweitzer, broadcast enthusiastically against U.S. activities in Vietnam. The rest of us were aghast, unable to believe that anyone in the United States armed forces, in our special situation, could take such a stand. There were cries of "Traitors!" and angry calls for them to be hung by their balls. Reviled and damned, particularly by those of us who had endured years of torture, the pair offered no regrets and refused to let up. Derisively, we slugged their tapes *The Bob and Ed Show.* Within months, however, Schweitzer freely admitted to us that he had made a mistake and regretted it. He never again took an open stand against policy laid down by the senior officers. But Miller, joined by Wilber, clung stubbornly and demonstratively to their renegade tack. We speculated that they had not been rewarded with early release because the Vietnamese hoped the two collaborators would brainwash some of us.

In the spring of 1971, before our return to the Zoo, a directive came down from the senior ranking officer stripping Miller and Wilber of their ranking authority. We were ordered not to recognize their rank. Clearly, they had violated the military Code of Conduct. Loss of respect was not enough. They also had to forfeit the privilege of rank.

Though the Code of Conduct was devised as a general guide for combat personnel, it did specify that POWs had to assist one another. And it was quite precise on other points, particularly on disclosure of information by POWs. The prohibition against giving aid and comfort to the enemy flatly barred collaboration by any means, including propaganda.

Successive senior ranking officers, beginning in late 1967, or early 1968, fleshed out these vague generalities to meet new dilemmas. No single order, for instance, could determine at what point a tortured POW should submit and sign a confession or broadcast a tape. Every situation was novel, demanding different levels of resistance. Was it worth risking a broken back for refusing to make a broadcast? Should a POW hold out and invite mutilation or death rather than confess anything? The flexible new rules set general parameters while allowing us wide personal judgment as the victims on the spot. Some of the other rules covered the need to maintain communications and the prohibition against accepting early individual release. Collectively, we called the new guidelines "Plums." It was a word chosen with deliberate cunning to outwit the Vietnamese. Occasionally they succeeded in intercepting our communications. What we needed was a red herring of a word, something so baffling and irrelevant to our captivity that it would not compromise us if overheard.

Most of the Plums had been developed by the time we moved back to the Zoo in September, 1971. Miller and Wilber moved into a separate room of the Pigsty while I was put in the same dreary space as Jerry Coffee, Norm

McDaniel, Harry Johnson, Brad Smith and Michael Lane on the other side of the building.

A few weeks after settling in, our SRO Maj. Roger Ingvalson ordered Jerry and me to brief Miller and Wilber on our own experiences as POWs. The SRO wanted to make sure that neither Miller nor Wilber could ever plead ignorance about our captors' behavior. At that point I had been held seven years and Jerry for a year and a half less. Between us, Jerry and I had gone through a number of camps and been knocked around enough to expose everything about the brutality.

We stood around in the compound, talking informally. Jerry and I recounted every form of torture we had been through, describing the manacles around our legs and the manner in which they trussed us up with ropes or ratchet handcuffs around our arms. We let them know about the whippings with sticks and rubber hoses and the merciless beatings with fists and rifle butts, when we ached just as much for a little sleep. Methodically, we traced their use of food as a weapon, from the earliest weeks when they had kept me on a starvation diet of blackbirds and slush to break my spirit, to more recent years when the staple diet was a bowl of lukewarm rice with live roaches and sewer weeds. We described conditions at every camp we had been in. Above all, we made sure they knew that the Vietnamese had tried hard to bust our communications links so they could isolate us, making each POW more susceptible to indoctrination.

The marathon briefing stretched into a third day before we were through. Both Jerry and I were exhausted. Miller and Wilber were as well briefed as anyone could be. Overall, however, I got the feeling that neither of them was much moved by the horror stories. They didn't demonstrate any particular understanding or disgust for the enemy. And I got the impression they did not believe everything we told them. Both of them brushed off much of the treatment with a blanket justification: everyone knew the consequences of breaking camp regulations. It was as simple as that.

Both Miller and Wilber continued to flaunt their independence and defy the Plums. We had to beware they were out of sight during communications between the buildings for fear they would report us. On several occasions, POWs in another building signaled across wanting to know more about the maverick duo. They said Miller and Wilber had seen them signaling and turned them into the guards. Fortunately, at that late stage of captivity, the Vietnamese did not punish anyone caught communicating. But no one could be sure from day to day whether it was a firm new policy or just a temporary lull.

In the course of maintaining contact with as many other buildings as possible, I frequently communicated from the Pigsty to the Pool Hall by standing on Harry Johnson's shoulders to reach the open air vent, a six-by-eight-inch opening created when they blocked up the windows. From that height, I looked down over the eight-foot-high brick wall across to the air vents of the Pool Hall. Before sending or receiving the communications by hand signals, I had to make sure that I was not seen by the two guards in the nine-foot high tower near the wash area. I also had to look out for Miller and Wilber.

Once, Jerry and some other guys were spotting for me as I prepared to sneak behind the north wall of the wash area, out of sight of the guards, to go across from the Pigsty to the Office to communicate routinely. Jerry said the way was clear, except for Miller, who was sitting reading outside on the northwest corner of the Pigsty. When I was done, I crept back, but noticed Miller standing outside his room. He was looking around. I didn't give it much thought until later when Jerry told me that Miller had admitted to him that he had seen me communicating. In the same time frame, Jerry was pulled into quiz. When he walked into the room, Miller was sitting behind the table next to the camp commander. Thereupon the camp commander told Jerry he knew that I was communicating with the Office. It did not matter because I was never called up to account for it or punished.

It might have been possible to ignore Miller and Wilber if they had not themselves gone out of their way to advertise their trustee status. It conferred on them special camp privileges, among which was the freedom to move around and constantly try to convert us to their line of thinking. Beginning in those final months of 1971, it was routine for us to be let out of the rooms at dawn. We could walk in the compound area immediately behind the Pigsty before being locked up again at noon for the two-hour siesta period. Then we would be released into the compound again until dusk, when we had to return to the rooms. The routine differed only on Sundays when we were let out for two periods of about an hour each to wash our dishes.

One of the most distasteful experiences during the entire period of my captivity was being locked up by Miller and Wilber. They took turns acting as our jailors. They locked us up at night, released us in the morning and repeated the procedure before and after the siesta hours. Neither of them was accompanied by guards when they carried out these shameful deeds. As far as I'm concerned, there was no evidence they had been coerced into it; it was their volunteer work. After they bolted and padlocked the doors, they stood around for hours on the porch outside the windows, gabbing at length about the misconduct of the U.S. and urging us to cooperate more with the Vietnamese. If we wanted better treatment, they enticed, we would have to follow camp regulations. Miller and Wilber got into lengthy arguments with some of those locked up on the other side of the window. I could not help overhearing everything because there was nowhere to run. Occasionally I let fly some barbed comments but I preferred not to enter into the fray.

To me, their collaboration with the Vietnamese extended even beyond being mere propagandists. I felt they took active steps to squelch our brotherhood and unity. The guards, for instance, had developed a standard practice, before letting us out of our rooms, of closing the gates in the walls separating the Pigsty from the Stable and the Pool Hall. This prevented us from walking into the other compounds. It also foreclosed those rare chances to signal through the open gates. Like some others, I had on occasion been successful at this. But Miller and Wilber had no qualms about shutting these gates if they found them open. Nobody forced them. Again, they acted willingly and enthusiastically.

Their reputations stank and they were looked upon as vermin by the rest of us.

On Christmas Day, 1971, I was summoned to the headquarters room. The day before I had received a Christmas card. I expected more mail because it had become customary over the years to hand out accumulated letters on Christmas and on Tet, the Vietnamese New Year. Six months had passed since I had sat down in the Hanoi Hilton and written the letter asking my parents to tell it to me straight. A full three months had slipped by since our return to the Zoo. Perhaps good news awaited me. I felt content and even slightly upbeat because it was the season of goodwill. I nodded politely to Spot, the assistant camp commander with the large white patch on the left side of his chin, caused by an absence of pigmentation. It had been sometime since I had seen him.

"Sit down," he said.

I sat down on the stool.

"Alvarez, you have a letter from your mother," he said blandly. "Your wife has decided not to wait for you. She has probably gone off with another man."

He dropped the letter on the table. I hesitated a moment and then opened it.

Tangee has decided not to wait. No one has seen her. We hope and pray that you will stay strong and well and that you will come home to us soon.

It hit me like dynamite. I read and re-read those few lines and reeled. Each time I read the words *"Tangee has decided not to wait,"* they seemed to spring out of the text and impale me. What did it mean? The letter mentioned nothing about another man or remarriage. I was confused and hurt, struggling to figure out what had happened. The letter raised so many questions. I read it again, memorizing the text, and then handed it back, as was customary, when he dismissed me.

Of all the possibilities I had considered during her years of silence, this was one I had not entertained as seriously as her illness, disappearance or death. It was possible that her feelings toward me had cooled. But what did it mean when it said, *"no one has seen her"*? Had she run off with someone else? Or had she taken off and become a wandering derelict or even a prostitute? Maybe she had become so ashamed of something she had done in her loneliness that she would not talk to anyone in the family. She had always been the type to lean on others for support. I recalled how the husband of one of her sisters had once told me "She has the mind of a child." This would explain why *no one* had seen her. But who was *"no one"*? Did this mean just Mom, Dad, Delia and Madeleine or did it extend to the entire family, including her sisters who were especially close to her?

Perplexed and dazed, I wandered around aimlessly, like a vagrant. At least she wasn't dead. Thank God for that! And she could not be in a hospital because Mom would surely have revealed that. What if she had gone off with another man? My guts churned at the thought. Often, in their attempts to inflict mental anguish, Rabbit and the other interrogaters would needle us. "Do you think your wife will wait for you? We think she is off with someone else. She's divorced you. She's living as a prostitute." Try as we might, we could not dismiss these jibes lightly. They played on our minds, particularly at night, when we lay down with nothing to do but think and brood. The thought that our wives might be bedding down with lovers preyed especially hard on those of us with young and attractive childless spouses. We were all prepared for the worst; we recognized that it was an awful long time for a marriage to stay together, especially when there was no physical togetherness. It was a thought that haunted many a man as the years drifted by. Mom's letter gave these repressed fears a jump-start.

The guys tried to comfort and console me, doing their best to find a silver lining. "It's going to be okay, Ev. She'll come back. Don't worry." Others mumbled, "Gee, I'm sorry, Ev." Fortunately I had chores to occupy my mind. There were dishes to wash when it was my turn. And there was activity around me, particularly at the ping-pong table. But I gradually withdrew, becoming a lot quieter, lost in the turmoil of my new uncertainty.

Sometimes I held her photograph, the one I received two years earlier where she was dressed in a mini-skirt. It was a good photo; it captured the essence of everything I loved about her—the playful smile, the shapely body, the soft femininity. She must have been driven to this on impulse. I was sure she had acted out of despair, impelled perhaps out of a sense of being trapped by circumstances that really had nothing to do with her feelings towards me. I had not done her any harm. And I was sure she meant no harm to me. We could correct this act of desperation. Together, with help from the family, we could straighten this out. It had to be a terrible mistake. I needed reassurance from home.

January 4, 1972

Mom,

    Since Tang promised to stick it out many times, was her decision impulsive? Did I discourage her? Who is in touch with her—has anyone seen her? Fill me in as much as possible.

On the unsteady screen of my mind's eye, I replayed over and over again the highlights of our courtship and marriage. We had a lot of fun and I knew she loved me as much as I fawned over her. Our ardor had survived an earlier nine-month separation during my first training cruise in the western Pacific. Tangee gave the most demonstrative proof of this one Sunday when she walked with me down the driveway of her sister's home as I prepared to drive back to Lemoore. Seldom had she looked so appealing, her white dress contrasting sensuously with her raven-black hair. She spread her arms to enfold me in a tight embrace and kissed me fervently. I had preserved that rapturous scene in slow-motion detail. It was the moment when her gestures told me unequivocally that she wanted to be my mate.

I winced at the memories which were still fresh. If only I was able to reach her I knew we could reverse whatever action she had taken.

January 18, 1972

Mom,

    Because of the situation, I hold no ill feelings towards Tang. I love her and always will. I would like her back if there is any possible way. If she is happier without me, then I'm happy for her. I know how unhappy and frustrated she was. We are only human. If she still loves me I can forgive her. You know the situation. Tell me if you need anything. Regards to her family.

Winter settled in. Men huddled indoors under blankets. Outdoors, they shuffled against the chill, cupping their hands to blow on them, the warm air rising like little puffs of steam. Even the guards, with their layers of clothing, shivered and hunched up against the biting cold. I kept much to myself, pacing back and forth along the compound wall, so wrapped up in my own thoughts that I was often oblivious to the foul weather.

I remembered an incident from our honeymoon in Las Vegas, when we were watching a floor show with topless dancers. Neither of us had seen anything like it before. Tangee suddenly turned to me and said, "If anything happened to you, that's what I'd like to do." I laughed, but when I turned to look at her it was obvious she was not jesting. It was a curious remark but I never gave it much thought at the time. Now, put in perspective, I saw beyond her sweet, down-to-earth personality. Being well aware of her own sex appeal, she did not have to do much more than dress advantageously to attract a lot of attention. The photograph she sent me showed her off in a typical cheesecake pose, flaunting her bare legs and shapely bust. What if she had followed up on her pledge in Las Vegas and dropped out to become a showgirl? Perhaps this was the reason no one had heard from her. Anything seemed possible. I had so little to go on that I had to consider even the most unlikely outcome.

When Tet rolled around again that winter I half expected an answer to all these questions because it had become traditional to give us a big meal together with letters from home. Rabbit was heartlessly forthright.

"Alvarez, here is a letter from your mother. Your wife has left you for another man. Divorced you!"

My stomach heaved and I almost threw up. All my carefully orchestrated defenses collapsed. No amount of preparation could withstand such a verbal uppercut. It hit right on target. Unsteadily, I opened the letter. It was in Mom's handwriting.

Hijo,

How difficult it is to tell you about Tang. She went to Mexico to get a Mexican divorce and remarriage. She either has a child or is expecting a child.

"MEXICAN DIVORCE? REMARRIAGE? EXPECTING A CHILD?" Is that what it was all about? For how long had I gone almost out of my mind wondering what had happened to her? All this time, while I was pining for her, she was alive and well and she was in someone else's bed! I felt a hollowness in my belly as if I had been slashed and gutted. I never imagined that Tangee would go to the extreme of wiping out our marriage, of erasing everything we had done together and meant to each other.

Mom's disclosure was a savage blow to my ego. It hurt deep down to the bone, knowing Tangee had dumped me so unceremoniously, without any lead-up or explanation, without even the grace of a goodbye. With the advantage of freedom and distance she had simply uncoupled me, leaving me stranded and bewildered in a godforsaken land far from home. I just could not reconcile myself to the manner in which she had done it nor the way in which I was let into the act. I felt ambushed. It was a low blow uncharacteristic of her. The Tangee I loved and left behind was warm and openly affectionate, completely without guile or malice. But the woman who divorced me, who took off with someone else and had his child, was heartless and cold-blooded.

When had she got the divorce? How many months or years past? Could it be made final without serving me documents? A torrent of questions surfaced. But they paled in comparison with the sting of losing her. I went through the motions of eating and breathing but my whole being focused on her. Some nights I tossed and turned restlessly, unable to blank her out of my mind. It was even more difficult to fraternize with the guys who, sensing my deep hurt, were understanding enough to let me ride out the pain alone.

Rejected by Tangee and separated by choice from the other POWs, I hugged the compound wall, beating a path as I trudged back and forth. I was so lost in the misery of my own misfortune that I didn't give a damn about anyone or anything. Without her, there were no dreams. She had snuffed them out. For seven-and-a-half years, I had held fast to the hope of an exciting, sensual reunion with her. I would smother her with kisses and hug her until it hurt. She had been the underpinning of my entire future. She was much more than a loved one. She was the light at the end of the tunnel. I relied on her as a mooring in all those years of lies and propaganda, torture, confessions, starvation, filth and incarceration. She was waiting beyond the walls and the barbed wire, a reminder of calmer, more innocent times, before we were swept up in America's longest war.

Now that she had cut me loose, I drifted pathetically. No hardship cut so deeply as her abandonment. But for all that, it was against my nature to feel anger towards her. She had obviously wanted to get on with her life and have children. She had always longed for children. We had tried, but in the short time we had been together as man and wife she had not succeeded in getting pregnant. I wondered what would have been our destiny if we had been blessed with a child.

March 9, 1972

Mom—

    I got your January letter—I hope he loves her as much as I do, and is good to her.

Jerry and Dave sometimes walked with me, trying in their gentle ways to steer me back to normality. "God, Ev, it's tough, but hey, man, we're still alive. We're still going to get back," they'd say. They went to great lengths to excuse themselves for claiming to understand the depth of my sadness. These two good men tried to ease me into putting reason above emotion. "When we get out of here we're going to have such a source of strength to draw on," one or the other would say. "In fact, we already have it, whether we get out or not. If we return with honor that in itself will be such an accomplishment that it will put everything else into perspective." Fearful of hurting me, yet persisting with the confidence borne of deep friendship, they urged me to remember how one day I would put all this behind me and regard it as nothing more than a minor setback. But they could see from my eyes that I wasn't there any more and that I needed time to be alone. Try as I might, I could not look on the bright side. How could I get excited thinking about repatriation when the door had slammed on all my hopes?

I had lost my freedom and now my wife, but my faith in a just and merciful God remained steadfast. While I paced outside I prayed silently, seeking guidance. "What shall I do now?" Prayer and the strong loyalty of my friends pulled me through the grim months of dejection and self-examination. Gradually, the pain eased somewhat and though my whole world had disintegrated, I was beginning to face up to the reality. I told Jerry I was thinking of becoming a monk. I would live in a monastery and write about my experiences. Having heard me narrate the fictional saga of the Hispanic boy I'd cooked up to pass the time, he replied, "Yeah, Ev, you would be good at that."

March 28, 1972

I just want to thank you about Tang. At last I know. Mom, I'm sure that it was hard on you also. It's sure difficult when you're doing as I was—living a dream—when just out of the clear sky your dream is shattered and you find that your world has vanished. The reality is hard to face—but you must; then pick yourself up, and go on. Someday, I will return home.

One day in April, I was pacing outside by myself when I looked up and noticed the blue sky for the first time since I got the bad news. It was spring and everything was beginning to open up. I saw buds holding the promise of color on the bare trees. The grass was beginning to grow where there had been nothing but mud. It was getting warm and the birds chirped. When I heard murmurings I seemed to shake off a trance and suddenly became aware of other people. It all happened so quickly that it felt like I was being carried along on a swift current. I was wrapped up in the frenzied burst of spring.

I stood revitalized. It did not hurt to think about Tangee any more. She was finally out of my system. I was free of her ghost. I was going to live! My prayers for guidance had been answered because I was now looking forward instead of backward. Maybe I would be a monk and maybe I wouldn't. It didn't matter. The heaviness was gone and I felt good. Once more I mixed with the guys, unburdened by doubts and freed from the terrible past.

In the heady spirit of the moment, I started to plan vacation trips I would take as soon as we got home. So what if I was alone. I could still visit all those places I'd always wanted to see—northern California and Oregon, and then on to Europe! I was bubbling over with ideas for the future. I would buy a car, new clothes, a boat. How much did a light plane cost? I didn't know what I wanted to do and yet I was going to do everything. There seemed to be neither limits nor boundaries. I might still be in a prisoner of war camp but I was now back up to speed. Actually, I felt much younger than my real age because I was so in tune with the season. I was raring to go!

May 16, 1972

Hijo,

Your letter of 3-28 arrived yesterday. It was good you had a dream to live when you did need one. Your world hasn't vanished. Time heals the worst of all. . . .

Love from all, Mom.

17
COUNTDOWN

THE FRANTIC WAIL OF AIR RAID SIRENS AND THE VOLLEYS
of distant flak tipped us off to a resumption of the bombing in mid-April.
Overjoyed, we cheered like football fans when a new outfit arrived at the Zoo
to take up anti-aircraft positions. I was elated and joined in the enthusiastic
cries. "This is it, baby! Nixon's gonna get 'em this time! Get 'em boy! Get
'em!" we yelled. The vast majority of us believed the only way we were going
to get out of the POW camps was by pounding the North without mercy.
The Paris Peace Talks were a farce. As far as we were concerned, they could
talk until kingdom come but the communists would never be persuaded at
the conference table. They would budge only if the U.S. showed it had the
will to use its air power as it should have done years back.

In June, they trucked us back to the Hanoi Hilton, probably as a security
measure. It was actually a blessing in disguise because now I shared a room
with some three dozen Americans. Though they tried to seal off each group
from the other we managed to keep in continuous contact. Much of this was
done verbally and we could even see into the other rooms because the barriers
were mere straw mats strung between bamboo supports.

Sometimes I was among those who got into arguments with the few among
us opposed to the bombing. Mark Gartley was one of them. He betrayed us,
in violating the Plums later that year, by accepting early release when his
mother came to Hanoi for him.

After a couple of spats, I realized it didn't help to argue. We all had to
live together in the same room. Even though I had taken up the gauntlet
several times, the more prudent course for the good of everybody in our room
was to avoid verbal clashes.

With Tangee recessed into the deepest folds of my memory, I no longer
worried anxiously about the passage of time and did not hunger for liberation.
I had no wife to rush home to, nor children to dote on. The return to single
status gave me a peace of mind I had not experienced in all my years of

bondage. I had the benefit of time to plan leisurely for my future. Eight years in chains had changed me into a more patient person, so that like many people of the East, I cared little for the movement of the hands on a clock. I had become like the craftsmen of old, to whom time was nothing but a change of seasons. I knew, in the ninth summer of my confinement, that I could hold out for many more if need be. Tangee had been my Achilles heel. Now that she was gone from my life I had no weak spot. I had the will and the stamina to ride out this war, no matter how long it took. If the new round of bombing hastened that end, so much the better.

The wide, unshuttered windows gave us an occasional view of flak or missiles streaking up to their targets. And occasionally an unmanned reconnaisance drone came right over the prison. But the bombing was, for the most part, infrequent in our vicinity. Sometimes we heard the A6s screaming in on night raids and saw the sky lit up with flashes and flickering fires from burning targets. When the giant B52s rolled in, the ground shook and rumbled as their deadly cargo struck home. There were some close calls and once a stray bomb hit something across the street from us. We were supplied with mahogany planks, about ten feet long and one-and-a-half feet wide, which we propped at angles against the walls then sat under for protective cover in the event one of the steel tresses or tiled roofs crashed down during a bombing raid.

Wave after wave of day and night air raids took their toll on the morale of the AAA units, which were equipped mostly with ineffective light weapons and machine guns. Towards the latter part of the year they were exhausted, moaning and groaning about the futility of their tasks and showing every sign that they no longer wanted to man their posts. It was heartening to see the proof of our belief that only massive use of air power would make the enemy knuckle under.

An improvement in our living conditions and diet signaled a weakening of the communist hold over us. If all were going well for them, they would have no need to upgrade our conditions. As the bombing continued we were allowed much more freedom to move around. Our diet grew to include a preponderance of potatoes and canned food, including fish from China and meat from East Germany. We were permitted to take cold showers and took turns cleaning the pots and pans in the communal kitchen.

New shootdowns were now spared the ritual interrogation and torture of years past. Instead, they were thrown in with the rest of the guys, some still wearing their flight suits. They brought us up to date on political and social trends in the U.S., feeding us a mass of data on new clothes styles, cars, sports, the cost of living and the upcoming presidential election between Richard Nixon and his Democratic challenger, George McGovern.

But we were still light years away from grasping the social trends that had taken place during our prolonged absence. This became abundantly clear one day when the Vietnamese called us into a tent in the courtyard to receive letters and packages. A POW emerged leering.

"There's a copy of *Playboy* magazine in there!"

A bolder man pilfered it and showed it around the gathering swarm of POWs. Holy smokes! I could hardly believe what I saw on the cover! There was very little left to the imagination. I could not recall *Playboy* being so explicit when I last saw it. I wondered at the scope of the transformation going on in America. Photographs guys received in the mail showed their sons with shoulder-length hair and their daughters outfitted in skirts that barely covered their thighs. We had heard about the hippies and the flower children and now and again been shown news clips of the anti-war rallies and marches and campus revolts. But being penned up within the walls of a foreign prison, where everyday sounds were alien, and the standard garb a drab military khaki, we could not even begin to plumb the depths of the American scene.

Increasingly, I began to feel like I had been squeezed into a mason jar eight years back and left on the mantelpiece. One day, some of the veteran POWs climbed up a partition between the rooms and looked over at the new shootdowns. In the course of the conversation one of the oldtimers told them I was also being held in the Hanoi Hilton. Apparently I was a household word because many of the newcomers asked to see me. Somewhat reluctantly, I climbed up and looked over. What I saw was astonishing. Everyone looked so young! Many of them looked like they were scarcely out of high school! I knew that most of them were majors, captains and lieutenant commanders but it was hard to reconcile these ranks with their open, boyish faces. Dressed in shorts, they stared up at me. A wave of awed silence fell upon them. No one said anything but I could detect from their expressions that I had become something of a freakish legend. After all, the period of my captivity spanned the entire length of this undeclared war. I was a living link all the way back to that murky encounter in the Gulf of Tonkin. As I got down, I was overcome by a sense of my own longevity, just like the time I saw my own aging looks in the mirror after five years.

Not long after this encounter, the room full of newcomers made contact with some other Americans who had been brought up from captivity in South Vietnam. They were being held outside of Camp Unity, in a section of the Hanoi Hilton beyond the vocal or visual range of my room.

"Hey," one of our neighbors said, "tell Ev there's a guy here they brought up from South Vietnam who's been held longer than Alvarez! His name's Jim Thompson."

I wondered about Thompson because I had not heard anything about him since reading the brief mention of his captivity in a *Vietnamese News Agency* handout of October, 1964. Thompson, a U.S. Army captain, had been detained in South Vietnam five months longer than I was held in the North. I was glad to hear that he had pulled through, especially when they reported he seemed to be okay. We never did manage to meet up, however, because the Vietnamese moved him elsewhere.

In October the partitions came down and we talked a lot more with the doves. There were some among them who were outspoken against the war and unafraid to espouse their views. They supported McGovern in the election; they saw the conflict dragging on interminably. In their view, the president had been given long enough to end the war and get the POWs home.

This was the same argument quoted by Robbie Risner's oldest son in a *Christian Science Monitor* article just before the presidential election. The Vietnamese made sure we all got copies. While Robbie predictably disagreed with his son, he took the same view I had when I learned that Delia had been campaigning against the war. He defended his son's democratic right to hold contrary opinions.

None of the so-called doves among the POWs made any moves to play into the hands of the Vietnamese, nor did they offer themselves as propagandists as we believed Miller and Wilber had done. Though in a conspicuous minority, these anti-war advocates cheered if McGovern's name was mentioned on the camp radio broadcasts and predictably booed references to Nixon. When they learned of Nixon's landslide victory the doves were downcast and complained that the electorate had been duped.

While I could in no way agree with their dovish views, I could not help but feel sad for them. As more time elapsed they uttered their deep-seated frustrations: "Ugh! This war's never going to end! We've had it!" The veterans among us knew that pessimism made survival tougher and freedom that much more elusive. Morale, however, did plummet as December dawned because there seemed to be deadlock in the negotiations, putting an end to our hopes for release by Christmas.

In the midst of this stalemate, the lights suddenly went out on December 18, as the siren wailed again for the first time in weeks.

"Atta boy!"

"Ya-hoo!"

"Sock it to 'em guys!"

Unlike previous raids, there was no interval between the siren and the rumble of the incoming B52s. Everyone scrambled for cover, knocking into each other and cussing in the darkness. There were mixed emotions of euphoria and panic. Only split seconds after the sirens wailed the bombs struck the city, setting off massive explosions, firestorms and reverberating rumbles of shock waves.

"Those aren't A6s! They're 52s!"

"Ya-hoo!"

But we were not united in our excitement at the surprise attack. There were dismal groans from the doves.

"Oh shit, here we go again!"

With every pause in the night raid, the lights went on again and we came out from under our mahogany planks smiling and upbeat. But then the rumble resumed and we took cover when the lights went out again. The succession of bombers continued through most of the night. In the morning the tired guards, grumpy from lack of sleep, ordered us out a room at a time for only ten minutes each. Anticipating more aerial attacks, they wanted us under lock and key, in tight control for security purposes. But Hanoi was burning and we still got to see the glow from our open windows. The sky over the capital rained bombs for eleven straight days, with a pause only for Christmas Day. From the stream of anti-American abuse over the radio, we learned that multiple targets had been hit, including factories, railroad yards, communications links, warehouses, port facilities and even, according to the announcers, residential areas, the city's largest hospital and the Cuban embassy.

Some Thai POWs overheard some of the guards discussing the raids and passed the word around that this time the Vietnamese were really hurting. Finally! It may have come late in the war but at last the U.S. was playing it right. If we had only done this years before the war might have been all over before the end of the previous decade.

If the stick-and-carrot approach of bombs and peace talks was ultimately successful, this would probably be our final Christmas in Vietnam. We decided to decorate the room as best we could and looped the clothes-hanging wire several times before placing it against a wall and draping it with blankets. As a final touch, we decorated it with ornaments made from kneaded bread and water rolled out to harden and then fashioned into multiple designs. We pledged to deliver gifts to each other after we were free and home again. And in a moving substitute for the warmth of absent families, we sang Christmas carols. The deep voices of male choristers carried well beyond the walls of our room.

Even the doves were quiet and expectant when the bombing stopped. What now? Some of us figured the massive bombing would not have stopped unless the communists had somehow signaled they had had enough. Others were as pessimistic as ever, refusing to believe that bombs would make any difference. The Vietnamese made no announcements but they did begin shuffling men from one room to another until we totaled more than forty. I noticed that newcomers in my room were always the early shootdowns: Bob Shumaker, Jim Stockdale, Robbie Risner, Larry Guarino. From being one of the more senior men in the building, I slipped fast in the pecking order, so that soon I was the second lowest-ranking officer in the room. "Bob," I joked with Shumaker one day, "this is the weirdest organization I've ever been in. The longer I stay here, the further down the ladder I go in the chain of command!"

The biggest surprise was seeing Scotty Morgan again. They had taken him away years back, soon after Ron Storz disappeared, when he was very ill and could not down his food. We all thought Scotty had died and had long since mourned his passing. Now he stood among us, not like a phantom from the graveyard but plump and looking almost obese next to the emaciated POW who returned with him. Both had been hospitalized, but being isolated and out of touch with other Americans, had been unable to report back on their whereabouts. Scotty's companion gave signs of mental disturbance. Even though his skinny body showed signs of malnutrition, he hardly ate, preferring to hide his food and anything else he could snatch. If we looked under his mat we might find food or a spoon or soap. And when we tried to talk to him he looked at us quizzically, with his head cocked slightly to the side.

One night, trucks arrived and I saw the guards carry out stacks of clothing and shoes, enough, surely to equip every POW with a new outfit. The following day, close to midnight, we heard a commotion and looked outside. What a surprise! Guys we had not seen for years had been bussed in. They must have added up to several hundred. While they washed up at the trough outside our windows we learned they had been held at the Dog Patch, another camp in the hills close to the Chinese border. They had been told it would be their last move before going home. As we clung to the window bars and looked down on the straggling line of new arrivals, I called out Tom Barrett's name.

Someone brought him over.

"Jeez, Tom, you're getting bald!"

"Yeah. How you doin'?"

"Okay. Hey, Tom, How's everything at home?"

"Oh, Marcia got married."

"I know, I heard," I said, wondering how he had taken the news that his fiancee had left him. "Don't feel bad, Tom. My wife didn't wait for me either."

"Yeah, I heard. I don't know what to say, Ev."

Though the guards yelled at us to get down and away from the windows we ignored them. In the feeble light of midnight I caught sight of Dick Ratzlaff.

"Ratz!"

"Who is it?"

"Ev."

"Hey, you've got a moustache and a goatee!"

"Yeah! What d'ya say Ratz!"

"I'd know you anywhere, you son of a gun!"

"How's Judy?"

"Fine."

"Got lots of pictures?"

"I'll show you sometime. Hey, Ev. Sorry about your wife. I heard."

"Yeah, well. . . . "

Suddenly we heard bamboo cracking and a man's cry for help. In the darkness one of the new arrivals had fallen through the bamboo covering of a deep well. Luckily he clung to the split bamboo and was quickly yanked up to safety. It was a night of surprises and joyful reunions. The guards kept pressing us to back away from the windows, telling us to be quiet, but we would have none of this. It was, as written in the biblical Book of Ecclesiastes, "a time to embrace. . . . and a time to speak."

The arrival of POWs from the Dog Patch fueled speculation that our release was imminent. But none of us could guess whether the oldtimers would be sent home first or last. I remembered how five years back, Spot had warned me I might be the last to go home because I had not cooperated with him. Suddenly his taunting threat of many winters past loomed large and fresh. It seemed likely, though, that we had been herded into rooms in chronological order of shootdown to make it easier to release us in increments when the time came.

A few days before the end of January, 1973, they ordered everyone in our room outside. An array of Vietnamese officials bunched around the camp commander, Spot and a studious-looking Vietnamese with horn-rimmed glasses. The camp commander smiled broadly and began to read in the squeaky, clipped tones of the vernacular. Spot translated. As expected, they announced the main points of the agreement signed days earlier in Paris by representatives of all combatants to impose a cease-fire, end the war, repatriate the POWs and restore peace.

We listened intently but when he had finished there were no cheers, no whooping, no backslapping. We just stood there looking back at them.

"Is this not good?" one of the Vietnamese asked. "Soon you will be going home."

He was met with blank stares and an eerie silence. The dramatic announcement had fallen flat and they could not understand why. None of us felt any cause for jubilation. We had already gone through too many emotionally draining false alarms. Our spirits had been raised so high only to come crashing down. Each time had been more painful. Disillusionment had bred skepticism, which had hardened into unresponsive flintiness, even callousness. As soon as we were dismissed we went back to our room and resumed the bridge tournament.

A few days later, they pitched a tent in the courtyard and summoned each man in for a few moments at a time. When my turn came, for what I later dubbed the "exit interview," I was amazed to see so many faces from the distant past, including Owl, Fox, and some of the interrogators. To a man, they were all smiles and even jovial, asking solicitously how I was and whether I remembered them. Whether this was a hoax or genuine, I could not bring myself to do anything other than nod without expression. I had long since learned to keep my guard up. Even when one of them asked whether I was happy to be going home I answered monosyllabically, "Yes."

Several POWs later reported that the Vietnamese had indirectly paid high tribute to our individual and collective spirit when they remarked a few times, "You Americans, you're not like the French." We knew this was a compliment. It was their way of acknowledging that they had not been able to make us break ranks.

Our SRO, Robbie Risner, wisely took action to prevent the Vietnamese from duping us into being used for propaganda. He directed that no one was to talk to any newsmen who might come into the prison before our release, nor agree to be photographed. And when the prison authorities brought in a troupe of Vietnamese entertainers to dance and juggle, we all filed back to our rooms, denying them a chance to film us living an apparently easy life.

Careful as we were to guard against false hopes, there was no denying the new mood which permeated the POW community. Several months back camp officials had let us have old packages of food, clothing and letters, long retained without our knowledge. As a consequence, we were better protected against the cold that winter and plentiful supplies of food made all the difference to our temperaments. Nobody ever went hungry. We feasted on candies and coffee, freeze-dried food and canned meat, common foodstuffs which seemed to us like the very gift of life. Given free rein in the prison kitchen we were able to boil water for coffee and heat much of our canned meat.

With our bellies full and our minds no longer focused on getting nourishment, our thoughts turned again to the world outside and the opposite sex. For most of us it had been so long without women that the very thought of returning to a normal life led to frequent daydreaming. It was hard to imagine that once again we would have freedom of movement, that we would make our own decisions and set our own agendas. The very thought of once more being able to roam free, even to jump in a car and cruise down a coastal highway, was as exhilarating as thinking of a roll in a farmyard haystack. That I would actually have all my options and choices restored was fulfilling in itself. The prospect of doing the most routine of daily activities filled me with tingling anticipation. I would get up whenever I pleased, make my own selection of clothing, eat whatever I wanted, and go wherever I fancied. Doorlocks and window bars and all the other hated symbols of restriction would be relegated to the past. I was going to be free, so free that as soon as I was out of Vietnam I would draw in great gulps of fresh air and fill my lungs to capacity with new life!

It was already dark when they called out the names of the first ten shoot-downs two weeks later. We walked into a small room. A hush fell over everyone as Spot addressed us. "A delegation from the United States is in Hanoi. Tomorrow morning you will leave. We will take you to the airport and you will go on your plane. Tonight we will give you new clothing to wear home."

Should we dare believe that the moment had arrived, that the countdown to departure had begun? Holding part of ourselves in check we lined up for clothing and excitedly swapped jackets and shirts, pants and shoes, trying to find the right fit for each man.

"You will be leaving very early," one of the guards announced. "You must sleep now."

But there were items to pack and farewells to be said. We packed our personal possessions into the little satchels given to each of us. I put in the little ditty bag, the cylindrical cigarette container made of dough, a spoon, my watch cap and cigarettes. And then I packed my little tin cup. It had been with me for so long that it had taken on the sentimental value of a baby's cup.

Bill Metzger, who was not among the first group leaving, asked me to call his wife. Another wanted me to phone his fiancee.

"Al," said Howie Dunn lying next to me, "we're going to make it! By God, we've made it!"

"Howie, I'll believe it when I see it."

When all was quiet, I thought about the first meal I would eat outside. For years I had fantasized, almost salivated, thinking about eating a 16-oz. steak with eggs, home-fried potatoes, lettuce, sliced tomatoes, buttered toast with jam, a large glass of orange juice, a glass of milk and a cup of steaming hot coffee. But now all I dreamed of eating was a plain hot dog and washing it down with an ice cold Coke. It would taste so good and it would be the ultimate proof that I was back home.

It was still dark when they beat the wake-up gong but everyone was immediately up and about. This might really be our last day in captivity. Never before had we been outfitted with going-away clothes and satchels to pack personal items. Nobody felt like eating even though the Vietnamese offered bread and bananas. When it was light they told us to go out into the courtyard and line up in groups of twenty. Suddenly our departure became a real probability and we hurriedly said farewells to those scheduled for later release.

Guards led us through to the smaller courtyard in front of my old cell, room 24.

While we stood and waited, sick and injured POWs limped out of the New Guy Village area. Some were on crutches. Two were carried on stretchers. Then, to our disgust, we saw Miller and Wilber, uninjured and healthy. Knowing that they were going to be released with our group brought on a chorus of curses and groans. They were misfits and, whatever their rank or date of shootdown, did not deserve to be up front with the first group to go home.

We idled for so long that after an hour gloom set in. The Vietnamese announced there had been a delay. It was turning into another false alarm. Guys stood around in twos and threes, some suggesting they might as well return to the room. Others sidled off under an archway to the bathroom. I sat alone, wrapped up in deep reminiscences of all the time I had spent in Vietnam since those earliest weeks in room 24. After all the horrors of the past eight-and-a-half years it was amazing to recall how a small, harmless gecko had startled and scared me in room 24!

I, too, finally made for the bathroom. It was a typical Vietnamese toilet, with foot pads. I squatted amongst the filth and rotting paper and had not finished my business when I heard someone hollering for me.

"Hey, Ev! Alvie! Come on! We're leaving!"

Jeez! What a time to get caught in the head with my pants down and no clean paper. The hell with it! I finished up but could not close the zipper on my pants. Too bad. I rushed out, still trying to work the zipper, but relieved to find them still lining up by twos. I took my place next to Bob Shumaker at the very front. Though several years older than me and a lieutenant commander at the time of his shootdown six months after my capture, Bob's sandy hair had already grayed over. But he still looked sprightly because of his boyish face and lean six-foot frame.

"Ev," said Jerry Denton, the most senior ranking officer among us, "We're going to march out in formation. You count cadence. I'll call you all in formation then turn on you. You'll be the right guide. Look sharp!"

"Bob! Is he serious?"

"I guess so."

"But I've never counted cadence!"

I had done well in everything at pre-flight training school—academics, sports, physical fitness, but not the spit-and-polish side, projecting the public image of the military. It just wasn't my bag. I was a jet pilot, not a parade ground drill sergeant! Though momentarily flustered, I remembered that a right guide was the guy who would carry the banner if we had one.

"Right face!" Denton boomed.

The double gates ahead were open.

"Cut 'er off, Ev!" ordered Denton.

"Forward march!" I shouted, finding the discipline somewhat incongruous.

"Count cadence!" Bob urged.

"Okay. One . . ."

Denton's voice boomed over mine from the back of the line: "Hup, two, three, four! Hup, two, three, four!"

"The hell with cadence," I thought. I was headed out those big, open, double doors!

We scrambled aboard the bus, Bob and I taking up the front seats. It felt strange to be aboard a bus without handcuffs or blindfolds for the first time in so many years. I looked out the window and saw the rest of the fleet of buses and white ambulances with Red Cross pennants. Try as I might, I could not suppress the butterflies swirling in my stomach. It looked like we were taking part in a genuine departure!

Our convoy attracted just enough attention as we drove through the streets so that people stopped to look up at us with passive, unemotional expressions. As we crossed a bridge over the Red River we got our first glimpse of significant war damage—a collapsed and buckled bridge. And then we stopped short of the airfield, again to be told there was a delay. We sat on benches in one of a cluster of buildings, wondering whether this excursion was doomed. I wondered how long we would have to wait before returning to the Hanoi Hilton. They offered us French bread with meat, but I settled for a cool beer and Dien Bien cigarettes to still my nerves.

More than two hours passed before we boarded the buses again and continued on to Gia Lam airport. It was scarred from the recent bombing. The tower building had been sprayed and seemed to stand precariously with gaping holes. Some of the hangars had been hit. There was little activity. Our buses halted one behind the other next to a hangar. Then, just as hunters with trained eyes could spot a deer in tall grass, so we too, on our own familiar terrain, quickly spied a U.S. Air Force C130 parked across the field several hundred yards ahead.

Suddenly we caught movement in the sky and someone shouted, "There it is! There it is guys!" A giant plane, now clearly visible, was coming in on final approach. The sight was electrifying. We stared hard, hoping that nothing would happen to this big bird coming down to pluck us up and carry us home.

"Look at the star!" someone screamed. "It *is* ours!"

"Come on down, baby, easy does it!"

"Man, what a beautiful sight!"

As it touched down and threw up a cloud of dust we cheered at the top of our lungs. It was the first C141 I had ever seen and it was love at first sight. It taxied past us before wheeling lazily in an almost complete circle and coming to a halt some fifty yards ahead of us. As soon as the engines cut our buses moved forward a bit, close to a roped-off area with a table surrounded by Vietnamese and American officials on our left. We got out of the bus and lined up in pairs as our guards hovered close. Just then a burly American Air Force colonel wandered over to our area. He was still about thirty feet away and though he didn't utter a sound he pointed to his watch and winked, as if to say, "Don't worry guys, just go along with this crap a little bit longer."

The guards marched us up to the table where we were surprised to see the Rabbit seated next to an American officer. Both were studying sheets of paper. The names of our injured and wounded were called first and they were carried over to the C141. Then Rabbit called out our names, beginning with mine.

"Step forward," said Rabbit.

I broke ranks as smartly as I could and returned the salute of the U.S. colonel standing next to Rabbit.

"Go on home," the American said softly.

A bulky sergeant took me gently by the arm. "C'mon, sir, we're gonna take you home."

I fought hard to hold back tears.

We passed by some of the crew from the C141 and a few jostling foreign reporters with tape recorders and microphones, who wanted me to comment on my years in captivity and my feelings as I prepared to fly out of Vietnam. But our SRO had already briefed us not to talk to anyone except the U.S. military or government representatives. There would be time for press conferences later, after the military debriefs and not before the last of the POWs had left Vietnam.

I stopped dead in my tracks at the rear of the C141. A beautiful blond flight nurse, in a form-fitting uniform with hair tied up at the back, stood at the top of the lowered ramp. She was busying herself with something and unaware of my presence. In my rapture, she looked like a delicate apparition. It had been almost nine years since I had set eyes on an American woman and every gesture, every slight movement she made was divine.

"Bob!" I called behind me, "take a look at that!"

"Wow! Yeah!" he almost yelped.

I walked up the ramp and she turned around and saw me. When she reached out and took my arm to help me aboard I felt like I might oxidize into thin air. She smelled so good; so clean and fresh and perfumed. Wallowing in the fragrance of her scent and the closeness of her flesh, I let her lead me by the arm to my seat. Bob sat down next to me.

"How old do you think she is?" I asked him when she left.

"Oh, maybe twenty-three, twenty-four."

"Nah, she's not that old. Maybe she's twenty-one or twenty-two. Well, I bet she's no more than twenty-five at the most."

When she came back escorting another POW, I asked her, but her smile was so tender, so captivatingly feminine, that I almost missed her reply.

"Thirty-two," she said with a light giggle, and then she was gone.

"I guess we've been away too long," said Bob.

"But jeez, Bob, have you *ever* seen anything that looked as good as that!"

The crew buttoned up the hatches, started the engines and taxied up the runway. I prayed we would not have a breakdown. We were so close. We really were going home.

The engines roared to a crescendo and when they released the brakes the giant cargo plane rumbled down the runway, gathering speed like an ungainly pelican preparing to fly. As soon as we broke ground a thunderous cheer erupted. Even the sick and maimed joined in. Everyone was laughing and grinning and whooping it up. Some cried with joy. There was a lot of handshaking and back-slapping.

"Son-of-a-bitch! We made it!"

"We're on our way guys!"

"YA-HOO!"

We walked around light-headed and ecstatically happy, aware now that we were on our way to Clark Air Force base in the Philippines. The doctors on board told us we would have to go through physical examinations before they could allow us normal meals but as a stop-gap they let the flight attendants offer us chocolate and apples. Every moment seemed to be filled with new thrills and warm sensations. As we flew over the Gulf of Tonkin, I almost choked up when the crew passed on a radio transmission from the U.S.S. *Enterprise* down below: *Welcome back, guys!*

Dr. Roger Shields, the State Department civilian in charge, started quizzing us about guys we had known in the POW camps whom we had not heard of for some time. Two names came to mind immediately: Ron Storz and J.J. Connell.

"They are both dead," he said. "We have word from the Vietnamese that they died in captivity."

Everyone who knew them froze, looking at Shields as if paralyzed by stun guns. We didn't know. They had been taken away and no one had seen them since. Even though we had to assume the worst we thought they might still be alive. We were always hopeful. Tears glistened in my eyes when I heard their fate. Nobody said a word for a couple of minutes. My mind flashed back to the Shed where I used to talk to J.J. I could see his melancholy face and his rough hands. When he talked to me he had such concern for my well-being. How could he be dead? They must be lying! And Ron Storz? The first time I had seen him he had walked by me in the Briar Patch, mistaking me for a Vietnamese because I was talking with one of the guards. He had the build of a classical Greek statue and over the years his courage became legendary. He was the stuff of which real heroes were made. They must have suffered because neither J.J. nor Ron would have succumbed quickly. Those two had been among the bravest, indomitable until the very last time we had seen them. It grieved me no end thinking about their demise. Our homecoming would not be complete. I felt like I had just woken up from surgery and been told they had amputated a leg. But I did not cry for long. The protective shell had grown rock-hard with years of conditioning. I would weep for them in the only way I knew how—by saluting their memory and their courage and vowing never to forget them.

Shields briefed us on what to expect when we landed. "Guys, when you get off, there's going to be a red carpet, military brass, a lot of TV cameras and hundreds, maybe thousands of well-wishers. What we're going to do is go off in order of shootdown. That means Ev Alvarez, you get off first. There'll be a lot of cameras and you'll get a chance to say a few words. Then the buses will take all of you to the hospital."

"What do I say?"

"Whatever you want. Just prepare a few words."

The four-hour flight passed quickly. Bob and I, locked in our own private thoughts, were much quieter after the initial thrill of departure. Jerry Denton brought us out of our cocoons with an announcement. "There's been a little change of plans here," he said. "As the senior officer, I'll go off first when we land. I'll say a few words. Then you'll go off in order of shootdown. So it'll be myself, then Alvie, then Bob, then the next guy and so on."

I thought nothing of it. Certainly it would have been a high honor to have led those men off the plane and to have spoken on their behalf. But if Denton wanted to pull rank, he was fully entitled to and it did not bother me either way.

As we approached the coastline, a wave of exhilaration swept through the plane. The moment of touchdown was greeted with a thunderous roar. We had made it back alive!

I could neither see nor hear Denton but when he had finished his speech someone beckoned me, "You can come on out now!" I looked at the flags, the welcoming throngs, and the admiral waiting to receive me at the edge of the red carpet. I almost sprang down and gave a snappy salute. "Lieutenant j.g. Everett Alvarez, Jr., reporting back, sir!"

18
HOMECOMING

I WAS SURPRISED BY THE MASS OUTPOURING OF GENUINE affection for us. Thousands of men, women and children, in military and civilian garb, thronged the airport and lined the route to the hospital. We had heard so much about antiwar protesters and those who despised any link with the war that we did not expect the rousing welcome given us. Especially moving were the hand-scrawled signs held high by kids: WE LOVE YOU! Many of those along the route gave the thumbs-up sign. It was a sweet and wonderful homecoming because it was so unforeseen.

As we set foot in the hospital I took a deep breath. How good it felt to inhale the clean, fresh air after the stench of human fertilizer in Vietnam! And the walls and floors! I marveled at their scrubbed and shiny look. We were still in the tropics but what a marked difference already!

My first priority after dumping my gear in a room of half a dozen beds, each enclosed by a curtain, was to take a shower. This was going to be with *hot* water, not like the cold dribble we got from the makeshift outdoor shower at the Pigsty. Armed with sweet-smelling soap and a tube of shampoo, I stood under the sprinkler for a full hour, cleansing the grime and washing away the smell of the past. Over and over I shampooed my hair, massaging my scalp vigorously, as if it was infested with fleas. The stream of hot water flowed over my shoulders and down my body like a steamy balm, relaxing the muscles and softening my skin. Serenely drowsy, I sensed for the first time the full impact of my restored freedom. The cuffs were broken, the ropes severed. Nobody hovered close to hurry me up, to bark orders or to regulate my movements. I could take my own sweet time and indulge myself. I had not experienced such physical and mental well-being since the hotsie baths at Atsugi. And to think, I could shower the following day and luxuriate all over again!

Now my thoughts turned to food. I had not eaten a square meal the whole day and was famished. I had it all planned. I could hardly wait to get into the steak and eggs and the side orders. But we were told to wait first for a preliminary medical check and it was several hours before the team of doctors appeared.

"Let's see now. Do you have any major problems?"

"No."

"Any big injuries?"

"No."

"Can you move everything?"

"Yeah."

"Is there *nothing* wrong with you right now?"

"Well doc, probably the biggest problem right now is the worms."

"Worms?"

I told them about all the parasites that had wriggled out into my pants since 1967, always after a seizure of belly cramps.

"Mmm, we'd better put you on a bland diet and start giving you some pills."

They gave me a slip with the words *bland diet* and I went with the others down to the dining room. As I picked up a tray a guy took my slip and handed me my meal. The centerpiece was a hamburger pattie, smaller than the palm of my hand, a dollop of mashed potatoes and a few string beans. Beside this was a glass of skimmed milk. I found a table and sat down. But then I saw other guys passing by holding trays heaped with steaks and eggs, salads, banana splits, milkshakes and everything we had dreamed of. A horde of them swarmed around an ice cream bar to pile on even more food.

"What's going on?" I asked Air Force Lt. Bob Peel sitting with me. "How come they're all eating that?"

Bob looked devastated. "I don't know. You got a bland diet, too?"

"Yeah, but the hell with this!"

"C'mon!" I said, "Let's get in that line!"

"Right behind you!"

The orderly who had directed us to our table tried to steer us away.

"You're on a bland diet, sir, you can't line up here."

"The hell we can't! If they can, we can! We've been eating garbage for years!"

"Yes, sir!"

I filled my plate with a huge steak, french fries, three eggs, toast, a milkshake and coffee. Ah! It tasted so good! We didn't eat—we *devoured*. Midway through the feast, some of the medical staff stopped at our table and to our surprise a nurse reprimanded us, "You're not supposed to be eating that! You're on bland diets!"

"Yeah, but if all of them can eat it then so can we!"

"Well," one of the doctors hesitated, "I guess it must be okay if you can keep it down."

We were too busy with our food to take them seriously.

No one but doctors and nurses were allowed up to our sixth floor rooms and soon after the meal a radio blared music and bottles of booze appeared. Our stomachs were full and our bodies clean. It was time to party.

Though I turned in about 3 A.M., I automatically woke up at the crack of dawn. It took about a year to get rid of this conditioned reflex. The curtain was still drawn around my bed when two nurses appeared, stuck a thermometer in my mouth and left. Then I heard Larry Guarino's groggy voice in the cubicle next to mine.

"Get away from me!"

"But sir, you have to take this thermometer. Sir, we have to take your temperature."

"I said get away from me!"

Again they pleaded.

"Look," said Larry, "if you don't leave me alone I'm going to bite you in the ass!"

Seconds later, I heard one of them scream, "Ouch!" while the other giggled.

The first full day passed in debriefings with military intelligence and breaks for medical and dental tests. They told me my teeth would need a lot of work. The Vietnamese had pulled out two of my broken teeth, once without any painkiller, but the beatings and crushed pieces of rock served up in our food had broken many of my fillings. Fortunately, the absence of sugar had prevented tooth decay but I would need to have some teeth ground down and fitted with crowns and two bridges.

After they measured us for new uniforms to be worn for arrival ceremonies back in the U.S. I wanted to phone home, but I put it off when I saw the long line of ex-POWs waiting to do the same. Such a long time had passed since I had spoken to my family that another day would not make any difference to me. Besides, many of the hospital nurses were Spanish-speakers from Puerto Rico and the word was that lots of them wanted to meet Alvarez. I was impatient to get on with the party.

I gave little thought to my own family's restless wait in Santa Clara. Certainly, I had become hard-hearted and emotionally drained. Blocking them out of my mind for so many years to prevent nostalgia had taken its toll. And being cast adrift by Tangee took away the urgent need to return home. With my normal senses blunted, I did not stop to consider the feelings of those who had been so loyal to me. By the time I made the call I had already slept two nights in the Philippines.

Chole, Lalo, Delia and Madeleine, joined by Cecilia, her husband Albert, Linda, George, Al, Virginia and their children, had already gathered for their final vigil at Bohannon Drive. The different time zones would force them to stay up long after midnight if they wanted to see the C141 arrive at Clark Air Force base live on television. They grouped around the TV in the corner of the living room, laughing and chattering excitedly. But well into the night, when it appeared the landing would be much later than scheduled, they spread the sleeping bags on the floor. Though no one fell asleep, Lalo told Madeleine to be sure to watch the TV screen and alert them whenever the plane came into view.

Madeleine switched the channel to something more interesting, but just in case something unexpected happened she left the radio on low volume. Suddenly she caught an announcement over the radio that the POWs had landed in the Philippines. Frantically, she switched channels but the landing ceremony was over. Lalo was beside himself, asking how such a thing could happen. They had missed the momentous climax to their eight-and-a-half-year wait. Madeleine trembled, feeling a mix of guilt, shame and embarrassment. Of course she had not done it deliberately but she knew that she alone was to blame. She had fouled up the biggest moment of his return.

But it was only a temporary setback. When the network showed a replay of the landing, their disappointment evaporated in a swell of jubilation. They cheered and wept when the cameras zoomed in on Everett as he stepped out of the plane. And then, to their collective amazement, he walked briskly down the steps! To be sure, he was very thin but he descended as if in perfectly good health. A warm glow settled over those in the modest home on Bohannon Drive. They embraced each other and let the tears streak down their flushed faces. It was a scene very reminiscent of that August day when they were all much younger, and the news had come through that Everett was in captivity, but alive. Now he was on his way home—not in a body bag but on his own two feet.

The pack of reporters and cameramen descended once more on the quiet and tidy street, waiting outside to record the family's reactions when Everett telephoned from the Philippines. They kept up the vigil even though two nights passed uneventfully.

With each passing hour, the suspense intensified. The telephone became the focal point of the household. All they could do was wait for the tell-tale ring to hear him once again. So many calls came in from well-wishers and friends, the media and even total strangers that they went through a roller coaster of expectations and false alarms.

On one occasion, after it had not rung for some time, Chole picked up the receiver. A voice asked formally and deferentially whether it was the

Alvarez home. It had to be the operator clearing the call for Everett! Tension mounted. But to their astonishment it was an official from a convalescent home. The message was brief and sad. Chole and Cecilia's older brother, Joe, had unexpectedly passed away. The news hit like successive shock waves. They had last visited him a few months back when he had seemed as well as could be expected. Since his transfer from a long stay in the Veterans Hospital, Joe had alternated between lucidity and incoherence. At times he recognized his sisters and spoke about familiar matters. More often he reverted to the odd babblings they had first noticed way back when he lost his job in the Great Depression. Yet he was physically fine and in good health.

Immediately, they agreed to keep their bereavement secret from Everett. The time would come when they would have to tell him but this was not the moment to talk about death. That meant keeping it to themselves and away from the media. Cecilia and her husband decided to return to Salinas to make arrangements for the burial there. The rest of the family would follow inconspicuously for the funeral. Cecilia marveled to herself how God had His way of doing things and changing people's plans.

The moment she and Al walked out the front door they were engulfed by reporters trying to lock up their side-bars to the major breaking story. Al told them Everett had not yet called, but they had to go back to Salinas briefly on private business. It was the first comment out of Bohannon Drive in two days and newsworthy or not, the hungry pack of newsmen pounced on it like a scrap of red meat. Local radio stations competing to top their news breaks, quickly reported Al's comments, which he heard over his own car radio on the drive south.

The family had already broken the news of MaMona's death in a letter Everett should have picked up on arrival in the Philippines. The military had advised sending a short letter to returning POWs to pre-empt questions the airmen were certain to ask in their first telephone calls home. The family knew Everett would ask about his grandmother. They had withheld the news of her death for five years, even though he had written asking whether she was still alive. Notwithstanding the lapse of time, everyone knew he would mourn her passing with a long and quiet hurt. Uncle Joe, on the other hand, was an aging relative for whom he felt acute sympathy but no special affection. He might even look upon Joe's death as a merciful release. Be that as it may, they decided to spare him news of another death in the family because he had only just emerged from his own darkness.

No one was over anxious when two days passed without his calling. Most likely he was in need of more thorough medical attention than other POWs.

It was going to be harder for him to adjust because he had been held longest. As understanding as they were, they could barely wait out those few days. When the call finally came they could not suppress their tears.

"Hi, Mom!" Everett shouted, the way people do on international calls.

"Hijo!" she said, her voice cracking, "Is it really you?"

Though dry-eyed himself, he could tell his mother was breaking down.

"Are you well, Hijo?"

"I'm well, Mom."

"I saw you on the television. You walked well down the plane."

"I'm fine, Mom. Don't worry about me. But I have a lot of gray hair!"

"Don't worry about it. You are part Indian so you won't go bald. It's okay to have gray hair so long as you aren't bald-headed!"

He laughed and then, almost tongue-tied, he said softly, as if confirming something to himself, "Mom, Tang didn't wait, eh?"

"No, Hijo, she didn't."

"Oh, Mom," he sighed.

They would talk later. There was so much ground to cover. Chole dabbed her eyes as the phone passed from mother to father and then to the sisters.

"Del, I'm really proud of you," he said.

"Are you *really* proud of what I did?" she asked, dumbfounded.

They were speaking at cross purposes. Everett had only a vague idea of her public commitment to the anti-war movement.

"Well, I'm proud of you all for sticking in there," he said. "It must have been tough on all of you."

Poignantly, he repeated the passing remark about Tangee, adding, "I hope her present husband loves her as much as I did."

Delia gulped, feeling the hurt that was still there.

Flustered, Madeleine took the phone. It was like talking to a stranger. She barely knew him. He was in his mid-thirties. She had just entered her twenties. But, caught up in the general flap and excitement, she told him she could not wait to see him soon.

"I'll be home shortly. I'm just going through routine examinations right now," he said.

That night someone snapped a polaroid picture of Everett with Robbie Risner, who had been such an inspiration to him. More than five years had elapsed since they were tethered together during the frightening parade through the streets of Hanoi. Both men had survived the terrible ordeals of solitary confinement and torture. Now, bathed and dressed in clean clothing and their hair combed neatly, they rested their arms on each other's shoulders. An outsider would have been hard-pressed to guess at the enormity of their suffering as they smiled broadly for the photographer, their gaunt faces suddenly looking youthfully lean and taut.

"Ev," said Risner, thirteen years his senior, "we're sending you home on tomorrow afternoon's flight. I'll be in a following plane. I want you to know we're going to send Miller and Wilbur back with you."

"Why with me?"

"Look, you're not the senior officer, but we want you to be the spokesman for the group. When you land I want you to be the one to say something to the American people and the press. I don't want them to say anything. I've told them not to say a word to anybody. Will you do that?"

"Sure, Robbie."

"Fred Cherry is really the senior guy, besides Miller and Wilber, but I want you to be the spokesman. You've done a good job. I'll see you back stateside."

The giant C141 Starfighter stopped at Hickam Air Force Base in Hawaii about 2 A.M. to refuel for the remainder of the long haul to California. Everett could hardly believe his eyes as he stepped out of the plane to a wildly cheering crowd of thousands of well-wishers waving American flags. Among them was Capt. Nick Nicholson, air operations officer on the staff of the commander in chief, Pacific Fleet. Accompanied by his wife, Evelyn, he was desperately trying to cut through red tape to meet with Everett during the brief stopover. Nick buttonholed an Air Force colonel.

"I know what the rules are but I don't give a damn! I want to see him! I have to see him!"

The colonel listened with growing understanding as Nick gave a quick run down of how he had been Everett's flight leader when they had flown over the *Maddox* and the *Turner Joy* in the Gulf of Tonkin almost nine years back, how, during the very first air raid over North Vietnam, when they had flown in the same attack group over Hon Gai, Nick had been the last person to have radio contact with Everett before he bailed out.

The colonel was obviously moved. "I'm not supposed to do this," he said, "but I'll go in. If he agrees to talk to you then I think we can work it out."

"Fair enough," said Nick, aware of the strict prohibition against anyone speaking with returning POWs before they had been fully debriefed.

Nick paced anxiously as he vividly recalled that clear August day when they had approached the coast of North Vietnam. The hilly range had reminded him of the way Chinese artists always painted unrealistic mountain peaks and pinnacles. Ignoring the curves and crooked lines of the landscape, the painters employed only straight brush strokes, making the mountains look like triangles. Yet remarkably, as his Skyhawk zoomed closer to Hon Gai, Nick saw that the hills and mountains had been faithfully reproduced. They really were exactly as the Chinese depicted them.

With the bay almost upon them, Nick focused his attention on the target area but didn't see any PT boat targets until Everett's high-pitched voice crackled into the headset, "They're at anchor in the bay!" Nick caught sight of them but in his eagerness to press the attack, flew in much too low for safety. He compounded his error by pulling up to the left, as Navy pilots invariably did after making bombing or landing patterns. "You idiot, man! You've got your head up and locked!" Nick said to himself, remembering that the plan had been to pull out to the right at Hon Gai, to confuse the Vietnamese in case they knew all about traditional Navy flight procedures.

As he pulled out, Nick looked over his shoulder to see whether his rockets had struck the target. But his attention focused instead across the bay towards the town of Hon Gai. There were two distinct layers of weird clouds. Nick thought they had a smog problem similar to Los Angeles. Then he saw bursts of smoke puffing at the same altitude as the smog. It was live flak, something he had seen only in movies! And it was coming thick and heavy from the Hon Gai area, pre-cut to explode at two levels! The flak came so quickly, just as the planes rolled in for the attack, that Nick had no doubts the Vietnamese were expecting them.

One after another the Skyhawks rolled in, strafing and bombing, when unexpectedly, Everett's voice shrieked across the air waves.

"409, this is 411. I've been hit! . . . I can't control it! I can't control it!"

Nick wanted to say something, *anything*, before Everett bailed out. It was vitally important to let him know that someone had picked up his alarm. "You know what to do, Alvie!" said Nick.

It was the last thing Everett heard before ejecting.

Nick looked frantically for Everett's stricken plane, scanning the sky above and sweeping his gaze left and right. He heard Everett's beeper for several seconds. That meant he had ejected. But still he saw nothing. He made a quick swoop over the bay, hoping to get a fix on a parachute or aircraft wreckage, but still drew blanks.

Nick felt bad about his missing friend and colleague and as the weeks evolved into months and years, he plunged deeper into a somber, obsessive melancholy, forever asking himself why fate had spared him and visited disaster on Everett. Though he tried hard to absolve himself he could not shake off a feeling of guilt, of being somehow responsible for Everett's loss. Before Hon Gai, he had always wanted to go to Monterey for postgraduate studies. There was something enchanting about that slice of California. The scenery never failed to charm him and fill him with a sense of well-being and he knew it would be especially conducive to academic research. But after Everett went down, and Nick had the opportunity to resume his studies, he no longer had the heart for it. He wrote to the squadron's executive officer, pleading for a return to combat conditions. Driven by the example of Everett's sacrifice, Nick pressed on with a fierce determination to give more highly of himself than ever before. He was posted back to active roles on ships and planes and whenever he felt downhearted or out of sorts, he took comfort by comparing his lot with Everett's. Nick had his health, his freedom, his wife and his four children. It was a hell of a lot better than anything Everett had.

At the time Everett stepped off the plane in Hawaii, Nick had no indication that the following year he would take command of the U.S.S. *Ranger,* an aircraft carrier as large as the *Constellation.* When he did, it would be the fulfillment of a career dedicated for the most part to Everett, whose memory had spurred him to succeed.

While Nick paced back and forth, waiting for the green light to meet with the returning POW, Everett was being feted as a VIP in the terminal building.

"Sir, there's a Capt. Nicholson to see you. He says he knows you."

"Capt Nicholson? *Nick* Nicholson!"

"Yes sir. Would you like to see him?"

"Would I! Sure!"

Nick and Evelyn were waiting alone in a large white room lit with bright lights. There was only one chair and a single table. The only two entrances were doors at opposite ends. Suddenly the door at the far end opened. Everett came in. Immediately when they saw one another they strode quickly and quietly forward, their arms outstretched. They locked in a bear hug and sobbed, both overcome by the profound emotions of this moment of reunion. For Nick it was the rounding out of a dismal period of his life. His valiant friend was back. The vigil was over. For Everett it was a link back to his happiest years, when he was a young and carefree pilot. Nick was the visible reminder of everything that had preceded Vietnam. In a flash he remembered his own wild and innocent youth, when he had borrowed Nick's little red sports car and almost totaled it on a drive up to see Tangee in the middle of the night. Fate plowed over the last eight-and-a-half years, but the period before still belonged to him. Everett had not cried in the Philippines. He would not cry in California. But he bawled like a baby as he gripped his former squadron operations officer who had remained so loyal. There was something very special about this friendship. Nick gently took him by the shoulders and stood back to look at him but Everett side-stepped to embrace Evelyn, herself in tearful disarray.

"You know, this is the first time I've cried," Everett said almost apologetically.

Nick did not know how to break the ice in the face of such overwhelming emotions.

"Alvie," he said in jest, "I've been waiting eight-and-a-half years to debrief that last flight we were on. I think it's totally unsatisfactory for a wingman to keep his leader waiting so long!"

"I guarantee it won't happen again!" Everett retorted, a big smile breaking over his face. "But Nick, why did you go off and leave me like that!"

They looked each other over. Everett was gaunt but looked much better than Nick had anticipated. Still, there was no doubt the ordeal had taken its toll.

"Hey Nick," Everett asked, "what did you mean when you radioed 'You know what to do'? What was I supposed to do!"

Nick swallowed hard.

"You remember that?"

"Sure! It's the last thing you said to me. God, for years I thought to myself 'What the hell was I supposed to do?' "

"You did okay," Nick replied, his voice full of compassion.

With only a single chair in the room, the three of them remained standing as Everett pounded Nick with a volley of questions about their former squadron. He wanted to know as much as possible about every individual, where they were and what they were doing. To Nick's astonishment, Everett's memory was phenomenally precise and accurate. He remembered the names of everyone, many of whom Nick had long since forgotten, together with the minutest details of events long past. It was like listening to a tape recording brought up from a time capsule. Everett talked constantly, the words coming out of his mouth like a machine gun on automatic fire, as if he had to absorb and convey as much as possible in the limited time available. It flabbergasted Nick and Evelyn. They remembered how quiet and even shy he had been when they all lived on the desolate stretches of Lemoore Naval Air Station.

Everett spoke very little about himself and Nick warily let him ask the questions, fearful of the experiences he might have endured and the raw wounds that might be no more than skin deep. Briefly, Everett described how he had been seized by the Vietnamese as he bobbed helplessly in the ocean. They had grabbed him roughly, yanked him into the boat, tied him up and pushed him down. But he had dropped his wedding ring into the Gulf waters to prevent any revelation of his marital status.

"I've got to show you this picture," Everett said suddenly as he fumbled in the left hand pocket of his khaki, short-sleeved, open-necked summer uniform shirt. As he did so he looked down at the two rows of ribbons pinned above the pocket.

"Hey, Nick, what do these damn things mean! I've got all these ribbons. I don't know what I did to earn this stuff!"

Carefully, as if handling delicate porcelain, Everett took a handkerchief out of his shirt pocket and unfolded it. Inside was the polaroid photograph of him standing next to Robbie Risner, their arms around one another's shoulders.

"I would go to the ends of the earth to follow this man," he said, looking at the photograph with such devotion that it was clear he regarded the colonel with awesome respect. "Robbie Risner was our senior ranking officer. He was a great leader and a very brave man."

Everett spoke sparingly about life as a POW, not mentioning anything about torture or common brutalities.

"You know," he said with a twinkle in his eye, "bread is wonderful! It's absolutely wonderful! Not only can you eat it but you can mold it and make things out of it." And then he described how he had passed some of the time rolling bread and water and fashioning it into cigarette containers, toothbrush stands and other useful items.

An MP opened the door.

"Commander Alvarez, sir, it's time to leave."

Nick and Everett embraced once more. This time they did not cry; they were exhaustively happy, content beyond measure.

I had no difficulty scribbling a few notes for the speech Robbie had asked me to deliver on arrival at Travis Air Force base. I wanted to pay humble tribute first of all to merciful God, and then to the president and the American people. None of them had forsaken us. We had kept faith and they had remained loyal. Unexpectedly, Wilber approached.

"Ev," he said softly, "can I see the words you've written down? Your message."

I held out the piece of paper. "You mean this?"

He scanned it.

"Yes."

"Go ahead."

He copied my notes and as he handed them back said, "I just wanted to keep it. You know, copy it."

I had always suspected that Wilber admired me. Even though he was a deeply religious man I felt that he may also have been mentally disturbed, as if he never quite had it all together. I could not help but feel sorry for him, though I was to have great respect for his lovely wife and family for standing by and supporting him through the years of ostracism and abuse that would follow. Miller, on the other hand, was, in my opinion, a devious person fully aware of his own actions.

As we approached the familiar beige crinkle of the California coastline, the captain invited me up to the flight deck briefly to take control of the C141. Compared to my sleek barracuda-like Skyhawk, the lumbering craft moved like a ponderous whale. But I felt the same euphoria that overcame me in basic flight training, when piloting a plane had taken on sensuous overtones and aerial maneuvers became graceful art forms.

The land ahead stretched out expansively and invitingly. I had survived and would wade again in the beckoning surf and walk once more on the fertile soil which held the promise of bountiful seasons to come. California! Its very name conveyed the lull of palms and the ease of the tropics. I was home again, back in the poet's blessed "land of the free."

I felt a great warmth and gratitude as I read my few prepared words to the multitudes of well-wishers at the air base and to those millions who watched our arrival live on national television:

> "For years and years we dreamed of this day and we kept the
> faith. Faith in God, in our president and in our country.
> It was this faith that maintained our hope that someday our
> dreams would come true and today they have.
> We have come home.
> God bless the president and God bless you Mr. and Mrs. America.
> You did not forget us."

19
REUNION

EVERETT DID NOT MIND THE THOUGHT OF STAYING AT Oak Knoll Naval Hospital in Oakland for weeks, if not months, since he would be free to come and go as he pleased. It would be his living quarters while he underwent extensive medical tests. The doctors wanted to check for any damage done by the bad diet and the beatings. They would have to examine his nervous system and take a close look at his jaw bone which periodically slipped out of place ever since that savage beating seven years back. They also wanted to find out more about the parasites he had been passing while in captivity. The dermatologist would be looking at the cause of rashes he had contracted in Vietnam. Above all, he needed a lot of dental repair work.

Within minutes of his arrival, a hospital psychiatrist told Everett his parents and sisters were down the hall waiting to see him.

"Do you want some time by yourself first?" he asked. "You can sit down and relax and we'll bring them in when you're ready."

Everett wondered what all the fuss was about. Why wait? What did he need to relax for?

"Let's go ahead," he said.

"You're sure you're ready?" asked the psychiatrist.

"Sure," said Everett.

The minutes had dragged like hours for Lalo, Chole, Delia and Madeleine. Outwardly they looked composed, despite their jitters, but the longer they waited for him in the privacy of the hospital, the more the suspense heightened and they tingled, feeling giddy and light-headed. Though separated for some time and barely on speaking terms with one another, Chole and Lalo had gotten together again for their son's sake, believing it would be better to pull the wool over his eyes for the time being. They began to fidget, though they did not even glance at each other.

Madeleine smoothed her dress and flicked her long black hair back over her shoulders. She was a twelve-year-old when Everett was shot down. Now she was twenty-one and engaged to be married. She wanted to make a good first impression, presenting herself as a mature young adult. But what would she say? How should she greet him? A Navy psychologist had warned them to expect him to be depressed and ill. He might even be carrying worms and parasites. "My God!" thought Madeleine, "What kind of person is coming back? How sick will he be? Will he have scars? Will he recognize me?" She wished the Navy had given them a current report on his physical and mental state instead of alarming them with unsubstantiated concern for his sanity.

Delia wondered how much Everett knew about her anti-war activities. Did he know she was a founding member and driving force behind an organization of families of POWs united against the war? Could her brother have learned that she had criss-crossed the country, speaking against the war at rallies from San Francisco to Miami? Or that she had appeared together with Jane Fonda on the Merv Griffin TV show to focus attention on the plight of the POWs and proclaim her opposition to the war? What would he think when he found out she had gone to Paris during the peace talks and lobbied representatives of the Vietcong in her crusade to speed the end of the war? She wondered how he would react to the abuse heaped on her for her views. Would he say she deserved it? The wives of most other POWs, outraged at her public campaign, had materialized at meetings where she was a featured speaker so that they could ridicule and scorn her. Anonymous callers had cussed her by phone while others sent her hate mail. Her many enemies had branded her unpatriotic and even a communist.

Delia began to have mixed emotions when she looked at the Stars and Stripes because it came to symbolize all the anger and hostility unleashed by the war. But she never doubted that the war was wrong and the killings in vain. She would have taken the same vehement stand even if Everett had not been a POW. She had not tempered her activism because of alternative views he might hold. To her, the war was transparently insane. Tens of thousands of Americans had died for a flawed policy. That had set her on fire. Even if Everett had perished in captivity, she would have continued the protests with the same driven commitment. Perhaps she would not have been asked to take such a prominent role, but she would have been just as passionate in protesting the conflict. How often people had said to her during his captivity, "What if your brother doesn't have anything to do with you?" And every time she had replied, "That's his decision. I have mine to make." Outsiders might have a hard time understanding how she could have worked so hard for a cause that could invite Everett's disapproval, if not disgust, but it did not stop Delia.

She had devoted so much time to her cause that she had even quit her job and then worked only part-time. Meanwhile she was studying full-time for her masters degree in Urban and Regional Planning at San Jose State University. As the most articulate and energetic of the family, she had for years done the legwork and made decisions on Everett's behalf, particularly after Tangee relinquished her responsibilities. It had all been so wearying.

With Everett's return imminent, the pressure finally told. One day, some months back, Delia was scheduled to fly to Boston for a rally, but she was simply too exhausted and skipped the flight. Chole was cooking and Delia was washing her hair in the kitchen sink as they talked of the war and what it had done to them. In mid-sentence Delia broke down and started to cry.

"You put the whole burden on me!" she wailed forlornly, her head lowered in the sink.

Chole winced but understood. Her daughter had assumed so many of the responsibilities for the whole family. She had carried too much for too long. She reached out to embrace her daughter from behind. Then she dug her head in Delia's back and squeezed and kissed her half a dozen times. Hearing the commotion, Lalo walked into the kitchen to find out what was happening.

"You'd better stay here and listen to Delia," Chole said firmly. "Look what we have done to our daughter. It's not fair. She has carried too many of our problems for too long. Look now what it's done to her."

Lalo looked downcast. It was not the moment to reopen the wounds of war and argue its rights and wrongs. It was all but over. He could never have joined their camp but he saw now that perhaps he had left too much to Delia. They should have lightened her load. His heart went out to his daughter but he said nothing as he watched her cry and then duck her head under the water to stifle the sobs.

With the signing of the peace accords and the certainty of Everett's repatriation, the pressures on all of them subsided dramatically. It would take time for them to wind down and return to a semblance of normality they had not known since August 5, 1964. But for the moment they wondered what kind of a son and brother would return. Even though they had spoken by telephone and seen fleeting glimpses on television, the sharpest images of Everett remained those before his capture, when he was lean and buoyant, a robust, healthy young man, raised in the warm Californian outdoors. Try as they might, they could not cloud this image with any other. It put them on edge because there had to be changes. The television pictures had not zoomed in on his face or his limbs. How many teeth might be missing, or bones broken? What had happened to his mind? Would there be brain damage? What really lay behind the smiles he had flashed on arrival in the

Philippines? A nerve-wracking sense of dread tempered their joy.

When a hospital orderly called them Delia cautioned Madeleine, "Let Mom and Dad go first. We'll follow behind."

Their footsteps resounded up the quiet hallway.

The moment had come. Chole was in tears as they embraced. He was thin yet not as gray-haired as she expected. Never mind, he was in one piece!

"Hijo!"

"Mom."

She held him tightly and squeezed.

She gave way for the others to have their turn. Lalo, looking uncharacteristically formal in suit and tie, wiped his eyes and embraced his son. How good it was to hold him again! Everett had come back alive! He was so damned relieved and happy. Dammit, why did he have to cry right now! In his confusion he almost blurted out, "Gee you look thin!" The tears streaked down his face.

Delia pressed forward to enfold her brother.

"You're fatter!" he teased.

Moist-eyed, Delia tried to smile but her chin wobbled as she fought to hold back tears. Same old brother! So abrupt! Not even a hello!

Nervously, Madeleine reached out and hugged and kissed her older brother. Everett looked her up and down. There was no disguising his amazement.

"Look how big Madeleine is!"

She smiled girlishly, her natural elegance masking an awkwardness and even turmoil. What should she say if she could not ask about his experiences?

They arranged the chairs in a circle and sat down self-consciously. Everyone wiped away tears except Everett. His eyes were dry but wide open and shifty, darting nervously from one side to the other as if he expected someone to pounce from behind. They were all abashed and tongue-tied. On guard, the family was sensitive to every thought or spoken word that might hurt him. They had so much to ask but dared not. Better for him to initiate any discussion about his ordeal. They waited for him to say something but he, too, did not know how to get started. Subdued and uncomfortable, each one hoped the other would say something. Anything.

Everett did not cry at the family reunion because he simply did not feel any overwhelming surge of emotion. Certainly it was good to see them again but it was as if he had withdrawn behind a shell, the emotional barrier he had erected to pull him through this terrible odyssey. In all that time he had lived from one day to the next, not knowing whether there would ever be a tomorrow. Being keenly attuned to the present in order to survive into the future, he had deliberately sacrificed the past. That meant tucking the family into the furthest recesses of his memory. Unsure of his own fate, he also had to consider the possible demise of his parents. In nearly all those years, when letters were few and far between, there was no way of knowing whether they were still alive. Better, then, to steel himself in advance. Discarding the family, however, drew him no closer to others. Some of the POWs he held in the highest esteem had disappeared. Word of their murders had come around much later. It was just as well that he had held his feelings in check and not gotten too friendly. Any of his roommates could have gone the same way, at any moment. Better to let that outer shell grow and solidify so that he could distance himself from overly familiar relationships. Combat pilots understood this phenomenon. They lived with the constant expectation of sudden death. None of them dared get too close to others because a guy could be here today and incinerated tomorrow. The only way to handle it was to get a grip on the emotions, to control them fiercely, even if others mistook this attitude for coldness. The net effect was that they beat down tender feelings and other emotional weaknesses that might undermine their defenses.

By the time Everett met his parents and sisters, his shell was encrusted with age. And his tear ducts had all but dried up. Yet he could not stop looking at Madeleine. How she had grown!

"What's that?" he asked, looking at her legs.

"What's what?" she questioned.

"On your legs," he said, pointing. Her mini-skirt was a third of the way up her thighs.

"Pantyhose," said Madeleine.

Everett looked puzzled. "Pantyhose? What's that?"

Smiling, Madeleine lifted her skirt to show him.

"Uh-huh!"

The family laughed good-naturedly, careful not to give the impression that they might be poking fun at him. Everett had so much to catch up on but the incident was funny and it loosened them up a bit.

They spoke about Madeleine's wedding plans. She was to be married in the snug mission church on the campus of the University of Santa Clara where Everett had graduated. Madeleine recalled how she was only six years old when she fell in love with the oak-beamed church with white stucco walls and red tiled roof, vowing then that she would get married inside it. Now she was about to fulfill that wish. For a brief moment the excited bride-to-be stimulated the conversation but then the moment was gone and again the talk became strained. Both parents and sisters wanted desperately to change the subject to Everett, to find out how he was and what he had been through. But as long as he didn't open up they would wait. Chole was just so thankful he was there. It was enough for her to see him and to hold him. Her son had returned!

When Everett spoke he had the same boyish half-smile they remembered so well. "Well Mom, I got you on the front pages of the newspapers!"

Chole chortled. Deep down he reminded her of MaMona. Both had pulled through the most exacting of circumstances. He had the same calm grit and determination that stamped him with a survivor's pedigree.

Everett didn't want to talk about his captivity but he had to get one thing off his chest. Looking at his Dad he said, "Maybe I could have come home earlier, many years earlier, but I couldn't have looked you in the eye. I don't think I could have lived with myself if I had voluntarily given them the propaganda statements they wanted. I just couldn't do it. I wouldn't have been a man. I wouldn't be here under these circumstances."

Lalo looked triumphantly at Chole. With wet eyes and on the verge of tears, he turned to his son: "You made me very proud. But I couldn't tell them that. I just couldn't make them understand."

The three women sat motionless, transfixed by the terse disclosure. No one said anything. Everett felt no need to say more. He had unburdened himself of the one pressing explanation he had to give without delay. Now that it was done he retreated inwards again, like a tortoise.

Another long silence followed, then Everett asked in dribs and drabs about individual clan members. Their responses were short and meaningless. Everyone was fine. They all sent their love. There was nothing substantial to say about any single person, which made them feel all the more the formality of the questions and answers. They listened intently to his voice. It sounded normal. No rasping or short breath. His movements seemed coordinated. All the outward signs looked good.

A Navy photographer asked permission to come into the room and with great deference positioned the family for a group picture. It brought them physically closer to one another but as soon as the photographer left, they reverted to the stiff, labored dialogue.

While speaking to his sisters he kept an ear cocked to his parents' squabbling. Everett wasn't fooled by their "togetherness." He looked at Delia, rolled his eyes and with a smile whispered, "I see things haven't changed!" Delia sniggered then let her laughter roll out.

They could have had the meal brought up to the room but all of them preferred to go down to the hospital cafeteria. Everett again looked around furtively. He seemed to be uneasy. When they were given menu cards to fill in their individual orders, Everett gave his to Madeleine. "Here, Mad, you fill mine out." Over the next few days he repeated the line, thinking it cute to refer to her as his secretary. A Navy psychiatrist confided otherwise to Delia, explaining that Everett could not make the decision what to eat because for almost nine years those decisions had been made for him. By leaving the choice to Madeleine he was covering up his own inability to decide.

Though restless and agitated by the unfamiliarity of sitting down to a normal meal, Everett was sharply observant. His alert eyes scanned people and objects in short, penetrating bird-like movements. He kept impressions to himself but at one point turned to compliment Delia: "You did a good job with Madeleine, teaching her table manners."

The media had speculated that Everett might shun Delia because of her outspoken anti-war stance. They attributed to her a remark, which she disavowed immediately when it was published, that "all hell might break loose" between them when they met. There had been snide remarks from naval personnel that she was going to get what she deserved. Others talked behind her back and made her aware that they would not feel sorry for her if her brother rejected her. Delia herself had a clear conscience and looked forward to the long-awaited reunion. But the afternoon passed without even a hint of any discordance. Neither Everett nor his family made any mention of the controversial stands taken during the long war.

The passage of days did nothing to change Everett's outward behavior. He was just as acutely nervous and anxious when he met Cecilia's family in the spacious hospital lobby. They stood up when he was escorted in but he looked dazed and off balance. Uncle Al strode up to him and exclaimed with relief, "Junior!" even though Everett had asked everyone, way back when he was in junior high school, to stop calling him that because the kids would make fun of him. But somehow Uncle Al never could get out of the habit. Once a "Junior" always a "Junior," even if the boy had grown into a man and returned home a hero.

After the hugging and kissing, they sat facing each other on sofas but they, too, quickly settled into an embarrassingly cold silence, as if waiting their turns at the confessional. This time the ice broke when Everett's goddaughter, Denise Sanchez, skipped up and spontaneously threw her arms around him. It gave them all a reason to laugh and smile. Her small sister, Raquel, seated on her mother's lap next to Everett, tugged at his shirt and got a little noisy. Her mother tried to hush her, but Everett touched her hand lightly and countermanded, "Don't stop her. I'd much rather hear kids screaming than men screaming. It's a welcome sound." After a pause, he added, "You'd better not hold onto me too long. I think I have worms!"

It was the opening they had been hoping for and Linda asked, "What kind of food did they give you?"

"Oh, a bowl of water, sometimes with little bugs floating in it," he said, his eyes shifting as he described the swill that passed for soup. The doctors in the Philippines had told him he had to have his insides checked because of the things he had consumed. They would have to cleanse him of parasites and assess any damage done from the long period of an unhealthy diet.

Linda proffered a small gift-wrapped box from one of her neighbors who was of German descent.

Everett unwrapped it slowly and drew out a carved and painted wooden egg, sliced in half across the width. A tiny hand-carved cross lay loose on top of the egg. He studied it thoughtfully.

"I've seen one of these before," he said to the astonishment of his relatives.

"You have?" said Linda, apprehensively.

"Yes. A priest who saw us came in with one just like this."

In the silence that followed he turned it around and looked hard, absorbed in his private memories. Linda fretted, certain that she had unintentionally touched a raw wound. She cowered when he looked up to scan the anxious faces of his assembled relatives. He himself looked bewildered, as if caught in the harsh lumination of a theater spotlight. His gaze settled on Linda's two daughters, Cherrie and Michelle.

"Where's Mona?" he asked.

"There's no Mona," Linda replied. "Why did you think there's a Mona?"

"I remember distinctly there is a Mona," said Everett. "That's what Delia wrote me."

Gently they explained that Cherrie's middle name was Mona and Delia was the only person in the entire family who called her by her middle name. Linda had two, not three children. Everett smiled faintly, acknowledging the correction.

"Well, you finally became an architect!" Everett said to Denise's father, his cousin Al. Everett told them about the home he had built for himself at Lake Tahoe. Of course it was all in his mind, but it was one of the ways he had passed time in the loneliness of captivity. He had done more than design a vacation home. He had also written the great American novel, a saga of a Mexican immigrant family. But again, this was in his own mind and nothing at all had been committed to paper. There was no real gusto in his voice. They got the impression that he was just trying to make conversation. But they were not about to intrude. They were content to see him trying to relax and enjoy himself.

Everett knew Cecilia had recently purchased a large motor home; she had sent him photos of it. Now he asked if he could borrow it. He was not very forthcoming, but said he had vague plans to travel around a bit, to see chunks of America and just take it easy.

He was apparently of sound mind and they wished him well. They were thankful for small mercies. Now they could go back home and pick up their lives. The agony was over, the void filled, the burden lifted. God had answered their prayers and spared their man.

Everett surprised them all by accepting an invitation to a barbecue at Al and Virginia's Walnut Creek home the following day. They imagined the medical checks would keep him hospitalized for some time and did not expect him to roam free for several weeks at least. Everyone was excited. If he could socialize like old times, and even perhaps take a dip in the patio pool, he could not be too badly hurt. But when Delia called to drive him over, Everett begged out. Though he did not say it in so many words, it was clear he needed a period of adjustment before resuming a normal social life. Delia telephoned the disappointing news to her cousin. "He's not feeling well," she explained. "Too much has happened too soon. He feels he needs to stay in the hospital."

The stilted conversations continued on for days but the first time Everett was alone with his father he blurted out, "Okay, tell me 'I told you so!' "

Lalo knew he was referring to that time when he had advised Everett not to get married before finishing his stint in the Navy because long separations led to marital problems.

"No," said Lalo solemnly, "I'll never tell you that."

There was a pause, then Everett said, "All the time I was over there I was wondering how you were getting along here with three women."

"It wasn't too easy," Lalo replied. "You know, your sister Delia was demonstrating. I thought it would work against you."

He said no more and did not encourage a reply. There was no reason to dwell on the past.

"Dad," Everett continued, "my first wish is to go shake that man's hand."

"Which man?"

"The president."

"Why?"

"If it hadn't been for him we would never have gotten out. When Nixon ordered the bombing they treated us even better. We started getting better food because they knew our government meant business."

"I was always for the bombing," said Lalo.

"Yeah, I figured you would be, Dad."

No way was Lalo going to wade in and ask his son anything about his POW experiences. That Navy psychiatrist had really shaken him up, scaring him so he trembled just thinking about what kind of a boy he was going to get back. He would let Everett make the openings for fear that anything he might ask would bring back horrifying memories his son was trying to repress.

Everett talked haltingly of his first months of captivity, telling his father about the cross he had carved on the outside wall of his cell at the Hanoi Hilton and how he had prayed there every day. Then he skipped a year and explained how POWs communicated by tapping on the walls. Lalo tried to cut him short, fearing the effect any discussion of Everett's POW experiences might have on his mental well-being.

"Son, the Navy told us to be real careful what we talk about."

Everett laughed.

"What are you laughing at?"

"I just thought of something! In the Philippines they said 'What do you guys want to eat?' We all said steak!"

"The psychiatrist said they planned on giving you baby food!" Lalo interjected.

"Everyone wanted steak," Everett continued. "And then we were in our pajamas and heard there was a party going on. The nurses wanted some men over to have some fun, so some of the guys slipped out in pajamas and had a ball! When it ended they snuck around the bushes back to the hospital. The back door was locked. They wondered how the hell they were going to get back in! But what the hell, what could happen to them if they got caught? Would they be put in prison! So they walked in the front door!"

They chuckled together, father and son, welcoming the relief of some down-to-earth humor. Lalo picked up a few of the open letters and photographs from adoring women and other well-wishers. There were so many from all over the country that they filled a number of mailbags. And still the fan mail poured in.

"What about Tangee?" Everett asked. "When did you find out?"

Lalo steeled himself. It had to be broached sooner or later. Slowly and gently he recounted his earliest suspicions, then followed through with her move up to Lafayette, her disappearance, receipt of the damning letter to her sister, and finally having the Pentagon cut off her monthly allotments. Damn, how it hurt telling, knowing how much it must be skewering his son's guts. He didn't want to say more because he figured it was too much, too soon.

Everett seemed interested only in fixing dates so he could pinpoint a chronology. For the rest he was silent. Characteristically, he was undemonstrative and kept his feelings to himself, as he had done from early childhood. He told Lalo he would remain in the Navy. "I've been here this long I might as well stick it out until retirement. There's no point in getting out now."

Lalo could not restrain himself. Timidly he asked, "Are you hurt?"

Everett explained how he suffered a bad back when ejecting over the Gulf of Tonkin. He shrugged it off, saying it was so long ago. He kept quiet about the harassment, the starvation diet, the isolation, the tattered winter clothing, and the physical torture which had left him with broken teeth, a dislocated jaw and permanent damage to the nerves near his elbows.

Later, when he was alone with Delia, he asked many more questions about Tangee, still trying to hone the chronology of her desertion. He was relaxed and at ease and Delia withheld nothing. This time he also spoke about his tentative plans, saying he wanted to get the legal wrangle of the divorce over as quickly as possible. A lawyer was already working on it. He had no desire to talk to Tangee. It was plain that he wanted a clean break with the past. But as he had done with his father, Everett showed no emotion. It did not surprise Delia that he would want to lick his wounds in private.

He held off discussion about Delia's role in protesting against the war until immediately after his news conference at the hospital. There he bluntly charged anti-war activists with prolonging his captivity by giving the enemy hope of ultimate victory. But when reporters asked about Delia's stand, he reasoned, "I'm convinced, to a large degree, her activities were based on emotion. We were there for a long time and she wanted us home. Of course, she lives in a free country. She has the right to express her opinions."

Delia was not at that conference and could only speculate what his thoughts might be towards her. Obviously he would not approve of her actions, but she was sure he would not disown her. They had grown up together and shared too many tough times for him to show a lack of understanding. Besides, she was more than a sister. For all his conservative traditionalism and her spirited social activism, she was in many respects his alter ego. Though they had gained national exposure from different ends of the spectrum, they shared a basic earthiness and sound common sense.

When they got together after his news conference, Everett made it clear to his sister that he had not said anything negative about her.

"I told them we live in a democracy and one thing we fought for over there was freedom of expression. This is a democracy and you have the right to express your own opinions."

But she felt his disapproval. He was less subtle in his disdain for Jane Fonda and everything she had come to symbolize. Delia knew it would have made no difference to him if she had told him that Jane Fonda herself had been used by the Vietnamese as a letter carrier to bring home letters from POWs, including one from Everett.

He told her he could have been freed years earlier, before even Mark Gartley, the POW released as a propaganda gesture in September 1972, after his mother appeared in Hanoi with anti-war activists.

"I met him," Delia said breezily. "He was very nice and cordial with me."

"Yeah, I know. But he left us," said Everett tersely. He didn't tell Delia that three months before Gartley's release the Vietnamese had taken Everett to "quiz" and again raised the possibility of freeing him. They had asked him what he would do if his mother or sister came for him. Would he agree to go? No, he would not. Either they all left together or nobody left. He didn't have the stomach to explain to her that it was a common understanding that they would all leave together, and then this guy Gartley had broken ranks and violated their trust. Gartley could never again be one of them. Surely his conscience would trouble him in the years ahead. Everett thought he might even have trouble just trying to crack a smile.

But Delia, too, was exasperated. "Everyone had to do what they felt they had to do," she said, unable to hold back her tears.

Try as he might, Everett could not see it from her side; he would not give ground.

"Even though you think you may be right, you don't understand my view. Your activities didn't help us. They hampered our efforts to end the whole thing," he countered.

Throughout, they controlled their voices, neither shouting nor interrupting each other. They tried very hard to keep the argument on a rational level.

At one point he cut her short.

"You can argue that policy right or wrong all day but it doesn't help. It was not the right thing to do."

Delia would not budge. "We got so tired after being told for so long by the Navy to keep quiet. When was it all going to end?"

He was not swayed.

"Well let's put it this way," she said, "If I had been the one in the POW camp and you were home, what would you have done?"

Everett did not reply. He looked hard at her but said nothing. He did not know what he might have done. And if he had done anything, he did not know if he could have done as much as she did. But there was no way he could go belly up and switch viewpoints. For him the issues were cut and dried. While she may have strained herself to the limit to end the war and free him, her stand had helped undermine the war effort and indirectly encouraged the enemy to hold out.

Delia could not press the subject any longer. In time, perhaps, he might come to understand. For the moment they were too far apart and their feelings too raw. But she asked him one more time, "Reverse the roles. Would you have abandoned me?"

He did not reply.

Pointedly, she did not report their brief dialogue to the media. It was their very private, if painful, agreement to disagree. They would have to try to let bygones be bygones.

Everett waited for the call to go through to Bill Metzger's wife, Bonnie, in Annandale, Va. He remembered with a smile how Bill had so often lain on the bed and for an eternity licked his bowl and spoon clean. All the other guys had picked up the habit. It wasn't that the food was so good. There just wasn't much else to do. And then Bill would stare for hours on end at a photograph of his wife and repeat over and over, "I wonder if she's gaining weight. I hope not. I hope she's holding her weight down."

When the call came through Everett introduced himself.

"I lived with Bill for a while and I just wanted you to know he's fine and doing real well. He asked me to give you a call and tell you he's okay. He said he'll be home in a few weeks. His leg is healed pretty well."

"Tell me about it," Bonnie asked.

Bill had already written but Everett repeated what she must have known already. His right leg was a little shorter than the left because it broke when he was shot down and the Vietnamese had left the fracture unattended.

"He's okay," Everett encouraged. "He's a strong guy with a lot of pluck."

Bonnie seemed assured.

"Anything else?" she asked.

Momentarily at a loss for conversation, especially with someone he had only heard of but never met, Everett blurted out, "How's your weight?"

"Oh, my weight. It's okay," she said defensively, losing her composure and wondering why Everett would ask such a personal question.

A little flushed and red-faced, Everett asked himself the same question. But it was too late.

He placed the second call to Bob Fant's fiance, Becky, hoping not to make another faux pas.

"Becky, this is Everett Alvarez. I was with Bob in Vietnam. He'll be home soon but he asked me to let you know his broken arm is coming along nicely. He still doesn't have full use of it but he says not to worry yourself. Believe me, he's fine. I've seen him exercising that arm so often I can vouch for him."

"Which arm is it?" she asked.

There was a pause. Everett's memory went into a tailspin. Suddenly there was a blank. He couldn't remember! Flustered, he tried to recall. Left? Right?

"Oops, I don't remember!"

About six weeks after his return, Everett accepted an invitation from his cousin Al for just the two of them to go to lunch in San Francisco. It was the first time they had been alone together in almost a decade and Al drove across the bay for a nostalgic return to the Mission district. Everett had played there as a schoolchild during World War II, sometimes with Al, who lived nearby. Both their fathers were pipe fitters during the war, building liberty ships at the Kaiser shipyards.

Everett's mind drifted back thirty years to the time when he used to dash across the cablecar tracks on Portrero Avenue to the junkyard at the base of Bernal Heights hill. Together with the neighborhood kids he had hung out on a groove in the hill where they dug caves for their hideout. At other times they squatted in the shallow ponds on the hill behind the scrap yard, picking up tadpoles and old pieces of junked autos. Everett was the smallest of the group on his block and did not know that the district was divided into gangs. Once he invited a second grade friend to come and play at his home, even though the little boy was from just three blocks away. As soon as they got into Everett's territory the older kids ganged up and chased off the intruder. They made Everett promise never again to bring in an outsider. When they were all a little older, the gang had fun jumping on the back of the streetcars. With the conductor turning a blind eye to their mischief, they hung on to the grating as it careened downhill, then dropped off and ran to the Saturday afternoon movie.

It was wartime and the bay was jammed with ships. San Francisco itself was a sea of sailors' uniforms. One day, Chole dressed him in a sailor suit and took him downtown for a studio photograph. As they walked along Market Street, passing sailors nudged each other and smiled at the cute little boy in the sailor outfit. Everett remembered just as well how that global war had ended. It was summer and he was playing on the familiar Bernal Heights when the entire city reverberated with chiming church bells, piercing sirens and the honking horns of motorists gone berserk. He ran home to find his mother laughing, with tears in her eyes. "The war's over!" she cried, almost too overcome with excitement to talk. Lalo had been deferred from military service because they rated his work of critical importance. But now, on the eve of his acceptance into the merchant marine, the conflict was over. Dad would not be leaving home!

Everett recalled how his Dad had taken him down to see the warships of the Pacific fleet anchored in the bay. Many were open to the public and they had gone to see the most famous, the U.S.S. *Missouri,* upon which General MacArthur had accepted the Japanese surrender. But there was such a long line of people waiting to board that they had instead walked over to her sister ship, the U.S.S. *South Dakota.* Everett was awed by the huge guns and the length of the decks. And then, to his everlasting wonder, he got his first close-up look at a baby flat-top carrier anchored nearby. It was the biggest man-made thing he had ever seen!

Flooded with memories of those halcyon days, Everett gazed at the homes and the shops as Al cruised up and down the once-familiar hills. Many buildings were much the same as before, small copies of double-story, all-wood Victorian homes. But the occupants had changed. They used to be predominantly Italians. Now they were mostly Mexican-Americans. The movie theater had vanished. Gone, too, was the little hobby shop on 24th Street where Everett and Al's late brother, Danny, had bought their model airplane sets. Everett felt a pang of regret for the passing years. He had not been there to see it happen. There would be much more, he realized, that would no longer be familiar.

They lunched at Fishermen's Wharf and as they quaffed beers Al told him how he had visited Chole and Lalo every two or three weeks, just to be with them and to comfort them. But he had also seen the marriage deteriorate and he hoped, now that Everett was back, that everything would be fine again. But Everett held out no hope. He knew his parents too well. The discord, they both knew, went way back to the time when they had lived in the Mission district.

"You know," Everett volunteered unexpectedly, "in order to survive in Vietnam I had to make all of my family non-existent. They were dead in my mind. That way I could not dwell on them. It made captivity that much easier."

He began to open up, but only a fraction, and not for longer than a few minutes. He told of his fear of dying if his crippled plane had exploded while he was trapped inside, or if he had bailed out too late and hit the land. He gave his cousin just a whiff of how hard things had been, letting on how his captors had harassed him unnecessarily.

Everett had little idea of what he would do in the future though he thought he would probably remain in the Navy and perhaps enroll in postgraduate studies.

"What about flying. Would you like to fly again?" Al asked.

"Yeah, but I don't think I'd like to be assigned to a carrier."

Al recognized the Everett he had known before his marriage to Tangee. Once again he was spare with words and said no more than was necessary. But when he talked of his refusal to accept early release in exchange for propaganda statements he was less reserved. He was fulsome in praise of the president for having the sense and courage to bomb the Vietnamese relentlessly, for that was the only way to win the peace and get the POWs out.

"What transpired had to be done," said Everett, "and if it had taken ten years I would have done it and still survived."

Al came away from the lunch deeply moved by Everett's unyielding sense of duty and commitment, his allegiance to his fellow officers, his feelings of deep respect for the president and his fierce patriotism.

20
WEDDING BELLS

IN THE GLUM AND MELANCHOLY AFTERMATH OF THE WAR, with the rhetoric over but divisions still raw, Americans rallied as one in welcoming home the POWs. The joy was real, and the exultation deep. Desperate for tranquility after a decade of turmoil, people across the land rejoiced in the return of their living symbols of hope, faith and courage. Everett had endured the longest in North Vietnam so they would acclaim him the loudest. From the moment he touched his native soil they gave him the love and warmth that had been denied him so long. His homecoming was tangible evidence that the war was finally over. Much later they would build memorials to the fallen and belatedly accept the veterans. But for the moment they opened up fleetingly and spontaneously to honor the liberated POWs. It was a surge of collective tenderness that momentarily purged their anger and frustration. Nowhere was this more apparent than in the homecoming parade in Everett's honor in Santa Clara, when 100,000 cheering people lined the route after earlier ceremonies rededicating a park in his name.

His mailbags were stuffed with the handwritten notes of affection from a compassionate public. Children sent pictures in crayon of flowers and flags. Men and women begged him to visit their homes and smallholdings so they could add their tributes and share their meals. From the humblest to the mightiest, invitations poured in for him to be guest of honor at conventions and fund-raisers, sports events and religious and ethnic gatherings. The months ahead would be a dizzying whirlwind of speeches and accolades at receptions and banquets. He needed the time to readjust; he had to winnow down the multitude of requests. Proud as she could be, Madeleine accompanied him to the reception given by Gov. Ronald Reagan at Sacramento. At the glittering Academy Awards party, he was lionized by legendary movie stars eager to shake his hand.

On March 29, 1973, just six weeks after setting foot on Travis Air Force base, he was summoned by the Navy to Washington, D.C. The last of the POWs was home and it was time to expose the awful truth about the prison camps. While other POWs spoke at similar press conferences throughout the country, Everett appeared at Bethesda Naval Hospital in Maryland, just north of the nation's capital. Briefly he recounted the worst of what he had suffered. There had been so much barbarism and senseless savagery. Yet even as he spoke he could not know that there were wounds that would never heal. The bones of his jaw and the nerves in his arms would never be normal. The jawbone would randomly slip out of position and the undersides of both arms would forever bear the scars of remedial surgery. He would never forget the likes of brave compatriots like Ron Storz and J.J. Connell who did not return. But just as assuredly, his own disfigurement would be a constant reminder of the horrors he now recalled.

Everett was scheduled to return to California the following day at 10 A.M. To be sure he got back in time for a date in San Francisco and an official welcome home celebration in Salinas, he switched from a flight leaving Baltimore to one leaving an hour earlier from Dulles International just outside of Washington, D.C. As he sat in the waiting area he heard his name paged. He was asked to report to the ticket counter.

An attractive United Airlines employee greeted him with a smile.

"Commander Alvarez?"

"Yes."

"Hello, Commander. I'm Tammy Ilyas, your passenger service representative with United. Would you please come with me, sir."

A directive had come down from the president of the airline ordering VIP treatment for any ex-POW traveling on United. Tammy knew the ropes. For some years, one of her main responsibilities was to provide extra attention to VIP passengers to preserve their patronage of the airline. The job called for tact, patience and a flexible personality. At Dulles it also meant having a sharp eye for the hundreds of congressmen, diplomats, executives and other luminaries who passed through the busy terminal serving the nation's capital. Often she invited VIPs into her comfortable office before departure if they preferred its privacy to the Red Carpet Room. Inevitably, she got on first-name terms with many regulars. Some had even dated the easygoing physician's daughter, inviting her to parties on Embassy Row and Capitol Hill.

But all of the luster of rubbing shoulders with the high and the mighty paled in comparison with walking beside the real-live hero by her side! Tammy could scarcely believe it. Long before his return she was familiar with his story because she had distributed bumper stickers and bracelets to publicize the plight of the POWs. She had seen Everett's plane arrive at Travis

Air Force base on TV and when he delivered his short speech she had the strangest feeling they would meet someday.

Tammy ordered coffee and closed the door. She sat at her desk while he made himself comfortable in a chair.

"We are so proud to have you fly United," she said, wondering whether he might see through her unaccustomed nervousness.

Everett smiled, still bewildered by all the attention yet reveling in the courtesies and chivalry after Vietnam. They talked about the airline industry and all the new planes that had come into service in the years he had been away. The hour flipped by and Tammy walked him over to the departure gate for his flight to San Francisco. She had already switched him to first class and ordered a bottle of champagne delivered on board. Now she introduced him to Sparky Matsunaga, a congressman from Hawaii, and gave him her business card. "If you ever get back to Washington give me a call. I'll show you around," she said.

"That would be nice. Well, thanks a lot," said Everett, thinking she was strikingly good-looking and pleasant and obviously a very capable person to hold down such an impressive job. She was the kind of woman he would like to get to know better if he ever saw her again.

Tammy returned to her office with a childlike sparkle in her eyes. She picked up the phone and got through to her married sister.

"Thelma! I've just met the man I'm going to marry!"

Her older sister giggled. "Again? You're crazy!"

"Thelma, this is for real!"

"Well tell me about him."

The words came easily because he had made such a vivid impression. It was his demeanor more than anything. She would never forget the strong sense of inner security and self assurance he projected; it made her feel so marvelously at ease in his company. She was as comfortable with him as she was with her family back in suburban Pittsburgh. And what a fine gentleman he was! He reminded her of how people used to be before everything got turned upside down in the sixties. You could see that Everett had not been part of that upheaval because he was so well-mannered! And oh, was he good-looking! He was lean and dark and he carried himself so confidently.

Thelma got the picture and was excited. Maybe this was for real! But how could she *possibly* hope to meet him again! Tammy was already thirty-three and had never been married. The family had begun to despair that she would ever walk down the aisle other than as a bridesmaid. She had been engaged several times, but on each occasion had backed out. None of the men had really measured up to her ideal. Coming from a very traditional family just one generation away from its roots in Syria, and its faith still firmly implanted in the Eastern Orthodox Church, of which her father was a national board member, Tammy looked upon marriage as permanent. The man of her choice would have to show signs of being not only a good husband but a caring father. Holding fast to all the disappearing values, and disregarding the cynicism of her generation, Tammy yearned for true fulfillment through a strong marriage and a close-knit family. She wouldn't have it any other way. That was how she had been raised. That was all she desired.

Two weeks later she approached California Congressman Burt Talcott in the airport lobby. He said he was flying out to a Jaycees testimonial dinner.

"In whose honor?" she asked casually.

"One of the ex-POWs, Cmdr. Everett Alvarez, Jr."

Tammy smiled. "Oh, I met him recently," she said coyly. "What a fine man! Would you please tell him that I said hello."

Later that day she took a call from San Francisco.

"Tammy? Burt Talcott here. How do you spell your last name again?"

"Why?" she asked.

"Oh, never mind," he replied, with a tantalizing hint in his voice that he was up to some mischief.

Talcott had known the Alvarez family for a quarter century, stretching back to the days when he lived in Salinas. A former POW himself in Europe during World War II, he had been a leading proponent of the planned parade through Washington at the time of the petition drive. He had already welcomed Everett home and when they met again at the Carmel Valley testimonial dinner he passed on Tammy's message, feeling a little bit like the matchmaker. Everett smiled. He remembered Tammy Ilyas, the pretty passenger service representative with the wide smile and a warm nature. She was the sort of person who easily made friends with people from all walks of life. And he liked the way she spoke, with a kind of measured expressiveness. So she wanted to see him again! He made a mental note. Who could tell, perhaps he would be going East again sometime.

Meanwhile he had his hands full on the West coast with dates in San Francisco, Oakland and San Jose. The celebrations were still going full swing in his home state. One of the highlights was his invitation to throw out the first ball at the season opener between the Oakland A's, World Series champs, and the Minnesota Twins. Everett had been deeply moved as he stood spotlighted on the pitcher's mound while the rest of the lights were doused and the national anthem played. It had reminded him of that Sunday at the Briar Patch, when he had stood at attention, faced the United States and proudly sung the *Star Spangled Banner*. Only, then, he had stood on alien turf in a hostile land and the anthem had been followed by miserable boredom and silence. Now the tumultuous cheers of friendly Americans thundered around the packed stadium and Everett blinked hard to contain his tears.

Everett had a problem when his invitation arrived for President Nixon's dinner/dance at the White House in honor of all former POWs. His first thought was to invite his mother or one of his sisters to accompany him. How proud they would be as presidential guests in Washington, D.C. But then he realized that his mother would feel awkward in the executive mansion because of her political views. The war had been traumatic and she blamed the political leadership. Delia would feel similarly uncomfortable socializing at an event hosted by a man she had railed against so vehemently. Madeleine had already had her turn, escorting Everett to the governor's mansion in Sacramento.

That left the multitude of girlfriends. There had been so many one-night stands and countless opportunities for other fleeting romances that Everett was overwhelmed. Daily arrivals of mailbags were filled with love letters from single and divorced women yearning to meet him. It was the same with most returning single POWs and those who had been deserted by wives and fiances. He could not hope to respond to all the invitations. He could not even cope with the adoring women who brazenly approached him at most gatherings he went to, whether it was a staid civic reception or a noisy nightclub. It had been eight-and-a-half years since he had held a woman and just so much as kissed her. Now he partied voraciously. Since showering and feasting in the Philippines he seemed to have had time for little else. On occasion, he had dated the same woman more than once, but to invite one of them to the White House would inflame those he passed over. Prudently, he decided to invite an outsider from across country. That way none of the Californians would feel snubbed. Why not the United Airlines woman at Dulles International Airport?

Tammy was at her hairdresser when the call came through from the Navy. United Airlines, holding fast to policy, had refused to give Everett her home number but relented when the Navy called later on his behalf. An answering service had directed the call from her home to the hairdresser.

"Please hold for Cmdr. Everett Alvarez, Jr.," said the military operator.

"He's going to invite me!" Tammy wanted to squeal. The Washington media was already agog about the extravaganza planned at the White House. It would be one of the biggest bashes since President Taft and his wife Helen invited 5,000 guests to celebrate their silver wedding anniversary.

"Miss Ilyas?"

"Commander Alvarez! I think I know what you're going to say!"

"How would you know?"

"I just know!"

"Will you come to the White House dinner/dance with me on May 24th?"

"Oh, I'd *love* to!"

Tammy was exhilarated. She could scarcely believe he had singled her out after their one brief encounter! Besides the White House, there would be a formal reception at the State Department, with a presidential briefing for the men and a tea hosted by the First Lady for spouses and partners. There was also the promise of more activities. She talked him into flying in three or four days before the event so they could get to know one another better.

Thelma was as excited as Tammy. "You have to wear something spectacular!" the older sister coaxed. "Buy something no one else will have!"

They shopped as if possessed, finally selecting an elegant floor-length white satin dress with a high collar and French cuffs. After finding a pair of matching shoes, they raced home to try on the complete outfit. Around her neck Tammy clipped the string of pearls given by her parents upon graduation from high school. Then she slipped into Thelma's white mink jacket. She looked exquisite!

April 24, 1973

Dear Tammy,

First let me say that it was certainly pleasant to talk to you once again (our telephone conversations) and I certainly do hope I didn't inconvenience you when we called your hairdresser, typical military procedures, you know—hurry up and wait. . . . I hope to have the opportunity to spend more time with you, aside from the activities of the "party." Would you like to show me Washington? . . . Take care and I will look forward to hearing from you.

Sincerely, Everett.

By mid-May, Everett had checked out of the hospital and moved into his mother's house. Officially he was on three months rehabilitative leave, but he got no rest as he responded to the flurry of invitations to make celebrity appearances all over the country. And he made frequent trips back to the hospital for a continuing outpatient watch on his health.

Uppermost in his mind was the need to get his divorce from Tangee finalized as soon as possible. It was a messy reminder of a traumatic past and an abscess on the joyful present. Her attorney had called his lawyer to tell him her new husband, who worked in an auto repair shop selling spare parts, wanted Everett to stop it.

"Stop what?"

"All of this publicity."

"Hey, wait a minute. I'm not doing anything. She did it herself. I'm not making an issue of it. I purposely played it down at the press conference."

Tangee asked only that Everett pay her attorney's fees of $750 and court costs. She was just as impatient as Everett to get the American divorce behind her. Everett's attorney, a Navy reservist who refused to bill other than to cover disbursements, advised him it was possible to go after Tangee for receiving some of his pay under false pretenses. But Everett was not interested. It would only drag out the proceedings. "I'm healthy and well. I've got a new life. Why pursue it? The money's probably gone anyway," he reasoned.

Ten days after he met Tammy, the civil divorce came through. It was final.

> *Delmonico's Hotel*
> *Park Avenue at 59th Street*
> *New York, N.Y. 10022*
> *May 7, 1973*

Dear Tammy,

Hi! It was so good to talk with you this evening. As soon as I hung the phone up I turned on the TV and the USA-USSR basketball game was just starting, so if my letter seems a bit discontinuous at times it's because something exciting happened and disrupted my train of thought. . . . Tammy, please don't feel that you have to go to the expense of getting another new dress for the afternoon tea party. It can get costly very easily and I hate to see you spend a lot of money. (What an exciting game—very close!).

Also, please don't feel you are imposing on my time when I'm there. I'm looking forward to spending a lot of time with you. (Score is now tied 64–64!). Do you have any favorite restaurants you would like to dine at? You know Tammy, the more I think of this Washington, D.C. visit, the more enthusiastic I get. Like I heard one man say one time—I get the goose-bumps. (USSR now ahead by 4! It's almost over!).

I should be back home in a few days (73–73 now with 25 seconds left! Just went into overtime!). . . .

It's getting late now and I have another busy day tomorrow so as soon as the game ends I will hit the sack. (USA just won 89–80 in overtime!!) . . .

Say, has this stuff about Watergate affected your water bill any?

> *Bye now—Always, Everett*

P.S. Do you like basketball?

United Airlines gave her the week off to be with him before the White House party. For much of the time, he was tied up in military engagements and briefings. But when they were together they criss-crossed Washington, seeing the sights as they drove slowly down spacious avenues. It was spring. Bicyclists weaved lazily between strollers along the paths of the green expanses near the monuments and by the Tidal Basin. The cherry blossoms of early spring were already gone but there was still plenty of pristine foliage. Tammy and Everett ambled hand in hand, blissful in the fullest moment of the new season. The days sped by like scudding clouds. Tammy was unabashedly in love. Yet she was not alone in wanting to be by his side. Well-wishers who recognized the former POW came up to wish him well. In fashionable Georgetown, effusively gracious maître d's picked up the tab at clubs and restaurants, and some admiring diners cut into the time the couple had to themselves.

Their heads spun from the whirlwind of activities. At the State Department, Tricia Nixon tearfully confided to Tammy how the Nixon family frequently read Everett's heartwarming letter of appreciation to the president for bringing the POWs home with honor and dignity.

Later, inside the Washington Hilton, Tammy glanced at the dresses worn by scores of other women as they waited for shuttle buses to take them the ten blocks down Connecticut Avenue to the White House. Thelma had been right. Her dress was entirely appropriate for the occasion and Everett was obviously delighted. He himself looked magnificent in his dress white jacket and miniature medals.

There was a momentary crisis when Tammy spotted an elegant lady coming down the escalator wearing the identical white satin dress. The woman was also going to the White House! Everett looked on with an expression of helpless sympathy as she approached Tammy and gently held her hands.

"Oh, my dear, it looks *much* better on you than it does on me! You look marvelous!" the stranger said, retrieving the moment with exquisite charm.

Disarmed by the gracious gesture, Tammy stammered, "You're so beautiful. The dress looks stunning on you!"

Even with the media hype over the White House affair, no one could have foreseen what a memorable gala it would be. The president opened up every room to his guests, with the exception of the family quarters. To accommodate the more than thirteen hundred invitees around 120 round tables, a giant yellow and tangerine striped marquee was pitched over the south lawn. A number of military bands played background and dance music while a sprinkling of movie and political stars mixed with the nation's newest heroes. National Security Adviser Henry Kissinger shook Everett's hand and let on, "I know your mother well. She gave me a rough time!" John Wayne, seated with them at table 32, had tears in his eyes when introduced to Everett. Later he whispered to Tammy, "I have such admiration for Cmdr. Alvarez that every time I look at him I just can't help but cry."

The following night they boarded *Le Bateau* for what they hoped would be a quiet evening cruise along the broad swath of the Potomac. But when autograph hunters beseiged him Tammy became protectively jealous of their privacy. Discomforted and annoyed, she soon lost patience.

"Alvarez," she said pointedly as they danced, "you must think you're a big shot because everyone's making such a fuss over you. Why don't you just tell me now that you love me and get it over with!"

He grinned as he held her tighter. "I do love you! Honest to God, I do!"

They spoke daily by telephone. Everett invited her to join him in Texas for a reception given by billionaire Ross Perot but Tammy would not go because her father was hospitalized for back surgery. A few weeks later Everett asked her to fly out to California to meet his family. It was a bad moment for Tammy to be staying with Chole. She and Lalo had been living under the same roof for the benefit of their son, trying to make him believe all was well at home. But it was nothing more than a charade. Their love had long since wilted and the marriage was dead. In the same month that their son dined and danced as the guest of the president at the White House, Lalo walked out of Bohannon Drive for the last time. Finally Chole had the peace and quiet that had eluded her nearly all her married life. But now she was alone, her husband gone forever and her daughters scattered. She looked forward to having her son back to fill the void.

There was so much to talk about. Neither Chole nor Lalo, nor even Delia or Madeleine had sat down with Everett to review the lost years. Until he gave a hint that he wanted to talk about it, they were determined to hold their tongues. For his part, Everett did not enquire about their wartime activities nor the strains upon their individual lives. Once they briefly mentioned their drive to get signatures for a petition to free him but Everett changed the subject. Caught up in the frenzied present and a long distance romance, he was content to bury the past, even to erase it from his memory if possible.

His schedule left little time to be with his family. They craved his love and intimate companionship but his time was at a premium. As his mother, Chole inwardly felt she had a lien on his time. It seemed only natural and right, for surely he would want to return to the fold. But Everett could not return to the old ways. Aside from all the speeches and functions that had him jetting wearily across the country, he had articles to write, continuing medical check-ups, and a brand new life to get on with. Delia was living alone. Madeleine was about to get married and his father had walked out. He thought about looking for an apartment in San Francisco.

At first the family received Tammy as just another of Everett's girlfriends, requiring no special affection or attention. But at Everett's request she visited regularly on weekends after the White House function, staying each time at Chole's house. An unspoken tension to the point of resentment built up. In their eyes she was an intruder, with none of their cultural stuffing nor shared anguish of the past eight-and-a-half years. They had barely set eyes on him and now a stranger from the East threatened to tear him away forever. As the romance grew more serious, Tammy began to sense that they looked upon her as a body snatcher, out to steal a son and a brother from under their noses. Everyone held their peace, but none of them felt comfortable with the fast-developing turn of events.

June 27, 1973

Hi Sweetheart,

Hope you made it home alright . . . When I got home I found a letter from Jim Bailey—"Bales"—who had taken some pics at the White House dinner. I thought you might like to show them at home. . . . I'll call you Sat. eve or maybe Sunday A.M.!

Luv you—Everett

Three months after first meeting at Dulles airport they talked openly of marriage though they still held off on a formal engagement. Everett was concerned about his remarriage in the eyes of the Catholic Church. He did not know whether the Church would agree to annul his marriage to Tangee.

When he flew to Washington in July they went to see the Bolshoi Ballet perform at Wolf Trap's outdoor theater and as they sat on the benches at intermission Everett turned gravely to Tammy.

"I don't think we can get married because the Catholic Church won't allow it."

He had no solid proof how the church would react to his formal request for annulment but it was a strong intuitive feeling. Tammy, anyway, did not want to get married in a Catholic Church. If Everett absolutely insisted, she would give way, but her preference was for the Eastern Orthodox Church, in which her late maternal grandfather had been a priest. She was adamant about one thing. She would not agree to be married by a Justice of the Peace. That would leave the marriage incomplete and mortify her parents. However much she loved Everett she would insist that their marriage be sanctified in the eyes of God. That meant a church wedding. For the moment they decided to wait for the formal ruling of the Catholic Church authorities.

Archbishop Joseph McGucken, whose San Francisco diocese embraced Santa Clara, had promised Everett he would study the former marriage to see whether it was binding in the eyes of the Catholic Church. To annul the marriage they would have to find fraud or deceit by one of the spouses. That meant asking both the husband and wife whether they had honestly intended to have a lifelong relationship with children.

The official reply came in a letter signed by Msgr. Richard Knapp after reviewing answers put to Tangee through her attorney.

Her reply indicates that she intended a permanent lifelong union with you at the time of your marriage, and that she certainly did not exclude children from the marriage.

This would seem to leave us no avenue of approach with regard to a church investigation of that marriage.

It is indeed unfortunate that you should be the one called upon to suffer in this situation, since it would seem that you are totally the innocent party in the break-up of the marriage.

However, our office can do no more than point out that our investigation shows no real grounds for challenging the validity of that marriage according to the norms of church law.

I wish I could be more encouraging but I really feel that it would be unfair to you to hold out hope for a solution when indeed none seems to exist.

Please be assured of my continued prayers for your acceptance of this unfortunate situation.

Everett spoke once more with the monsignor.

"What does this mean?" he asked for final clarification.

"In the eyes of God you are still married to that woman, even though it is unfair and unrealistic," replied the monsignor.

"What should I do?"

"You could take her back."

"That's totally out of the question."

"I understand," the monsignor agreed.

Even though he had braced himself for bad news Everett had still not quite fully expected it. He reviewed the decision with Jesuits and other priestly intellectuals whom he knew well from his years at the University of Santa Clara. Many promised they would continue to administer the sacraments to him, regardless of whether he remarried out of the Catholic Church. Some of those same clerics had earlier urged him to seek a ruling from a diocese more liberal than the conservative one in San Francisco. But he had refused, contending he had nothing to hide.

He talked it over with Tammy and authorities from the Eastern Orthodox Church. Not one of them objected to a marriage in Tammy's church. Everett felt comfortable with himself. In the eyes of God he was sure he was clean. He had nothing to be ashamed of. The Catholic Church had relied on man-made laws to deny him annulment and remarriage. Man-made laws were subject to change and interpretation. He knew that he himself had not changed. And he was certainly not going to maneuver, looking for a new avenue of approach to seek Catholic approval. He had not broken his bonds with God during his long travail. He did not feel that a merciful and compassionate God, full of understanding and love, would want him penalized for life simply because man-made laws forbade him to remarry. With a clear conscience and an unyielding devotion to his faith, he decided there was no honest impediment to remarrying in the Eastern Orthodox Church.

They were staying overnight at cousin Al and Virginia's house in Walnut Creek with all four set to enjoy a bottle of wine and the TV premiere of Barbara Streisand's *Funny Girl.* Two hours before the movie started Everett excused himself saying he would be gone half an hour. He wanted to say hello to Tangee's sister, Mercedes, who lived nearby. The oldest of six sisters, she had always been very friendly and was the outstanding loyalist who had tipped off Everett's family to Tangee's infidelity. When Everett had dropped by her house some weeks back she had sobbed uncontrollably, telling him how ashamed she still felt on account of Tangee's behavior.

Everett had not meant to stay long but it was like old times: he felt relaxed and comfortable as he chatted with Mercedes and her husband and son. They talked about anything and everything, with the exception of Vietnam and Tangee. He felt so at home that he did not notice the hours ticking by and it was well after midnight when he got up to go.

During his absence, Tammy grew progressively angrier, feeling let down, neglected and ignored. He had invited her all the way to California and then abandoned her while he went off to see his ex-wife's sister. Tammy's weekend flights gave her precious little time with Everett. In a day and a half she had to catch the Red Eye Special back to Dulles. When Everett returned the movie was over, Al and Virginia had long since gone to bed, and she was groggy and sleepy. But she was still hurting. "That's it!" she cried. "I'm not coming back anymore. You've hurt and embarrassed me!"

Everett was at a loss for words. He knew he had blown it and he felt like a dolt. Deep inside he wondered why he had become so insensitive to others since getting back to the U.S.A. Perhaps it was because he was so spoiled. There had been so many women that he never had to worry about their feelings. He didn't even have to try and charm them because there were countless others waiting to be dated. Tammy, though, was different. This was the woman he knew he wanted to settle down with and raise a family. She was the only one he cared deeply about and loved. He was not going to lose her through his own thick-headedness.

As Tammy headed for her bedroom, in tears, Everett said, "Okay, let's get married!"

But she dropped off to sleep, unsure whether he had spoken to her, and unable to distinguish voices from sounds still coming out of the TV set.

She woke up perplexed, wondering what had taken place the night before. She remembered she had been angry at him and yet she felt strangely excited and serenely content. Had he really proposed marriage to her?

Al had already gone off to work and Everett was making a call at Oak Knoll Naval Hospital. Tammy and Virginia sat in their robes drinking coffee. Still bewildered by the events of the night before, Tammy said, "I think he asked me to marry him, but I don't remember. How can I find out without looking foolish?" They decided she had no alternative but to ask him when he came back. When he returned, she backed off. Then, when they got in his LTD, a gift from the Ford Motor Company, he turned to her and asked, "Shall we get the ring here or wait?" Ecstatic, she leaned over and kissed him, scarcely able to believe that she had won over the man who had stolen her heart at their first encounter.

They bought the 14k. brushed gold engagement ring set with a diamond and drove over to Bohannon Drive to break the news to Chole. She was in her favorite rocking chair and showed no emotion as they entered. Though he fully intended telling his mother, Everett froze. He could not announce what she obviously dreaded to hear.

"Everett," Tammy whispered, "Tell your mother!"

It was to no avail. Everett could see his mother's discomfort. He did not know how to handle it. He felt trapped between wanting to tell her the good news yet knowing she could not adjust to the speed of it all. Chole heard Tammy twice more urge Everett to tell his mother but she feigned ignorance. The awkward silence persisted until they invited her to dine out with them at an Italian restaurant. Everett promised Tammy he would announce the engagement at some stage during the meal. But even though Tammy ostentatiously crossed her hands Chole made no acknowledgment that she had seen the ring. When Everett finally announced the wedding plans Chole made no comment and changed the subject. Her pain was so deep that she could not rejoice with her son. It had all happened too soon, and it had foiled all those years of hope when she had cried and dreamed of having him home again. He was no sooner home than he was off again. And they had never discussed those painful eight-and-a-half years. Not once. She would never know what he had gone through. And he was equally unaware of the family's long travail.

In the waning years of his life, sixty-nine-year-old Dr. Shakir Ilyas was mellow and content. A man of his age looked not to the future but to the days that had gone before. He thanked God for the blessings bestowed on his household. In the beginning he had known only the cycles of poverty and the sting of neglect in the Syrian village of his birth. In his nineteenth year he had followed his father to Washington, Pennsylvania, where he helped in the store as he learned to mouth the strange alphabet of his adopted land. Intelligent and observant, Shakir had triumphed and gone on to medical school at Georgetown University. There, the six-footer with a French-Arabic accent had met and later married Roujina Koury, a first generation American also with roots in Syria. She was the jewel in his life, the loyal support and the faithful wife. She bore him two daughters before the World War tore him from her. When there was peace the doctor, now a lieutenant colonel, returned from England but with such severe arthritis that he could not be the orthopedic surgeon he had hoped to be. Shakir prospered instead as a general practitioner. One of the pillars of the Eastern Orthodox Church in America, the respected physician was nowhere more at peace than in the library of his Munhall home in suburban Pittsburgh. His books gave him the knowledge to be wise and the instructions to be humble in the eyes of his God. His library was his sanctuary and it provided something of the same purity that he received from his church.

He had met the young airman when he came as a house guest. But he had been careful not to be influenced by the magic of the returning hero's renown. Long captivity, however cruel and unjust, did not alone qualify him to be judged a good man. Shakir was too wise to make the quick judgment that made fools of lesser men. He preferred to take the measure of the soft-spoken commander even as he plied him with gracious hospitality. Only then did he take his youngest daughter aside and give her his blessing. "He has to be a good man because he likes people in spite of all he has suffered," he told her. "You will see, if he is good to his mother he will be good to you. I myself am happy. This is a kind man and a good person. You have chosen well."

It was a refrain she would hear from many of the elders in her family who wanted to give the benefit of their seasoned years. In her clipped Arabic accent, her grandmother Tukla, the widow of the Eastern Orthodox priest, passed down the simple lore that she herself had received when she was a young woman. "You love your husband. You go where your husband goes. You cook the meals your husband wants. He is a good man."

Shakir had given his firstborn, Thelma, an extravagant wedding, befitting the love that he had for her and the joy that she brought him. Now it was the turn of the last of his beloved children and he would do no less. He reserved Pittsburgh's exclusive Allegheny Club at Three Rivers Stadium for the sumptuous post-nuptial dinner/dance and engaged strings from the Pittsburgh Symphony Orchestra to entertain the 250 guests. On the eve of the wedding, while most of the celebrants clapped rhythmically to the sounds of the Middle Eastern mandolin and drums at Shakir's home, Lalo approached his daughter-in-law to be.

"So tomorrow's your big day, Tammy! How do you feel? After all, you know what he's been through."

"He'll be alright."

"Are you sure you want him?"

"Dad, I've waited this long. I know the right man has come."

"All I wish is that you make my son happy. He deserves it."

The congregants and guests filled St. George's Orthodox Church late the following afternoon, October 27. Chole and Lalo sat next to one another, brought together one final time to witness the miracle of their son's new-found happiness. They faced a brilliant golden altar screen richly decorated with icons. A trail of white silk overlaying the red carpet all the way up the aisle to the altar symbolized the bridal couple's new path in life. Flanking either side of the aisle were the sword-bearers, five former POWs—Tom Barrett, Bill Metzger, Dick Ratzlaff, Chuck Rice and Charlie Zuhoski—and a close squadron mate, Bob Reynolds. Resplendent in black jackets, gold cummerbunds and small medals, all stood ramrod straight, ceremonial swords unsheathed and pointed diagonally up to form an arch. It was a splendid spectacle of military bearing and colorful pomp. But a deeper feeling stirred in Everett as he passed beneath the arch of swords. It was the sense of lasting kinship with this small band of former comrades-in-arms. More liberated POWs sat in the pews with other guests. But two in particular, Dave Carey, his best man, and Jerry Coffee, his usher, stood near the altar close by their friend, just as they had done in the bitterest moments in the Hanoi Hilton when Everett had suffered from a woman's betrayal.

Surrounded in the church by such a phalanx of loyal friends, a man could be forgiven if tears welled up in his eyes. The road home from bondage had been long and arduous, painful and grim. Everett could not redeem the years nor forget the horrors. But that was the past. Now he wore a jeweled crown, like his bride, as the priest intoned three times, "O Lord, our God, crown them with glory and with honor." There were many in the congregation who wept.

Far to the south, a U.S. flag fluttered over the domed capitol in Washington, D.C. It had been raised in Everett's honor on the day of his wedding. At dusk it was hauled down and furled respectfully and neatly. Then it was sent as a gift to the newly-married lieutenant commander. He had been steadfastly faithful to his country. He had served it well, with honor and dignity and above all, with valor.

EPILOGUE

IT SEEMED LOGICAL TO STAY ON IN THE NAVY AND COMplete the seven remaining years of a twenty-year commitment. Together with many other former POWs, I went to Kingsville, Texas, for fifty hours of refresher flight training in the TA4 trainer, the two-seater version of my former A4 Skyhawk. Sitting once more in the cockpit and taking control of the aircraft was as natural as riding a bike or driving a car after a long break: it all came back with the speed of instinct. Once again I thrilled to the feel of effortlessly maneuvering at high altitude. It was just as I had felt as a child when taking my first hop over Salinas with Fergie the crop-duster. But flying no longer gripped me as it had in my youth. The chance to remain shorebound and close to home while raising a family appealed more than the prospect of returning to sea and competing for line commands. I looked forward with mounting anticipation to being a doting father.

Former POWs had a virtual free hand to pick and choose their future fields within the Navy. Some did go back to sea. Others even committed themselves to multiple years of studies to become doctors and lawyers. At the time I did not have the stomach for such a long haul. More technically oriented, and determined to get my masters degree, I entered the Operations Research & Systems Analysis Program at the Naval Post-Graduate School in Monterey, California, in the spring of 1974. Far from being duller after years of enforced isolation, I found I was actually a little sharper than I had been as an undergraduate.

We were blessed with the birth of our first son on June 20, 1974, and named him Marc Ilyas. Though a coincidence, his initials, MIA, would remind him that his father had, for a while, been declared Missing In Action. Marc survived his own narrow brush with death thirteen years later when a summer camp bus he was riding in veered down an embankment in Pennsylvania. The most severely injured, Marc underwent multiple operations to save a badly gashed leg. Though bedridden for months, he rallied strongly, achieved excellent academic results, and resumed most sports with guts and enthusiasm.

On July 6, 1976, two years after his birth, I again witnessed the miracle of new life with the arrival of our second son, Bryan Thomas. It was ten years to the day that I had run the gauntlet of the howling mob in the streets of

Hanoi. Joy beyond measure had followed years of unspeakable barbarity.

Shortly after Bryan's birth I graduated and relocated to Fort Belvoir, Virginia, for a six-month course at the Program Managers' School, followed by assignment to the Naval Air Systems Command in Crystal City, Virginia. With barely two years until retirement, I decided to prepare for a legal career and enrolled as a night student at George Washington University law school in Washington, D.C. After five years of part-time studies I was admitted to the District of Columbia Bar.

On June 30, 1980, I formally retired from the Navy.

Six months later, after Ronald Reagan's election to the presidency, I was offered the position of Deputy Director of the Peace Corps and after confirmation by the U.S. Senate served in that capacity for a year-and-a-half. Then I was asked to consider appointment as Deputy Administrator of the Veterans Administration. I held that post until I left the Administration in 1986 to accept an offer from the Hospital Corporation of America as Vice President for Government Operations in Washington, D.C. In September, 1987, I formed my own management consulting company.

The succession of honors conferred upon me over the years has left me with a sense of high privilege and concern for the educational needs of others. After my return, I started a scholarship foundation for the benefit of needy students at the University of Santa Clara, funding it with part of the honoraria earned from speaking engagements. I am on the board of the Armed Services YMCA and was appointed by President Reagan to serve on the Board of Regents of the Uniformed Services University of Health Sciences. My alma mater, the University of Santa Clara, conferred upon me an Honorary Doctorate in Public Service and made me a life member of the Board of Fellows. The same institution named me the Alumni of Distinction after my appointment to the Veterans Administration. I was inducted into the California Public Hall of Fame and in 1987, a high school, scheduled for completion in the early 1990s, was named for me in my birthplace, Salinas. In El Paso, Texas, a housing project was dedicated in my name.

My parents divorced soon after they separated. Dad remarried and now lives in retirement in San Jose. Mom still resides in the house on Bohannon Drive, Santa Clara, where Naval officers knocked on the door in 1964 to tell her I had been shot down. Late in life she got her driver's license and in a further show of independence and determination, she attended night school on and off for five years. It was a proud day for all of us when, in her 60th year, Mom received her certificate in Early Childhood Programs from West Valley Joint Community College in Los Gatos. Until her retirement in 1986, she taught mostly Hispanic children from pre-school to 6th grade level, who had difficulties with the English language or who were slow learners.

Both my sisters are women of accomplishment. Delia graduated with a masters degree in Urban and Regional Planning from San Jose State University, the year I returned. She is currently Director of Public Health for the Santa Clara County Health Department, managing a $27 million budget for a population of 1.4 million people.

Madeleine, who divorced and remarried, graduated in Accounting from San Jose State University and is an accountant with Ford Aerospace in Palo Alto, California.

Misfortune struck a number of former POWs after their release, none of which filled me with more grief than the blow dealt Dick Ratzlaff. The childless South Dakotan was held captive a month shy of seven full years and shortly after release he and his wife divorced. The discolored spot that had grown larger over his chest was removed and found to be a malignant cancer. Dick was told that if he could make it through five years there was a good chance it would not recur. He remarried a Navy widow, went to law school and became a member of the Navy Judge Advocate General's corps. But the deadly melanoma reappeared and spread. Just six-and-a-half years after his liberation from captivity, Dick passed away.

Red Berg never did get to run the airfield he dreamed of while we shared a miserable cell in the Zoo, because the airfield changed hands and the new owners were not interested in his proposal. On arrival home he discovered his wife had deserted him, leaving their two sons with her parents. Red remained in the Air Force while graduating with a degree in Business Administration from the University of Washington at Seattle. He remarried and after a long stay on Mercer Island, moved down to southern California to take a position as vice-president with a finance company.

I was best man at Tom Barrett's marriage to Susan, a nurse he met during his hospitalization at Scott Air Force Base outside of east St. Louis, Illinois. He, too, completed his twenty-year military career in an academic environment. After several years of marriage he and his wife adopted two Vietnamese girls before their only son was born. After retirement, Tom returned to live in his childhood neighborhood and is now a stockbroker in a suburb of west Chicago.

The best man at my own wedding, Dave Carey, married his fiancee who waited five-and-a-half years for his return. They have two children. He flew on active duty in the Navy before retiring with the rank of Captain. Now residing near San Diego, he conducts motivational seminars for corporate executives.

Gerry Coffee returned to his wife, three sons and a daughter in Hawaii and completed his Navy service with the rank of Captain. While still in the military he became actively involved in speaking about the values that we believe saw us through the worst of times in Vietnam, and he is now on the lecture circuit full-time.

John "Nick" Nicholson retired after commanding the aircraft carrier, U.S.S. *Ranger*. He and his wife, Evelyn, bought a small farm close to Lemoore Naval Air Station. He is involved with youth and Navy programs and works part-time at a local high school comprising mostly disadvantaged minority children. His personal goal is to try and get at least one of his students placed each year in the Naval Academy at Annapolis, Maryland, and he has been quite successful at it.

Robinson "Robbie" Risner retired from the Air Force with the rank of Brigadier General, overcoming surgery for removal of a brain tumor. He lives in Austin, Texas, where he is an active leader in educating youth against the dangers of drug and other substance abuses.

Years after the conflict, I am still asked how I feel about the Tonkin Gulf incidents, which led to U.S. military involvement in the Vietnam War. A number of top intelligence experts who were close to the events at the time have since reviewed the evidence and concluded that it is unlikely that the U.S. destroyers, *Maddox* and *Turner Joy*, were attacked by North Vietnamese torpedo boats on the night of August 4, 1964. Their findings do not trouble me and I have never felt cheated or frustrated because I was shot down and captured in a reprisal raid for an earlier action that may not have taken place. If the events didn't happen, then so be it. The episode, as far as I am concerned, is part of history.

ABOUT THE AUTHORS

EVERETT ALVAREZ, JR., is a native of Salinas, California. He retired from the Navy in 1980 in the rank of commander. His numerous awards include the Silver Star, two Legions of Merit (with combat "V"), two Bronze Stars (with combat "V"), the Distinguished Flying Cross, and two Purple Hearts. His degrees include a Bachelor of Science degree in Electrical Engineering, a Master's degree in Operations Research and Systems Analysis, a Juris Doctor from George Washington University, and two honorary doctorates. He served as deputy director of the Peace Corps and deputy administrator of the Veterans Administration under President Ronald Reagan and is currently president of Conwal, Inc., a consulting firm that he founded in 1987. In addition to *Chained Eagle*, he is the author of *Code of Conduct*, which is the story of rebuilding his life after Vietnam. He lives in Rockville, Maryland.

ANTHONY S. PITCH is a former writer in the books division of U.S. News and World Report. He has also been a broadcast editor and newsman for the Associated Press in Philadelphia and London. His books include *The Burning of Washington: The British Invasion of 1814*. He lives in Potomac, Maryland.